FOLK MUSIC IN AMERICA

GARLAND REFERENCE LIBRARY
OF THE HUMANITIES
(VOL. 496)

FOLK MUSIC IN AMERICA
A Reference Guide

Terry E. Miller

GARLAND PUBLISHING, INC. • NEW YORK & LONDON
1986

Library of Congress Cataloging-in-Publication Data

Miller, Terry E.
Folk music in America.

(Garland reference library of the humanities ;
vol. 496)
Includes indexes.
1. Folk music—United States—Bibliography.
2. Folk music—United States—Discography. I. Title.
II. Series: Garland reference library of the humanities ;
v. 496.
ML128.F74M5 1986   016.781773   84-48014
ISBN 0-8240-8935-9 (alk. paper)

Printed on acid-free, 250-year-life paper
Manufactured in the United States of America

781.773
mil

CONTENTS

Contents

ACKNOWLEDGMENTS

Research for this bibliography was accomplished in six
libraries: The Library of Congress, The Ohio State University
Library, University of Akron Library, Cleveland Public Library,
Case-Western Reserve University Library, and Kent State University
Library. Sincere thanks is hereby extended to the personnel of
these libraries. Special recognition is given to Kent State
University for allowing liberal use of the OCLC computer terminal.

While most of the expenses relating to the preparation of this
work were borne by the compiler, he wishes to acknowledge help from
a small grant given by the College of Fine and Professional Arts,
Kent State University, which provided support for library work
during the Summer of 1984.

Three individuals deserve special recognition. First I wish
to thank Joseph Hickerson of the Archive of Folk Culture in the
Library of Congress for his advice early on in planning this work.
Still, it is cautioned that imperfections remain the responsibility
of the compiler. Secondly, without the help of Dr. Terry Lee Kuhn
of Kent State University this work might not have seen the light of
day before my retirement, planned for roughly 2005 A.D. Dr. Kuhn
first convinced me of the madness of attempting such a work without
a computer, helped me select an appropriate system, and spent
endless hours giving advice, making repairs, and especially in
writing programs to do the Author and Subject indices. Finally, I
owe profound gratitude to my wife, Sara, who, besides accepting the
fate of "academic widowhood" during the preparation period, also
helped collect materials in libraries and especially aided in the
proofreading of the manuscript. Her love and never-ending
encouragement are the main reasons why the compiler, often
suffering from fatigue and discouragement, did actually finish the
project. It is to her that I dedicate this work.

INTRODUCTION

Practical Information for the User of This Bibliography

1. <u>Criteria for inclusion</u>. If the compiler of this
bibliography ever entertained any hopes of creating the ultimate
"complete" listing of materials pertaining to American folk music,
his illusions were shattered near the beginning of the collection
process. What would complete mean? It would mean including every
item published in every language--books, book reviews, booklets,
articles in learned journals, articles in encyclopedias, articles
in magazines, record jacket notes, doctoral dissertations, master's
theses, scholarly papers, articles in Festschrifts, and even
articles in newspapers. It became quickly apparent that "complete"
would not happen in one volume or with a single compiler.

A selection process involving all of the above but based on
"quality" was also quickly seen as hopeless. No one person,
however qualified, can possibly decide what is "good" and what is
"bad" relative to all fields of American folk music. Even within a
narrow sub-field or genre, the "experts" cannot agree on this
matter. Playing God was definitely out.

Certain types of materials had to be eliminated from the
outset. While doctoral dissertations are mostly available from
University Microfilms, master's theses are not. Although many of
the latter can be described as significant contributions, only a
mere handful have been included simply because they can only be
seen by requesting them from the institution which granted the
degree.

Articles in magazines--and of the folk type there are dozens--
could not be included without creating an unreasonably thick book,
and only a low percentage of these articles could be described as
of primary importance or scholarly. Consider what would happen
just by including every article pertaining to American folk music
ever published in <u>Sing Out!</u>, and this is only one of many such
periodicals. As for record notes, scholarly papers, reviews, and
newspaper articles, they are also far too numerous for inclusion,
and some of them are difficult, if not impossible, to obtain.

INTRODUCTION

What, then, is included? 1) Books (including many of modest length), 2) doctoral dissertations, 3) scholarly articles in the more learned journals and Festschrifts, and 4) articles in certain important encyclopedias. Brief articles, i.e., under nine pages, were included only for areas lacking great quantities of material. Among the items listed, however, are additional bibliographies and discographies which will refer unusually avid readers (and also those in pursuit of trivia) to the lesser types mentioned above and to ephemera.

What time period is covered? Because the compiler has sought to list only items which can be found with reasonable ease, few items from before 1900 will be found, except those which have been reissued in facsimile editions. The general emphasis has been on more recent studies, although significant works, especially books, from the earlier decades of the century, have been included. In the case of periodical literature, only a few journals (e.g., Journal of American Folklore and Musical Quarterly) have been searched back to the beginning at or before the turn of the century. Every attempt has been made to include the most recent publications, including some that have been announced but are not yet available.

2. Use of the Bibliography. The bibliography has been divided into nine Sections, each pertaining to an "area." Some of these are fairly unified (such as Section 7, Singing Schools) and others are more like collections of related phenomena (such as Section 4, which includes bluegrass, country, and the folk revival). Each Section was subdivided, but how many subcategories depended partly on the length and complexity of the subject (such as Section 3, Folksongs and Ballads) and partly on the obvious appearance of unifying ideas. Most Sections, however, include a "General and Miscellaneous" category.

Users can search for materials both from the Table of Contents and from the Index. The former, through its headings and sub-headings, will direct users to specific genres, geographical areas, and other distinctions. There are two Indices, one for authors' names and one for subjects. In the case of subjects which are also covered in a Section or subsection (e.g., blues or ballads), the appropriate inclusive numbers will be given; but items pertaining to the subject outside these will be individually listed.

Each Section is introduced by a brief essay providing a perspective on that material. Because the compiler is an ethnomusicologist with extensive training in music (rather than folklore or anthropology), certain of these perspectives bear this particular bias. The compiler is aware that the vast majority of authors listed here are not ethnomusicologists, a fact which only became apparent gradually and with some surprise. It is nonetheless hoped that this listing will be useful to people in a variety of fields pursuing many different goals.

Regardless of how many times an author's name appears in succession, it has been written out fully and exactly as used in the article or book. The custom of using underlines for successive entries was not followed in order to make the reader's job easier, especially over page breaks. Similarly, abbreviations were kept to a bare minimum. The annotations are meant to provide the user with some understanding of the nature of the item without attempting more than a minimum of judgement as to its merits. Space limitations simply would not permit more elaborate reviews of each book or article.

After the user finds items pertinent to his/her needs, what next? Obviously, one can visit the nearest public or college/university library hoping to find the item waiting on the shelf. If it is not there, then what? Probably there is no library in the world, except possibly the Library of Congress, which will have ALL of these items. Some are commonplace; some are scarce. All exist.

If one cannot visit other nearby libraries, again hoping for a run of good luck, the best thing to do is request materials on inter-library loan. If one is lucky enough to have access to an OCLC terminal, the item can be searched and the libraries owning it revealed. The main limitation is that every library is not a member of OCLC, and the terminal will probably not be able to tell you which volumes of a given periodical the library in question owns. Dissertations sometimes turn up in libraries, but many may have to be ordered from University Microfilms, 300 North Zeeb Road, Ann Arbor, Michigan (48106), either in microfilm or xerographic printout (book form). UM needs the author's name, the title, the university, and the year.

3. Keeping Up with New Material. Obviously, nothing appearing after this book was prepared (July, 1986) could be listed, and that sometimes means periodical issues that are behind schedule. The best ways to keep up with the newest publications are: 1) watch for notices of new books and check to see if your library displays newly received materials, 2) consult newly arrived issues of periodicals, 3) consult the journals which attempt to maintain bibliographies of current materials. Each issue of Ethnomusicology, for example, has a section on current literature, and some of the folklore journals sometimes include this also.

4. <u>Your</u> <u>Help</u> <u>is</u> <u>Needed.</u> The compiler welcomes communications from
users who may wish to offer corrections and additions. If further
editions are published, these emendations will be included. Please
send this material to Dr. Terry E. Miller, School of Music, Kent
State University, Kent, Ohio 44242.

Defining the Scope of This Compilation:
An Essay

Based solely on the phrase "American folk music" found in its
title, there is little question that most potential users of this
book have some idea concerning its contents. Few would reach for
such a title expecting to find material on jazz, rock and roll,
Charles Ives, or Tin Pan Alley. Most would expect to find material
on Anglo-American balladry, Afro-American spirituals, American
Indian music, and Appalachian "folk hymns." Many of us, like
Kenneth Clark ["What is civilisation? I don't know. I can't
define it in abstract terms--yet. But I think I can recognize it
when I see it. . . ."][1] may not be able to define folk music
clearly, but we recognize it when we hear it. It is further likely
that a folklorist selecting this book might harbor different
expectations from an anthropologist who in turn has contrasting
views from an ethnomusicologist. Even within a discipline it may
be difficult to predict expectations, because of various
subgroupings (e.g., structuralists and functionalists).

Musings as to what constitutes "folk," "traditional,"
"popular," "ethnic," and a host of other such terms are more easily
accomplished over cocktails or in a seminar than in a work such as
this in which one is forced to make clear and irrevocable decisions
regarding what goes into the book and what does not. The contents
of a book cannot be left up in the air or balanced between two
opposing points of view. One might easily surmise that the
inclusion or exclusion of a kind of music determines whether or not
it is folk. Unfortunately, this would seem to be the case, but
that is not necessarily the intention of the compiler.

To the extent that the concept of folkness exists at all, and
that is likely more common among "intellectuals" than "ordinary
people," it is part of a process that tends to divide people into
categories, and these divisions often carry with them valuative
connotations. At its best, folk suggests the late eighteenth- and
early nineteenth-century fascination with common people, an aspect
of what is denoted by the term "romanticism," with its desire to
return to nature, respect for the "noble savage," and the tendency
to escape from corrupted "civilization" in the cities by fleeing to
the "pristine" countryside. It was part of a search for local

xiv

roots on the part of northern European peoples tired of emulating the supposedly superior civilizations of Mediterranean peoples, especially that of the French. It is also tied up with nationalism. At its worst, folk is a patronizingly affectionate term for inferior people, those who cannot read and write, those who are not artistic, and individuals who live in isolation, or at the fringes of a "great" society.

While many "purists" decried the alleged misuse of the term "folk music" during the 1950s and 1960s, the "folk revival" was merely symptomatic of a "romantic" mind set, an escape from what was seen as an abusively powerful establishment and a way of empathizing with "oppressed" common people. Similarly, "folk" became within the music industry a commercial term that bore as much relation to its original model as the sickeningly sweet, chocolate-covered "granola bars" of the 1980s bear to their health-conscious predecessors. It might be asserted that genuine folk music, like simple, grain-filled, honey-sweetened granola bars, both served a limited community with particular interests until appropriated by "big business" which transformed both into products saleable to a general population willing to accept such distortions. Those who want the "pure" form of each must abandon the supermarkets and folk festivals and retreat to the isolated, marginal areas lacking such amenities, while the rest of us have come to accept that granola bars are sweet and folk music is performed on stages with amplification and with a sales table in the vestibule.

In my more cynical states of mind, I have come to believe that the idea of "folk" can only exist in the minds of people who know (or fear) that they are not folk. Those who collect, analyze, read, and publish scholarly papers about folk traditions are usually those who do not consider themselves members of the folk species. And if they are, many of us would consider them to have lost their folkness. The Apprenticeships in the Folk Arts, given by many state arts agencies, require an awareness on the part of "folk artists" that they are folk artists; otherwise, the very people whom we hope will apply do not, precisely because they consider themselves neither folk nor artists, let alone masters. These qualities are bestowed, in most cases, by open-minded admirers from outside folkdom.

Then, is there any point to this book--does it distinguish one body of music from other bodies--or is reality, as Charles Seeger concludes: "Thus, musically speaking, the people of the United States are divided into two classes: a majority that does not know it is a folk; a minority, that thinks it isn't."[2] Obviously, the subject of this book cannot be merely American music or music in

INTRODUCTION

America, for that would either require many volumes or merely duplicate David Horn's fine work, The Literature of American Music. Thus, in the following paragraphs I will attempt to define my thinking on the subject, and why I included what I did, together with appropriate verbal hand-wringing, hedging, and "on the other hands." The reader is warned in advance, however, not to expect a unified, consistent system based on a closed definition that rationally explains all the contents of the book.

Many attempts have been made to define the folk in general and folk music in particular. While I do not intend to compose a Review of Literature on the subject, please permit a few scattered examples. An important attempt to formulate an "official" definition was undertaken by the International Folk Music Council at their conference in Sao Paulo in 1954.

Folk music is the product of a musical tradition that has been evolved through the process of oral transmission. The factors that shape the tradition are: (i) continuity which links the present with the past; (ii) variation which springs from the creative impulse of the individual or the group; and (iii) selection by the community, which determines the form or forms in which the music survives.3

The Harvard Dictionary of Music (2nd ed.) formulates a definition with many points of similarity, but notes that the study of folk music requires special methods, those of ethnomusicology.

It is perhaps interesting to note that ethnomusicology, as it is usually practiced in the United States, is a much younger discipline than folklore, and it was folklorists who influenced the thinking of the IFMC in 1954. The field of folklore in the United States was originally centered on the study of Anglo-American traditions. Moreover, because the earlier phase of ethnomusicology, known as comparative musicology (from the German, Vergleichendes Musikwissenschaft), flourished in Europe, its interests were non-American for the most part. While ethnomusicology in the United States began on these same European foundations, with much influence from folklore and its related disciplines, the field only expanded into the consciousness of most musicians after Mantle Hood's students at UCLA, imbued with their teacher's ideas of bi-musicality, began taking positions throughout the country in the 1960s. Hood's interests, and those of most of his students, however, were non-American. Consequently, it comes as no surprise (though the proportions of it did surprise me) that the vast majority of writing about American "folk" music has been done by people other than ethnomusicologists--folklorists, anthropologists, literary critics, linguists, ethnologists, and amateur enthusiasts.

With our bent for classifying musical genres, we are often inclined to argue over just which ones fit into the folk category as opposed to those which fit into the other three "usual" categories--primitive, popular, and art. More and more people, however, recognize not only the futility of neatly dividing up music in this way, but some, ethnomusicologists in particular, strongly reject certain of the terms, especially "primitive," as condescending or elitist. It has been pointed out by some (e.g., Klaus Wachsmann[4]) that this need to categorize musics is peculiar to Europeans and North Americans and little felt or felt not at all in other societies except where Western ideas have penetrated. Many ethnomusicologists, influenced by social anthropology, have come to see music as related to the culture from which it comes, and have shed their concern for distinctive categories such as folk. Music is music. It is transmitted by various means. While the primary musical source material of those trained in musicology tends to be written documents, implying the primacy of musical literacy, the primary source material of the ethnomusicologist tends to be living musicians within their cultures, making irrelevant the distinction of literate/non-literate.

It has been argued that folk music consists of specific kinds of music with stylistic traits that define it as folk. It has also been argued that folk music is really a process, an attitude, or a manner of performance practice. The former lends itself to selecting what goes into or does not go into a book such as this, but also assumes the absolute distinctness of categories. To a certain extent I have opted for the former as a practical solution, but with all the hand-wringing and squirming alluded to earlier. In the process of categorization, some musics appear black, others white, but most appear as shades of gray.

I have attempted, for the sake of argument, to make distinctions on the basis of several criteria. One of them is the method of transmission, since most definitions of folk music mention oral transmission. Folk music is thought to be transmitted orally and therefore usually heard in live performances. Popular music is transmitted to a certain extent by scored arrangements but also orally, but is mostly disseminated by the media. Art or classical music is transmitted by written scores and performed live. (I have omitted the factor of recordings, since this may be either significant or insignificant, an after-the-fact matter).

The difficulties with this division are legion. Folk material is often learned from recordings and the media, and all classical music notation depends to some extent on oral tradition for its performance practice. If individual variation in performance is a factor in folk music, it certainly occurs as well in classical music, for otherwise why would one prefer Serkin over Cliburn or the Cleveland Orchestra over that of Philadelphia? Oral transmission versus written transmission seems to be a false issue, based perhaps on our belief that literacy is superior to illiteracy, or that the practitioners of genuine folk music are unschooled.

A possibly more fruitful avenue is a distinction founded on an economic base, i.e., the cost of making the music. Money has much to do with how music is made and disseminated, to what extent the makers of music are rewarded and possibly freed from other kinds of labor to become music specialists. We might view the situation as described in the following paragraphs.

A symphony or opera is labor intensive, requiring the services of a large number of individuals who have liberal amounts of time to devote to creating and performing complex, demanding music. In order to have the time, they must be supported, although they do not create any wealth (products) in return. In earlier times the only people capable of supporting such an establishment were royalty, both sacred and secular. Thus, complex, hand-made, and lavish music was the exclusive privilege of the elite. Because their preferences were for elaborate music (as well in sculpture, painting, and other manifestations of "art"), and because they were the ones holding power and thus able to call the shots, they dubbed their music (always modestly)--"classical," meaning the highest form or ideal form.

People of modest means, whether in the village, the city, or on the farm, obviously could not afford an elaborate musical establishment. Indeed, they could rarely support full-time specialists. Most practitioners of music were necessarily amateurs, because they derived their principal support from another enterprise. In some societies, although not to any extent in the United States, certain groups which were considered near outcasts and not permitted to participate in the mainstream activities of the dominant group, such as the Jews and Gypsies in Eastern Europe, were permitted to make their livings as musicians. But because their financial base was modest, they too made modest music, although their abilities might match those working for the elite.

People of modest means, when they did not hire musicians, had to make their own music. Because it was played by amateurs or semi-professionals, it was naturally simpler and more practical (e.g., for weddings, funerals, dancing) than was the music of the elite, who could afford grander music on a regular basis. These people might best be described as the folk and folk music as home-made music.

In the city much of the same was true, but the base of support among the working poor was proportionately greater. Consequently, a musical establishment gradually evolved in urban areas which was intended for the non-elite, reflected their relative simplicity, tended to be functional, but was purveyed by specialists. These relatively better paid musicians depended upon large numbers of people pooling their modest resources in order to support a segment of the economy that we now describe as the "service sector." This new musical establishment, because it depended on satisfying great numbers of customers, created the products which were most likely to bring them income. Consequently, the music could be described as "trendy" or "in fashion," and might be seen as a symbol of the time. Whereas rural musicians tended to reinforce links with the past through their music's <u>tradition,</u> urban specialists appealed to their supporters on the basis of current taste. This kind of music is what we generally call "popular" music.

In the modern United States, entrepreneurs have applied the same marketing techniques to music that had previously proved so beneficial to other segments of the economy. A Rolls Royce, because it is hand-crafted, costs too much for anyone other than the rich, just as opera, for similar reasons, requires support from the wealthy quite apart from the proceeds from ticket sales. Just as Henry Ford developed mass production in order to reduce the per-item cost, and just as "discount" stores depend on volumn to balance their lower prices, promoters have seen that extremely elaborate and financially rewarding musical activities could be supported by the American masses who could be dealt with the same way that toothpaste and beer producers deal with them--through advertising, the media, and a vast sales network. Thus, the gigantic costs could be spread over a vast number of people while at the same time bringing back enough extra money to make the producers wealthy. As Americans have become more affluent, the mass-marketed music has kept pace, and its promoters can now mount extravaganzas rivaling those of seventeenth-century Venice and eighteenth-century France.

With few exceptions, the musics included in this particular "folk music" bibliography are those which have been forgotten or ignored by the media and the mass producers, because they refuse to succumb to the quick-income solution of fashion and mass appeal. Supporters of "classical" music usually remain ignorant of or at best condescending towards these musics. They are more concerned with artistic quality in music which has often been de-contextualized. Because "folk" music tends to be simple and classical music enthusiasts tend to equate complexity and virtuosity with artistry, the former pales in comparison.

INTRODUCTION

In a way, then, this collection is about the forgotten musics of America. They remain known to small groups of enthusiasts but are mostly ignored by the vast majority of us who have forgotten how to make our own music and who prefer to experience music vicariously, especially through the media. Any of us, then, can be folk by relying more on ourselves for our entertainment, by re-establishing closer relationships with the people around us—our own community—and by regaining a concept of music as individual and group expression rather than as a consumer product to be bought and sold like bottles of shampoo and cans of beer, or perhaps more accurately, as a drug to calm or arouse.

Terry E. Miller
Center for the Study of World Musics
Kent State University
Kent, Ohio 44240
July 12, 1986

1. Kenneth Clark, <u>Civilisation</u> (New York: Harper and Row, 1969), p. 1.

2. Charles Seeger, "The Folkness of the Nonfolk and the Nonfolkness of the Folk," in <u>Studies in Musicology, 1935-1975,</u> ed. Charles Seeger (Berkeley: University of California Press, 1977), p. 343.

3. Maud Karpeles, "The Distinction Between Folk and Popular Music," <u>Journal of the International Folk Music Council</u> 20 (1968):9.

4. <u>The New Grove Dictionary of Music and Musicians,</u> s.v. "Folk Music," by Klaus P. Wachsmann.

Folk Music in America

I. GENERAL RESOURCES

While most of the material listed in this collection can be classified into fairly specific categories, some of it cannot because it pertains to the field of folk music in general or covers the entire United States in some way. This material follows in Section I.

The bibliographies listed here are of a national or regional nature. Bibliographies pertaining to specific genres will typically be found in the appropriate Sections. For example, De Lerma's monumental black music bibliography is listed in Section VIII on Afro-American music. However, Feintuch's bibliography on folk music in Kentucky is listed here rather than in Section III because it embraces all genres, not just folksong and ballad, which is the concern of Section III.

This bibliography does not attempt to list recordings and films of American folk music individually. Such a folly would result in a multi-volume library rivaling the Encyclopedia Britannica. It does, however, list available discographies and filmographies, again including those of a national nature here and those pertaining to specific genres in the appropriate Sections.

Bibliographies

1. American Music Before 1865 in Print and on Records: a Biblio-discography. I.S.A.M. Monograph #6. New York: Institute for Studies in American Music, 1976. 113 pp.

    Most of these 543 entries cover classical and other written traditions, but a fair number pertain to the singing school as well as other kinds of folk music. There are four sections: performing editions (including arranged folk songs), facsimile reprints, music in books, and music on records.

2. Appalachian Literature and Music: a Comprehensive Catalogue. Berea, Ky.: Appalachian Book and Record Shop, 1981. 80 pp

3

A shop catalogue, but includes annotated bibliography of hundreds of items, including music, Appalachian culture and studies, biographies, literature, photo collections, children's books, records, and instrumental instruction books.

3. Come-All-Ye: a Review Journal for Publications in the Fields of Folklore, American Studies, Social History and Popular Culture. Vol. 1 (1980)-present.

A major resource that lists new publications in a number of areas and provides brief reviews as well. Published by Legacy Books, Box 494, Hatboro, Pennsylvania 19040-0494. Became quarterly with Vol. 6-1.

4. EVANS, Charles. American Bibliography. 14 vols. Chicago: Blakely Press; Worcester, Mass.: American Antiquarian Society, 1903-1959; reprint ed., New York: Peter Smith, 1941-1959.

Not concerned with music per se, Evans' original compilation, 1903-1934, catalogues all books, pamphlets, and broadsides printed in colonial and post-colonial United States from 1639 to 1799. Evans' work actually occupies vols. 1-12. In 1955 Clifton K. Shipton published vol. 13 to include the year 1800 and in 1959 a cumulative index was added. In 1954 the American Antiquarian Society together with Readex Microprint Co. started producing microprints of all works in Evans under the title Early American Imprints, 1639-1800. The titles that include music notation are found in Donald L. Hixon's Music in Early America: a Bibliography of Music in Evans and Priscilla Heard's American Music, 1698-1800.

The series was originally projected to run through 1820, but others have completed it up to 1834. Ralph R. Shaw and Richard H. Shoemaker together compiled a 22-volume American Bibliography: A Preliminary Checklist for 1801 (and for each successive year). These, together with addenda and indices (title and author) were published in New York by Scarecrow Press from 1958 to 1963, and include more than 100,000 entries, 3,297 of them with music. Most are songsters and tunebooks. Shoemaker, Gayle Cooper, and others continued the series with volumes for each year from 1820-1834, also published by Scarecrow from 1964 to 1982.

5. FEINTUCH, Burt. Kentucky Folkmusic: an Annotated Bibliography. Lexington: University Press of Kentucky, 1985. 105 pp.

Includes 709 briefly annotated entries classified under collections and anthologies, fieldworkers, collectors and scholars, singers, musicians and other performers, text-centered studies, and studies of history, context, and style.

6. FLANAGAN, Cathleen C. and John T. American Folklore: a
   Bibliography, 1950-1974. Metuchen, N.J. and London:
   Scarecrow, 1977. 406 pp.

Includes 3,639 entries, some lightly annotated. Pertinent are those under "Ballads and Songs," pp. 90-162.

7. FULD, James J., and DAVIDSON, Mary Wallace. 18th-Century
   American Secular Music Manuscripts: an Inventory. MLA
   Index & Bibliography Series #20. Philadelphia: Music
   Library Association, 1980. 225 pp.

Description of 20 collections in 9 states and District of Columbia. Includes contents, item by item, comparison with Sonneck and Wolfe, and has an index.

8. GILLIS, Frank, and MERRIAM, Alan P. Ethnomusicology and
   Folk Music: an International Bibliography of Dissertations and Theses. Middletown, Conn.: Society for Ethnomusicology and Wesleyan University Press, 1966. 148 pp.

Although it is now out-of-date, it includes some 873 items without annotations indexed by institution and subject.

9. HARTLEY, Kenneth R. Bibliography of Theses and
   Dissertations in Sacred Music. Detroit Studies in Music
   Bibliography #9. Detroit: Information Coordinators, 1966.
   127 pp.

Though the subject area is world-wide, quite a few items are on American subjects. It is organized state by state, and while including no annotations, has a number of indices.

10. HAYWOOD, Charles. Bibliography of North American Folklore
    and Folksong. New York: Greenberg, 1951. 1,292 double-
    column pages; rev. ed., New York: Dover, 1961 in 2
    volumes, 748 pp. and 1,301 pp.

Begun in 1939 and compiled by Haywood and his students in American folksong at Queens College, this ten-year project, which became his 1951 Columbia doctoral dissertation, includes more than 40,000 mostly non-annotated entries on virtually every kind of folk music. The index alone is 131 pp. Book I covers general subjects, including ballad, dance, and song games, regional types (including Alaska and Canada), ethnic musics (including Afro-American and European), occupational songs (e.g., cowboy, hobo, railroad), and miscellaneous subjects (e.g., Shakers and white spirituals). Book II includes American Indians arranged into ten cultural areas. The entries include much that is folklore and not folk music, but is particularly valuable for its inclusion of many journal articles. Although the revised edition is from 1961, the cut-off date for entries remained 1948.

11. HEARD, Priscilla S. American Music, 1698-1800: an Annotated
    Bibliography. Waco, Tex.: Baylor University Press and
    Markham Press Fund, 1975. 246 pp.

After a history and description of Evans' monumental collection (see #4), there is a list of all entries in Evans with notation or pertaining to music. In chronological order, the author provides the Evans' number, the microprint number, the title, date, description, and annotation. In addition, a bibliography and list of other printings or editions are provided. Material is in three sections: I. Entries with notation (pp. 19-102), II. Entries pertinent to music (pp. 103-88), and III. Entries not in microprint (pp. 182-218). Finally, there is a bibliography and index.

12. HEINTZE, James R. American Music Studies: a Classified
    Bibliography of Master's Theses. Detroit: Information
    Coordinators, 1984. 312 pp.

Although this list covers all kinds of music, including classical, among the 2,370 entries are many pertaining to folk music. This source is especially valuable because it is relatively up-to-date and includes items not in the present work. Some entries are lightly annotated.

13. HICKERSON, Joseph. "American Folklore: a Bibliography of
    Major Works." Washington, D.C.: Library of Congress,
    Archive of Folk Culture, 1975. 22 pp.

Lists the major folklore studies on the United States, including many pertaining to folk music or including it. Many of these are also listed in the present work. Lacks annotations.

14. HICKERSON, Joseph, et al., ed. "Current Bibliography and Discography." In Ethnomusicology.

The listing of current bibliography by the Society for Ethnomusicology began in 1953 in its "Ethno-Musicology Newsletter" and has been a regular feature edited by J. Hickerson and others since 1967. Arranged by geographical area, these extensive lists appear three times a year in issues of the society's journal.

15. HICKERSON, Joseph. "Journals and Magazines." In Folk Song U.S.A., 2nd ed., pp. 505-10. By John and Alan Lomax and Charles and Ruth Seeger. New York: New American Library, 1975.

Important list of 132 magazines and journals concerned with folklore and folk music, mostly American.

16. HICKERSON, Kathryn W., and CONDON, Kathleen. "Folklife and Ethnomusicology Serial Publications in North America." Washington, D.C.: Library of Congress, Archive of Folk Culture, 1982. 16 pp.

An invaluable list of roughly 300 items with addresses.

17. HIXON, Donald L. Music in Early America: a Bibliography of Music in Evans. Metuchen, N.J.: Scarecrow, 1970. 623 pp.

Earlier than, but similar to, Priscilla Heard's index (see #11), Hixon lists all items in Evans that include musical notation. The body of the work consists of six sections. I. Alphabetical list of items under composers, editors, or compilers, together with contents; II. Similar list for items not yet in microprint; III. Biographical sketches of composers; IV. Composer/ editor and composer/compiler indices; V. Title index; VI. Numerical index. While Heard's list also includes items that mention music (though without notation), Hixon's collection obviously includes some information not found in the former study; consequently, both are valuable and can be used to complement each other.

18. HORN, David. The Literature of American Music in Books and Folk Music Collections: a Fully Annotated Bibliography. Metuchen, N.J.: Scarecrow, 1977. 556 pp.

Based on the collection of the Exeter University Library in Great Britain, this monumental effort attempts to survey the entire range of American music, including American Indian, folk, jazz, popular, and classical. Restricted primarily to books (and therefore not including periodical literature), Horn's work lists 1388 fully annotated items plus an appendix of 302 items without annotations. The annotations, which in many cases constitute complete book reviews, are the book's main strength. A great number of items are necessarily duplicated in the present work, but everything listed in Horn will not be found here. While Horn's book, having been published in 1977, is not current, a supplement through 1980 has been advertised as forthcoming. Although the index, which combines subjects and authors, is a bit frustrating, the book is well organized into subject categories with numerous subheadings.

19. JACKSON, Richard. United States Music: Sources of Bibliography and Collective Biography. I.S.A.M. Monograph #1. New York: The City University of New York, Brooklyn College, Department of Music, Institute for Studies in American Music, 1973; rev. ed., 1976. 79 pp.

A relatively light but useful catch-all source listing ninety bibliographies and collective biographies. Organized into historical, regional, and topical studies, and includes annotations.

20. KARPEL, Bernard, ed. Arts in America; a Bibliography. 4 vols. Washington, D.C.: Smithsonian Institution Press, 1979.

Although a relatively recent book, its entries lean to the side of the "out-of-date." Vol. 4 includes Section R, "Music," which is broken down into two subheadings: I. General Works and Regional Studies, and II. Topical Studies (e.g., "Music of Ethnic and Religious Groups" and "Folk Music and Folk Song"). Items are annotated.

21. KEALIINOHOMOKU, Joann W., and GILLIS, Frank J. "Special Bibliography: Gertrude Prokosch Kurath." Ethnomusicology 14-1 (1970): 114-28.

8

Exhaustive list of major publications, brief articles,
manuscript materials, and major field trips undertaken by Prof.
Kurath (b. 1903), who specialized in ritual and dance, especially
American Indian dance and music.

22. LLOYD, Timothy Charles. A Bibliographic Guide to Ohio
    Folklife. Traditional Arts Program, Publications in
    Folklife #2. Columbus: Ohio Foundation for the Arts,
    1978. 91 pp.

    Covering a wide range of subjects, including music, these
entries are annotated.

23. MATTFELD, Julius. The Folk Music of the Western Hemisphere:
    a List of References in the New York Public Library. New
    York: New York Public Library, 1925. 74 pp.

    This classified list is devoted to periodical literature,
monographs, and song collections dealing with many kinds of
American folk music, including that of cowboys, Creoles, Eskimos,
American Indians, and Afro-Americans.

24. MEAD, Rita H. Doctoral Dissertations in American Music: a
    Classified Bibliography. I.S.A.M. Monograph #3. New
    York: The City University of New York, Brooklyn College,
    Department of Music, Institute for Studies in American
    Music, 1974. 155 pp.

    Although this work covers all kinds of American music,
Section III, "Ethnomusicology" (pp. 111-22), is devoted to folk
music, especially Afro-American, ballads, and American Indian. All
1,226 entries are indexed by author and subject.

25. MERRIAM, Alan P. "Special Bibliography: an Annotated
    Bibliography of Theses and Dissertations in
    Ethnomusicology and Folk Music Accepted at American
    Universities." Ethnomusicology 4-1 (January 1960): 21-35.

    List of 180 items covering all areas of the world, including
American music. A Supplement by Frank Gillis appeared in the same
journal, 6-3 (September 1962): 191-219 that includes 197 items with
an index.

9

26. The Music Index. Detroit: Information Service, 1949–
    present.

Index of periodical literature, both scholarly and popular,
published in monthly installments with annual accumulations.
Indexed by subject, this is an important source for articles on
American folk music, though the series is several years behind in
annual accumulations.

27. Répertoire international de littérature musicale/Interna-
    tional Repertory of Music Literature/Internationales
    Repertorium der Musikliteratur. 1967--present.

Begun in 1967 and now published by the City University of
New York, RILM (as it is usually called) indexes primarily
scholarly literature. Broader in coverage than The Music Index,
it includes articles in collections, Festschrifts, yearbooks,
periodicals, symposium collections, books, dissertations, theses,
and reviews, but does not include the lighter kinds of periodicals
indexed in The Music Index. Many items include annotations.

28. SONNECK, Oscar George Theodore. A Bibliography of Early
    Secular American Music: Eighteenth Century). Revised and
    enlarged by William Treat Upton. Washington, D.C.:
    Library of Congress Music Division, 1945; reprint ed., New
    York: DaCapo, 1964. 616 pp.

Begun in 1905, this exhaustive bibliography of early printed
music includes American hymns, songs, airs, marches, anthems,
ballads, as well as classical genres. There are also a great
number of indices which make the work extremely useful. Its
relationship to folk music is found in the folk-like genres that
were written down and published.

29. Southern Folklore Quarterly. "Folklore Bibliography for the
    year."

Usually the third issue of the year, in September, is devoted
to a classified and annotated bibliography of recently published
materials in folklore, including folk music.

30. WEICHLEIN, William J. A Checklist of American Music Peri-
    odicals, 1850-1900. Detroit Studies in Music Bibliography
    #16. Detroit: Information Coordinators, 1970. 103 pp.

This alphabetical list includes some periodicals of importance to folk music research, especially of singing school music.

31. WOLFE, Richard J. Secular Music in America, 1801-1825: a Bibliography. 3 vols. New York: New York Public Library and Astor, Lenox & Tilden Foundations, 1964. 1,234 pp.

A numbingly extensive work of 10,357 items that continues the bibliography by Sonneck and Upton (#27), this collection is concerned with secular music published in America. Consequently, some items are by non-American composers. While much of this material is tangential to folk music, it does include some of interest.

Discographies

32. ALLEN, Daniel. Bibliography of Discographies. 2 vols. New York and London: R. R. Bowker, 1981. Vol. 2: Jazz. 239 pp.

In addition to jazz, this work includes entries for blues, gospel, and other folk types.

33. "American Folk Music and Folklore Recordings 1983: a Selected List." Washington, D.C.: Library of Congress, American Folklife Center, 1984.

This series of pamphlets, which began in 1984 (for the year 1983), lists and describes about thirty new and outstanding recordings (discs and tapes) selected by a committee of prominent folklorists. Also included are addresses of producers.

34. BOGGS, Beverly B., and PATTERSON, Daniel W. An Index of Selected Folk Recordings. Chapel Hill: University of North Carolina, Curriculum in Folklore, 1984. 75 pp.

This item is a manual that explains a 55 microfiche index of 500 selected recordings with 8,350 performances in total. It is indexed under titles and key lines, performers, geography, instrumental subjects, speech subjects, vocal subjects, album titles, and a master list. An appendix indexing 100 currently available recordings is provided for libraries whose holdings would not warrant the complete index.

11

35. Check List of Recorded Songs in the English Language in the
    Library of Congress, Archive of American Folk Song, to
    July 1940. 3 vols. Washington, D.C.: Library of Congress,
    Archive of Folk Song, 1942; reprint ed. in 1 vol., New
    York: Arno Press, 1971. 598 pp.

    Based on material collected from 1933 until the summer of
    1940 in thirty-three states and the West Indies, the entries cover
    many important types of American folk song. Each entry notes
    title, name of the singer, place, collector, and year of the
    recording. Additional indices allow searching by state and
    country.

36. DANIELS, William R. The American 45 and 78 rpm Record
    Dating Guide, 1940-1959. Discography #16. Westport,
    Conn.: Greenwood, 1985. 157 pp.

    Lists some 93,000 individual discs produced by 2,500
    American record companies. Arranged alphabetically by company,
    subsidiary, and includes related releases and dates (to the
    month). In addition, there are short histories of the record
    companies.

37. DAVIS, Elizabeth A. Index to the New World Recorded
    Anthology of American Music: a User's Guide to the
    Initial One Hundred Records. New York: W. W. Norton,
    1981. 235 pp.

    Produced with grant monies from 1975-78, this
    comprehensive collection of records must be considered central to
    any library with an interest in American music. The recordings
    are indexed by number, by titles, performers, composers, writers
    of liner notes, photographers, and by genre.

38. Folk Music, a Catalog of Folk Songs, Ballads, Dances,
    Instrumental Pieces, and Folk Tales of United States and
    Latin America on Phonograph Records. Washington, D.C.:
    Library of Congress, Music Division, 1964. 110 pp.

    A selection of 166 recordings deemed to be the best of
    the 16,000 in the Library indexed here, with 1,240 titles in all.

39. KORSON, Rae. Folk Music, a Catalog of Folk Songs, Ballads,
    Dances, Instrumental Pieces, and Folk Tales of the U.S.

and Latin America on Phonograph Records. Washington,
D.C.: Library of Congress, Music Division, 1964. 107 pp.

40. LIFTON, Sarah. The Listener's Guide to Folk Music. New
York: Facts on File, 1983. 140 pp.

Series of short articles and record reviews covering
Britain, Ireland, and the U.S.A. (pp. 94-137). Includes mountain,
black, blues, urban revival, and old-timey traditions.

41. MOSES, Julian Morton. Collectors' Guide to American
Recordings, 1895-1925. New York: American Record
Collector's Exchange, 1949. 199 pp.

Rather dated listing of 7,000 records and 235 performers,
giving serial and matrix numbers. Brief biographical sketches of
each artist are included.

42. A Preliminary Directory of Sound Recordings Collections in
the United States and Canada. New York: New York Public
Library, 1967. 157 pp.

Organized by state, each entry provides name and address
as well as the types of materials included. While there are no
indices, making it hard to use, it lists many obscure but valuable
collections.

43. RUST, Brian. The American Record Label Book. New
Rochelle, N.Y.: Arlington House, 1978; reprint ed., New
York: Da Capo, 1984. 336 pp.

Alphabetical catalogue of American record labels and
histories, some extensive, some brief, by an English professor.
Covers from end of nineteenth century to 1942, from Aco to
Zonophone.

44. SCHURK, William L. "From the Popular Culture Turntable."
Journal of Popular Culture Supplement 4-1/4 (Summer, 1970
and Spring, 1971).

Classified and annotated list of records of many types
including blues, country-western, folk, gospel, jazz, popular, and
soul.

45. SPOTTSWOOD, Richard K. "A Catalogue of American Folk Music
     on Commercial Recordings at the Library of Congress, 1923-
     1940." M.A. thesis, Catholic University, 1962. 440 pp.

     Although theses are difficult to obtain and not normally
included in this work, Spottswood's thesis is significant for its
scope and thoroughness, and thus mentioned here.

46. TALLMADGE, William. A Selected and Annotated Discography of
     Southern Appalachian Mountain Music. Berea, Ken.: Berea
     College Appalachian Center, 1985. 69 pp.

47. TUDOR, Dean, and TUDOR, Mary. Grass Roots Music.
     Littleton, Colo.: Libraries Unlimited, 1979. 367 pp.

     Annotated survey and buying guide for librarians to 1,700
records covering such areas as ethnic, British folk traditions,
American folk traditions, American folk revival, old time,
bluegrass, southwestern music, country, sacred, and troubadour
(i.e., singer-songwriter). In addition, there is a bibliography, a
directory of labels, a list of specialist record stores, and of
artists.

Filmography

48. CENTER FOR SOUTHERN FOLKLORE. American Folklore Films and
     Videotapes: an Index. Compiled by Carolyn Lipson.
     Memphis: Center for Southern Folklore, 1976. 338 pp.;
     2nd ed., American . . . :a Catalogue. New York: R. R.
     Bowker, 1982. 355 pp.

     A vast list with descriptions of films and videotapes,
including timing, type and source. Indexed.

49. INTERNATIONAL FOLK MUSIC COUNCIL, LONDON. Films on
     Traditional Music and Dance: a First International
     Catalogue. Ed. by Peter Kennedy. Paris: UNESCO, 1970.
     261 pp.

     The section on the United States lists twelve films (pp.
230-4), giving location, type, duration, characteristics,
producer, distributor, and a brief synopsis. The subjects include
Afro-American blues, fiddle, banjo, Kentucky mountain music,
American Indian music, and jazz.

14

50. "Review of Folk Music on Film." Journal of American
    Folklore 87-345 (July-Sept., 1974--present).

    The journal began reviewing films of interest to
folklorists in 1974 and has continued doing so to the present.

Reference Works

51. BAGGELAAR, Kristin, and MILTON, Donald. Folk Music: More
    than a Song. New York: Thomas Y. Crowell, 1976. 419 pp.

    An encyclopedia of names, festivals, music publishers, and
organizations, especially in the folk music revival. Cross
referenced.

52. CLAGHORN, Charles Eugene. Biographical Dictionary of
    American Music. West Nyack, N.Y.: Parker, 1973. 491 pp.

    Brief biographical notes on 5,200 composers, lyricists,
musicians, singers, and teachers, living and deceased.

53. Grass Roots International Folk Resource Directory. New
    York: Grass Roots Productions, 1985.

    Covering the entire world, this ambitious collection lists
clubs, festivals, folksong and dance societies, concert promoters,
radio stations, media, record and book publishers and distributors,
instrument makers and repairers, and includes helpful articles,
such as "getting gigs." Revised annually.

54. HICKERSON, Joseph C. "North American Dealers of Folk Music
    and Folklore Books." Washington, D.C.: Library of
    Congress, Archive of Folk Song, 1980.

    Listing of sixteen companies with addresses.

55. HICKERSON, Joseph C., and CONDON, Kathleen. "Folklife and
    Ethnomusicology Archives and Related Collections in the
    United States and Canada." Washington, D.C.: Library of
    Congress, Archive of Folk Culture, n.d. 13 pp.

    State by state list of sources including seven directories
of archival resources in folklife and ethnomusicology.

56. HICKERSON, Kathryn W., and CONDON, Kathleen. "Folklife and Ethnomusicology Societies in North America." Washington, D.C.: Library of Congress, Archive of Folk Culture, 1982. 14 pp.

List of some 300 societies, with addresses.

57. House of Musical Traditions Catalog: a Guide to Musical Instruments of the World. Takoma Park, Md.: House of Musical Traditions.

A shop catalog updated and re-published according to business needs, its more than 100 pages a vast array of American folk instruments, instruction books, collections of music, and other materials. Address is 7040 Carroll Avenue, Takoma Park, Maryland 20912.

58. JONES, F. O. A Handbook of American Music and Musicians. Canaseraga, N.Y., 1886; reprint ed., New York: Da Capo, 1971. 182 pp.

Biographies of individuals and histories of musical institutions, firms, and societies.

59. KRUMMEL, D. W., GEIL, Jean, DYEN, Doris J., and ROOT, Deane L. Resources of American Music History. Urbana: University of Illinois Press, 1981. 463 pp.

Listing of 1,689 collections from the United States, its territories, and Canada and organized geographically (by state). These include university archives and libraries, publishers' libraries, private collections. There is a description of holdings for each item. Completing this well-researched resource is a 69-page index in fine print. This collection is indispensible for locating sometimes obscure but significant collections throughout the country.

60. LICHTENWANGER, William, HIGBEE, Dale, HOOVER, Cynthia Adams, and YOUNG, Philip T., compilers. A Survey of Musical Instrument Collections in the United States and Canada. Ann Arbor, Mich.: Music Library Association, 1974. 137 pp.

A list of 572 collections followed by an index of names and instruments, along with origins.

61. RABIN, Carol Price. A Guide to Music Festivals in America. Stockbridge, Mass.: Berkshire Traveller, 1979. 199 pp.

   Although devoted to all kinds of music festivals, pp. 164-81 list 15 "Folk and Traditional" festivals, and pp. 182-94 list 9 "Bluegrass, Old-Time Fiddlers, and Country" festivals. The descriptions are fuller than those of Smith and Barton's International Guide to Music Festivals (#66).

62. RABSON, Carolyn and KELLER, Kate Van Winkle. The National Tune Index: 18th Century Secular Music. New York: University Music Editions, 1980. 78 microfiche.

63. RABSON, Carolyn, and KELLER, Kate Van Winkle. The National Tune Index User's Guide: Eighteenth-Century Secular Music. New York: University Music Editions, 1980. 108 pp.

   Supported by the Sonneck Society, the authors created the National Tune Index to catalogue some 40,000 items from 520 printed and manuscript collections from the eighteenth century. Folk tunes and sacred tunes will be indexed in the future. Maintained in an electronic storage system, the index is in six categories: American imprints, musical theatre, country dances, airs without words, manuscripts, and songs. There are 5 indices: text (first lines), music (incipits in scale degrees), music (incipits in stressed note order), music (incipits in interval sequence), and source. Much of the material is of British Isles origin, naturally, and most of it thus far of tangential interest to folk song scholars. The User's Guide explains the National Tune Index and provides examples.

64. RASOF, Henry. The Folk, Country, and Bluegrass Musician's Catalogue. New York: St. Martin's, 1982. 192 pp.

   Extensive list, illustrated, of magazines, festivals, instruction materials, instrument makers, parts suppliers, etc. for guitar, banjo, mandolin, violin, dulcimer (lap zither), hammered dulcimer, autoharp, harmonica, bass, ukelele, psaltery, balalaika including strings and accessories. Also, dealers in used and vintage instruments are appended.

65. SANDBERG, Larry, and WEISSMAN, Dick. The Folk Music Sourcebook. New York: Alfred Knopf, 1976. 260 pp.

Organized into four sections, the collection provides much information in a folksy form. I. Listening, mostly a list of records of various kinds of music (Afro-American, American Indian, Chicano, Canadian, Cajun, Anglo, Western Swing, Contemporary, and Revival); II. Learning, a list of songbooks, reference books, and how-to books; III. Playing, information on playing the five-string banjo, dulcimer, guitar, mandolin, and others; IV. Hanging Out, a list of organizations, folk festivals, folk music centers, films, video tapes, and archives.

66. SMITH, Douglas, and BARTON, Nancy. International Guide to Music Festivals. New York: Quick Fox, 1980. 245 pp.

A general resource, pp. 48-128 include folk festivals listed by state and in Canada. Offers a description and information for travellers, but must be considered incomplete since it omits university and college festivals.

67. TUFT, Harry M. Catalogue and Almanac of Folk Music Supplies and Information for the Fiscal Year 1966. Denver: The Denver Folklore Center, 1965. 220 pp.

Provides information about folk music instruments and supplies, but emphasizes collections of both Afro-American and Anglo folk music on record. The former include, besides jazz, various kinds of blues and folk singers. The latter include some 950 recordings with annotations. There is also a bibliography of 258 folk song titles and an index to songs and articles in Broadside, issues 1-57.

68. WASSERMAN, Paul, ed. Festivals Sourcebook. Detroit: Gale Research Co., 1977. 656 pp.

Music festivals constitute a small part of this vast resource, specifically pp. 324-75, organized by place. In addition it lists fairs, festivals, and celebrations in agriculture, antiques, community dance, the arts, theatre and drama, arts and crafts, ethnic events, film, folklife, food and drink, history, Indians, marine, seasons, and wildlife. There are brief descriptions, dates, and addresses.

69. WILSON, Joe, and UDALL, Lee. Folk Festivals: a Handbook for Organization and Management. Knoxville: University of Tennessee Press, 1982. 278 pp.

A practical guide to organizers of folk festivals, this manual treats the history of folk festivals, administration, programming, publicity, hospitality, production, and provides examples of materials.

General and National Studies

70. BENSON, Norman Arthur. "The Itinerant Dancing and Music Masters of Eighteenth Century America." Ph.D. Dissertation, University of Minnesota, 1963. 488 pp.

Indirectly related to folk music research, this study concentrates on the musicians patronized by the upper classes in Charleston, Boston, New York, Philadelphia, Williamsburg, and elsewhere. These performers brought the fashions of Europe during their heyday in the eighteenth century, fashions which formed the popular taste of the nineteenth century.

71. BERGER, Melvin. The Story of Folk Music. New York: S. G. Phillips, 1976. 127 pp.

A lightweight study of personalities, instruments, and the influence of politics in the evolution of American folk music.

72. BRADY, Erika. "The Box that Got the Flourishes: the Cylinder Phonograph in Folklore Fieldwork, 1890-1937." Ph.D. Dissertation, Indiana University, 1985. 245 pp.

Study of the phenomenon of field recording, the relationships between collector and informant, and the changing needs of the discipline. The author asserts that "field cylinder recordings are the product of a complex human encounter in which the fieldworker and informant cooperate in order to fulfill their own agendas."

73. BROOKS, Henry M. Olden-Time Music: a Compilation from Newspapers and Books. Boston: Ticknor & Co., 1888; reprint ed., New York: AMS Press, 1973. 283 pp.

Based on books and Boston and Salem newspapers, this collection sought to show how much "progress" had been made since the time when our grandparents had it so bad musically. Although there are fascinating quotes, the documentation is slight. Coverage is broad, both secular and sacred, classical and folk.

19

74. CARNEY, George O. The Sounds of People and Places:
    Readings in the Geography of Music. Washington, D.C.:
    University Press of America, 1978. 336 pp.

A study of American music from a geographer's point of
view, based on maps, this unique study is divided into nine parts.
They include six articles on country music, two each on popular and
rock musics, and one each on gospel and folk revival musics. There
is also a list of record companies.

75. CHASE, Gilbert. America's Music: from the Pilgrims to the
    Present. Rev. 2nd ed. New York: McGraw-Hill Book Co.,
    1966. 759 pp.

The standard survey of American music for many years,
Chase's study maintains a high level of scholarship but presented
with relatively few attractive features, e.g., illustrations and
musical examples. Certain subjects pertinent to this study are
thoroughly covered, such as early psalm singing, singing schools,
and nineteenth-century folk hymnody, but there is rather little on
Anglo-American instrumental or vocal music and ethnic music. There
is in addition a chapter on the African heritage and the spiritual.

76. COFFIN, Tristram Potter, ed. Our Living Traditions: an
    Introduction to American Folklore. New York: Basic Books,
    1968. 301 pp.

A collection of 25 short articles by leading folklorists
on folklore as a field of study, ballads, Afro-American religious
music, folksong and dance, as well as a section on "Folklore and
Modern Times," i.e., hillbilly and urban revival musics.

77. DAVIS, Ronald L. A History of Music in American Life. 3
    vols. Huntington, N.Y. and Malabar, Florida: Robert
    Krieger Publishing Co., 1980-1982. Vol. I, The Formative
    Years, 1620-1865, 301 pp. Vol. II, The Gilded Years,
    1865-1920, Vol. III, The Modern Era, 1920-Present. 444 pp.

Based mostly on secondary sources, this ambitious and
comprehensive survey was written by a specialist in history and
American studies, and thus the concern for "music in American
life." It is therefore a non-technical social history. Vol. I
includes the Puritans, Billings, and much classical music. "A
Nation of Sections" covers many small groups. Some quotes appear
to be undocumented. Vol. III treats, among other things, popular

songs, country, rock, and soul. More a summing up than breaking of new ground.

78. The Federal Cylinder Project: a Guide to Cylinder Recordings in Federal Agencies. Studies in American Folklife #3. Washington: Government Printing Office, 1984--present. (In progress)

Vol. I. BRADY, Erika, LAVIGNA, Maria, LEE, Dorothy Sara, VENNUM, Thomas, Jr. Introduction and Inventory. 110 pp.

An index of collections totalling 10,000 plus field-recorded wax cylinders that have been copied onto tape at the Library of Congress.

Vol. VIII. LEE, Dorothy Sara, with Introduction by DeVALE, Sue Carole. Early Anthologies. 96 pp.

Descriptions of Benjamin Ives Gilman's cylinder recordings from the 1893 World's Columbian Exposition and the "Demonstration Collection" edited by E. Moritz von Hornbostel issued by the Berlin Phonogramm Archiv shortly after World War I.

79. FERRIS, William, and HART, Mary L., eds. Folk Music and the Modern Sound. Jackson: University Press of Mississippi, 1982. 215 pp.

Collection of 15 essays organized under six headings: The Anglo Connection (Kenneth Goldstein and A. L. Lloyd on folk music in Britain), Ethnic Voices (Mark Slobin, Charles Keil, and Richard Spottswood on Jewish, Slovenian, and the ethnic-popular relation-ship), The Religious Sound (articles by Doris Dyen on Sacred Harp singing, Charles K. Wolfe on white gospel, and Anthony Heilbut on black gospel), Pure Country (William Ivey and Bill C. Malone), Myths and Heroes (Dena Epstein on myths on black folk music), and Blacks and Blues (3 articles by David Evans, Imamu Amiri Baraka, and Robert Palmer). Together these papers were the basis of a conference held at the University of Mississippi in 1980.

80. GLEASON, Harold, and BECKER, Warren. Early American Music: Music in America from 1620 to 1920. 2nd ed. Music Literature Outlines, series III. Bloomington, Ind.: Frangipani Press, 1981. 201 pp.

In outline form and intended for students, this survey covers psalmody, singing schools, German sects, folk hymns, and Shakers. Each section has a bibliography.

81. GRAME, Theodore C. _America's Ethnic Music._ Tarpon Springs, Fla.: Cultural Maintenance Associates, 1976. 232 pp.

The first phase of the SCAMP Project, Study Collection of American Musical Pluralism, this volume surveys the ethnic and musical diversity in the United States, from blacks to ballads to Greeks. There is a classified bibliography.

82. _Grove's Dictionary of Music and Musicians._ 5th ed. S.v. "Folk Music U.S.A." by Charles Seeger [Vol. 3, pp. 387-98]

Although this edition has been superceded both by _The New Grove Dictionary of Music and Musicians_ (#102) and _The New Grove Dictionary of American Music_ (#101), Seeger's article in the 1954 edition is important for its viewpoint. Among the topics he treats are Afro-American music, the field collection of folk music, American elements in Anglo-American folk music, instrumental music, and the musics of foreign language minorities.

83. HAMM, Charles. _Music in the New World._ New York: W. W. Norton, 1983. 722 pp.

The most comprehensive, single volume study currently available and a worthy successor to Chase's pioneering _America's Music._ Examples linked to the New World Records series, the Library of Congress Folk Music in the Americas series, and other earlier sets of recordings. Substantial material on American Indians, colonial psalm singing, Anglo-American oral traditions, Afro-American music, singing schools and shape note music, popular song, the roots of jazz, hillbilly and country-western, jazz, and rock. There are numerous musical examples and illustrations.

84. HERZOG, George. _Research in Primitive and Folk Music in the United States._ Washington, D.C.: American Council of Learned Societies, Bulletin #24, April, 1936. 97 pp. [pp. 561-657].

Early survey of the "new" field of ethnomusicology, its history in the United States, problems, goals, collectors and collections. Herzog asserts that primitive and folk musics are different categories. There is an extensive bibliography that is strongest in American Indian music.

85. HITCHCOCK, H. Wiley. Music in the United States: a Historical Introduction. Englewood Cliffs, N.J.: Prentice-Hall, 1969. 270 pp.; 2nd ed., 1974. 286 pp.

While this survey concentrates on "cultivated" (i.e., classical) music, there is some coverage of sacred and secular traditions in New England, but surprisingly, the word "ballad" is not found in the Index.

86. HOWARD, John Tasker. Our American Music. 3rd ed., rev. New York: Thomas Y. Crowell, 1946. 841 pp.

Originally published in 1929, Howard's tome was the first genuine attempt at being comprehensive. But only fourteen pages are devoted to psalmody, and one chapter, "Our Folk Music" (pp. 613-42) discusses the music of American Indians, Afro-Americans, and others (e.g., Appalachians). There are no musical examples.

87. HOWARD, John Tasker. "Our Folk-Music and its Probable Impress on American Music of the Future." Musical Quarterly 7 (1921): 167-71.

This early article deplores the inadequacy that some Americans felt regarding their culture. He raises the question whether American Indian or Negro musics are American, and suggests that our composers might use folk materials in their works.

88. KEENE, James. A History of Music Education in the United States. Hanover, N.H.: University Press of New England, 1982. 396 pp.

In the course of tracing music education's history from colonial times to the present, the author considers at great length both the contributions of the eighteenth-century singing school school masters and Lowell Mason in the nineteenth century.

89. KINSCELLA, Hazel Gertrude, ed. History Sings. Lincoln: University Publishing Co., 1940. 528 pp.; rev. ed., 1970. 428 pp.

A rather light collection of articles by the compiler and others, many of which are reprints, on various facets of American folk music, including singing schools, American Indian singing, psalmody, balladry, Southern music, Texas music, and cowboy songs, as well as others by region. Most are quite brief.

90. LIFTON, Sarah. The Listener's Guide to Folk Music. New York: Facts on File, 1983. 140 pp.

A popular overview of folk music and the revival in both the United States and the British Isles.

91. LIST, George. "Folk Music." In Folklore and Folklife: an Introduction, pp. 363-80. Edited by Richard M. Dorson. Chicago: University of Chicago Press, 1972.

Intended as textbook material, List offers a definition of folk music (music that is transmitted orally) and instructs the student in doing transcription, determining scale, and musical analysis.

92. LIST, George, and ORREGO-SALAS, Juan, eds. Music in the Americas. Inter-American Music Monograph Series #1. Bloomington: Indiana University Research Center in Anthropology, Folklore, and Linguistics, 1967. 257 pp.

Comprises papers presented at the First International American Seminar of Composers and the Second Inter-American Conference on Ethnomusicology held at Indiana University, April 24-28, 1965. Papers of interest here are by Gillis, Haywood, List, Merriam, and Nettl.

93. McCUE, George, ed. Music in American Society, 1776-1976: From Puritan Hymns to Synthesizer. New Brunswick, N.J.: Transaction Books, 1977. 201 pp.

Collection of articles, the pertinent ones covering hymnology (Caswell), black music (Billings), American Indian (Frisbie), and "American Folksong: Some Comments on the History of its Collection and Archiving" (Hickerson).

94. McCULLOH, Judith, ed. Ethnic Recordings in America: a Neglected Heritage. Washington: Government Printing

Office, Library of Congress, American Folklife Center, 1982. 269 pp.

Compilation of essays on the history and current status of the ethnic recording industry. Many illustrations and an index.

95. MARROCCO, W. Thomas, and GLEASON, Harold. Music in America: an Anthology from the Landing of the Pilgrims to the Close of the Civil War, 1620-1865. New York: W. W. Norton, 1964. 371 pp.

Collection of music in notation with brief introductions to each section. Subjects include metrical psalmody, singing school music, music from Ephrata and of the Moravians, European-influenced music, the works of L. Mason and his contemporaries, and a good selection of folk hymns taken from nineteenth-century oblong collections. The selections in this fully documented collection are presented for practical performance.

96. MASON, Daniel Gregory. "Folk-Song and American Music (A Plea for the Unpopular Point of View)." Musical Quarterly 4 (1918): 323-32.

An essay written by a composer on the discovery and creation of an "American music," it examines analytically the Negro spirituals as sung by the Jubilee Singers and asks whether these might be the basis for new American compositions.

97. MEADE, Guthrie T., Jr. "Copyright: a Tool for Commercial Rural Music Research." Western Folklore 30-3 (July, 1971): 206-14.

Argues that there is a relationship between the printed and manuscript materials of the U.S. Copyright Office and folk music, especially for country music and to some extent for blues as well.

98. NETTL, Bruno. An Introduction to Folk Music in the United States. Detroit: Wayne State University Press, 1960; rev. ed., 1962. 126 pp. 3rd ed., revised and expanded by Helen Myers, entitled Folk Music in the United States, an Introduction, 1976. 187 pp.

Non-technical introduction to the idea of folk music, and to specific types: American Indian, British Isles, European, African, urban folk music, professional folk singers, and the collection and study of folk music.

99. NETTL, Bruno. Music in Primitive Culture. Cambridge: Harvard University Press, 1956. 182 pp.

Generously illustrated with musical examples, this early and general study of the subject includes American Indian music (pp. 105-19) and Afro-American music (pp. 120-33).

100. NETTL, Bruno. "Preliminary Remarks on the Urban Folk Music of Detroit." Western Folklore 16-1 (Jan., 1957): 37-42.

Exploratory article in which the author seeks answers to many questions about research on folk music in the context of Detroit. Shows how urban folk music differs in function and structure from rural folk music.

101. The New Grove Dictionary of American Music. 4 vols. (Available, September, 1986)

Partially new, partially derived from The New Grove Dictionary of Music and Musicians published in 1980 (#102), this comprehensive encyclopedia devoted to American music includes folk music as one part of the larger picture. Within its 2,600 pages will be some 5,000 articles and 600 illustrations. According to advance publicity, the work will include 90 articles on ethnic musics, 205 on instruments and instrument makers, 90 on Country music, and 95 on blues and gospel.

102. The New Grove Dictionary of Music and Musicians. 20 vols. 1980.

The successor to Grove's Dictionary of Music and Musicians, 5th ed., The New Grove is a world-scope encyclopedia by hundreds of scholars. There are numerous articles relative to American folk music, the most important of which follow. The longer articles include photographic illustrations and musical examples, and most examples include chronologically arranged bibliographies. Most subjects appear within major articles devoted to geographical areas, but certain genres are treated in separate articles of varying lengths.

"Ballad I" by Bertrand H. Bronson (2:70-75) surveys the subject from an international perspective, with American balladry woven into this larger picture.

"Blues" by Paul Oliver (2:812-19) discusses definitions, origins, and then traces the history of the blues from the earliest recordings.

"Cajun" by Bill C. Malone (3:611) provides a brief, historical overview.

"Country Music" by Bill C. Malone (4:854-5) is brief and basic.

"Gospel Music" is divided into white and black, the former by Harry Eskew (7:549-55) and the latter by Paul Oliver (7:555-59). Both are historically based.

"Hawaii" by A. Peter Brown (8:319-20) is an historical overview with emphasis on European traditions written by a musicologist. Information on traditional music is found in the article "Polynesia, 5: Hawaii" (15:62-5).

"North America, I. Folk Music" by various authors (13:292-95) is an overview.

"North America, II. Indian and Eskimo Music" by various authors (13:295-320) is organized by geographical area. The writing is technical, and includes transcriptions as well as photos of instruments and dance.

"Shape-Note Hymnody" by Harry Eskew (17:223-28) is historical and descriptive.

"United States of America" by various authors (19:424-52) is the most substantial article. Section I. Art Music, includes psalm singing and singing school music. Section II. Folk Music (pp. 436 ff. by Charles Seeger) treats the broad-spectrum, including Afro-American, instrumental music, and the folk revival.

103. Racial and Ethnic Directions in American Music. By T. J. Anderson, Chairman. College Music Society Report #3. 1982. 76 pp.

    With its emphasis on the place of minorities in the music professions and in the education system, the report surveys American Indians, Asian-Americans, Hispanics, Afro-Americans. While information about the musics is limited, the author reports

on changes in attitudes towards these musics vis-a-vis the
education system.

104. ROONEY, James. __Bossman: Bill Monroe & Muddy Waters.__ New
York: Hayden Book Co., 1971. 159 pp.

Although popular and photo oriented, an interesting study
of two leaders, one (Bill Monroe) of bluegrass and one (Muddy
Waters) of urban blues. Includes many direct quotes.

105. SEEGER, Charles. __Studies in Musicology, 1935-1975.__
Berkeley: University of California Press, 1977. 357 pp.

Collection of published articles by a brilliant but
sometimes difficult-to-follow thinker. Articles pertinent here
include "Music and Class Structure in the United States" (pp. 222-
36", "Contrapuntal Style in the Three-Voice Shape-Note Hymns of
the United States" (pp. 237-51), "The Appalachian Dulcimer" (pp.
252-72), "Versions and Variants of 'Barbara Allen' in the Archive
of American Song to 1940" (pp. 273-320), "Professionalism and
Amateurism in the Study of Folk Music" (pp. 321-29), "Folk Music
in the Schools of a Highly Industrialized Society" (pp. 330-34),
and "The Folkness of the Nonfolk and the Nonfolkness of the Folk"
(pp. 335-44). While certain of them examine specific matters of
folk music, others are philosophical and thought-provoking.

106. STEVENSON, Robert. __Protestant Church Music in America.__
New York: W. W. Norton, 1966. 168 pp.

Brief, but detailed and thoroughly documented study which
includes psalm singing, singing schools, shape-notes, and Afro-
American musics. The bibliography is especially valuable.

107. WHITMAN, T. Carl. "The Energy of American Crowd Music."
__Musical Quarterly__ 4 (1918): 98-116.

Early and broad-minded study of the kinds of music
avoided by "snobs," e.g., folksong, popular music, religious
music, the talking machines (phonographs), movie music, and
municipal music. These are examined briefly in the context of
certain cities.

108. WOLFE, Richard J. Early American Music Engraving and
     Printing: a History of Music Publishing in America from
     1787 to 1825 with Commentary on Earlier and Later
     Practices. Urbana: University of Illinois Press, 1980.
     344 pp.

     Comprehensive history of the subject with much information
on the techniques, presses, paper, and people who used them. While
not about folk music per se, it is germaine to the study of singing
school books.

State and Regional Studies

109. ADAMS, Kermit Gary. "Music in the Oklahoma Territory:
     1889-1907." Ph.D. dissertation, North Texas State
     University, 1979. 238 pp.

     With Oklahoma City and Guthrie as the focus, this study
of music at the turn of the century is based on newspapers, books,
periodicals, letters, sheet music, concert programs, college
catalogues, church records, and photographs. It covers cultivated
as well as folk genres.

110. BARNES-OSTRANDER, M. E. "Domestic Music Making in Early
     New York State: Music in the Lives of Three Amateurs."
     Musical Quarterly 68 (1982): 353-72.

     Based on material in the Music Division of the Library of
Congress dating from the 1780s to the 1820s, this article
describes music making in the home. While the music is not folk
per se, this study provides a valuable look at a folk-like
environment.

111. BROUCEK, Jack W. "Eighteenth Century Music in Savannah,
     Georgia." Ed. D. dissertation, Florida State University,
     1962. 251 pp.

     Included is the study of early church music, particularly
that of the Wesleys, the musics of various ethnic groups (e.g.,
Indians, Afro-Americans, and the Scottish), and social music
(e.g., music for dance).

112.   BURTON, Thomas G., ed.   Tom Ashley, Sam McGee, Bukka White:
       Tennessee Traditional Singers.   Knoxville: University of
       Tennessee Press, 1981.   256 pp.

       This set of articles, with Introduction and Conclusion
written by Burton, treats three traditional musicians: Tom Ashley,
a white folksinger (by A. N. Manning and M. M. Miller); Sam McGee,
a country musician (by C. K. Wolfe); and Bukka White, a black blues
singer (by F. J. Hurley and D. Evans).   Photos and transcriptions.

113.   CARDEN, Joy.   Music in Lexington Before 1840.   Lexington,
       Ken.: Fayette County Historic Commission, 1980.   148 pp.

       Treats both classical and folk musics, the latter
including singing schools and religious folk music.

114.   CARNEY, George O.   Oklahoma's Folk Music Tradition: a
       Resource Guide.   Stillwater: Dept. of Geography, Oklahoma
       State University, 1979.   104 pp.

115.   COLLINGS, Henrietta.   Georgia's Heritage of Song.   Athens:
       University of Georgia Press, 1955.   87 pp.

       A collection of folk songs, spirituals, and other songs,
including some composed by Georgians.   Drawings by Virginia Hall.

116.   CREWS, Emma Katherine.   "A History of Music in Knoxville,
       Tennessee, 1791-1910."   Ed.D. dissertation, Florida State
       University, 1961.   253 pp.

       Comprehensive study that touches on such diverse topics
as church music, dance, celebrations, music merchants and
merchandise, concerts and art music, organizations, theatre, music
education, general attitudes, singing schools, music societies,
the Brotherhood of Fiddlers, and piano making.

117.   EDWARDS, George Thornton.   Music and Musicians of Maine.
       Portland: Southwark Printing, 1928; reprint ed., New
       York: AMS, 1970.   542 pp.

       This early study provides much useful and detailed
material on psalms, singing schools, as well as other kinds of
music, especially classical.

118. HICKERSON, Joseph. "Alan Lomax's 'Southern Journey': a
     Review-Essay." Ethnomusicology 9-3 (Sept. 1965): 313-22.

     Review of eleven records (Prestige International
Documentary Series Int 25001-25012) that resulted from a major
recording trip undertaken by Lomax in 1959 during which he
collected Georgia sea island music, ballads, instrumental music,
music from the Ozarks, Sacred Harp singing, blues, and choral
music of the Church of God and Saints of Christ. This set
includes a series published earlier, in 1959, called "Southern
Folk Heritage" (Atlantic HS #1).

119. HOOGERWERF, Frank W., ed. Music in Georgia. New York: Da
     Capo, 1984. 343 pp.

     Collection of periodical reprints from 1934-77, including
several pertaining to folk music in Georgia. Subjects include
Sacred Harp singing, Wesley's hymns, camp meetings, Judaeo-Spanish
ballads, Anglo ballads, black song, and do-re-mi shape notes.

120. KAUFMAN, Charles H. Music in New Jersey, 1655-1860.
     Rutherford, N.J.: Fairleigh Dickinson University Press,
     1981. 297 pp.

     Part I is devoted to sacred music, especially psalmody,
and is organized by denomination. Part II treats secular genres,
including singing schools and instrument makers. A number of
historical documents are reproduced.

121. LAMBERT, Barbara, ed. Music in Colonial Massachusetts,
     1630-1820. 2 vols. Publications of the Colonial Society
     of Massachusetts, vols. 53-54. Boston: Colonial Society
     of Massachusetts, 1980-85. 1,194 pp.

     Vol. I. Music in Public Places, 1980.

     Vol. II. Music in Homes and in Churches, 1985.

     Compiled from papers given by noted scholars at a
conference on May 17-18, 1973, in Boston, Vol. I covers a variety
of topics, including country dance and military music, Revolutionary War songs, and broadside ballads, while Vol. II is devoted
to songsters, early American psalmody, drums, cries, and bells.

122. MALONE, Bill C. <u>Southern</u> <u>Music</u> <u>American</u> <u>Music.</u> Lexington:
      University Press of Kentucky, 1979. 203 pp.

         Major study of southern music, both in its own right, and
as the fountainhead for national musics, intended for a general
reading audience. Traces the origins of southern music from the
many influences on it, especially British and African, to its
appreciation outside the south beginning in the 1830s. From near
the turn of the century the south spawned blues, jazz, hillbilly,
rock, and other genres which came to be appreciated and embraced
by all Americans.

123. NATIONAL SOCIETY OF THE COLONIAL DAMES OF AMERICA. <u>Church</u>
      <u>Music</u> <u>and</u> <u>Musical</u> <u>Life</u> <u>in</u> <u>Pennsylvania</u> <u>in</u> <u>the</u> <u>Eighteenth</u>
      <u>Century.</u> 3 vols. Publications of the Pennsylvania
      Society of the Colonial Dames of America #4.
      Philadelphia: The Society, 1926-47.

         Substantial collection of essays providing a
comprehensive view of religious music in Pennsylvania. Vol. I
(274 pp.) concentrates on Johannes Kelpius, Justus Falckner, and
early German and Swedish settlements. Vol. II (303 pp.) concerns
German and Swiss Pietists, Dunkers and Mennonites, the Moravians,
and musical practices. Vol. III. (597 pp.), compiled in part in
1938 and completed in 1947, studies English traditions, including
ballads, church music, Freemason songs, Jewish, Welsh, Roman
Catholic, and Lutheran musics, and other matters, such as early
composers.

124. REYES-SCHRAMM, Adelaida. "The Role of Music in the
      Interaction of Black Americans and Hispanos in New York
      City's East Harlem." Ph.D. dissertation, Columbia
      University, 1975. 273 pp.

         While this study focuses on the musical interaction of
two groups in New York's East Harlem, it is concerned with the
larger issue of urban ethnomusicology and the methodological
problems associated with it as well as music in everyday life and
how groups interact.

125. ROHRER, Gertrude Martin, ed. <u>Music</u> <u>and</u> <u>Musicians</u> <u>of</u>
      <u>Pennsylvania.</u> Port Washington, N.Y.: Kennikat Press,
      1940; reprint ed., 1970. 121 pp.

         Relatively brief non-technical studies that include

Indian music (by Rohrer), "native folk music" (by Marian E.
Ottoson), Quaker music and gospel.

126.   SPELL, Lota M. Music in Texas: a Survey of one Aspect of
          Cultural Progress. Austin: By the Author, 1936. 157 pp.

        With a distinct bias for "cultural progress," the author
treats briefly the musics of the Indians, missions, Spanish-
Mexicans and Anglo-Americans. Texas folk music is specifically
studied on pp. 127-36.

127.   SWAN, Howard. Music in the Southwest, 1825-1950. San
          Marino, Cal.: Huntington Library, 1952. 316 pp.

        Regional study of many kinds of music including Mormon
(pp. 3-58), mining camps, missions, and cowboys. Orientation is
cultural and textual.

128.   SWAN, John C., ed. Music in Boston: Readings from the
          First Three Centuries. Boston: Trustees of the Public
          Library, 1977. 99 pp.

        Collection of quotations from various sources concerning
the Bay Psalm Book, Cotton Mather, Thomas Symmes (on regular
singing), William Billings, and other matters.

129.   WILSON, Ruth Mack, and KELLER, Kate Van Winkle.
          Connecticut's Music in the Revolutionary Era. Hartford:
          American Revolution Bicentennial Commission of
          Connecticut, 1979. 142 pp.

        Scholarly study full of direct quotations from and
facsimiles of contemporary material. Concentrates on psalmody,
singing schools, and secular music.

130.   WOLFE, Charles K. Kentucky Country: Folk and Country Music
          of Kentucky. Lexington: University Press of Kentucky,
          1982. 199 pp.

        Written by an English professor, this study concentrates
on hillbilly, Western swing, gospel, bluegrass, honky tonk, and
Nashville styles.

II. MUSIC OF THE AMERICAN INDIANS AND ESKIMOS

Of all the areas covered by this collection, American Indian
music is by far the most thoroughly researched from both musical
and anthropological points of view. Just as the field of folklore,
which now embraces the entire world, at first concentrated on
Anglo-American traditions, the field of ethnomusicology once
concentrated much of its energy on American Indian music. Indeed,
one of the major roots of ethnomusicology was largely created by
American Indian specialists trained in both music and anthropology.
Furthermore, these people were the pioneers in ethnomusicological
scholarship in the United States, some going back to the late
nineteenth century. Their names appear often in this biblio-
graphy--Frances Densmore, David McAllester, George Herzog, Bruno
Nettl, Alan Merriam, Gertrude Prokosch Kurath, Willard Rhodes,
among others.

Interestingly, the earliest research among American Indians
had a European focus, for the American Theodore Baker wrote his
1882 dissertation while a student in Germany and Carl Stumpf wrote
his 1886 study based on Indians visiting Germany. In 1890, an
American, J. Walter Fewkes, became the first scholar to use the
phonograph for field recording, among Indians in Maine and the
Southwest, and Benjamin Gilman, who worked with Fewkes' cylinders,
was the first "armchair" ethnomusicologist to study field
recordings.

Although research on American Indian music was being done for
its own sake or as part of larger studies of particular tribes, a
significant stimulus came from a new generation of American composers seeking to create a distinctly American idiom around the
turn of the century, a period of musical nationalism. Antonin
Dvorak had suggested that American composers seek American
inspiration, and quite a few thought American Indian music would
serve this purpose. Unfortunately, ethnocentrism prevented most
trained musicians from approaching the music on anything
approximating neutral terms. John Comfort Fillmore, for example,

argued not only that the Indians really meant to sing within the European diatonic scale system, but that their music had clear harmonic implications which he could easily realize on the piano. Some critics thought Edward MacDowell's Suite No. 2 ("Indian") was genuine "red" Indian music but not beautiful while others realized that it was beautiful but not genuine. Composers tended to take a patronizing position, saying that, while American Indian music obviously required cleaning up, because it was so "rough," it nevertheless had enough "natural" beauty of its own to provide usable material when transformed by a skillful composer.

A higher percentage of material listed here is technical in a musical sense than is found in any other section. The reader will find numerous transcriptions and detailed analyses along with extensive contextual description. The level of scholarship is overall higher than in any other section as well. Indeed, much of this research has been and continues to be held up as a model for students of ethnomusicology.

Bibliography and Discography

Note: The following unannotated lists were prepared by the Archive of Folk Song in the Library of Congress, Washington, D.C., and are available by mail.

131. "A Brief List of Material Relating to Seneca Indian Music." 23 entries.

132. "A Brief List of Material Relating to Shawnee Indian Music." 12 entries.

133. "A Brief List of Material Relating to the Music of the American Indians of the Northwest Coast." 31 entries, including many relating to Canada.

134. "A Brief List of References to the Music of the Cherokee Indians." 1970. 18 entries.

135. "A List of References to the Music and Songs of the California Indians Culture Area." 1967. 5 pp.

136. "Selected List of References on Eskimo Music." 1968. 22 entries.

137. "A Selected List of Works on American Indian Music, not Including Eskimo." 1970. 5 pp.

138. CAVANAGH, Beverly. "Annotated Bibliography: Eskimo Music." Ethnomusicology 16-3 (Sept. 1972): 479-87.

    List of 118 sources, including some bibliographies, covering Alaska, Greenland, and Canada.

139. FRISBIE, Charlotte J. Music and Dance Research of Southwestern United States Indians: Past Trends, Present Activities, and Suggestions for Further Research. Detroit Studies in Music Bibliography #36. Detroit: Information Coordinators, 1977. 109 pp.

    A review of the research literature from 1880 to 1969 under "The Past," and from 1970 to 1976 in "The Present." Includes a 42-page unannotated bibliography.

140. HICKERSON, Joseph. "Annotated Bibliography of North American Indian Music North of Mexico." M.A. thesis, Indiana University, 1961. 464 pp.

    Roughly 1300 items, including a tribal index and list of items concerning the investigation of North American Indian music.

141. KORSON, Rae, and HICKERSON, Joseph C. "The Willard Rhodes Collection of American Indian Music in the Archive of Folk Song." Ethnomusicology 13-2 (1969): 296-304.

    A description of the contents of ten LP records.

142. LEE, Dorothy Sara. Native North American Music and Oral Data: a Catalogue of Sound Recordings, 1893-1976. Bloomington: Indiana University Press, 1979. 463 pp.

    A list of the holdings in the Archives of Traditional Music covering North and Central America including the Eskimos. Published from a computer print-out, and for the specialist.

143. RHODES, Willard. "North American Indian Music: a Biblio-
     graphic Survey of Anthropological Theory." Music Library
     Association Notes 10-1 (Dec. 1952): 33-45.

     Serious and valuable review of literature from Baker's
study in 1882 to 1952, emphasizing older material.

144. STEVENSON, Robert. "English Sources for Indian Music until
     1882." Ethnomusicology 17-3 (July 1973): 399-442.

     Review of literature and bibliography covering the period
c.1588 to 1882, with musical examples and quotations.

145. STEVENSON, Robert. "Written Sources for Indian Music until
     1882." Ethnomusicology 17-1 (Jan. 1973): 1-40.

     Review of literature and bibliography for materials from
the sixteenth to nineteenth centuries, many of which were the
sources for Baker's 1882 study, with emphasis on the observations
of early French and Spanish travellers. Also includes several
early examples in facsimile.

General Books and Articles

146. ARCHABAL, Nina Marchetti. "Frances Densmore: Pioneer in
     the Study of American Indian Music." In Women of
     Minnesota: Selected Biographical Essays, pp. 94-115.
     Edited by Barbara Stuhler. St. Paul: Minnesota
     Historical Society, 1977.

     A study focusing on Densmore's Western European art music
training and the influences of her mentors, Alice Cunningham
Fletcher, John Comfort Fillmore, and Carl Seashore. Also a
description of her methods of analysis. While Densmore focused on
the Dakota and Chippewa, she wrote on a host of other tribes too.

147. BAKER, Theodore. Uber die Musik der Nordamerikanischen
     Wilden. Leipzig: Breitkopf und Hartel, 1882; reprint
     ed., New York: Da Capo, 1977; new edition, with trans-
     lation by Ann Buckley, Buren, Netherlands: Frits Knuf,
     1976. 150 pp.

     Baker (1851-1934) is best known for his biographical
dictionary which first appeared in 1900 and continues in new

37

editions to the present, but his doctoral dissertation, written in Leipzig in 1882, was the first serious study undertaken of American Indian music. Based on field studies among the Seneca in New York State, Baker's book was an important stimulus for a new generation of American classical composers who sought to develop an American idiom based on Indian melodies. Edward MacDowell, for example, borrowed some of his themes for his Second ("Indian") Suite from Baker's transcriptions. Baker also used a number of earlier written sources.

148. BARBEAU, Marius. "Asiatic Survivals in Indian Songs." Musical Quarterly 20 (1934): 107-16; reprinted in Queen's Quarterly 47 (1940): 67-76.

Valuable study with text translations of singing on both sides of the Bering Strait. Shows a clear relationship between North American and Siberian singing.

149. BIERHORST, John. A Cry from the Earth: Music of the North American Indians. New York: Four Winds, 1979. 113 pp.

An enlightened book for children with well-done translations, a survey by topics, and good photos.

150. BROWN, Donald N. "Ethnomusicology and the Prehistoric Southwest." Ethnomusicology 15-3 (Sept. 1971): 363-78.

A study in which both contextual (music as one aspect of a socio-cultural system) and comparative (similarities and differences among groups) approaches are applied, especially to Indian artifacts from the Southwest. The author notes that although instruments were added from time to time, the instruments already existing in the 7th century (e.g., flutes, whistles, and rattles) continue to the present.

151. BUTTREE, Julia M. The Rhythm of the Red Man: in Song, Dance and Decoration. New York: A. S. Barnes Co., 1930. 280 pp.

In library card catalogues, this collection may also be found under SETON, Mrs. Julia Moss. A sincere attempt to make Indian music accessible by describing it and providing meaningful words. It also describes and illustrates ceremonies, songs, musical instruments, and art.

152. CADMAN, Charles Wakefield. "The 'Idealization' of Indian
     Music." Musical Quarterly 1 (1915): 387-96.

     Essay by a composer on the uses of Indian themes in
composition.

153. COLLAER, Paul. Amerika: Eskimo und indianische
     Bevolkerung. Musikgeschichte in Bildern, Band 1.
     Musikethnologie, Lieferung 2. Leipzig: VEB Deutscher
     Verlag, n.d. [1967]. 211 pp.

     In German, but includes 90 excellent photos and captions
of instruments and musicians covering North, Central, and South
America. See following entry for translation.

154. COLLAER, Paul. Music of the Americas: an Illustrated Music
     Ethnology of the Eskimo and American Indian Peoples. New
     York: Praeger, 1971. 212 pp.

155. CRONYN, George William. The Path of the Rainbow: an
     Anthology of Songs and Chants from the Indians of North
     America. New York: Boni & Liveright, 1918. 347 pp.; 2nd
     ed., New York: Liveright Publishing Co., 1934. 360 pp.

     After a 32-page introduction by Mary Austin, there is a
collection of translated texts from the Eastern Woodlands,
Southeast, Great Plains, Southwest, California, Northwest Coast,
and Far North Indian areas, interpreted by several writers.

156. CURTIS, Natalie. "American Indian Cradle Songs." Musical
     Quarterly 7 (1921): 549-58.

     An examination of seven lullabies with both melody and
text from various tribes.

157. CURTIS, Natalie. The Indians' Book. New York: Harper and
     Brothers, 1907, 1923; reprint ed., New York: Dover, 1968.
     584 pp.

     Mostly a classified catalogue of songs with texts and
tunes and some discussion.

158. DENSMORE, Frances. The American Indians and Their Music. New York: The Woman's Press, 1926; reprint ed., New York: Johnson Reprint Corp., 1976. 143 pp.

The best of the early surveys, written in non-technical language.

159. DENSMORE, Frances. "Music of the American Indians at Public Gatherings." Musical Quarterly 17 (1931): 464-79.

Non-technical article that considers in general the poetry, drama, dance, and games of the Papago, Sioux, Yaqui, Ute, and others, with some examples.

160. DENSMORE, Frances. "The Songs of Indian Soldiers during the World War." Musical Quarterly 20 (1934): 419-25.

An appreciation of the Indians' contribution to the war effort (World War I) and a description of their songs about the war, with transcriptions.

161. DENSMORE, Frances. "The Study of Indian Music." Musical Quarterly 1 (1915): 187-97.

Broad essay on Indian music and the author's experience with it up to that time.

162. DENSMORE, Frances. "The Use of Music in the Treatment of the Sick by American Indians." Musical Quarterly 13 (1927): 555-65.

Broad survey of song and drumming in the context of healing, with examples and photos.

163. DENSMORE, Frances. "The Words of Indian Songs as Unwritten Literature." Journal of American Folklore 63-250 (Oct.-Dec. 1950): 450-8.

The author offers this study of text to counter-balance the previous emphasis given to melody and instruments.

164. ERICKSON, Edwin Erich. "The Song Trace Song Styles and the Ethnohistory of Aboriginal America." Ph.D. dissertation, Columbia University, 1969. 441 pp.

Highly technical, but broad study comparing American Indian styles with New World culture history in songs from both South and North America based on Alan Lomax's Cantometrics.

165. FICHTER, George S. American Indian Music and Musical Instruments. New York: David McKay, 1978. 115 pp.

Children's book of a general nature with line drawings of instruments and a few songs.

166. FIFE, Austin E., and REDDEN, Francesca. "The Pseudo-Indian Folksongs of the Anglo-American and French-Canadian." Journal of American Folklore 67-265 (July-Sept. 1954): 239-51 and 67-266 (Oct.-Dec., 1954): 379-94.

Based on research in Utah, Idaho, and California, this study focuses on white attitudes towards Indians and the musical genres in which Indians are treated. Includes examples.

167. FILLMORE, John Comfort. "The Harmonic Structure of Indian Music." American Anthropologist, new series, 1 (1899): 297-318; reprinted in Music 16 (1899): 453-72.

Written by a protege of Alice Fletcher in 1888, this article turns out to be an unintended case study in musical ethnocentrism and elitism. The author's source material was Indians met at the World's Columbian Exposition, specifically the Kwakiutl, Navaho, and Midway Plaisance. The author extrapolates an "intended" but unrealized harmonic structure in Indian music.

168. FILLMORE, John Comfort. "Primitive Scales and Rhythms." In Memoirs of the International Congress of Anthropology, pp. 158-75. Edited by Charles Staniland Wake. Chicago: Schulte Publishing Co., 1894.

Like the above article, this blatantly ethno-centric study is based on Indian music out of context, the Vancouver Indians in this case. After hearing their songs, Fillmore went to the piano and began harmonizing based on assumed harmonic implications he found in the melodies. When he played them for the Indians, they were "delighted" and told him he had it exactly right. An article so bad that it's worth reading as an example.

169. FILLMORE, John Comfort. "What do Indians Mean to do When They Sing, and How Far do They Succeed?" Journal of American Folklore 8-29 (Apr.-June 1895): 138-42.

Ethno-centric, non-technical comparison of Omaha singing with Anglo-American singing.

170. FLETCHER, Alice Cunningham. Indian Games and Dances with Native Songs: Arranged from American Indian Ceremonials and Sports. Boston: C. C. Birchard, 1915; reprint ed., New York: AMS, 1970. 145 pp.

An instruction book for amateurs with a few melodies transcribed.

171. FLETCHER, Alice C. "Indian Songs and Music." Journal of American Folklore 11-41 (Apr.-June 1898): 85-104.

An overview with concentration on the alleged "psychical aspects" of Indian song and on "emotional expression." Several transcriptions as well, arranged for piano.

172. FLETCHER, Alice Cunningham. Indian Story and Song from North America. Boston: Small, Maynard and Co., 1900; reprint ed., New York: AMS, 1970; London and New York: Johnson Reprint Corp., 1974. 140 pp.

A non-scholarly essay based on a paper given in 1898 that describes arranged Indian music for composers who might use the themes and wish to know the original context.

173. GILLES, Martha Mead. "A Synthesis of American Indian Music as Derived from Culture: Examination of Style, Performance Practices, and Aesthetic for Music Education." Ph.D. dissertation, University of Oklahoma, 1977. 237 pp.

Ambitious project in which the author, basing her work on available literature and transcriptions, attempts to describe a six-stage evolution in Indian musical development, and further delineates cultural regions based on performance practices.

174. HATTON, Orin T. "In the Tradition: Grass Dance Musical Style and Female Pow-Wow Singers." Ethnomusicology 30-2 (Spring/Summer, 1986): 197-222.

Comprehensive and well documented study of the Northern Plains Grass Dance, its origins, diffusion, history, role of women, musical style, and use of drums. There is an extensive bibliography as well as some transcriptions and illustrations.

175. HATTON, O. Thomas. "Performance Practices of Northern Plains Pow-Wow Singing Groups." Yearbook for Inter-American Musical Research. 10 (1974): 123-37.

Descriptive, non-technical study of the Grass Dance or War Dance of some 25 tribes of the Northern Plains.

176. HERNDON, Marcia. Native American Music. Norwood, Pa.: Norwood Editions, 1980. 233 pp.

General study with overview based on topical, theoretical, and historical divisions, such as "Music and Ceremonial" and "Music and the Lifecycle." Traces the history of the study of Indian music.

177. HETH, Charlotte, ed. Selected Reports in Ethnomusicology III-2. Los Angeles: University of California at Los Angeles, 1980. 201 pp.

A collection of seven articles, all by top scholars but mostly written for specialists. They include McAllester, Powers, Vennum, Jr., La Vigna, Yeh, Draper, and Herndon. There is also a "Selected Bibliography and Discography" divided into two sections, one for the specialist, one for the general reader.

178. HIGHWATER, Jamake. Ritual of the Wind: North American Indian Ceremonies, Music, and Dances. New York: Viking, 1977. 192 pp.

Heavily illustrated (photos and drawings) study of ceremonies, primarily Navaho, but little on music per se.

179. HOFMANN, Charles. American Indians Sing. New York: John Day Co., 1967. 96 pp. and recording of 7 songs.

General essay describing music in the context of daily life and ceremonies, the instruments, song-poetry, and dance in ritual.

180. HOFMANN, Charles, ed. Frances Densmore and American Indian Music: a Memorial Volume. Contributions from the Museum of the American Indian, Heye Foundation, #23. New York: Museum of the American Indian, 1968. 127 pp.

Scholarly study and biography of a great American researcher with emphasis on her work, research, works, and letters. Also included is a selection of representative articles (pp. 67-100), a bibliography, and a collection of photographs.

181. HOFMANN, Charles. "Frances Densmore and the Music of the American Indian." Journal of American Folklore 59-231 (Jan.-Mar., 1946): 45-50.

Review of Densmore's work until then and description of previous influences on her. Basically an appreciation.

182. HOUSTON, James A. Songs of the Dream People: Chants and Images from the Indians and Eskimos of North America. New York: Atheneum and Don Mills, Ontario: Longman, 1972. 83 pp.

Juvenile collection of translated songs from various tribes illustrated with drawings and one notated song.

183. KURATH, Gertrude P. "Antiphonal Songs of Eastern Woodland Indians." Musical Quarterly 42 (1956): 520-6.

Based on field work done in 1948, this is a study of one kind of song, especially in the Stomp Dance.

184. McALLESTER, David P. "A Different Drum: a Consideration of Music in the Native American Humanities." In The Religious Character of Native American Humanities: an Interdisciplinary Conference Held April 14-16, 1977, pp. 155-83. Tempe: Humanities and Religious Studies, Arizona State University, 1977.

185. McALLESTER, David P. "Indian Music in the Southwest."
     Colorado Springs: Taylor Museum, 1961 [15 pp.]; reprinted
     in Readings in Ethnomusicology, pp. 215-26. Edited by D.
     P. McAllester. New York: Johnson Reprint Corp., 1971.

     Introductory, non-technical museum booklet which includes
an introduction and short sections on Pueblo, Apache, and Navaho
musics.

186. McALLESTER, David P. "North American Native Music." In
     Musics of Many Cultures: an Introduction, pp. 307-31.
     Edited by Elizabeth May. Berkeley: University of
     California Press, 1980.

     Introductory article for non-specialists, organized by
area (e.g., Eastern Woodlands, The Plains, The Southwest) with
some transcriptions and photos as well as discussion of particular
dances. Bibliography, discography, and filmography.

187. NETTL, Bruno. "American Indian Music North of Mexico: Its
     Styles and Areas." Ph.D. dissertation, Indiana
     University, 1953. 239 pp.

     One of the first, and possibly the best, attempts to see
American Indian musical style in perspective. The author divides
styles into six areas by criteria other than language or
geography. This work was reduced and published as "North American
Indian Musical Styles" (see 189). A later reconsideration is
found in the "Musical Areas Reconsidered" article following.

188. NETTL, Bruno. "Musical Areas Reconsidered." In Essays in
     Music in Honor of Dragon Plamenac on his 70th Birthday,
     pp. 181-9. Edited by Gustave Reese and Robert J. Snow.
     Pittsburgh: University of Pittsburgh, 1969.

     In this article the author, because of new material and
rethinking, reconsiders some of the conclusions found in his 1953
dissertation and its resulting publications.

189. NETTL, Bruno. "North American Indian Musical Styles."
     Journal of American Folklore 67-263 (Jan.-Mar., 1954);
     45-56; 67-265 (July-Sept. 1954): 297-307; 67-266 (Oct.-
     Dec. 1954): 351-68; reprinted as booklet: Philadelphia:
     American Folklore Society, 1954. 51 pp.

A version of the author's doctoral dissertation (see #187).

190. NETTL, Bruno. "Notes on Musical Composition in Primitive Culture." Anthropological Quarterly, new series, 27-2 (1954): 81-90.

Broad essay dealing with the contrasts of improvisation and composition among American Indians, Afro-Americans, and Africans, with two transcriptions.

191. NETTL, Bruno. "Polyphony in North American Indian Music." Musical Quarterly 47 (1961): 354-62.

An area by area survey of references to polyphony in the literature on North America, but shows that polyphony is much more common in Central and South America.

192. NETTL, Bruno. "Some Influences of Western Civilization on North American Indian Music." In New Voices in American Studies, pp. 129-37. Edited by Ray B. Browne, Donald M. Winkelman, and Allen Hayman. Lafayette, Ind.: Purdue University Press, 1966.

An essay in which the author explores the effects the meeting of whites and Indians have had on the latter's music, such as the use of English words, hymns with Indian words, the adoption of white dances, and the general impoverishment of Indian music.

193. NETTL, Bruno. "Stylistic Variety in North American Indian Music." Journal of the American Musicological Society 6 (1953): 160-8.

A brief version of the author's doctoral dissertation (see #187) with a map and several transcriptions.

194. POWERS, William K. "The Study of Native American Music." Keystone Folklore 20-1/2 (Winter-Spring, 1975): 39-56.

Intended for the non-specialist, this practical study offers material in three categories: 1) a survey of the state of research on Indian music, 2) an introductory bibliography, 3) list of recorded sources of both historical and contemporary songs.

195. RHODES, Willard. "North American Indian Music in Transition." Journal of the International Folk Music Council 15 (June 1963): 9-14.

A study of one specific kind of Indian song, those with English words, a genre the author believes had been ignored until then. This kind of song, he asserts, acts as a measure of acculturation.

196. ROBERTS, Helen H. Form in Primitive Music: an Analytical and Comparative Study of the Melodic Form of Some Ancient Southern California Indian Songs. New York: American Library of Musicology and W. W. Norton, 1933. 180 pp.

Technical and analytical study by one of the major scholars on American Indian music.

197. ROBERTS, Helen H. Musical Areas of Aboriginal North America. Publications in Anthropology, vol. 12. New Haven: Yale University, 1936; reprint ed., New Haven: HRAF Press, 1970. 41 pp.

Survey of American Indian styles, but far less extensive than that of Nettl's dissertation of 1953.

198. WHITINGER, Julius Edward. "Hymnody of the Early American Indian Missions." Ph.D. dissertation, The Catholic University of America, 1971. 344 pp.

While the author refers to Indians as "savages," he has written a useful history of the role of hymnody in converting Indians to Christianity. He divides this work into three groups: 1) Spanish and Mexican Jesuits in the South, 2) French Jesuits in the North and Great Lakes regions, 3) English in the mid-Atlantic area.

The Music of Individual Tribes

Note: Because there is no universally accepted division of tribes and because some studies involve more than one tribe, all materials relating to specific tribes are listed here. The reader will find, however, that each individual tribal unit studied here is listed in the index.

199. BAHR, Donald M., GIFF, Joseph, and HARIER, Manuel. "Piman Songs on Hunting." Ethnomusicology 23-2 (May 1979): 245-96.

A text-centered study of three sets of songs, with texts quoted in their entirety in both the native tongue and English on pp. 270-96.

200. BAHR, Donald M., and HAEFER, J. Richard. "Song in Piman Curing." Ethnomusicology 22-1 (Jan. 1978): 89-122.

A study of song in the context of curing, with some analysis of melody and rhythm, but the emphasis on text.

201. BARRETT, Samuel A. "The Dream Dance of the Chippewa and Menominee Indians of Northern Wisconsin." In Bulletin of the Public Museum of the City of Milwaukee, vol. 1, (article #4), pp. 252-415. Milwaukee: Public Museum of the City of Milwaukee, 1911; reprint ed., New York: Garland, 1979.

Extremely detailed ethnographic study of a particularly elaborate ceremony, day by day, with excellent photos and an index. Little directly on music, however.

202. BARTLETT, Charles E. "Some Seneca Songs from Tonawanda Reservation." New York State Archeological Association Bulletin 5 (Nov. 1955): 8-16.

Report of a field trip and description of findings, classification of recordings by type of song.

203. BEATTY, John. Kiowa-Apache Music and Dance. Greeley; Museum of Anthropology, University of Northern Colorado, 1974. 80 pp.

Scholarly, somewhat technical survey with numerous examples of music.

204. BLACK BEAR, Ben, Sr., and THEISZ, R. D. Songs and Dances of the Lakota. Rosebud, S.D.: Sinte Gleska College, 1976. 137 pp.

Overview of the tribe's music and discussion of 46 songs, but without musical examples.

205. BOYD, Maurice. Kiowa Voices: Ceremonial Dance, Ritual and Song, Vol. 1. Ft. Worth: Texas Christian University Press, 1981. 164 pp.

Based on oral histories collected among the Kiowa by Kiowa, this series of chapters, each treating a different dance, provides many direct quotations from the elders of the tribe. The book's strength lies more in its discussion of history and context than in providing musical insights.

206. BURTON, Frederick R. American Primitive Music with Especial Attention to the Songs of the Ojibways. New York: Moffat, Yard, and Co., 1909; reprint ed., Port Washington, N.Y.: Kennikat Press, 1969. 283 pp.

A survey of American Indian music, its scales, rhythms, structures, and place in Indian life, with the Ojibways as the prime source. Rather technical and with many examples.

207. CHAMPE, Flavia Waters. The Matachines Dance of the Upper Rio Grande: History, Music, and Choreography. Lincoln: University of Nebraska Press, 1983. 101 pp. 1.7" disc.

Based on more than 30 years of observations at a number of Pueblos, especially San Ildefonso, this study focuses on the matachines dance, which is apparently of European origin but has become part of the Pueblo dance repertory. While it is an attractive book, its organization presents the dance in a pseudo theatrical format.

208. DAVIDSON, John F. "Ojibwa Songs." Journal of American Folklore 58-230 (Oct.-Dec. 1945): 303-5.

Brief treatment, with melodic transcriptions of eight songs.

The following 16 books by Frances DENSMORE (1867-1957) are listed separately but without annotations. Densmore, a protege of Alice Cunningham Fletcher and a classical music graduate of Oberlin College, Oberlin, Ohio, was America's first significant scholar on American Indian music, Theodore Baker notwithstanding. While her interest began as early as 1893 stemming from reading Fletcher, it was in 1904 that she first notated an Indian song, one sung by Geronimo, and in 1905 began her first field trip, among the Chippewa of Minnesota. By 1907 the Smithsonian's Bureau of American Ethnology noticed her fine work, and made her a Collaborator, which title she held until her death. Her studies are based entirely on field work. Although they are musically oriented, and therefore quite technical with many transcriptions, she also provided considerable ethnograhic data. Although much of her work was done in the earlier years of the century, it is still considered valid. Nonetheless, modern scholars have sometimes pointed out biases in her descriptions and analyses stemming from her classical training, a fault which scholars even today find difficulty in avoiding. The value of her books is perhaps indicated by the fact that most have been reprinted and purchased by all libraries desiring the basic materials for the study of American Indian music.

209. DENSMORE, Frances. Cheyenne and Arapaho Music. Southwest Museum Papers #10. Los Angeles: Southwest Museum, 1936. 111 pp.

210. DENSMORE, Frances. Chippewa Music. 2 vols. Smithsonian Institution, Bureau of American Ethnology Bulletin 45/53. Washington, D.C.: Government Printing Office, 1910/ 1913; reprint ed., New York: Da Capo, 1972. 216 & 341 pp.

211. DENSMORE, Frances. Choctaw Music. Smithsonian Institution, Anthropological Papers #28, Bureau of American Ethnology Bulletin #136. Washington, D.C.: Government Printing Office, 1943; reprint ed., New York: Da Capo, 1973. 188 pp. and 21 plates.

212. DENSMORE, Frances. Mandan and Hidatsa Music. Smithsonian Institution, Bureau of American Ethnology Bulletin #80. Washington, D.C.: Government Printing Office, 1923; reprint ed., New York: Da Capo, 1972. 192 pp.

213. DENSMORE, Frances. Menominee Music. Smithsonian Institution, Bureau of American Ethnology Bulletin #102. Washington, D.C.: Government Printing Office, 1932; reprint ed., New York: Da Capo, 1972. 230 pp.

214. DENSMORE, Frances. <u>Music</u> <u>of</u> <u>Acoma</u>, <u>Isleta</u>, <u>Cochiti</u> and <u>Zuni</u> <u>Pueblos</u>. Smithsonian Institution, Bureau of American Ethnology Bulletin #165. Washington, D.C.: Government Printing Office, 1957; reprint ed., New York: Da Capo, 1972. 117 pp. and 4 plates.

215. DENSMORE, Frances. <u>Music</u> <u>of</u> <u>the</u> <u>Indians</u> <u>of</u> <u>British</u> <u>Columbia</u>. Smithsonian Institution, Bureau of American Ethnology, Anthropology Paper #27. Washington, D.C.: Government Printing Office, 1943; reprint ed., New York: Da Capo, 1972. 99 pp. and 9 plates.

216. DENSMORE, Frances. <u>Music</u> <u>of</u> <u>the</u> <u>Maidu</u> <u>Indians</u> <u>of</u> <u>California</u>. Los Angeles: Southwest Museum, 1958. 67 pp. (Note: this is Densmore's last work and was published posthumously, for she had died the previous year.)

217. DENSMORE, Frances. <u>Music</u> <u>of</u> <u>the</u> <u>Santo</u> <u>Domingo</u> <u>Pueblo</u>, <u>New</u> <u>Mexico</u>. Southwest Museum Papers #12. Los Angeles: Southwest Museum, 1938; reprint ed., Ann Arbor, Mich.: Edwards Brothers, 1983. 186 pp.

218. DENSMORE, Frances. <u>Nootka</u> <u>and</u> <u>Quileute</u> <u>Music</u>. Smithsonian Institution, Bureau of American Ethnology Bulletin #124. Washington, D.C.: Government Printing Office, 1939; reprint ed., New York: Da Capo, 1972. 358 pp.

219. DENSMORE, Frances. <u>Northern</u> <u>Ute</u> <u>Music</u>. Smithsonian Institution, Bureau of American Ethnology Bulletin #75. Washington, D.C.: Government Printing Office, 1922; reprint ed., New York: Da Capo, 1972. 213 pp.

220. DENSMORE, Frances. <u>Papago</u> <u>Music</u>. Smithsonian Institution, Bureau of American Ethnology Bulletin #90. Washington, D.C.: Government Printing Office, 1929; reprint ed., New York: Da Capo, 1972. 229 pp.

221. DENSMORE, Frances. <u>Pawnee</u> <u>Music</u>. Smithsonian Institution, Bureau of American Ethnology Bulletin #93. Washington, D.C.: Government Printing Office, 1929; reprint ed., New York: Da Capo, 1972. 129 pp.

222357

222. DENSMORE, Frances. Seminole Music. Smithsonian Institution, Bureau of American Ethnology Bulletin #161. Washington, D.C.: Government Printing Office, 1956; reprint ed., New York: Da Capo, 1973. 223 pp.

223. DENSMORE, Frances. Teton Sioux Music. Smithsonian Institution, Bureau of American Ethnology Bulletin #61. Washington, D.C.: Government Printing Office, 1918; reprint ed., New York: Da Capo, 1972. 561 pp.

224. DENSMORE, Frances. Yuman and Yaqui Music. Smithsonian Institution, Bureau of American Ethnology Bulletin #110. Washington, D.C.: Government Printing Office, 1932; reprint ed., New York: Da Capo, 1972. 216 pp.

225. DRAPER, David E. "Breath in Music: Concept and Practice among the Choctaw Indians." In Essays in Honour of Peter Crossley-Holland on his Sixty-Fifth Birthday. Selected Reports in Ethnomusicology, Vol. IV, pp. 285-300. Edited by Nicole Marzac-Holland and Nazir A. Jairazbhoy. Los Angeles: University of California, 1983.

Exploration of breath as a structural device, and the meanings of breath in Choctaw music, where it is prominent.

226. FENTON, William Nelson. The Iroquois Eagle Dance, an Offshoot of the Calumet Dance. Smithsonian Institution, Bureau of American Ethnology Bulletin #156. Washington, D.C.: Government Printing Office, 1953. 324 pp.

Originally a doctoral dissertation (Yale University, 1937, 264 pp.), this study focuses on one aspect of Iroquois dance and music based on field work in western New York 1933-6.

227. FENTON, William N. Songs from the Iroquois Longhouse: Program Notes for an Album of American Indian Music from the Eastern Woodlands. Smithsonian Publication #3691. Washington, D.C.: Government Printing Office, 1942. 34 pp.

Introduction to Iroquois song texts; technical except as it relates to musical matters.

228. FEWKES, J. Walter. "The Miconinori Flute Altars." Journal
      of American Folklore 9-35 (Oct.-Dec. 1896): 241-56.

      Detailed description of an elaborate ceremony at the
Tusayan, Miconinori Pueblo of the Hopi.

229. FEWKES, J. Walter. "The Oraibi Flute Altar." Journal of
      American Folklore 8-31 (Oct.-Dec. 1895): 265-84.

      Description of ceremony of the Tusayan Indians at Oraibi.

230. FEWKES, J. Walter. "The Walpi Flute Observance." Journal
      of American Folklore 7-27 (Oct.-Dec. 1894): 265-88.

      Detailed description of the ceremony and its ritual
significance among the Tusayan Indians.

231. FLETCHER, Alice C. The Hako: a Pawnee Ceremony. Assisted
      by James R. Murie, Music transcribed by Edwin S. Tracy.
      N.p.: n.p., 1904. 372 pp.

      Fletcher (1845-1923) was, along with Theodore Baker, one
of the significant pioneers in the study of Indian music. This
work, based on research done in 1898 in collaboration with "an
educated Pawnee" (Murie), concerns a ceremony of the Chaui band of
the Pawnee. Like many researchers of the time, Fletcher was
hopeful that her material could be utilized in compositions. "The
songs are commended to the general student of music and
particularly to the young composers of our country as offering
native themes worthy of musical treatment" (p. 16).

232. FLETCHER, Alice C., and LA FLESCHE, Francis. A Study of
      Omaha Indian Music. With a Report on the Structural
      Peculiarities of the Music by John Comfort Fillmore.
      Harvard University, Peabody Museum of Archaeology and
      Ethnology Papers 1/5. Cambridge: Peabody Museum, 1893;
      reprint ed., New York: Kraus Reprint, 1967. 152 pp.

      Survey of the genres of Omaha music, with a musical
supplement (pp. 79-151). The music examples were arranged
(inappropriately) by Fillmore.

233. FOGELSON, Raymond. "The Cherokee Ballgame Cycle: an Ethnographer's View." Ethnomusicology 15-3 (1971): 327-38.

An ethnographer's description of an all-night ceremony connected with a ballgame. Related to Herndon's article (see #247) which studies the musical and dance aspects.

234. FRISBIE, Charlotte J. "An Approach to the Ethnography of Navajo Ceremonial Performance." In The Ethnography of Musical Performance, pp. 75-104. Edited by Norma McLeod and Marcia Herndon. Norwood, Pa.: Norwood Editions, 1980.

A long introduction explores the idea of the "ethnography of performance," one which the author feels is novel to ethnomusicology (pp. 75-81). The author then assesses these ideas in a case study involving the Navajo.

235. FRISBIE, Charlotte J., ed. Southwestern Indian Ritual Drama. Albuquerque: University of New Mexico Press, 1980. 372 pp.

The results of a seminar sponsored by the School of American Research, April 3-8, 1978, these 12 articles include: Barbara Tedlock's "Songs of the Zuni Kachina Society," Claire R. Farrer's "Composition, Rehearsal, and Performance," and Leanne Hinton's "Vocables in Havasupai Song."

236. FRISBIE, Charlotte J. "Vocables in Navajo Ceremonial Music." Ethnomusicology 24-3 (Sept. 1980): 347-92.

Scholarly study of "nonsense" syllables in a number of Navajo song types, which are found to have various levels of meaning. Indeed, this is an important study in explaining the meaning of Indian song texts.

237. FRYETT, Jere Thomas. "The Musical Culture of the Crow Indians in Montana." Ph.D. dissertation, University of Colorado, Boulder, 1977. 257 pp.

A delineation of the many functional types of songs among the Crow, both those now obsolete and those still surviving. Also a discussion of song composition, i.e., mainly from visions, and a description of musical instruments.

238. GARCIA, Antonio and Carlos. "Ritual Preludes to Tewa Dances." Ethnomusicology 12-2 (1968): 239-44.

Non-technical, anthropological introduction to a relatively secret ritual genre of the Tewa Indians of the San Juan and other Pueblos. These ceremonies take place for four nights in the kiva and involving only the War Chief and certain others preceding the plaza dance.

239. GAUS, Dorothy Shipley. "Change in Social Dance Song Style at Alleghany Reservation, 1962-1973: the Rabbit Dance." Anthropology Studies #33. Ph.D. dissertation, The Catholic University of America, 1976. 2 vols., 719 pp.

A study of change between the years indicated during which part of the reservation was moved, creating deep social disruption. While many old songs survived, new ones were added. The Rabbit Dance song repertory changed totally during this time, but other genres saw only stylistic change. In addition, the use of meaningful words and the merging of styles and types occurred.

240. GILMAN, Benjamin Ives. "Hopi Songs." Journal of American Archaeology and Ethnology 5 (1908).

241. GILMAN, Benjamin Ives. "Zuni Melodies." Journal of American Archaeology and Ethnology 1 (1891): 1 ff.

Gilman (1852-1933), though a psychologist by training, accompanied J. Walter Fewkes in 1890 on an expedition to the Pueblo Indians and was the first to use a gramophone to record Indian songs in the field. Using Ellis' recently devised "cents" system to measure intervals, Gilman asserted that the slight deviations from the equal-tempered scale of Europe were significant and part of the style, though John Comfort Fillmore, whose ethno-centric musical studies of Indian music are now held in disrepute, disputed this. In this sense, Gilman was a forward-looking ethnomusicologist not only for his day, but for ours.

242. GOODMAN, Linda. "Music and Dance in Northwest Coast Indian Life." Tsaile, Ariz.: Navajo Community College Press, 1977. 38 pp.

Introductory level study for the non-specialist.

243. HAEFER, J. Richard. "Papago Music and Dance." Tsaile, Ariz.: Navajo Community College Press, 1977. 37 pp.

Brief, non-technical introduction to the culture and music, with photos.

244. HALL, Jody C., and NETTL, Bruno. "Musical Style of the Modoc." Southwestern Journal of Anthropology 11 (1955): 58-66.

Analysis, with transcriptions, of material collected in 1934 by Leslie Spier in California among a tribe whose musical style was found to be exceptionally simple.

245. HALPERN, Ida. "On the Interpretation of 'Meaningless-Nonsensical Syllables' in the Music of the Pacific Northwest Indians." Ethnomusicology 20-2 (May, 1976): 253-72.

An attempt, after 26 years of study, to interpret the so-called "nonsense syllables" meaningfully. Text oriented, but with musical transcriptions as well.

246. HEIDSIEK, Ralph George. "Music of the Luiseno Indians of Southern California--a Study of Music in Indian Culture with Relation to a Program in Music Education." Ph.D. dissertation, University of California, Los Angeles, 1966. 452 pp.

Based partly on fieldwork, partly on existing collections, this is a description and analysis of 12 songs arranged into eight study units with information for teachers.

247. HERNDON, Marcia. "The Cherokee Ballgame Cycle: an Ethnomusicologist's View." Ethnomusicology 15-3 (1971): 339-52.

A description of an all-night Cherokee ritual dance which precedes an important ballgame. Also discusses musical style. Related to Fogelson's "The Cherokee Ballgame Cycle: an Ethnographer's View" (see #233).

248. HERZOG, George. "A Comparison of Pueblo and Pima Musical
    Styles." Journal of American Folklore 49-194 (Oct.-Dec.
    1936): 283-417.

    First an analysis of Pueblo style, then Pima, then a
comparison of them with a summary. Although technical, there is a
valuable bibliography, and pp. 341-415 are transcriptions.

249. HERZOG, George. "A Comparison of Pueblo and Pima Musical
    Styles." Ph.D. dissertation, Columbia University, 1937.
    134 pp.

    Comparative study centered around vocal techniques,
tonality, rhythm, form, genres, with commentary.

250. HERZOG, George. "Plains Ghost Dance and Great Basin
    Music." American Anthropologist 37 (1935): 403-19.

    Studies the relationship of Ghost Dance music among the
Plains Indians to that of the Great Basin area Indians, and shows
that the Ghost Dance is not native to the former.

251. HERZOG, George. "The Yuman Musical Style." Journal of
    American Folklore 41-160 (Apr.-June 1928): 183-231.

    Transcriptions and analyses of 85 songs, 39 of them given
in the article. Technical.

252. HETH, Charlotte Ann. "The Stomp Dance Music of the
    Oklahoma Cherokee: a Study of Contemporary Practice with
    Special Reference to the Illinois District Ceremonial
    Ground." Ph.D. dissertation, University of California at
    Los Angeles, 1975. 589 pp.

    Based on extensive field work in the early 1970's by a
participant-observer plus library data used primarily as
background material. The Stomp Dance is a vital part of the
Oklahoma Cherokee culture, and it is here transcribed, analysed,
texts translated, and instruments and rituals described.

253. HETH, Charlotte Ann. "Stylistic Similarities in Cherokee
    and Iroquois Music." Journal of Cherokee Studies 4-3
    (Summer, 1980): 128-62.

254. HODGES, Daniel Houston. "Transcription and Analysis of Southern Cheyenne Songs." Ph.D. dissertation, University of Oklahoma, 1980. 267 pp.

    Although written in Music Education, this apparently ethnomusicological study is devoted to the little-studied Southern Cheyenne, rather than the better-known Northern Cheyenne in Montana. The writer collected 130 songs from various sources, transcribed and analysed 60 of them, and organized them into six categories. Then he examined nine stylistic variables and concluded that the Southern Cheyenne have maintained a style untouched by American culture.

255. HOFMANN, Charles. "American Indian Music in Wisconsin, Summer 1946." Journal of American Folklore 60-237 (July-Oct. 1947): 289-93.

    A report on the Stand Rock Indian Ceremonial at Wisconsin Dells in which five tribes and 250,000 persons participated.

256. HOFSINDE, Robert (Gray-Wolf). Indian Music Makers. New York: William Morrow and Co., 1967. 96 pp.

    Written by a native of the Ojibwa or Chippewa nation of northern Minnesota, this is a lightweight description of instruments and a few songs, with drawings as illustrations.

257. HOWARD, James H., and KURATH, Gertrude P. "Ponca Dances, Ceremonies and Music." Ethnomusicology 3-1 (Jan. 1959): 1-14.

    An article which emphasizes dance more than music, with several examples.

258. JOHNSON, Charlotte I. "Navaho Corn Grinding Songs." Ethnomusicology 8-2 (May 1964): 101-20.

    Based on material collected in 1963, this is an analysis of 14 texts and melodies.

259. JONES, John Alan. "The Role of the Sun Dance in Northern Ute Acculturation." Ph.D. dissertation, Columbia University, 1950. 104 pp.

In Northern Ute culture the Sun Dance is of central importance. This is a cultural history, functional analysis, and description.

260. JURRENS, James W. "The Music of the Sioux Indians of the Rosebud Reservation in South Dakota and its Use in the Elementary School." Ed.D., Colorado State College [now University of Northern Colorado], 1965. 342 pp.

Field collected, but the goal is to make this music available for elementary teaching and to encourage better understanding between people. Songs transcribed and arranged with piano accompaniment and in other formats.

261. KEELING, Richard Hamilton. "Songs of the Brush Dance and their Basis in Oral-Expressive Magic: Music and Culture of the Yurok, Hupa, and Karok Indians of Northwestern California." Ph.D. dissertation, University of California, Los Angeles, 1982. 605 pp.

Description of the Brush Dance, which is used for a curing ritual, the ritual, the communal singing. The transcriptions and detailed analyses use both staff and Melograph notations.

262. KILPATRICK, Jack F., and Anna G. "Muskogean Charm Songs among the Oklahoma Cherokees." Smithsonian Contributions to Anthropology 2-3 (1967): 29-40.

Highly technical from a linguistic and textual point of view, with transcriptions of 9 songs.

263. KOLINSKI, Mieczyslaw. "An Apache Rabbit Dance Song Cycle as Sung by the Iroquois." Ethnomusicology 16-3 (Sept. 1972): 415-64.

Technical study based on recordings made 1966-67 at the Six Nations Reservation in Ontario, Canada, focusing on the Rabbit Dance cyle which the Iroquois got from the Apache. Four versions were recorded and studied, three by a single informant, the last by the informant's father. A high degree of stability from one performance to the next, even with a year's separation, was found.

264. KURATH, Gertrude Prokosch. "An Analysis of the Iroquois Eagle Dance and Songs." In The Iroquois Eagle Dance: an Offshoot of the Calumet Dance, pp. 223-306. Edited by William N. Fenton and Gertrude P. Kurath. Smithsonian Institution, Bureau of American Ethnology Bulletin #156. Washington, D.C.: Government Printing Office, 1953.

Extensive and highly technical analysis of songs, with numerous transcriptions.

265. KURATH, Gertrude P. "A Comparison of Plains and Pueblo Songs." Ethnomusicology 13-3 (1969): 515-17.

Brief comparison of one song from each tribe, from the Long Plains Reserve in Manitoba and San Juan Pueblo, Santa Fe, New Mexico. The differences suggest that Indian musical style categories need to be re-thought.

266. KURATH, Gertrude P. Iroquois Music and Dance: Ceremonial Arts of Two Seneca Longhouses. Smithsonian Institution, Bureau of American Ethnology Bulletin #187. Washington, D.C.: Government Printing Office, 1964; reprint ed., St. Clair Shores, Mich.: Scholarly, 1977. 268 pp.

A detailed, analytical study of both song and dance, with transcriptions occupying pp. 113-259.

267. KURATH, Gertrude Prokosch. "Local Diversity in Iroquois Music and Dances." In Symposium on Local Diversity in Iroquois Culture, pp. 109-37. Edited by William Fenton. Smithsonian Institution, Bureau of American Ethnology Bulletin #149. Washington, D.C.: Government Printing Office, 1951.

Description of dances and songs, with transcriptions. Written from an anthropological point of view.

268. KURATH, Gertrude P. "Tewa Choreographic Music." In Studies in Ethnomusicology, Vol. II, pp. 4-19. Edited by M. Kolinski. New York: Oak, 1965.

Technical study with many transcriptions and photos, with an emphasis on dance.

269. KURATH, Gertrude Prokosch, and GARCIA, Antonio. Music and Dance of the Tewa Pueblos. Santa Fe: Museum of New Mexico Press, 1970. 309 pp.

An exploration of the context of music and dance from both an anthropological and musico-technical point of view, with numerous transcriptions.

270. KWIATKOWSKA, Barbara Jolanta. "The Present State of Musical Culture among the Diegueno Indians from San Diego County Reservations." Ph.D. dissertation, University of California, Los Angeles, 1981. 345 pp.

Based both on fieldwork and old descriptions, this study concerns a tribe not previously studied. After enumerating and describing the various genres, there are transcriptions, analyses, and a description of style. The author concludes that change has occurred in the Diegueno Indian music.

271. LA VIGNA, Maria. "Okushare: the Turtle Dance Ceremony of the Tewa Indians of San Juan Pueblo." Ph.D. dissertation, University of California, Los Angeles, in progress.

272. LIST, George. "The Hopi as Composer and Poet." In Proceedings of the Centennial Workshop in Ethnomusicology, pp. 43-53. Edited by Peter Crossley-Holland. Victoria: Government of the Province of British Columbia, 1968.

273. LIST, George. "Song in Hopi Culture, Past and Present." Journal of the International Folk Music Council 14 (Jan. 1962): 30-5.

A preliminary study of Hopi song based both on fieldwork and materials in the Archives of Traditional Music at Indiana University.

274. McALLESTER, David P. Enemy Way Music: a Study of Social and Esthetic Values as Seen in Navaho Music. Peabody Museum of American Archaeology and Ethnology, Harvard University Vol. 41, No. 3. Cambridge: by the Museum, 1954. 96 pp.

This important, though relatively brief, work is a study of the relationships between music and cultural values, with the major focus on the Enemy Way Ceremony, which protects the Navaho from non-Navaho peoples. Based on field work and a questionnaire done in 1950, the author presents both cultural information and numerous transcriptions of the songs.

275. McALLESTER, David P. Peyote Music. New York: Viking Fund, 1949; reprint ed., New York: Johnson Reprint Corp., 1964/1971. 104 pp.

Originally the author's doctoral dissertation completed at Columbia in 1949 in anthropology, this comprehensive study describes the Peyote ceremony, its history, its songs and texts, the sources of style, and compares the styles of fourteen tribes.

276. McLEOD, Norma. "The Semantic Parameter in Music: the Blanket Rite of the Lower Kutenai." Yearbook for Inter-American Musical Research 7 (1971): 83-102.

Description of a ceremony of the Lower Kutenai, a tribe found in northern Idaho and southern Canada. Because the Blanket Rite is accompanied by textless music, but music which has meaning in terms of defining cosmology, it must be understood on a number of levels besides that of organized sound. The author hopes that this article will serve as a model for similar studies elsewhere.

277. MATTHEWS, Washington. "Songs of Sequence of the Navajos." Journal of American Folklore 7-26 (July-Sept. 1894): 185-94.

A study of texts and context of song sets from various rites.

278. MERRIAM, Alan P. Ethnomusicology of the Flathead Indians. Viking Fund Publications in Anthropology #44. Chicago: Aldine Publishing Co., 1967. 403 pp.

Classic and model study from an anthropological point of view of songs, dances, and instruments of a single tribe. Technical in its descriptions of individual songs. Major review of POWERS, William K. and KOLINSKI, M. in Ethnomusicology 14-1 (Jan. 1970): 67-99.

279. MERRIAM, Alan P. "Flathead Indian Music: Report of Field
     Research, Summer 1950." Mimeographed. Missoula, Mont.:
     1955. 66 pp.

     Report of an early field trip to the Flathead from June 19
to September 18, 1950, during which numerous recordings were made.

280. MERRIAM, Alan P. "The Importance of Song in the Flathead
     Indian Vision Quest." Ethnomusicology 9-2 (May 1965):
     91-99.

     A study of music in culture, with emphasis on the latter.

281. MERRIAM, Alan P., and SPIER, Robert F. G. "Chukchansi
     Yokuts Songs." In Actas del XXXIII Congreso Internacion-
     al de Americanistas, 2:611-38. San Jose, 1959. 2 vols.

282. MITCHEL, Frank. Navajo Blessingway Singer: the Autobio-
     graphy of Frank Mitchel 1881-1967. Edited by Charlotte J.
     FRISBIE and David P. McALLESTER. Tuscon: University of
     Arizona Press, 1978. 446 pp.

     An autobiography created by the editors from interviews
and written records of the greatest living singer of the Blessingway Ceremony, which is a preventative ceremony of great importance.
There is also an appendix of genealogical and census data, a
chronology, a list of people who worked with him, and a list of
documents relating to him.

283. MOSES, L. G. The Indian Man: a Biography of James Mooney.
     Urbana: University of Illinois Press, 1984. 293 pp.

     Mooney (1861-1921) was an early anthropologist who was
involved in research on the Ghost Dance, Peyote, and Native
American Church.

284. NETTL, Bruno. "Biography of a Blackfoot Indian Singer."
     Musical Quarterly 54 (1968): 199-207.

     Study of an individual (kept anonymous in the article)
based on interviews and recordings of all his songs, but written in
non-technical language.

285. NETTL, Bruno. "Blackfoot Music in Browning, 1965: Functions and Attitudes." In _Festschrift für Walter Wiora zum 30. December 1966_, pp. 593-8. Edited by Ludwig Finscher and Christoph-Hellmut Mahling. Kassel: Barenreiter, 1967.

Study of traditional musical life on the Blackfoot Indian Reservation at Browning, Montana, where the author interviewed six informants representing different aspects of the tribe in order to determine attitudes.

286. NETTL, Bruno. "Musical Culture of the Arapaho." _Musical Quarterly_ 41 (1955): 325-31.

An overview of the musical culture and role of music in one tribe found in Wyoming and Oklahoma, with six transcriptions.

287. NETTL, Bruno. "Observations on Meaningless Peyote Song Texts." _Journal of American Folklore_ 66-260 (Apr.-June 1953): 161-4.

Supplements McAllester's book, _Peyote Music_, with transcriptions and a brief discussion.

288. NETTL, Bruno. "The Shawnee Musical Styles: Historical Perspective in Primitive Music." _Southwestern Journal of Anthropology_ 9 (1953): 277-85.

Systematic overview of style, with emphasis on historical considerations, migrations, and the relationship of this to the concept of "primitive music."

289. NETTL, Bruno. "The Songs of Ishi: Musical Style of the Yahi Indians." _Musical Quarterly_ 51 (1965): 460-77.

Ishi, the last surviving Yahi Indian from California and called by some "the last wild Indian," was found in 1911 and taken to the Museum of Anthropology in Berkeley, where he recorded 60 songs between 1911 and 1914. This is an analytical study of the songs from the cylinder recordings.

290. NETTL, Bruno. "Studies in Blackfoot Indian Culture, Part I: Traditional Uses and Functions." _Ethnomusicology_ 11-2 (May 1967): 141-60.

Introductory article in a series of four which together constitute a major study of Blackfoot musical culture.

291. NETTL, Bruno. "Studies in Blackfoot Indian Culture, Part II: Musical Life of the Montana Blackfoot, 1966." Ethnomusicology 11-3 (Sept., 1967): 293-309.

292. NETTL, Bruno, and BLUM, Stephen. "Studies in Blackfoot Indian Culture, Part III: Three Genres of Song." Ethnomusicology 12-1 (Jan., 1968): 11-48.

Analytical study, with many examples, of the War Dance, Hand Game, and Medicine Pipe.

293. NETTL, Bruno. "Studies in Blackfoot Indian Culture, Part IV: Notes on Composition, Text Settings, and Performance." Ethnomusicology 12-2 (May 1968): 192-207.

Three-part study involving tune relationships based on motivic similarities, the relationship between text and musical form (with analyses of seven songs), and a study of performance practices from which is inferred the kind of changes that have taken place since the nineteenth century.

294. NETTL, Bruno. "Text-Music Relationships in Arapaho Songs." Southwestern Journal of Anthropology 10 (1954): 192-9.

Overview of Arapaho musical style, with special attention to the text-music relationship.

295. PAIGE, Harry Worthington. Songs of the Teton Sioux. Los Angeles: Westernlore Press, 1970. 201 pp.

A doctoral dissertation (State University of New York at Albany, 1967, 270 pp.) written by an English major, this study concentrates on songs in context and songs as literature, their meaning, ceremonial uses, and acculturation. Little on music.

296. PARTHUN, Paul Robert. "Chippewa Music in Minnesota." Ph.D. dissertation, University of Minnesota, in progress.

297. PIETROFORTE, Alfred. Songs of the Yokuts and Pintes.
     Healdsburg, Cal.: Naturegraph, 1965. 64 pp.

     Introduction and treatment of individual songs, with
melodic transcriptions.

298. RADIN, Paul. "The Ritual and Significance of the Winnebago
     Medicine Dance." Ph.D. dissertation, Columbia University,
     1911. 159 pp.

     A description of Winnebago rituals and how they are
organized, the kinds of speeches and songs that occur, and their
significance.

299. RANDLE, Martha Champion. "A Shoshone Hand Game Gambling
     Song." Journal of American Folklore 66-260 (Apr.-June
     1953): 155-59.

     Brief report on field work at Lone Pine, California, with
introduction and transcriptions.

300. RHODES, Robert. "Hopi Music and Dance." Tsaile, Ariz.:
     Navaho Community College Press, 1977. 30 pp.

     Introductory overview for non-specialists.

301. RHODES, Robert. "Selected Hopi Secular Music: Transcrip-
     tion and Analysis." Ed.D. dissertation, Arizona State
     University, 1973. 123 pp.

     Written by an educator who collected and transcribed Hopi
secular songs with the hope that they will both be preserved thusly
and used by educators in teaching children.

302. RHODES, Willard. "A Study of Musical Diffusion Based on
     the Wandering of the Opening Peyote Song." Journal of
     the International Folk Music Council 10 (1958): 42-9.

     Detailed analysis of the first song from the ritual,
stemming from McAllester's book Peyote Music, in which the present
author demonstrates changes from place to place.

303. ROBB, John Donald. "Rhythmic Patterns of the Santo Domingo Corn Dance." Ethnomusicology 8-2 (May 1964): 154-60.

Technical, analytical study of one ceremony.

304. ROBERTS, Don L. "The Ethnomusicology of the Eastern Pueblos." In New Perspectives on the Pueblos, pp. 243-55. Edited by Alfonso Ortiz. Albuquerque: University of New Mexico Press, 1972.

Based on research begun in the 1930s into this music, considered to be the most complex in all of North America, this study groups the ceremonial songs under these categories: Kachina dances, maskless Kachina dances, animal dances, corn dances, borrowed dances, and social dances.

305. ROBERTS, Don L. "Tewa Pueblo Round Dances." In Music and Dance of the Tewa Pueblos, pp. 292-302. Edited by Gertrude Prokosch Kurath. Santa Fe: Museum of New Mexico, 1970.

Transcription and analysis of six round dances, each having a different form. All of these have English texts, a phenomenon which began in the early twentieth century.

306. ROBERTS, Helen H. "Chakwena Songs of Zuni and Laguna." Journal of American Folklore 36-140 (Apr.-June 1923): 177-84.

Transcriptions and analyses of three versions of a particular song, one from the Zuni, two from the Laguna.

307. ROBERTS, Helen H., and HAEBERLIN, Herman K. "Some Songs of the Puget Sound Salish." Journal of American Folklore 31-122 (Oct.-Dec. 1918): 496-520.

Field research by Haeberlin done in 1916 among the Snohomish and Snoqualmu Indians, with transcriptions by Roberts as well as some discussion of the songs.

308. ROBERTS, Helen H., and SWADESH, Morris. "Songs of the Nootka Indians of Western Vancouver Island." In Transactions of the American Philosophical Society, new

series, Vol. 45, Pt. 3, pp. 199-327. Philadelphia: American Philosophical Society, 1955.

Although actually about Indians in Canada (not normally included in this bibliography), it is included because it is significant and is one of Roberts' major studies. Technical.

309. ROBINS, R. H., and McLEOD, Norma. "Five Yurok Songs: a Musical and Textual Analysis." Bulletin of the School of Oriental and African Studies 18 (1956): 592-609.

Based on songs recorded in northern California in 1951 by Robins, transcribed and analyzed by McLeod, this study's intention is to illustrate the relationship between language and music.

310. SHOEMAKER, Henry Wharton. "Pennsylvania Indian Folk-Songs." N.p.: n.p., 1925; rev. ed. as "Indian Folk-Songs of Pennsylvania." Ardmore, Pa.: Newman F. McGirr, 1927. 16 pp.

Account of field research near Corydon in Warren County, with some texts transcribed, but non-scholarly on the whole.

311. SPECK, Frank Gouldsmith. "Ceremonial Songs of the Creek and Yuchi Indians." In Anthropology Publications, Vol. 50, No. 2, pp. 157-245. Philadelphia: University of Pennsylvania University Museum, 1911.

Mostly music, with a four-page introduction and headnotes for 22 Creek dance songs, seven Yuchi dance songs, and 20 Creek medicine songs and formulas. The texts are given separately.

312. SPIER, Leslie. "The Sun Dance of the Plains Indians: its Development and Diffusion." Ph.D. dissertation, Columbia University, 1920. 76 pp.

Anthropological study of the Sun Dance, its organization, history, diffusion, and assimilation into the practices of the Plains Indians.

313. STEVENSON, George William. "The Hymnody of the Choctaw Indians of Oklahoma." D.M.A. dissertation, Southern Baptist Theological Seminary, 1977. 248 pp.

A study made from direct observation as well as from
library resources, with historical survey and evaluation of current
situation. A close examination of the Choctaw Hymn Book, the only
remaining collection in the Choctaw language, shows many types of
hymns are used, with many from the folk hymn repertory as well as
from southern shape-note collections.

314. STUART, Wendy Bross. "Coast Salish Gambling Music."
     Canadian Folk Music Journal 2 (1974): 3-12.

     Study made in British Columbia and Washington State
centered around the slahal or lehal, i.e., the Bone Game with
special attention to both the vocal and percussion aspects.

315. STUMPF, Carl. "Lieder der Bellakula-Indianer."
     Vierteljahrsschrift für Musikwissenschaft 2 (1886): 405-
     26; reprinted in Abhandlung zur Vergleichenden Musik-
     wissenschaft, Vol. 1 [Sammelbande fur Vergleichende
     Musikwissenschaft], pp. 87-103. Edited by Carl Stumpf
     and Erich M. von Hornbostel. Munchen, 1922.

     Stumpf (1848-1936) was a German psychologist,
acoustician, and musicologist who worked primarily in Western
music history, but recorded visiting Bella Coola Indians in Berlin
in 1886 on an early recording device. The article is primarily
analytical, since he could know nothing of the original context of
the music, and includes both transcriptions of music and
translations of texts. A landmark American Indian musical study.

316. TAX, Sol. "Primitive Social Organization with Some
     Description of the Social Organization of the Fox
     Indians." Ph.D. dissertation, University of Chicago,
     1935. 212 pp.

     Although an anthropology dissertation with special
interest in the Peyote cult of the Fox Indians, Appendix VI, which
treats ceremony, includes material on singing and drumming.

317. UNDERHILL, Ruth Murray. Singing for Power: the Song Magic
     of the Papago Indians of Southern Arizona. Berkeley:
     University of California Press, 1938; reprint ed., 1976.
     175 pp.; also New York: Ballantine Books, 1973. 148 pp.

     Primarily a study of song texts, with no musical examples.

318. VANDER, Judith. "The Song Repertoire of Four Shoshone
      Women: a Reflection of Cultural Movements and Sex Roles."
      Ethnomusicology 26-1 (Jan. 1982): 73-84.

      A non-technical study of recent cultural history as
viewed through the song repertories of four individual singers.

319. VENNUM, Thomas, Jr. "The Ojibwa Begging Dance." In Music
      and Context: Essays for John M. Ward, pp. 54-78. Edited
      by Anne Dhu Shapiro. Cambridge: Harvard University,
      Department of Music, 1985.

      Description and decoding of a solicitation dance, with
musical examples and photos as well.

320. VENNUM, Thomas, Jr. "Ojibwa Origin-Migration Songs of the
      mitewiwim." Journal of American Folklore 91-361 (July-
      Sept. 1978): 753-91.

      This scholarly study focuses on the mitewiwin ("Grand
Medicine Society") ceremonies performed by a priest. Primarily
about the ceremony and the texts rather than music.

321. VENNUM, Thomas, Jr. "Southwestern Ojibwa Music." Ph.D.
      dissertation, Harvard University, 1975. 2 vols. (Vol. 1,
      213 pp. [text]; Vol. 2, 254 pp. [music]).

322. VOEGELIN, C. F., and EULER, Robert C. "Introduction to Hopi
      Chants." Journal of American Folklore 70-276 (Apr.-June
      1957): 115-36.

      A text-centered study of chants, a musical phenomenon
that is between speech and song and is often improvised.

323. VOGET, Frederick William. "The Diffusion of the Wind River
      Shoshone Sun-Dance to the Crow Indians of Montana."
      Ph.D. dissertation, Yale University, 1948.

      Based on field work done in 1941 and 1946, this study is
concerned with how and why a particular dance was transmitted to
another tribe.

324. WALTON, Ede Lou. "Navajo Song Patterning." Journal of American Folklore 43-167 (Jan.-Mar. 1930): 105-18.

Derived from the author's University of California, 1921, doctoral dissertation entitled "Navajo Traditional Poetry," this article is primarily a structural analysis of poetry.

325. WARE, Naomi. "Survival and Change in Pima Indian Music." Ethnomusicology 14-1 (1970): 100-13.

A study of acculturation happening among the Pima, who in the 1960s were already rapidly losing their culture and music and replacing it with Mexican-American and rock-'n'-roll musics. The author discovered, however, two groups at Salt River attempting to preserve certain of the traditional styles.

Music of the Alaskan Indians and Eskimos

326. DAVIS, Carol Beery. Songs of the Totem. Juneau: Empire Printing Co., 1939. 48 pp.

A collection of songs (melodies and texts separately) of the Tlingets of southeastern Alaska in which the meanings of the totem poles are interpreted. There is also discussion of the songs and a number of photos.

327. DAVIS, Carol Beery. Totem Echoes. Juneau: by the author, 114 East 6th St. [99801], 1986.

A collection of native raw material "transcribed into art songs," along with photos, historical data, and other information from southeastern Alaska. Only 500 copies (at $100 each) have been printed.

328. EELLS, Walter Crosby. "Mechanical, Physical, and Musical Ability of the Native Races of Alaska." Journal of Applied Psychology 17-5 (Oct. 1933): 493-506.

Using the Seashore Measures of Musical Talent, the author studied the Aleuts, Eskimos, and Indians. His results reflect what would now be expected of a culturally biased test: "Definite inferiority for all three races in each test is shown at every grade level" (p. 502).

329. ESTREICHER, Zygmunt. "Eskimo-Musik." In Die Musik in
     Geschichte und Gegenwart, Vol. 3, Cols. 1526-33. [1954]

Written in German for the foremost music encyclopedia of
the time, this article includes general information, a description
of style, instruments, plus two illustrations, one transcription,
and a bibliography. Requires a good command of the language.

330. ESTREICHER, Zygmunt. "La musique des Esquimaux-Caribous
     (Collection Gabus)." Bulletin de la société
     néachateloise de géographie 54-1 (1948): 1-53.

331. ESTREICHER, Zygmunt. "Die Musik der Eskimo: eine
     vergleichende Studie." Anthropos 45 (1950): 659-720.

Major article, but quite technical and analytical, in
four sections: I. Methodology, II. Music style description, III.
Comparisons among various groups, IV. Conclusions. Transcriptions
are at the end of the article. In German.

332. HAUSER, Michael. "Formal Structures in Polar Eskimo
     Drum songs." Ethnomusicology 21-1 (Jan. 1977): 33-53.

Based on a 1937 collection of 126 songs by Erik Holtved
and field work in 1962 during which 335 songs were collected, this
study shows that drum songs are highly developed in form and are
closely related to language. Analytical and technical.

333. HOFMANN, Charles. Drum Dance: Legends, Ceremonies, Dances
     and Songs of the Eskimos. N.p.: by the author, 1974.
     95 pp.

Lightweight survey of song types with texts, translations
and a number of photos.

334. JENNESS, D. "Eskimo Music in Northern Alaska." Musical
     Quarterly 8 (1922): 377-83.

Overview of types of music found from Barrow to the
Canadian boundary based on field work, but the examples are
harmonized.

335. JOHNSTON, Thomas F. "Alaskan Eskimo and Indian Musical
        Performance: its many Social and Psychological Ramifica-
        tions." Folklore Forum 15-9 (1976): 117-31.

        In this article the author shows Eskimo and Indian musics
to be integrative and furthering the communal nature of
settlements in the rural areas.

336. JOHNSTON, Thomas F. "Alaskan Native Social Adjustment and
        the Role of Eskimo and Indian Music." Journal of Ethnic
        Studies 3-4 (Winter, 1976): 21-36.

        A study of texts made during the disruption caused by the
pipeline construction, this article explores "the social and
psychological role of Eskimo and Indian musical performance in
maintaining mental well being and in providing core cultural
identity."

337. JOHNSTON, Thomas F. "Eight North Alaskan Eskimo Dance
        Songs." Tennessee Folklore Society Bulletin 40-4
        (December 1974): 123-36.

        An examination of eight Eskimo songs from Point Hope,
focusing on cultural references, musical style, and commonalities.

338. JOHNSTON, Thomas F. Eskimo Music by Region: a Comparative
        Circumpolar Study. Canadian Ethnology Service Paper, no.
        32. Ottawa: National Museums of Canada [Mercury Series],
        1976. 222 pp.

        A series of 34 brief chapters on both areas (from Alaska
to Greenland) and topics (e.g., "tolerant missionization and
music," land claims and music, game songs).

339. JOHNSTON, Thomas F. "The Social Background of Eskimo Music
        in Northwest Alaska." Journal of American Folklore 89-
        354 (Oct.-Dec. 1976): 438-48.

        A study of context rather than content, describing the
role of the media, of government, and the relationship of music to
social organization.

340. JOHNSTON, Thomas F., PULU, Tupou L., et al. Inupiat aggisit atuutinich: Inupiat Dance Songs. Anchorage: National Bilingual Materials Development Center, University of Alaska, 1979. 96 pp.

   A collection of 21 songs with their music designed for practical performance and therefore including pictures of dance motions and explanations. Also describes dance costumes, the songs, drum styles, and composers.

341. KORANDA, Lorraine D. "Music of the Alaskan Eskimos." In Musics of Many Cultures: an Introduction, pp. 332-62. Edited by Elizabeth May. Berkeley: University of California Press, 1980.

   Introductory article for non-specialists, but still fairly technical in that it focuses on style and performing traditions and includes many transcriptions and some analyses. Also includes bibliography, discography, and filmography.

342. LAGUNA, Frederica de. "Under Mount Saint Elias: the History and Culture of the Yakutat Tlingit." Smithsonian Contributions to Anthropology, Vol. 7. 3 vols. Washington, D.C.: Smithsonian Institution, 1972. 1,395 pp.

   This comprehensive study of the Tlingit at Yakutat includes a section on music in Vol. 2, pp. 560-77. Considering the thoroughness of the remainder of the study, it is disappointing that the music section is non-technical and concerned mostly with text. A few inadequate transcriptions are included.

343. LANTIS, Margaret. Alaskan Eskimo Ceremonialism. Monographs of the American Ethnological Society, Vol. 11. New York: American Ethnological Society, 1947.

   This scholarly, anthropological study includes a brief section on music, pp. 98-104, where emphasis is given to text in spite of the sub-title, "Song, Dance, and Musical Instruments."

344. STEIN, Robert. "Eskimo Music." In The White World: Life and Adventures within the Artic Circle Portrayed by Famous Living Explorers, pp. 337-58. Edited by Rudolph Hersting. New York: Lewis, Scribner Co., 1902.

A report of field work done in 1900 among the Smith Sound
Eskimos at Ft. Magnesia. Additional information from an 1818
description plus eight pages of transcriptions.

345. THUREN, Hjalmar Lauritz. "La musique chez les Eskimos."
     S.I.M. [Société internationale de musique] Review
     Musicale Mensuelle 7-12 (Dec. 1911): 36-56.

Musical Instruments of the American Indians

346. BAKKEGARD, B. M., and MORRIS, E. A. "Seventh Century Flutes
     from Arizona." Ethnomusicology 5-3 (Sept. 1961): 184-6.

     A description of four flutes dating from c. 620-670 A.D.
in the Prayer Rock Valley of northeastern Arizona.

347. BROWN, Donald Nelson. "The Distribution of Sound Instru-
     ments in the Prehistoric Southwestern United States."
     Ethnomusicology 11-1 (Jan. 1967): 71-90.

     An attempt to draw together a reasonably complete picture
of early musical life from a variety of scattered sources.
Instruments included are only idiophones and aerophones. Evidence
provided partly in maps, photos, and drawings, with bibliography.

348. CONKLIN, Harold C., and STURTEVENT, William C. "Seneca
     Indian Singing Tools at Coldspring Longhouse: Musical
     Instruments of the Modern Iroquois." In Publications of
     the American Philosophical Society, Vol. 97-3, pp. 262-
     90. Philadelphia: American Philosophical Society, 1953.

349. DENSMORE, Frances. "Musical Instruments of the Maidu
     Indians." American Anthropologist 41 (1939): 113-8.

     Report of research done among the Valley Maidu at Chico,
California, in March 1937. Describes drums, rattles, musical
bows, flutes, and whistles but without pictures or examples.

350. HAEFER, J. Richard. "North American Indian Musical
     Instruments: Some Organological Distribution Problems."
     Journal of the American Musical Instrument Society 1
     (1975): 56-85.

AMERICAN INDIANS: MUSICAL INSTRUMENTS

A preliminary study in which the author attempts to summarize present knowledge on distribution, coordinate the methods of collecting data, and explore the implications of distribution analysis. Sub-headed for each major instrument category and includes maps and photos.

351. HURLEY, William M. "The Kickapoo Whistle System: a Speech Surrogate." Plains Anthropologist 13-41 (1968): 242-7.

A study of Kickapoo whistle and flute languages used in Mexico and Oklahoma for at least one hundred years.

352. LACZKO, Gina. "Apache Music and Musical Instruments." N.p.: Mesa Museum, 1981. 21 pp.

Illustrated pamphlet that goes with an exhibit.

353. McGRATH, James, ed. My Music Reaches to the Sky: Native American Musical Instruments. Santa Fe: Center for the Arts of Indian America, 1973. 57 pp.

More illustrations than text, but includes information on how to make a number of instruments. Part of a teaching kit that also includes actual instruments and a soundsheet.

354. MASON, Bernard Sterling. Drums, Tomtoms, and Rattles: Primitive Percussion Instruments for Modern Use. New York: A. S. Barnes, 1938; reprint ed., New York: Dover, 1974. 206 pp.

A practical guide for the construction and decoration of American Indian drums and rattles and related instruments. Drawings by Frederic H. Kock.

355. MERRIAM, Alan P. "Flathead Indian Instruments and their Music." Musical Quarterly 37 (1951): 368-75.

Scholarly study of the few and relatively simple instruments of the Flathead in Montana, with photos and melodic analysis.

356. VENNUM, Thomas, Jr. The Ojibwa Dance Drum: its History and
      Construction. Smithsonian Folklife Studies #2.
      Washington, D.C.: Smithsonian Institution, 1982. 320 pp.

      While the focus of this book is the Ojibwa drum, its
construction and decoration (pp. 156-249), most of the preceding
pages provide an overview of the Ojibwa and their music,
especially the drum dance. Concluding this thorough and scholarly
study is an excellent bibliography.

357. WATERMAN, Thomas T. "Native Musical Instruments of
      California and Some Others." Out West 28 (1908): 276-86.

358. WHEELER-VOEGELIN, Erminie. "Shawnee Musical Instruments."
      American Anthropologist 44 (1942): 463-75.

      Detailed description of the instruments of a people who
use virtually no European types and few traditional ones
generally. Unfortunately, without illustrations, but includes an
excellent list.

III. ANGLO-AMERICAN FOLKSONGS AND BALLADS

For some, this section may have been the only one expected in a "folk music" bibliography. Certainly it is a major one. Research into folk song and ballad has gone on since before the turn of the century, and therefore only American Indian music has been researched for a longer period in this country. But because far more scholars have worked in the Anglo-American folksong tradition than in American Indian music, this section includes a greater bulk of material. Indeed, it is unlikely that this section actually includes more than a respectable percentage of what has been published, although it is hoped that few major contributions have been omitted.

Research into ballad and folksong was begun by students of English literature. The germinal event in this history was the publication between 1882 and 1898 of The English and Scottish Popular Ballads compiled by Harvard professor, Francis James Child, based on work in the British Isles. Child's collection came to be virtually canonized, and the term "Child ballad" nearly came to denote a genre apart from ballads not published by Child. Early issues of the Journal of American Folklore, even in the 1890's, already included ballads collected by various individuals.

In 1914 the Bureau of Education in Washington, D.C., issued a bulletin listing 305 English and Scottish ballads and urged teachers to form ballad societies in each state in order to find and "rescue" ballads and folksongs. This stimulated a long-lasting obsession for collecting, which only began tapering off in the 1940's and 1950's. But some of the early ballad hunters, like early archaeologists hunting pots and sherds, were more intent on bringing back specimens for a literary museum than in recording the context or studying the informant. Collection after collection, both in book and article form, was published. Most included only the texts of ballads and songs classified by topic with brief headnotes. Some also included information about the original context. Too much energy, perhaps, was given to virtual contests to see which state's collectors could come up with the greatest number of "Child" ballads.

The present writer, as an ethnomusicologist, must be forgiven for expressing the extent to which he was taken aback by the number of publications dealing with folksong which had little or nothing to do with <u>music</u>. Perhaps because folklore has its roots in literature and folklorists have done most of the work on folksong and ballad, there has been so little emphasis on the musical. Most of the early collectors lacked musical training and, because compact field recording equipment was not yet invented, could neither make recordings nor transcribe the melodies as they were heard. Consequently, the musical portions of most ballads and songs were simply lost. At best, they were notated in a simple form that usually pertained only to the first stanza. The least studied aspect has been and remains the total "style" of performance, with its nuances of intonation, rhythm, and ornamentation.

The greatest amount of work done on the musical aspect has been accomplished by one man, Bertrand Bronson. But detailed analysis has also been done by George Boswell and, more recently, James Cowdery. Much of the earlier analytical work suffered from a preoccupation with determining mode based on the medieval system of "church modes." It was presumed for many years that folksong made use of "gapped" scales, i.e., incomplete modal seven-tone scales. It has taken many years for scholars to break the habit of attempting to force American folksong into the mold of a neat but perhaps inappropriate system.

Because the material on this subject area is so vast, it has been subdivided into what is hoped are useful categories. For items placed under the "Regional" subheading, the reader shall have to interpret terms such as "Midwest" and "South" in a generous manner, since there is sometimes no general agreement on what states might be included. Appalachia embraces the usual mountain states including the Carolinas, but Virginia, for example, is included under "Middle Atlantic." "Midwest" includes Ohio, Indiana, Michigan and the Plains States out to, but not including, Colorado. While some might include Texas under "South," it is here part of the "Southwest."

Occupational songs have been divided into the obvious rail, mining, sea, and lumberjack categories, but there is also a catch-all group that includes songs of soldiers, labor unions, and politics. However, the latter does not include those items identified with the Folksong Revival of the 1940's and 1950's which grew in part out of the leftist movements of the 1930's. These are included in Section IV. Admittedly, some of these items are borderline "folk."

While some book-length collections have no doubt been
inadvertently overlooked, a number of article-length studies have
simply been omitted because, were every article pertaining to
ballad and folksong that was published in every folklore journal
listed here, this section would soon constitute a separate volume.
Again, as an ethnomusicologist, I continue to wonder how many
"trophy-head" article-length collections from around 1925 need be
known before surfeit has been reached. All articles, but not
necessarily all of the brief queries and notes, from the Journal
of American Folklore have been listed, and most from the other
major journals in the field, but if the reader desires an even
more complete listing, he/she will have to consult the complete
bound collections of such journals as Southern Folklore Quarterly,
New York Folklore Quarterly, Western Folklore, and a host of other
state- or region-oriented journals.

By far the greatest resource for this area is the Archive of
Folk Culture, headed by Joseph Hickerson. The Archive is part of
the American Folklife Center in the Library of Congress. There,
and in the general collections of the Library including those of
the Music Division, one can locate all items listed here and
probably much, much more.

Bibliography and Discography

359. BEAN, Charles W. An Index to Folksongs Contained in Theses
and Dissertations in the Library of Congress.
Loughborough, Leicestershire, England: Dept. of Library
and Information Studies, Loughborough University of
Technology, 1982. 266 pp.

Although "theses and dissertations in the Library of
Congress" does not specify a corpus of documents beyond those
found elsewhere, this study provides a useful index to the
materials which the Library of Congress does have.

360. BOGGS, Beverly B., and PATTERSON, Daniel W. An Index of
Selected Folk Recordings. Chapel Hill, N.C.: Curriculum
in Folklore of the University of North Carolina, 1984.

Published as a set of 55 microfiche cards (of 10,864
pages of material) with a 75-page printed manual explaining the
resource. Geographically, the study covers the United States,
Canada, the British Isles, and the Caribbean and includes
folksongs, ballads, religious songs, worksongs, children's songs,
folktales along with some banjo tunes, early country music, blues,

dance, medicine-show tunes, and old string band music. Material
is organized by title and key lines, performers' names,
geographical sources, and by spoken, instrumental, and vocal
categories. Some 8,350 performers on 500 LPs are indexed.

361. BRUNNINGS, Florence E. Folk Song Index: a Comprehensive
Guide to the Florence E. Brunnings Collection. New York:
Garland, 1981. 357 pp.

Based on the private collection of Ms. Brunnings, which
includes more than just folk music, this labor of love (or
possibly obsession) that took 11 years lists 49,300 entries for
1115 books and journals and 695 records. From the title, one may
find the source.

362. COHEN, Norm. "Folk Music Discography." Western Folklore
30-3 (July 1971): 235-46. Reprinted in JEMF Reprint
Series #17-25.

A brief history of mainly hillbilly records from 1922-42,
organized by period.

363. HICKERSON, Joseph C. "A Bibliography of American
Folksong." In American Folk Poetry: an Anthology, pp.
775-816. By Duncan Emrich. Boston and Toronto: Little,
Brown & Co., 1974.

In two parts, the first portion offers bibliographic
coverage to each chapter as a supplement to that of Emrich. The
second part is a classified bibliography in four sections: general
works on American folk song, general collections, regional
collections, and general works and collections of Afro-American
folksong. Sections are introduced, but items lack annotations.
Lastly there is a list of publishers of books, records, journals
and magazines that specialize in folk music.

364. LAWLESS, Ray McKinley. Folksingers and Folksongs in
America; a Handbook of Biography, Bibliography, and
Discography. New York: Duell, Sloan and Pearce, 1960;
rev. ed., 1965; reprint ed., Westport, Conn.: Greenwood,
1968. 750 pp.

Although somewhat out-of-date, Lawless' work remains an
extremely valuable reference work. It begins with an extensive

alphabetical list of singers who appear in painting, literature, and Steuben Glass engravings, with short biographies, followed by a listing of folk instruments, and a bibliography of ballad and folksong collections. Additionally, he lists folklore societies, folk festivals, has a folksong title checklist, and a list of LP recordings. A supplement adds further singers, books, magazines, and recordings. Lawless does not distinguish between traditionalists and revivalists.

365. LOMAX, Alan and COWELL, Sidney Robertson. American Folk Song and Folk Lore; a Regional Bibliography. New York: Progressive Education Association, [1942]. 59 pp.

Rather dated and now rare annotated bibliography of songs, jokes and other genres in collections. After a brief discussion of folksong scholarship, items are organized by region, race, and other distinctions (e.g., occupational, ethnic).

366. LOWENS, Irving. A Bibliography of Songsters Printed in America Before 1821. Worcester, Mass.: American Antiquarian Society, 1976. 229 pp.

A songster is "a collection of three or more secular poems intended to be sung." Few of the 649 items described here include notation, but the study is well indexed.

General and Miscellaneous Studies

367. ABRAHAMS, Roger D. "Patterns of Structure and Role Relationships in the Child Ballad in the United States." Journal of American Folklore 79-313 (July-Sept. 1966): 448-62.

A study of "interpretation," the third step after collection and comparison, this "experimental" essay uses Child ballads as its subject.

368. ABRAHAMS, Roger D., and FOSS, George. Anglo-American Folksong Style. Englewood Cliffs, N.J.: Prentice-Hall, 1968. 242 pp.

Comprehensive study of the stylistic elements that comprise folksong, including relationship with audience, metrical structure of the verses, kinds of stories, community value systems, relationship of tune and text, and structure of the tunes. In a larger sense, it is a study of oral composition and transmission.

369. ALVEY, R. Gerald. "Phillips Barry and Anglo-American Folksong Scholarship." Journal of the Folklore Institute 10-1/2 (June-Aug. 1973): 67-95.

A preliminary investigation of the scholarship of Barry (1880-1937), a scholar who published rather little but had a far-reaching impact. Covers his career, his research, the influences on him, and reviews his work in order to understand it as a coherent whole.

370. BARRY, Phillips. Bulletin of the Folksong Society of the Northeast. Philadelphia: American Folklore Society, 1960; reprint ed., New York: Kraus, 1970. c250 pp.

With an introduction by S. P. Bayard, this collection gathers Barry's articles into one place. The user is warned, however, that not only are the articles rather old, but that there is neither table of contents nor continuous pagination.

371. BARRY, Phillips. "Folk-Music in America." Journal of American Folklore 22-83 (Jan.-Mar. 1909): 72-81.

Early theoretical study concentrating on modal analysis, with melodic transcriptions.

372. BARRY, Phillips. Folk Music in America. Washington, D.C.: Works Progress Administration, Federal Theatre Project, Folk-song and Folklore Department, June 1939. #80-S. 113 pp.

Series of mimeographed reprints from the Journal of American Folklore, with an introduction.

373. BARRY, Phillips. "Native Balladry in America." Journal of American Folklore 22-86 (Oct.-Dec. 1909): 365-73.

Texts and tunes for three ballads and variants.

374. BARRY, Phillips. "Some Aspects of Folk-Song." Journal of American Folklore 25-97 (Jul.-Sept. 1912): 274-83.

Study based on songs selected for their "aesthetic" value and to illustrate "manner and process in growth of folk songs."

375. BARRY, Phillips. "Some Traditional Songs." Journal of American Folklore 18-68 (Jan.-Mar. 1905): 49-59.

Unusually early presentation of four ballads and variants, including tunes, texts, and discussion.

376. BARRY, Phillips. "The Transmission of Folk Song." Journal of American Folklore 27-103 (Jan.-Mar. 1914): 67-76.

After a general discussion of the folksinger, this article becomes a collection of tunes and texts for eight songs.

377. BRONNER, Simon J. "Street Cries and Peddler Traditions in Contemporary Perspective." New York Folklore 2-3/4 (Summer, 1977): 2-16.

A study of urban street cries in New York City, who uses them and for what occasions. Includes some transcriptions.

378. BEATTY, Arthur. "Some Ballad Variants and Songs." Journal of American Folklore 22-83 (Jan.-Mar. 1909): 63-71.

Study of texts from both written and oral traditions.

379. BELDEN, Henry M. "Balladry in America." Journal of American Folklore 25-95 (Jan.-Mar. 1912): 1-23.

Traces the history of folksong scholarship in America to that point, especially in the above journal, lists the problems to be solved, and offers examples.

380. BEVIL, Jack Marshall. "Centonization and Concordance in the American Southern Upland Folksong: a Study of the Musical Generative and Transmittive Processes of an Oral Tradition." Ph.D. dissertation, North Texas State University, in progress.

381. BLUESTEIN, Eugene. "The Background and Sources of an
American Folksong Tradition." Ph.D. dissertation,
University of Minnesota, 1960. 210 pp.

In seeking to identify an American folksong tradition,
the author explores various eighteenth and nineteenth century
ideas, especially those of Herder, who thought that folksong is
the source of national literary traditions.

382. BOATRIGHT, Mody C., HUDSON, Wilson M., and MAXWELL, Allen,
eds. A Good Tale and a Bonnie Tune. Dallas: Southern
Methodist University Press, 1964. 274 pp.

Collection of articles by leading figures, such as T. P.
Coffin, John Greenway, W. Edson Richmond, D. K. Wilgus, Geo. Foss,
and Roger Abrahams. Completing the book is a substantial essay,
"Folksong and Folksong scholarship: Changing Attitudes" (pp. 199-
269) in addition to appendices.

383. BRONSON, Bertrand H. "Cecil Sharp and Folksong: a Review
Article." Western Folklore 27-4 (Oct. 1968): 200-7.

Partly a review of Maud Karpeles' book Cecil Sharp: His
Life and Work, partly a discussion of what folksong collecting was
and what it is now.

384. BURT, Olive Woolley. American Murder Ballads and their
Stories. New York: Oxford, 1958. 272 pp.

A lifetime study of ballads based on murders that
actually happened. Examples of texts, tunes, with headnotes.

385. CAREY, George G. "A Collection of Airborne Cadence
Chants." Journal of American Folklore 78-307 (Jan.-
Mar. 1965): 52-61.

Written by an author who ran with the troops, this study
was done at Ft. Campbell, Kentucky, with the 101st Airborne
Division in April 1961, and offers many examples of texts.

386. CAZDEN, Norman. "Regional and Occupational Orientations of
American Traditional Songs." Journal of American
Folklore 72-286 (Oct.-Dec. 1959): 310-44.

A reassessment of the relationship between regional and occupational songs and a critique of extant work. Based on songs from the Catskill region and includes a great number of charts.

387. COFFIN, Tristram Potter. The British Traditional Ballad in North America. Philadelphia: American Folklore Society, 1950. 187 pp. Rev. ed., 1963 (Bibliographical Series #2). 186 pp. Rev. ed., Austin: University of Texas Press, 1977. 297 pp.

Based on Coffin's 1949 English Literature Ph.D. dissertation at the University of Pennsylvania, this classic critical study of the ballad focuses on variability of plot and poetic structure. The 1977 edition includes a nearly 100 page supplement by Roger deV. Renwick.

388. COFFIN, Tristram P. "The Folk Ballad and the Literary Ballad: an Essay in Classification." Midwest Folklore 9-1 (Spring, 1959): 5-18; reprinted in Folklore in Action: Essays for Discussion in Honor of MacEdward Leach, pp. 58-70. Ed. by Horace P. Beck. Bibliographical and Special Series #14. Philadelphia: American Folklore Society, 1962; reprint ed., Millwood, N.Y.: Kraus, 1972.

Literary study of written ballads grouped into six categories: 1) those of no literary merit, 2) flashes of literary merit, 3) ballad poems, 4) rewritten ballads, 5) poems developed from ballads, and 6) poems using balladry as plane of reference.

389. COFFIN, Tristram P. "An Index to Borrowing in the Child Ballads of America." Journal of American Folklore 62-244 (Apr.-June 1949): 156-61.

Although these changes are considered by the author to be a corruption, Coffin lists borrowed material and cites sources.

390. COHEN, Norm. "Tin Pan Alley's Contribution to Folk Music." Western Folklore 29-1 (Jan. 1970): 9-20.

A discussion of how urban popular music from the 1860 to 1910 period drew upon folk sources and their inter-relationships.

391. DAVIS, Arthur Kyle, Jr. "Some Problems of Ballad Publication." Musical Quarterly 14 (1928): 283-96.

The author discusses five problems encountered in ballad research: 1) music notation, 2) ribaldry, 3) artificial geography, 4) patriotism, 5) academic versus popular interest.

392. DUGAW, Dianne M. "Anglo-American Folksong Reconsidered: the Interface of Oral and Written Forms." Western Folklore 43-2 (April 1984): 83-103.

An exploration of the interrelationships between written and oral traditions through female warrior ballads, oral, printed, and written. Includes six extensive examples.

393. ELDRIDGE, John William. "A Preface to the Study of Anglo-American Ballad Variation." Ph.D. dissertation, University of Oregon, 1978. 242 pp.

The writer, asserting that an adequate methodology for treating ballad variants had not been developed, procedes to create one.

394. FATOUT, Paul. "Threnodies of the Ladies' Books." Musical Quarterly 31 (1945): 464-78.

Probably more in the popular vein than folk, this study focuses on songs found in nineteenth-century ladies' magazines and their texts. Examples and facsimiles are included.

395. FERRIS, William R., Jr. "Folk Song and Culture: Charles Seeger and Alan Lomax." New York Folklore Quarterly 29-3 (1973): 206-18.

An introductory article to the views of Seeger and Lomax, especially the latter's Cantometrics, and their relevance to folksong research.

396. "Folksong and Ballad: a Symposium." Journal of American Folklore 70-277 (Jul.-Sept. 1957): 205-61.

Comprising an entire issue are eight articles by Leach, Coffin, Freeman, Greene, Greenway, Hyman, Lathrop, and Musick.

397. FORD, Mr. and Mrs. Henry. "Good Morning," Music Calls &
     Directions for Old-Time Dancing. Dearborn, Mich., 1941.
     96 pp.

     An illustrated guide to dancing with notation, diagrams,
and pictures.

398. FUKUDO, Hanako. "Lullabies of the Western Hemisphere."
     Ed.D. dissertation, University of Southern California,
     1960. 495 pp.

     Based on a sample of 154 items representing 28 groups of
people, this study attempts to show similarities in range, scale,
melodic repetition, rhythms, and the sentiment of the texts. Some
are American folk.

399. GEROULD, Gordon Hall. The Ballad of Tradition. Oxford:
     Clarendon Press, 1932. 311 pp.

     Scholarly work on the British ballad, especially the
stories, tunes, as history, their variations, musical and poetic
forms. Also a study of the broadside in Britain and America.

400. GLASSIE, Henry, IVES, Edward D., and SZWED, John F.
     Folksongs and Their Makers. Bowling Green, Oh.: Bowling
     Green University Popular Press, 1972. 170 pp.

     After an introduction on "Folklore and Popular Culture"
by Ray B. Browne, there are three substantial articles, one each
by the three authors. Those by Ives and Szwed concern songmakers
in Newfoundland, Canada, but that by Glassie ("'Take that Night
Train to Selma': an Excursion to the Outskirts of Scholarship") is
concerned with the instrumental and vocal musical activities of
the Weir family from near Cooperstown, N.Y. Glassie's article
previously appeared in Journal of Popular Culture 2-1 (Summer,
1968): 1-62.

401. GOLDENBERG, June Lazare. "Folk Song is Alive and Well and
     Living in the City." Journal of American Culture 4-4
     (Winter, 1981): 167-76.

     Historical introduction to and definition of urban folk
song, especially the topical ballad, which is explored from the
eighteenth and nineteenth centuries with textual examples.

402. GOMBOSI, Otto. "Stephen Foster and 'Gregory Walker'."
     Musical Quarterly 30 (1944): 133-46.

     A musicologist leaps into the Foster fray (was his work
based on Afro-American sources or not?), asserts along with G. P.
Jackson that Foster wrote songs based on his own European
heritage, and traces a Foster melody back to the sixteenth-
seventeenth century ballad, "Gregory Walker."

403. GOWER, (Lemuel) Herschel. "Traditional Scottish Ballads in
     the United States." Ph.D. dissertation, Vanderbilt,
     1957. 228 pp.

     Concerned with establishing whether the Child ballads
collected in the United States are of English or Scottish origin.
Concludes that "at least forty per cent . . . are of Scottish
origin."

404. HAWES, Bess Lomax. "Folksongs and Function: Some Thoughts
     on the American Lullaby." Journal of American Folklore
     87-344 (Apr.-June 1974): 140-8.

     Author shows that American "lullabies," rather than being
about sleep in terms of text, are lullabies by virtue of being
used at bedtime. Most are in 4/4 meter and involve a period of
chatting and game playing followed by lulling.

405. HENDREN, Joseph W. "The Scholar and the Ballad Singer."
     Southern Folklore Quarterly 18-2 (June 1954): 139-46.

     Reviews the way scholars had until then looked at
ballads, mostly as literature. Raises questions of who are the
folksingers, how is the ballad folksong, with brief review of the
literature.

406. HUDSON, Arthur Palmer. Folklore Keeps the Past Alive.
     Athens, Ga.: University of Georgia Press, 1962. 63 pp.

     Three lectures given October 24-26, 1961, at Mercer
University as part of the Eugenia Corothy Blount Lamar Memorial
Lectures. 1) "The Poetry of the Earth: Two Old Folksongs," 2)
"Glimpses of History in Folksongs of the South," and 3) Folksongs
in American Poetry and Fiction."

407. HUSTVEDT, Sigurd Bernhard. <u>Ballad Books</u> and <u>Ballad Men:</u>
<u>Raids and Rescues in Britain, America, and the Scandi-</u>
<u>navian North Since 1800.</u> Cambridge: Harvard, 1930. 376 pp.

Not a collection but text criticism of material from a
broad area. Discusses the work of great Child ballad scholars.

408. HYMAN, Stanley Edgar. "The Child Ballad in America: Some
Aesthetic Considerations." <u>Journal of American Folklore</u>
70-277 (Jul.-Sept. 1957): 235-39.

Discusses the changes ballads go through in coming to
America, particularly loss and corruption.

409. JACKSON, Bruce, ed. <u>Folklore and Society: Essays in Honor</u>
<u>of Benjamin A. Botkin.</u> Hatboro, Pa.: Folklore
Associates, 1966. 204 pp.

A Festschrift for Dr. Botkin at age 65, with ten
articles, most of them being listed elsewhere in the present work.

410. JAMES, Thelma G. "The English and Scottish Popular Ballads
of Francis J. Child." <u>Journal of American Folklore</u> 46-
179 (Jan.-Mar. 1933): 51-68.

An analytical study of what Child included and left out
of his classic collection; also examination of his consistency.

411. KINNE, Frances Bartlett. "A Comparative Study of British
Traditional Ballads and American Indigenous Ballads."
Ph.D. dissertation, Johann-Wolfgang-Goethe University
(Frankfurt am Main), 1957. 161 pp.

Text based study of the origin and development of
balladry, both British traditional and American indigenous.

412. LAWS, G. Malcolm, Jr. <u>American Balladry from British</u>
<u>Broadsides: a Guide for Students and Collectors of</u>
<u>Traditional Song.</u> Bibliographical and Special Series #8.
Philadelphia: American Folklore Society, 1957. 315 pp.

A classic study of the broadside ballad, both in Britain
and in America. It is defined, its origin studied, and its

distribution detailed. One section (pp. 63-83) looks at the broadside as traditional song, but this study is not a musical one. Appendix I (pp. 125-294) lists broadside ballads.

413. LAWS, George Malcolm, Jr. Native American Balladry; a Descriptive Study and a Bibliographical Syllabus of the Ballads Sung in the United States. Bibliographical and Special Series #1. Philadelphia: American Folklore Society, 1950. 276 pp. Rev. ed., 1964. 298 pp.

Based on the author's doctoral dissertation of 1949, the study is in two parts. The first, the descriptive part, deals with American ballad forms, variants, and types, with examples. The second, the bibliographical syllabus, is mainly a list of 185 native ballads collected from oral tradition, here grouped by nine topics. For each there is a sample stanza and summary.

414. LAWS, G. Malcolm, Jr. "The Spirit of Native American Balladry." Journal of American Folklore 64-252 (Apr.- June 1951): 163-70.

A study of the "Americanization" of British ballads.

415. LEACH, MacEdward, and COFFIN, Tristram P., eds. The Critics and the Ballad. Carbondale: Southern Illinois University Press, 1961; reprint ed., 1973. 284 pp.

Collection of 15 articles about the conflicting ideas in ballad and folksong scholarship, i.e., origin, variation, and transmission. Authors are prominent folklorists, e.g., Phillips Barry, Bertrand Bronson, Samuel Bayard, and Tristram Coffin.

416. LOMAX, John A. "Some Types of American Folk-Song." Journal of American Folklore 28-107 (Jan.-Mar. 1915): 1-17.

Text-based study of "new" ballads composed in America.

417. LOMAX, John A. Adventures of a Ballad Hunter. New York: Macmillan, 1947. 302 pp.

Autobiographical experiences of one of America's greatest collectors who lived from 1867 to 1948. Organized chronologically, but mostly around the types of songs collected.

418. LONG, Eleanor R. "Ballad Singers, Ballad Makers, and
     Ballad Etiology." Western Folklore 32-4 (Oct. 1973):
     225-36.

     Deals with the question of variation and where one ballad
variant ends and a new ballad begins. The author describes four
basic types of folk artistry: 1) perseverating (faithful
reproduction of learned versions), 2) confabulating (creative), 3)
rationalizing (making the text conform to preset values and
organization), and 4) integrative (free approach).

419. McGILL, Josephine. "'Following Music' in a Mountain Land."
     Musical Quarterly 3 (1917): 364-84.

     Interesting description by an early collector of music in
the Kentucky mountains of her work on horseback. Some
descriptions of instruments and ballad singing.

420. McGILL, Josephine. "Old Ballad Burthens." Musical
     Quarterly 4 (1918): 293-306.

     Study of the phenomena of repetition and refrains in
ballads collected in Kentucky.

421. McMILLAN, Douglas J. "A Survey of Theories Concerning the
     Oral Transmission of the Traditional Ballad." Southern
     Folklore Quarterly 28-4 (Dec. 1964): 299-309.

     Well-done review of literature and theories with numerous
quotations.

422. MILLER, Geoffrey. "'Are You All Unhappy at a $20 Bill?':
     Text, Tune and Context at Antique Auctions."
     Ethnomusicology 28-2 (May 1984): 187-208.

     Description of performance context and analysis of the
chant of the auctioneer. Defines how it is musical and cites
possible reasons for its existence.

423. MILLER, Kurt Robert. "Heroes Found in Song Texts from Folk
     Music of the United States." 2 vols. DMA dissertation,
     University of Southern California, 1963. 642 pp.

Studied texts to identify male heroes from among cowboys, hunters, labor, lawmen, lumbermen, outlaws, politicians, railmen, rivermen, seamen, and soldiers. Derived character traits and created a composite "folk hero of the United States" based on 300 collections. Competence, courage, and leadership were found most important.

424. NEWELLS, William Wells. "Early American Ballads." Journal of American Folklore 12-47 (Oct.-Dec. 1899): 241-54 and 13-49 (Apr.-June 1900): 105-22.

Early and general text study stimulated by Child's work.

425. PORTER, James, ed. The Ballad Image: Essays Presented to Bertrand Harris Bronson. Los Angeles: Center for the Study of Comparative Folklore & Mythology, University of California, Los Angeles, 1983. 262 pp.

Twelve articles by leading scholars on individual ballads, stability and variation in traditional song, folk music and the visual arts, individual singers, and programs of oral re-creation. Writers include D. K. Wilgus, Archie Green, T. P. Coffin, Judith McCulloh, and James Porter.

426. POUND, Louise. "American Folksong." Southern Folklore Quarterly 17-2 (Mar. 1953): 114-21.

Wide-ranging, general article focusing on change.

427. SMITH, C. Alphonso. "Ballads Surviving in the United States." Musical Quarterly 2 (1916): 109-29.

After a strong recommendation that scholars immediately begin collecting, the author provides an overview of the ballad in America, citing examples of texts and tunes.

428. SMITH, Reed. "The Traditional Ballad in America, 1933." Journal of American Folklore 47-183 (Jan.-Mar. 1934): 64-75.

Examination of new publications and discoveries since 1928, as well as a review and analysis of the contents of these new works.

429. SORCE-KELLER, Marcello. "The Problem of Classification in Folksong Research: a Short History." Folklore 95-1 (1984): 100-104.

Survey of literature and ideas concerning classification in both American and European ballad research.

430. STECKERT, Ellen J. "Tylor's Theory of Survivals and National Romanticism: Their Influence on Early American Folksong Collectors." Southern Folklore Quarterly 32-3 (Sept. 1968): 209-36.

Suggests that early collectors tended to be biased stemming from a priori theories, such as those of National Romanticism (the Noble Savage) and of Survivals. This is a hindsight evaluation of all the major collectors.

431. TALLMADGE, William H. "The Scotch-Irish and British Traditional Ballad in America." New York Folklore Quarterly 24-4 (Dec. 1968): 261-74.

Historical study of the Scotch-Irish in Appalachia and their importance in transmitting ballads.

432. TAYLOR, Archer. "Trends in the Study of Folksong, 1937-1950." Southern Folklore Quarterly 17-2 (Mar. 1953): 97-113.

Text-oriented study covering American and other types.

433. THIGPEN, Kenneth A., Jr. "A Reconsideration of the Commonplace Phrase and Commonplace Theme in the Child Ballads." Southern Folklore Quarterly 37-4 (Dec. 1973): 385-408.

Reconsiders the Perry-Lord theory as applied to ballads and other related genres.

434. TOELKEN, J. Barre. "An Oral Canon for the Child Ballads: Construction and Application." Journal of the Folklore Institute 4-1 (June 1967): 75-101.

Non-musical discussion of ballads as either traditional
or non-traditional, and presents a method of testing that aspect.
Seeks a reliable corpus of texts on which to make conclusions.
This article followed up by George W. Boswell's "A Note-Commentary
of J. Barre Toelken's 'An Oral . . . Application'," in the same
journal, 8-1 (June 1971): 57-65.

435. TOLMAN, Albert H., and EDDY, Mary O. "Traditional Texts and
Tunes." Journal of American Folklore 35-138 (Oct.-Dec.
1922): 335-432.

Continuation of an earlier study, dividing the subject
into four categories. Good for its bibliography of ballad
collections to date. A few tunes are given as examples.

436. TRUZZI, Marcello. "Folksongs of the American Circus." New
York Folklore Quarterly 24-3 (Sept. 1968): 163-75.

After a brief historical introduction, the author
presents and discusses the texts for songs organized as clown
songs and work shanteys.

437. VAN DER HORST, Brian. Folk Music in America. New York:
Franklin Watts, 1972. 79 pp.

A thin but comprehensive study of the history of American
folk music, from the American Indians and Puritans to contemporary
folk music and scholarship. Also, stories of individual singers
(e.g., Lightnin' Hopkins and the Carter Family).

438. VASSAL, Jacques. Folksong: une historie de la musique
populaire aux Etas Unis. Paris: Edition Albin Michel,
1971. 348 pp.

Comprehensive study of American folksong, of American
Indians, Afro-Americans, Anglo-American genres, and especially the
folksong revival movement. Brief biographies of revivalists such
as Woodie Guthrie, Cisco Houston, Pete Seeger, and Bob Dylan.

439. WELLS, Evelyn Kendrick. The Ballad Tree: a Study of
British and American Ballads, their Folklore, Verse, and
Music. New York: Ronald Press Co., 1950. 370 pp.

Written by an English professor, this study focuses on a variety of topics, such as Christian elements in ballads, the research of Sharp and Child, and includes some tunes.

440. WILGUS, D. K. Anglo-American Folksong Scholarship Since 1898. New Brunswick, N.J.: Rutgers University Press, 1959; reprint ed., Westport, Conn: Greenwood, 1982. 466 pp.

Based on the author's 1954 Ohio State University doctoral dissertation, this valuable study traces the problems confronting folksong scholars and the latter's changing ideas from 1898 until the 1950s. Major figures examined include Sharp and Child, and the development of ballad scholarship. He also includes the black spiritual. The discography, while extensive, is out of date.

441. WILGUS, D. K. "Ballad Classification." Midwest Folklore 5-2 (Summer, 1955): 95-100.

Originally a paper, the author proposes that the days of collecting are basically over, that the results, being scattered around, must be organized, and suggest that this be done according to narrative theme.

442. WILGUS, D. K. "The Future of American Folksong Scholarship." Southern Folklore Quarterly 37-4 (Dec. 1973): 315-30.

Comments that the old way of collecting focuses on "the thing," but that now there is emphasis on "the event." Summarizes earlier collecting and its biases, and surveys more recent work and changing attitudes and emphases.

443. WILGUS, D. K. "A Type-Index of Anglo-American Traditional Narrative Songs." Journal of the Folklore Institute 7-2/3 (Aug.-Dec. 1970): 161-76.

Based on a paper presented at a conference in which the author was the only American, this study proposes an alternative way of classifying ballads based on the "family" idea as opposed to the European thematic system.

444. WOLF, John Quincy. "Folksingers and the Re-Creation of Folksong." Western Folklore 26-2 (April 1967): 101-12.

Based on field work in the Arkansas area of the Ozarks, the author relates how the singers themselves explain change that takes place in ballads and folk songs. Organized by informants.

General Collections of Ballads and Folksongs

445. *American Musical Miscellany: a Collection of the Newest and Most Appoved [sic] Songs, Set to Music*. Northampton, Mass.: Andrew Wright, 1798; reprint ed., New York: Da Capo, 1972. 300 pp.

One of the some 500 pocket songsters issued up to 1820, but this one is exceptional because it includes notation for songs, some in parts, in addition to texts.

446. AMES, Russell. *The Story of American Folk Song*. New York: Grosset and Dunlap, 1955. 276 pp.

Chronologically organized and general collection of American folksongs (texts only) with running commentary.

447. ASCH, Moses, DUNSON, Josh, and RAIM, Ethel, eds. *Anthology of American Folk Music*. New York: Oak, 1973. 118 pp.

Collection of texts transcribed from Columbia recordings produced in the 1920s. Includes an account of recording in the South. Singers include the Carter Family, Dock Boggs, Blind Lemon Jefferson, Clarence Ashley, and Uncle Dave Macon.

448. BOTKIN, Benjamin A., ed. *Treasury of American Folklore: Stories, Ballads, and Traditions of the People*. New York: Crown, 1944. 959 pp.

One of the most popular collections ever published, it includes a vast amount of material. Part 6 is devoted to folksong and ballad, with three play rhymes, nine play parties, and 67 ballads and songs classified by topic. For each section there is historical introduction and other pertinent material.

449. BROWNE, C. A. *The Story of Our National Ballads*. New York: Thomas Y. Crowell, 1919; rev. ed., 1931. 315 pp.

Old-fashioned, non-documented, non-technical history of well-known American songs, e.g., "Yankee Doodle," "Hail Columbia," and "Tenting on the Old Camp Ground."

450. CAZDEN, Norman. The Abelard Folk Song Book. New York: Abelard-Schuman, 1958; reprinted in part as A Catskill Songbook. Fleischmanns, N.Y.: Purple Mountain Press, 1978. 2 vols. in one, 127 pp. each.

Vol. 1 is "Songs for Everyday" and Vol. 2 is "Songs for Saturday Night." Popular arrangements with guitar chords of such folksongs as "A Shantyman's Life" and "I Wish I Was a Single Girl."

451. CHASE, Richard. American Folk Tales and Songs. New York: New American Library of World Literature, 1956; reprint ed., New York: Dover, 1971. 240 pp.

Pp. 107-86 include ballads, songs, and hymns, giving text and tune in shape-notes, with a little commentary on each.

452. CHILD, Francis James. The English and Scottish Popular Ballads. 5 vols. Boston and New York: Houghton, Mifflin and Co., 1882-1898; reprint eds., New York: Folklore Press, 1956; New York: Cooper Square Publishers, 1962; New York: Dover, 1965.

Child, an American professor at Harvard, was the most important pioneer in ballad study. His collection of 305 ballads and numerous variants done in Britain set off in part the ballad collecting mania that swept American campuses in the early twentieth century. Besides presenting the complete text of each ballad, Child provided cross references to other versions, parallel versions in foreign languages, and summarized the story. Because Child died in 1896 before the series was completed, the final volume was accomplished by others and includes besides a list of published tunes, a set of 55 melodies in manuscript. While there is no doubt as to the central importance of Child's corpus, it came to be thought that ballads outside this collection were somehow less legitimate or important.

453. COCKRELL, Dale. "The Helen Hartness Flanders Ballad Collection, Middlebury College." Music Library Association Notes 39-1 (Sept. 1982): 31-42.

Flanders, a student of Phillips Barry, collected some 5,000 examples of music and 4,000 textual items between 1930 and 1941 in New England. The archive includes field recordings, unpublished papers, chapbooks, songsters, broadsides, published music, books, and Flander's own publications.

454. DARLING, Charles W., ed. The New American Songster: Traditional Ballads and Songs of North America. Lanham, Md., University Press of America, 1983. 388 pp.

A text anthology by a history professor for amateurs and students consisting of more than 320 classic ballads, broadsides classified by subject. Also includes native American songs, white country and black blues, work songs, and songs of struggle.

455. DEAN, Michael Cassius. Flying Cloud and One Hundred and Fifty other Old-time Songs and Ballads of Outdoor Men, Sailors, Lumber Jacks, Soldiers, Men of the Great Lakes, Railroadmen, Miners, etc. Virginia, Minn. Quickprint, 1922; reprint ed., Norwood, Penn.: Norwood Editions, 1973. 146 pp.

456. DOLPH, Edward Arthur. "Sound Off!" Soldier Songs from Yankee Doodle to Parley Voo. New York: Cosmopolitan Book Co., 1929. 621 pp.

After a very brief introduction, the compiler presents a great variety of songs arranged for piano and voice by Philip Egner with headnotes for each.

457. DOWNES, Olin, and SIEGMEISTER, Elie. A Treasury of American Song. Rev. and enlarged. New York: Knopf, 1943. 410 pp.

Collection of 194 songs (texts only) arranged by historical periods with piano accompaniment by E. Siegmeister.

458. EMRICH, Duncan. American Folk Poetry: an Anthology. Boston and Toronto: Little, Brown & Co., 1974. 862 pp.

Based on the holdings of the Archive of American Folk Song in the Library of Congress, this study focuses on the texts of ballads, songs, chants, hymns, and lullabies. Besides being classified by topic, the record numbers are supplied.

459. EMRICH, Duncan. _Folklore on the American Land._ Boston: Little, Brown & Co., 1972. 707 pp.

Chapters 27-31 (pp. 401-594) includes song texts, melodies, and commentary arranged under headings of historical, sea, cow country, love, and murder ballads.

460. FORCUCCI, Samuel L. _A Folk Song History of America: America Through its Songs._ Englewood Cliffs, N.J.: Prentice-Hall, 1984. 260 pp.

Running commentary on broad idea of American folksong with many examples (tunes, chords, and words) interspersed. The rather unappealing transcriptions are arranged chronologically.

461. FORD, Ira W. _Traditional Music of America._ New York: E. P. Dutton, 1940; reprint ed., Hatboro, Pa.: Folklore Associates, 1965; New York: Da Capo, 1978. 480 pp.

Poorly documented but important collection with a heavy concentration of fiddle tunes from Missouri. Includes also square dance calls and movements, round dances, play parties, children's play songs, and some ballads (tunes and texts). The collector is vague as to who, when, and where, for he was a local enthusiast. The reprint edition includes a useful introduction by Judith McCulloh.

462. GORDON, Robert Winslow. _Folk-Songs of America._ Washington, D.C.: Works Progress Administration, Folk-Song and Folklore Department, Publication 73-S, 1938. 110 pp.

Text study of a variety of song types, white and black.

463. GROVER, Carrie B. _A Heritage of Songs._ Bethel, Me., 1953; reprint ed., Norwood, Pa.: Norwood Editions, 1973. 216 pp.

464. HORSTMAN, Dorothy. _Sing Your Heart Out, Country Boy._ New York: E. P. Dutton, 1975. 393 pp.; New York: Pocket Books, 1976. 455 pp.

After an introduction, the song texts (no notation) are arranged in chapters by type (e.g., Songs of the Home, Religious Songs). The song texts are embedded within a running commentary.

465. JOHNSON, Helen Kendrick. <u>Our Familiar Songs and Those Who Made Them.</u> New York: Henry Holt & Co., 1909; reprint ed., New York: Arno Press, 1974. 660 pp.

Non-scholarly collection of arranged songs, many composed in the genteel tradition, and a few headnotes.

466. IVES, Burl. <u>Song in America: Our Musical Heritage.</u> New York: Duell, Sloan, and Pearce, 1962. 312 pp.

An extensive collection of songs arranged for piano and voice by Albert Hague, and lacking headnotes. Examples include "My old 'coon dog" and "Billy Boy."

467. KITTREDGE, G. L., ed. "Ballads and Songs." <u>Journal of American Folklore</u> 30-117 (July-Sept. 1917): 283-369.

Large collection of ballads collected by members of the AFS, including texts and some tunes.

468. KITTREDGE, G. L. "Various Ballads." <u>Journal of American Folklore</u> 26-100 (Apr.-June 1913): 174-82.

A set of six miscellaneous ballads, mostly of the Child type, but including "John Henry."

469. KRYTHE, Maymie R. <u>Sampler of American Songs.</u> New York: Harper & Row, 1969. 245 pp.

A somewhat scholarly discussion and collection of standard songs such as "Home Sweet Home," "Yankee Doodle," "Dixie," "The Lord's Prayer," and the "Ballad of the Green Berets."

470. LAIR, John. <u>Songs Lincoln Loved.</u> New York: Duell, Sloan and Pearce, 1954. 85 pp.

A collection of 47 songs, both secular and sacred, mostly reproduced from the original nineteenth-century copies.

471. LEISY, James F. <u>The Folk Song Abecedary.</u> New York: Hawthorn Books, 1966. 410 pp.

A collection of "standard" songs from America's "folk song heritage," with commentary for each song.

472. LOMAX, Alan. The Folk Songs of North America in the English
     Language. Garden City, N.Y.: Doubleday, and London:
     Cassell, 1960; reprint ed., Garden City: Dolphin
     (Doubleday), 1975. 623 pp.

A valuable collection of 317 songs including melodies with
guitar chords by Peggy Seeger and 100 piano-voice arrangements by
Matyas Seiber and Don Banks. Arranged by region and topically:
North, Southern Mountains, West, Negro South. All songs are
introduced with extensive information concerning performance,
function, and relationship to the local society.

473. LOMAX, John A., and LOMAX, Alan. American Ballads and Folk
     Songs. New York: Macmillan, 1934. 625 pp.

Collected by the authors throughout the USA and presented
as melody and text, these 273 songs are organized into 25 topics,
e.g., working on the railroad, levee camp, chain gangs, songs from
the mountains, blues, reels, cowboy, play parties, etc.

474. LOMAX, John A., and LOMAX, Alan. SEEGER, R. C., Music Ed.
     Our Singing Country: a Second Volume of American Ballads
     and Folk Songs. New York: Macmillan, 1941. 416 pp.

Well-documented collection transcribed from discs in the
Archive of Folk Song into monophonic notation (unless original was
sung in harmony). Organized into categories (e.g., religious,
social, men at work, outlaws, hollers and blues, Negro gang songs);
most have headnotes.

475. LOMAX, John A., LOMAX, Alan, SEEGER, Charles and Ruth
     Crawford. The 111 Best American Ballads: Folk Song
     U.S.A. New York: Duell, Sloan, & Pearce, 1947. 423 pp.
     Rev. ed., New York: New American Library, 1975. 528 pp.

An attempt to establish a cultural historical canon of
American folksong, this "popular" collection includes 111 songs
arranged "in traditional style" for piano and voice by the Seegers.
Songs arranged by category and include much discussion. Appendices
include an extensive bibliography, discography, list of journals
and magazines, and folk festivals, information now rather outdated.

Also published as _Best Loved American Folk Songs_. New York:
Grosset and Dunlap, 1947. 407 pp.

476. LUTHER, Frank. _Americans and Their Songs_. New York: Harper
     and Brothers, 1942. 323 pp.

A collection of 75 ballads and folksongs with piano
accompaniment and 50 unaccompanied melodies. Pp. 297-311, "The
Songs of America (1620-1900)" is a chronological list.

477. NILES, John Jacob. _The Ballad Book of John Jacob Niles_.
     Boston: Houghton Mifflin, 1961. 369 pp.; reprint ed., New
     York: Dover, 1970.

A compilation made over the years by a performer/collector
(b. 1892) who grew up within the tradition that includes 65 Child
ballads arranged with harmony, plus texts and variants.

478. POUND, Louise. _American Ballads and Songs_. New York:
     Charles Scribner's Sons, 1922; reprint ed., 1972. 266 pp.

Although there is a 36-page introduction, the texts to
these 120 ballads (organized by topic) lack introductions and
tunes.

479. SANDBURG, Carl. _The American Songbag_. New York: Harcourt,
     Brace & Co., 1927. 495 pp.

Important collection for its influence, there are 280
songs, ballads and ditties, some with piano accompaniment, some
monophonic, with rather little documentation.

480. SCOTT, John Anthony. _The Ballad of America: the History of
     the United States in Song and Story_. New York: Bantam,
     1966, 415 pp.; new ed., Carbondale: Southern Illinois
     University Press, 1983. 439 pp.

Broad collection of songs combined with narrative on
American history, arranged by historical periods and topically.
Each song introduced with history, versions, and characteristics.
Song texts and tunes provided.

481. SHARP, Cecil J., and KARPELES, Maud. Eighty Appalachian Folk
     Songs. London: Faber & Faber, and Cambridge: M.I.T.
     Press, 1968; reprint ed., Winchester, Mass.: Faber &
     Faber, 1983. 112 pp.

Performance collection arranged by type: ballads, love
songs, humor and faith, work and lullabies. Piano accompaniments
by Benjamin Britten and chord symbols by Pat Shaw.

482. SHARP, Cecil J. English Folk Songs from the Southern
     Appalachians, Comprising 273 Songs and Ballads with 968
     Tunes, Including 39 Tunes Contributed by Olive Arnold
     Dame Campbell, Edited by Maud Karpeles. 2 vols. London,
     1917. 2nd enl. ed. London and New York: Oxford, 1932;
     reprint editions, 1952, 1960, 1966. 410 pp. and 428 pp.

Although Child's collection of ballads is most often
thought of, it was not the American who went to Britain who had
the greater influence, but the Englishman (Sharp) who came to
America. A noted folksong researcher at home, Sharp (1854-1924)
came to New York in 1914 during a lecture tour. During the years
1916 to 1918, mostly with his assistant, Karpeles, Sharp collected
all kinds of songs in the eastern mountains. His work was the
immediate stimulus for the collecting mania that swept American
universities soon afterwards, and as such must be seen as a central
figure in American folksong research. Vol. 1 includes 72 ballads
with texts and tunes as well as extensive commentary. Vol. 2
includes 201 songs of various types (hymns, nursery songs, jigs,
and play parties).

483. SHEETS, Bill G. America's Most Beloved Folk Ballads.
     Lexington, Ken.: by the author, 1965. 82 pp.

Compiled by a singer-collector, this volume consists of
texts only organized under the headings of tragic, sentimental,
humorous, and cowboy.

484. SMITH, Elmer L. Early American Broadsides & Ballads.
     Lebanon, Pa.: Applied Arts Publishers, 1969. 42 pp.

Non-scholarly but interesting reproductions of early
broadsides and pictures illustrating them. Minimal commentary and
a few tunes included.

485. SMITH, Reed, and RUFTY, Hilton. _American Anthology of Old-World Ballads_. New York: J. Fischer, 1937; reprint ed., Ann Arbor: University Microfilms, 1967. 70 pp.

 English and American ballads in arrangements by H. Rufty.

486. SPAETH, Sigmund. _Weep Some More, My Lady_. Garden City, N.Y.: Doubleday, Page & Co., 1927. 268 pp.

 Collection of tunes and texts of various types of songs: Negro, ballads, temperance, and topical songs for a general audience.

487. TOLMAN, Albert H. "Some Songs Traditional in the United States." _Journal of American Folklore_ 29-112 (Apr.-June 1916): 155-97.

 Collection of texts organized as older ballads (Child type), modern songs, homiletic ballads, play-party songs.

488. WOLF, Edwin II. _American Song Sheets, Slip Ballads, and Poetical Broadsides: 1850-1870_. Philadelphia: Library Company of Philadelphia, 1963. 205 pp.

 A listing of 2,722 broadsides from the peak period, some illustrated, a few with tunes.

Regional Studies

Appalachia

489. BACKUS, Emma M. "Early Songs from North Carolina." _Journal of American Folklore_ 14-55 (Oct.-Dec. 1901): 286-94.

 Tunes and texts for seven songs from Grovetown, Columbia County, N.C.

490. BARTIS, Peter T. "An Examination of the Holler in North Carolina White Tradition." _Southern Folklore Quarterly_ 39 (1975): 209-17.

While most research on hollers has focused on blacks, here the author presents material on white hollers studied around Spivey's Corner and Dunn in eastern North Carolina in 1972-3, defining the holler, describing types, and providing several transcriptions.

491. BASCOM, Louise Rand. "Ballads and Songs of Western North Carolina." Journal of American Folklore 22-84 (Apr.-June 1909): 238-50.

Texts collected at a fiddler's convention, plus a description of the convention.

492. BOETTE, Marie, ed. Singa Hipsy Doodle & Other Folk Songs of West Virginia. Parkersburg, W. Va.: Junior League of Parkersburg, 1971. 193 pp.

Collection of 140 songs, tunes and texts, with headnotes, classified by topic. Field collected.

493. BURTON, Thomas G., and MANNING, Ambrose N., eds. The East Tennessee State University Collection of Folklore: Folk Songs. Commentary by Annette Wolford. Institute of Regional Studies, Monograph 4. Johnson City: East Tennessee State University, 1967. 114 pp.

Mostly ballads transcribed from field recordings that are part of the collection. Besides tune, text, and minimal notes, there is an attempt at scale analysis. Carefully done.

494. BUSH, Michael E. Folksongs of Central West Virginia. 2 vols. Ravenswood, W. Va.: Custom Printing Co., 1970.

Transcribed from field recordings, these volumes, with 41 and 44 songs respectively, present texts and tunes on opposite pages plus notes on the tune and the singer.

495. CAMBIAIRE, Celestin Pierre. East Tennessee and Western Virginia Mountain Ballads (The Last Stand of American Pioneer Civilization). London: The Mitre Press, 1934. 179 pp.

Idealistic view of mountaineers as pure. History and description of culture, with words of songs.

496. CARTER, Isabel Gordon. "Some Songs and Ballads from Tennessee and North Carolina." Journal of American Folklore 46-179 (Jan.-Mar. 1933): 22-50.

Thirty texts, including new ballads, from eastern Tennessee and western North Carolina.

497. CHAMBERS, Virginia Anne. "Music in Four Kentucky Mountain Settlement Schools." Ph.D. dissertation, University of Michigan, 1970. 154 pp.

Survey of the kind of music being taught in 1) Hindman Settlement School, 2) Pine Mountain Settlement School, 3) Alice Lloyd College, and 4) Henderson Settlement School. Author found that there was an emphasis on indigenous and informal music, especially the ballad, at #1 and #2, while #3 and #4 were less interested, although they did some quartet gospel hymns.

498. COMBS, Josiah H. Folk-Songs of the Southern United States (Folk-Songs du midi des Etats-unis). Ed. by D. K. Wilgus. Bibliographical and Special Series #19. Austin: University of Texas Press for American Folklore Society, 1967. 254 pp.

A reworking of a French language dissertation written at the Sorbonne in 1925 and published the same year by Les Presses Universitaires de France (230 pp.) written by a native singer of Hazard, Kentucky. Collected in seven states (Kentucky, Virginia, West Virginia, Tennessee, Arkansas, Oklahoma, and Texas) from 1910-25, there are 25 songs of English origin and 34 of American origin. This classic study deals only with texts, however. Also includes an article, "The Highlander's Music," originally published in Kentucky Folklore Record 6-4 (Oct.-Dec. 1960): 108-22, reprinted in the above book, pp. 85-95.

499. COX, John Harrington. Folk Songs Mainly from West Virginia. W.P.A. Federal Theatre Project, Publication #81. Washington, D.C.: Works Progress Administration, 1939; reprint ed., New York: Da Capo, 1977.

Introductory essay by Herbert Halpert.

107

500. COX, John Harrington. Folk-Songs of the South. Cambridge: Harvard University Press, 1925; reprint ed., Hatboro, Pa.: Folklore Associates, 1963 with introduction by Arthur Kyle Davis, Jr.; reprint ed., New York: Dover, 1967. 545 pp.

Originally a doctoral dissertation at Harvard, completed in 1923 with 711 pp., this major study was begun while the compiler was a professor at the University of West Virginia in the later teens. After a 17-page introduction, Cox presents 185 ballad and song texts (and variants) with extensive headnotes. There are 26 monophonic tunes included at the back associated with certain of the texts.

501. COX, John Harrington. Traditional Ballads Mainly from West Virginia. American Folk-Song Publications #3. Washington, D.C.: Works Progress Administration, 1939. 109 pp.

A collection of 49 versions of 29 ballads, most of them with melodies. Introduction by Herbert Halpert.

502. CUTHBERT, John A. West Virginia Folk Music: a Descriptive Guide to Field Recordings in the West Virginia and Regional History Collection. [Morgantown]: West Virginia University Press, 1982. 185 pp.

Founded in 1933, the above named collection includes four archives totalling over 1,000 recordings and many manuscripts. 185 records are described and the contents listed and indexed.

503. EDMANDS, Lila W. "Songs from the Mountains of North Carolina." Journal of American Folklore 6-21 (Apr.-June 1893): 131-4.

Three song texts and tunes collected at Roan Mountain.

504. FUSON, Harvey E. Ballads of the Kentucky Highlands. London: The Mitre Press, 1931; reprint ed.: Norwood, Pa.: Norwood Editions, 1974. 219 pp.

Collection of texts without tunes.

505. GAINER, Patrick W. Folk Songs from the West Virginia Hills. Grantsville, W. Va.: Seneca Books, 1975. 236 pp.

Collected from 1924-1950 without a recorder and until 1974 with one, the author includes tunes, texts, and headnotes for Child and other ballads, fiddle-tune songs, religious songs, and Negro music.

506. HENRY, Mellinger E. "Ballads and Songs of the Southern Highlands." Journal of American Folklore 42-165 (Jul.-Sept. 1929): 254-300.

23 examples of texts, with variants, a few with tunes, collected in Tennessee, North Carolina, Kentucky, and elsewhere.

507. HENRY, Mellinger Edward. Folk-Songs from the Southern Highlands. New York: J. J. Augustine, 1938. 460 pp.

180 songs and ballads collected in east Tennessee and western North Carolina by a sensitive folklorist influenced by Cecil Sharp's work. Includes texts, tunes, and context.

508. HENRY, Mellinger E. "More Songs from the Southern Highlands." Journal of the American Folklore Society 44-171 (Jan.-Mar. 1931): 61-115.

Collection of 36 song texts and some tunes of various types from Appalachia.

509. HENRY, Mellinger E. "Still More Ballads and Folk-Songs from the Southern Highlands." Journal of American Folklore 45-175 (Jan.-Mar. 1932): 1-176.

Book-length article presenting 93 songs (including a few tunes) of many types, black and white.

510. JAMESON, Gladys. Sweet Rivers of Song: Authentic Ballads, Hymns, and Folksongs from the Appalachian Region. Berea, Ken.: Berea College, 1967. 81 pp.

Songs arranged by the author for piano and voice.

511. JOYNER, Charles W. Folk Song in South Carolina. Tricentennial Booklet #9. Columbia: University of South Carolina Press, 1971. 112 pp.

Texts and tunes for 20 ballads, 17 religious songs, and 8 secular songs, all but 12 taken from print. Author stresses importance of black influence on white traditions.

512. KIRKLAND, Edwin C. "A Check List of the Titles of Tennessee Folksongs." Journal of American Folklore 59-234 (Oct.-Dec. 1946): 423-76.

According to the author, "this list presents the repertory of the state of Tennessee," and provides titles, references to publications, locations, and discography.

513. KITTREDGE, G. L., ed. "Ballads and Rhymes from Kentucky." Journal of American Folklore 20-79 (Oct.-Dec. 1907): 251-77.

Texts collected by Miss Katherine Pettit of Hindman, Knott County, Kentucky.

514. MUSICKE, Ruth Ann. "Ballads and Folksongs from West Virginia." Journal of American Folklore 70-277 (Jul.-Sept. 1957): 247-61; 70-278 (Oct.-Dec. 1957): 336-57.

Texts of 26 Civil War, temperance, Child ballad, and other English songs with musical examples.

515. OWENS, Bess Alice. "Songs of the Cumberlands." Journal of American Folklore 49-193 (Jul.-Sept. 1936): 215-42.

Twenty-four ballads and ditties with tunes, mostly non-ballad, collected in Pike County and derived from a collection that numbers over 400 items.

516. REECE, Cortez D. "A Study of Selected Folksongs Collected Mainly in Southern West Virginia." Ph.D. dissertation, University of Southern California, 1955. 2 vols. 443 pp. and 606 pp.

Field collected materials by a musicologist concerned with classification, variants, and notation.

517. RITCHIE, Jean. Singing Family of the Cumberlands. New
      York: Oxford, 1955; reprint ed., New York: Oak, 1963.
      258 pp.

      An autobiography of the author and her family, who are
noted performers of Appalachian ballads and instrumental music,
the book also includes the tunes and texts for 42 songs here and
there in the text.

518. ROBERTS, Leonard. Sang Branch Settlers: Folksongs and
      Tales of a Kentucky Mountain Family. Austin: American
      Folklore Society, University of Texas Press, 1974. 401 pp.

      Pp. 1-86 are an introduction to the personalities in the
family, pp. 87-198 a collection of folksongs and hymns (texts and
tunes), and pp. 199-308 folktales and riddles.

519. ROBERTS, Leonard W., AGEY, C. Buell, and SCHINHAN, Jan
      Philip. In the Pine: Selected Kentucky Folksongs
      Pikeville, Ken.: Pikeville College, 1978; 2nd ed., 1979.
      319 pp.

      Collection of melodies, words, and guitar chord symbols
with descriptive notes by Roberts, music transcriptions by Agey,
and advice from Schinan.

520. SCARBOROUGH, Dorothy. A Song Catcher in the Southern
      Mountains: American Folk Songs of British Ancestry. New
      York: Columbia University Press, 1937; reprint ed., New
      York: AMS Press, 1966. 476 pp.

      Collected from 1931 to 1935 in North Carolina and
Virginia, Part I is background information, Part II is ballads,
and Part III is songs. An appendix presents melodies and words.

521. SHEARIN, Hubert G., and COMBS, Josiah H. A Syllabus of
      Kentucky Folk-Songs. Lexington, Ken.: Transylvania
      Printing Co., 1911; reprint ed. as Transylvania University
      Studies in English #2, Folcroft, Pa.: Folcroft Library,
      1976. 43 pp.

      List of 333 items, exclusive of 114 variants, of all
types (18 divisions). Each entry includes the title, a roman
numeral indicating how many versions were found, the prosodical

character indicated by letters, the number of stanzas by an arabic number, and a brief synopsis of the contents.

522. SHELLANS, Herbert. Folk Songs of the Blue Ridge Mountains. New York: Oak, 1968. 96 pp.

Collection based on field work presented as tune with guitar chords, texts, and a little commentary, organized by type (e.g., love and marriage, work and play, crime and punishment).

523. SMITH, Reed. South Carolina Ballads. Cambridge: Harvard University Press, 1928. Reprint ed.: Spartanburg, S.C.: Reprint Co., and Freeport, N.Y.: Books for Libraries Press, 1972. 174 pp.

The first 100 pages constitute a description of ballads as they persisted in the 1920s, their composition, and transmission. The final 69 pages present numerous examples, with texts and tunes.

524. THOMAS, Jean. Ballad Makin' in the Mountains of Kentucky. New York: Henry Holt, 1939; reprint ed., New York: Oak, 1964. 268 pp.

Organized by subject, the author presents a large collection of texts with some tunes arranged with piano accompaniment.

525. THOMAS, Jean. Devil's Ditties, Being Stories of the Kentucky Mountain People with the Songs they Sing. Chicago: W. Wilbur Hatfield, 1931. 180 pp.

Fashioned for a general audience, this collection of 50 or so songs and ballads arranged with piano accompaniment by Philip Gordon also includes information on who collected the song, from whom, and the situation. The main text depicts the life of the mountain people.

526. TREAT, Asher E. "Kentucky Folksong in Northern Wisconsin." Journal of American Folklore 52-203 (Jan.-Mar. 1939):1-51.

Interesting story of the "Kentucks" who moved onto abandoned lumber tracts from c. 1888-1904, with 56 tunes and texts brought from Kentucky.

527. VISSCHER, William Lightfoot. Blue Grass Ballads and Other
      Verse. New York: H. M. Caldwell, 1900; reprint ed.,
      Miami: Mnemosyne Publ. Co., 1969. 222 pp.

      A collection of texts for local (Kentucky) ballads and
songs, but without introduction or notes.

528. WARNER, Anne. Traditional American Folk Songs from the
      Anne & Frank Warner Collection. Ed. by Jeff Warner and
      Jerome S. Epstein. Syracuse: Syracuse University Press,
      1984. 526 pp.

      Derived from an Archive having around 1,000 songs recorded
in North Carolina during the 1930s, the 195 songs presented here
are extensively documented, and include tunes and information on
the singers. The organization is by singer.

529. WHITE, Newman Ivey, gen. ed. The Frank C. Brown
           Collection of North Carolina Folklore. 7 vols. Durham:
           Duke University Press, 1952-64.

      One of the most significant collections of Appalachian
materials, vols. 2-5 pertain to folk music. Vol. 2, Folk Ballads
from North Carolina, ed. by Henry M. Belden and Arthur Palmer
Hudson (1952, 747 pp.), is comprised of 314 texts and brief
headnotes. Of these, 49 are Child ballads, and the remainder are
of American and North Carolina origin. Vol. 3, Folk Songs from
North Carolina, ed. by H. M. Belden and A. P. Hudson (1952, 710
pp.), includes 658 texts organized into 13 categories (e.g.,
courting, drinking and gambling; play-party and dance; work
songs). Vol. 4, The Music of the Ballads, ed. by Jan Philip
Schinhan (1957, 420 pp.), includes all available melodies whose
texts are found in vol. 2. These were transcribed from wax
cylinders, and information is given about the performer as well as
a brief analysis of the melody. Vol. 5, The Music of the Folk
Songs, ed. by J. P. Schinhan (1962, 639 pp.), includes 658 songs
relating to the texts in vol. 3. In addition there are 128 tunes
for other texts and 66 for children's game songs.

530. WOLFE, Charles K. Kentucky Country: Folk and Country Music
      of Kentucky. Lexington: University Press of Kentucky,
      1982. 232 pp.

      A comprehensive survey of the state's folk music,
including string bands, old-fashioned hillbilly music, western

swing, gospel, bluegrass, honky-tonk, and the contemporary
Nashville sound.

Middle Atlantic States

531.   BETHKE, Robert D.   Adirondack Voices: Woodsmen and Wood
          Lore. Urbana: University of Illinois Press, 1981. 148 pp.

Although about New York's lumbermen in general, pp. 55-138
pertain to folksong, including both texts and monophonic tunes.

532.   BOYER, Walter E., BUFFINGTON, Albert F, and YODER, Don.
          Songs Along the Mahantongo Valley. Lancaster, Pa.:
          Pennsylvania Dutch Folklore Center, 1951.   231 pp.

Background discussion of this area in central
Pennsylvania plus 61 songs (texts and monophonic tunes).

533.   CAREY, George G.   Maryland Folk Legend and Folk Songs.
          Cambridge, Md.: Tidewater, 1971.   120 pp.

The section on songs comprises pp. 88-end. After a four-
page introduction, there is a collection of texts with headnotes.

534.   CAZDEN, Norman, HAUFRECHT, Herbert, and STUDER, Norman.
          Folk Songs of the Catskills. Albany: State University of
          New York Press, 1982.   650 pp.

Most material collected from 1941-48, with further work
done up to 1962. This "annotated archive of regional lore" has a
musical emphasis, including the study of tune formation and
relationships. After a cultural introduction (pp. 1-35), songs
are presented by category, with tunes (some with accompaniments),
texts, and extensive commentary. A major resource.

535.   CAZDEN, Norman, HAUFRECHT, Herbert, and STUDER, Norman.
          Notes and Sources for Folk Songs of the Catskills.
          Albany: State University of New York Press, 1982. 188 pp.

Related to the previous item, this is a detailed
catalogue of 178 songs, their sources, variants, and texts. The
unannotated bibliography, pp. 127-88, of sources for songs is
especially outstanding.

536. CHAPPELL, Louis W. Folk-Songs of Roanoke and the Albemarle. Morgantown, W. Va.: The Ballad Press, 1939. 203 pp.

Collection of tunes and texts for various types, including ballads, sea songs, and religious songs. Sources given, but little else.

537. DAVIS, Arthur Kyle, Jr. Folk-Songs of Virginia: a Descriptive Index and Classification. Durham: Duke University Press, 1949; reprint ed., New York: AMS, 1965. 389 pp.

List of materials collected by the Virginia Folklore Society since their 1929 Traditional Ballads of Virginia. Whereas the earlier collection had only ballads, this one includes songs of all types, indicating classification, title, where and when collected and from whom. Songs given in abbreviated form, however.

538. DAVIS, Arthur Kyle, Jr. More Traditional Ballads of Virginia, Collected with the Cooperation of Members of the Virginia Folklore Society. Chapel Hill: University of North Carolina Press, 1960. 371 pp.

Discussion about and collection of 46 Child ballads, presented with text and tune.

539. DAVIS, Arthur Kyle, Jr. Traditional Ballads of Virginia, Collected under the Auspices of the Virginia Folklore Society. Cambridge: Harvard University Press, 1929; reprint ed., Charlottesville: University of Virginia Press, 1969. 634 pp.

The first of the series edited by Davis, this concentrates on ballads, including 148 traditional tunes for 451 text versions of 51 ballads, each with commentary.

540. GOLDSTEIN, Kenneth S., and BYINGTON, Robert H. Two Penny Ballads and Four Dollar Whiskey: a Pennsylvania Folklore Miscellany. Hatboro, Pa.: Folklore Associates for the Pennsylvania Folklore Society, 1966. 176 pp.

Collection of articles, seven of which are pertinent, by such scholars as Korson, Stekert, Goldstein, Bayard, and Krelove on topics including vocal music, revivalist fiddle players, scales and ranges of fiddle tunes, broadsides, and children's gamesongs.

541. GRAVELLE, Jean F. "The Civil War Songsters of a Monroe County Farmer." New York Folklore Quarterly 27-2 (June 1971): 163-230.

Extensive description and history of a manuscript of songs written by James Edmunds of Brighton, Monroe County, New York. The texts of 34 songs and variants are included.

542. HALPERT, Herbert. "Some Ballads and Folk Songs from New Jersey." Journal of American Folklore 52-203 (Jan.-Mar. 1939): 52-69.

About a dozen songs and ballads, a few with tunes, collected in Burlington and Ocean Counties.

543. HAUFRECHT, Herbert, and CAZDEN, Norman. "Music of the Catskills." New York Folklore Quarterly 4-1 (Spring, 1948): 32-46.

Collected when the authors worked at Camp Woodland in Ulster County, includes some examples with commentary and a six-page list of titles.

544. KAUFMAN, Charles H. "An Ethnomusicological Survey Among the People of the Ramapo Mountains." New York Folklore Quarterly 23-1 (March, 1967): 3-42; 23-2 (June 1967): 109-31.

Collected 1964-5 about 50 miles north of New York City among an outcast group of mountain people, called the "Jackson Whites." This is a thorough study of what they do musically, its meaning and function, as well as their genealogy. Much of the article reports on what was collected, with transcriptions and words of some songs, though the text of "The Dirty Son-of-a-Bitch" was omitted to keep the article respectable. The author also reports some use of seven shape-notes in religious music.

545. KORSON, George. Pennsylvania Songs and Legends. Philadelphia: University of Pennsylvania Press, 1949; reprint ed., Baltimore: Johns Hopkins University Press, 1960. 474 pp.

Collection of 13 articles by various writers on diverse topics, e.g., Pennsylvania-German songs, Amish hymns, Indian music, songs of canalmen, railroad men, lumberjacks, and oilmen. Some articles include discussion of tunes. A major contribution is Bayard's article on British folk traditions, pp. 17-61.

546. LEACH, MacEdward, and BECK, Horace P. "Songs from Rappahannock County, Virginia." Journal of American Folklore 63-249 (July-Sept. 1950): 257-84.

      Collection made in 1947 of 23 songs (texts only), both ballads and other kinds.

547. LUMPKIN, Ben Gray. "Folksongs of the Early 1830's." Southern Folklore Quarterly 33-2 (June 1969): 116-28.

      Study of six song texts in manuscript written 1831-2 from Dinwiddie County, Virginia.

548. MCNEIL, William K. "A Schoharie County Songster." New York Folklore Quarterly 25-1 (Mar. 1969): 3-58.

      Song texts and headnotes for a manuscript collection kept by Ida Finkell of Argusville from 1879 to 1883.

549. NESTLER, Harold. "Songs from the Hudson Valley." New York Folklore Quarterly 5-2 (Summer, 1949): 77-112.

      Collection of sea song texts from written sources, some quite old.

550. OSTER, Harry. "A Delanson Manuscript of Songs." New York Folklore Quarterly 8-4 (Winter, 1952): 267-82.

      Song texts from a manuscript collection of 40 songs bought at an antique shop in Delanson, Schenectady County, by Harold Thompson. Dating from c.1845-80, the songs are organized by theme and briefly discussed.

551. RING, C. V., BAYARD, Samuel P., and COFFIN, Tristram P. "Mid-Hudson Song and Verse." Journal of American Folklore 66-259 (Jan.-Mar. 1953): 43-67.

Collected 1920-30 in Dutchess, Ulster, and Columbia
Counties, New York, this is a selection of texts and some tunes
from a much larger archive. Included are Anglo-American, play
party, Dutch-American, local-sentimental, and ballad songs.

552. ROSENBERG, Bruce A. The Folksongs of Virginia: a Checklist
     of the WPA Holdings, Alderman Library, University of
     Virginia. Charlottesville: University Press of Virginia,
     1969. 145 pp.

An A-Z catalogue of 1,604 songs and similar materials
collected by the W.P.A. Included for each is information the
collector, time and place, and a bibliography.

553. SHOEMAKER, Henry W. Mountain Minstrelsy of Pennsylvania.
     Philadelphia: Newman F. McGirr, 1931. 319 pp.

This is a revised and enlarged third edition of North
Pennsylvania Minstrelsy: as Sung in the Backwoods Settlements,
Hunting Cabins, and Lumber Camps in Northern Pennsylvania, 1840-
1910. Altoona: Altoona Tribune, 1919. After a 44 page
introduction, there follows a collection of poems under such
categories as Pennsylvania Mountains, Fireside, Civil War, English
Folk, and Ballads.

554. THOMPSON, Harold W. A Pioneer Songster: Texts from the
     Stevens-Douglass Manuscript of Western New York, 1841-
     1856. Ithaca: Cornell University Press, 1958. 203 pp.

A text study of 89 songs organized by topic.

Midwestern States

555. BARBOUR, Frances M. "Some Fusions in Missouri Ballads."
     Journal of American Folklore. 49-193 (July-Sept. 1936):
     207-14.

An analysis of textual content.

556. BELDEN, Henry M. Ballads and Songs Collected by the
     Missouri Folk-Lore Society. 2nd ed. University of
     Missouri Studies #15-1. Columbia: University of Missouri
     Press, 1955; reprint ed., 1966. 544 pp.

One of the pioneer collections, here are 287 ballads and folksongs gathered over a forty-year period. Included are texts, variants, and some tunes with headnotes detailing relationships to previously printed versions as well as collection data.

557. BELDEN, Henry M. "Old-Country Ballads in Missouri." Journal of American Folklore 19-74 (July-Sept. 1906): 231-40; 19-75 (Oct.-Dec. 1906): 281-99; 20-79 (Oct.-Dec. 1907): 319-20.

Analysis of texts of Child type ballads.

558. BELDEN, Henry M. A Partial List of Song-Ballads and Other Popular Poetry Known in Missouri. Columbia: University of Missouri Press, 1907. Rev. ed., 1910.

559. BREWSTER, Paul G. Ballads and Songs of Indiana. Folklore Series #1. Bloomington: Indiana University Press, 1940. 376 pp.

Originally a doctoral dissertation completed the same year, this is a study of 100 ballads and songs plus their variants. A few have tunes included along with background information on each item.

560. BREWSTER, Paul G. "Traditional Ballads from Indiana." Journal of American Folklore 48-190 (Oct.-Dec. 1935): 295-317.

Fifteen of the best ballad texts and tunes from about 200 recently collected in southern Indiana.

561. EDDY, Mary O. Ballads and Songs from Ohio. New York: J. J. Augustine, 1939; reprint ed., Hatboro, Pa.: Folklore Associates, 1964. 330 pp.

Collected early in the century by a Harvard graduate and follower of Child, this group of 153 texts (with tunes for some) includes headnotes. The reprint includes a foreward by D.K. Wilgus.

562. GARDNER, Emelyn Elizabeth, and CHICKERING, Geraldine Jencks. Ballads and Songs of Southern Michigan. Ann

119

Arbor: University of Michigan Press, and London: Humphrey Milford, 1939; reprint ed., Hatboro, Pa.: Folklore Associates, 1967. 501 pp.

The songs were collected by Chickering and the 26-page introduction is by Gardner. Brief headnotes, texts, and some tunes for 201 songs and ballads from the lower peninsula.

563. LUMPKIN, Ben Gray. "Folksongs from a Nebraska Family." Southern Folklore Quarterly 36-1 (March 1972): 14-35.

The texts and tunes of songs known to the Cummings family of Beatrice, Nebraska.

564. McINTOSH, David S. Sing and Swing from Southern Illinois. Carbondale: Southern Illinois University Press, 1948. 72 pp.

A practical edition of notation and directions for performing a series of traditional dances.

565. McINTOSH, David S. "Southern Illinois Folk Songs." Journal of the Illinois State Historical Society 31-3 (Sept. 1938): 297-322.

Introduction to music in early Illinois, including singing schools and religious music, then a collection of ballads with tunes, texts, and comments.

566. McINTOSH, David S. Southern Illinois Singing Games and Songs. Carbondale: Southern Illinois University Press, 1946. 49 pp.

Music notation and directions for a series of dances.

567. NEELY, Charles. "Four British Ballads in Southern Illinois." Journal of American Folklore 52-203 (Jan.-Mar. 1939): 75-81.

An analysis of four texts.

568. NEELY, Charles Leslie. Tales and Songs of Southern
    Illinois. Menasha, Wis.: George Banta, 1938; reprint
    ed., Norwood, Pa.: Folcroft Library Editions, 1974;
    Norwood, Pa.: Norwood Editions, 1976, 1977; Philadelphia:
    R. West, 1978. 270 pp.

    A collection of songs with musical notation.

569. PETERS, Harry B. Folk Songs Out of Wisconsin. Madison:
    State Historical Society of Wisconsin, 1977. 311 pp.

    A recent and extensive selection of songs with tunes and
texts and source information, plus excerpts from a journal kept by
Franz Rickaby on a trip through Wisconsin in 1919 with pictures.

570. POUND, Louise. Folk-Song of Nebraska and the Central
    West: a Syllabus. Lincoln: Nebraska Academy of Science
    Publications IX,3, 1914. 89 pp.

    Written by a student of Belden, the six-page introduction
is followed by a list of songs by topic, with text examples.

571. POUND, Louise. "Traditional Ballads in Nebraska." Journal
    of American Folklore 26-102 (Oct.-Dec. 1913): 351-66.

    A report on the initial collection effort in Nebraska,
with some analysis of ballad texts.

572. POURCHOT, Mary Ellen. Music of a Young Illinois, 1830-
    1900. DeKalb: Gurler Heritage Association, 1980. 48 pp.

    Lightweight collection of folksong and singing school
songs, with a few in notation.

573. THOMAS, Cloea. Scenes & Songs of the Ohio-Erie Canal.
    Columbus: Ohio Historical Society, 1971. 22 pp.

    Eight songs collected and recorded by Capt. Pearl R. Nye.
After a three-page introduction, tunes and texts with photos.

574. WELSCH, Roger L. A Treasury of Nebraska Pioneer Folklore.
    Lincoln: University of Nebraska Press, 1967. 391 pp.

A substantial portion of this book is devoted to
folksongs, primarily chapter 1 which includes "Songs of Trail and
Prairie" (pp. 3-56), "Songs of the Farmers' Alliance" (pp. 57-79),
and "Square Dances" (pp. 80-138). Mostly texts are given, but a
few tunes with guitar chords as well, plus headnotes.

New England

575.   BARRY, Phillips. Folk-Songs of the North Atlantic States.
        Privately published, 1908.

576.   BARRY, Phillips. The Maine Woods Songster. Cambridge:
        Powell Printing Co., 1939. 102 pp.

Compilation of 50 camp and work songs of the Maine
lumberman with tunes, as well as some ballads. Headnotes give
substantial information on each song.

577.   BARRY, Phillips. "Traditional Ballads in New England."
        Journal of American Folklore 18-69 (Apr.-June 1905):
        123-38; 18-70 (July-Sept. 1905): 191-214; 18-71 (Oct.-
        Dec. 1905): 291-304.

Texts, tunes, and some discussion of 14 ballads collected
in New England.

578.   BARRY, Phillips, ECKSTORM, Fannie Hardy, and SMYTH, Mary
        Winslow. British Ballads from Maine: the Development of
        Popular Songs with Texts and Airs. New Haven: Yale
        University Press, 1929; reprint ed., New York: Da Capo,
        1982. 581 pp.

Well-documented study of 92 traditional ballads, 56 found
in Child's collection, with special emphasis on text-tune
relationships. One of the major collections from the period.

579.   BECK, Horace Palmer, Jr. "Down-East Ballads and Songs."
        Ph.D. dissertation, University of Pennsylvania, 1952.
        433 pp.

Compilation of 120 songs classified (e.g., songs sung
around home, songs of the logging camps and aboard ship, bawdy
songs), with documentation.

580. BOTKIN, Benjamin A. Treasury of New England Folklore: Stories, Ballads & Traditions of the Yankee People. New York: Crown, 1947. 934 pp. Rev. ed., 1965. 618 pp.

Part 5, pp. 525-91 of the revised edition, is "Songs and Rhymes" and includes texts, tunes, and a few notes of materials from collections and records.

581. ECKSTORM, Fannie Hardy, and SMYTH, Mary Winslow. Minstrelsy of Maine: Folk-Songs and Ballads of the Woods and the Coast. Boston: Houghton Mifflin, 1927; reprint ed., Ann Arbor: Gryphon, 1971. 390 pp.

Well documented, text study of woods songs (organized as oldest, middle, and later), deep sea songs, chanties, etc., collected in Piscataquis, Penobscot, and Hancock Counties mostly.

582. FLANDERS, Helen Hartness. Ancient Ballads Traditionally Sung in New England. 4 vols. Philadelphia: University of Pennsylvania Press, 1960-1965. 1262 pp.

Compiled in the 1930s period by one of America's most important collectors, and here edited by T. P. Coffin with musical transcriptions and analysis by Bruno Nettl. There are 92 Child ballads with nearly 500 variants from the Flanders archive at Middlebury College, Vermont, and about 300 melodies. Each volume is indexed and includes a list of sources by area.

583. FLANDERS, Helen Hartness. "Ancient Themes and Character- istics Found in Certain New England Folksongs." Journal of American Folklore 77-303 (Jan.-Mar. 1964): 32-8.

Originally a paper, this is a theme study of texts only.

584. FLANDERS, Helen Hartness. Country Songs of Vermont. New York: G. Schirmer, 1937. 50 pp.

A collection of songs with piano accompaniment.

585. FLANDERS, Helen Hartness. A Garland of Green Mountain Song. Northfield, Vt., 1934. 86 pp.

A collection of texts and tunes with piano accompaniment.

586. FLANDERS, Helen Hartness, and BROWN, George. <u>Vermont</u> <u>Folk-Songs</u> <u>&</u> <u>Ballads</u>. Brattleboro: Stephen Daye, 1930/31; reprint ed., Hatboro, Pa.: Folklore Associates, 1968. 256 pp.

Collection of 120 texts, 62 tunes, and little else for ballads, including some found earlier by Phillips Barry.

587. FLANDERS, Helen Hartness, and OLNEY, Marguerite. <u>Ballads</u> <u>Migrant</u> <u>in</u> <u>New</u> <u>England</u>. New York: Farrar, Straus, and Young, 1953; reprint ed., Freeport, N.Y.: Books for Libraries Press, 1968. 248 pp.

Texts and many tunes of 97 ballads collected all over New England in the 1940s and housed in the Flanders Collection at Middlebury College, with commentary.

588. FLANDERS, Helen Hartness, BALLARD, Elizabeth Flanders, BROWN, George, and BARRY, Phillips. <u>The</u> <u>New</u> <u>Green</u> <u>Mountain</u> <u>Songster</u>: <u>Traditional</u> <u>Folk</u> <u>Songs</u> <u>of</u> <u>Vermont</u>. New Haven: Yale University Press, 1939; reprint ed., Hatboro, Pa.: Folklore Associates, 1966. 278 pp.

Collected by Hartness in the 1930s on a Dictaphone and transcribed by Brown, this collection of songs and ballads, providing both texts and tunes as well as some commentary, was meant to describe the Vermont musical heritage.

589. HALE, Edward E., and his Children. <u>New</u> <u>England</u> <u>History</u> <u>in</u> <u>Ballads</u>. Boston: Little, Brown & Co., 1903. 182 pp.

Collection of broadside type texts.

590. HONERT, Peter van den. "A Pedagogical Study of New England Folksongs." D.M.A. dissertation, University of Missouri, in progress (in Choral Conducting).

591. IVES, Edward D. <u>Folksongs</u> <u>from</u> <u>Maine</u>. Northeast Folklore vol. 7. Orono: Northeast Folklore Society, 1966. 104 pp.

Collection of classified songs ("Local songs," "Native American Songs," "The British Tradition") with texts and tunes and biographies of singers. Eleven-page introduction.

592. LINSCOTT, Eloise Hubbard. Folk Songs of Old New England.
New York: Macmillan, 1939; 2nd ed., Hamden, Conn.: Archon
Books, 1962, 1974. 344 pp.

Popularized collection of singing games, country dances,
shanties, ballads, and folksongs with little commentary. Texts
and tunes with piano accompaniment and list of singers.

593. PIKE, Robert E. "Folk Songs from Pittsburg, New
Hampshire." Journal of American Folklore 48-190 (Oct.-
Dec. 1935): 337-51.

Eight non-ballad song texts without tunes collected in
northern New Hampshire.

594. QUINN, Jennifer Post. An Index to the Field Recordings in
the Flanders Ballad Collection at Middlebury College,
Middlebury, Vermont. Middlebury, Vt.: Middlebury
College, 1983. 242 pp.

This reference tool is to be used in conjunction with the
famous Flanders collection, and indexes some 4066 titles and 635
performers.

Southern States

595. ARNOLD, Byron. Folksongs of Alabama. University:
University of Alabama Press, 1950. 193 pp.

Collection of 153 ballads, black and white, and play
parties made in 1945 with notes for each song and cross references
to other publications. Organized by singer and presented in the
order recorded, providing both texts and tunes and biographies.

596. BOTKIN, Benjamin A. Treasury of Mississippi River
Folklore: Stories, Ballads & Traditions of the Mid-
American River Country. New York: Crown, 1955. 620 pp.

Pp. 555-602, "Where the Blues Begin," includes river work
songs with brief introductions, texts, and tunes for most. Scant
documentation.

597. BROWNE, Ray B. The Alabama Folk Lyric: a Study in Origins and Media of Dissemination. Bowling Green, Oh.: Bowling Green State University Popular Press, 1979. 480 pp.

After a 37-page introduction providing a general discussion of folksongs and their meaning, 192 classified songs, with melodies, texts, and headnotes. Originally a Ph.D. dissertation in English at U.C.L.A. entitled "Alabama Folk Songs" (1956).

598. HUDSON, Arthur P. "Ballads and Songs from Mississippi." Journal of American Folklore 39-152 (Apr.-June 1926): 93-194.

Collection of 88 tuneless song texts of various kinds.

599. HUDSON, Arthur Palmer. Folksongs of Mississippi and their Background. Chapel Hill: University of North Carolina Press, 1936; reprint ed., New York: Dover, 1977. 321 pp.

Originally a Ph.D. dissertation (1930) and field collected among the white population, this group of 156 ballads and 207 songs (texts only) is discussed in relation to the culture at large and especially in the lives of the people of Mississippi.

600. MORRIS, Alton Chester. Folksongs of Florida. Gainesville: University of Florida Press, 1950, 1971; reprint ed., New York: Folklorica, 1980 (Folklorica Publications in Folksong and Balladry #2). 464 pp.

Collected starting in 1933, there is a 16-page introduction, headnotes, texts, and tunes for 243 songs in two major categories: I. Songs of the New World (war, west, sea, outlaws, disasters, love, religion, work, nursery, play party, and fiddle) and II. Songs of the Old World (English, Scottish, Bahaman, Irish, and Anglo-Irish).

601. PERROW, E. C. "Songs and Rhymes from the South." Journal of American Folklore 25-96 (Apr.-June 1912): 137-55; 26-100 (Apr.-June 1913): 123-73; 28-108 (Apr.-June 1915): 129-94.

Song texts and some tunes for a vast collection of items from the southern Appalachian area; valuable source.

602. RANDOLPH, Vance. Ozark Folklore: a Bibliography. Indiana
     University Folklore Institute Monograph Series vol. 24.
     Bloomington: Indiana University Research Center for the
     Language Sciences, 1972. 572 pp.

     Pp. 1-40 of this extensive reference work, "Songs and
Ballads," include a great number of items, mostly annotated, but
among them is much ephemera.

603. RANDOLPH, Vance. Ozark Folksongs. 4 vols. Columbia:
     State Historical Society of Missouri, 1946-1950; reprint
     ed., 1980. 464, 448, 416, 414 pp.

     This monumental work shares with that of Frank C. Brown
in North Carolina the honor of being the most extensive folklore
collections on a particular region ever published. Edited by
Floyd C. Shoemaker and Frances G. Emberson, it includes at least
900 ballads and songs from Missouri, but with variants, the total
is closer to 1,700. About 800 of these have tunes. All are
extensively documented in headnotes. Vol. I, English and related
ballads, Vol. II, topical songs (including Civil War, Negro and
pseudo-Negro songs, temperance), Vol. III, lighter songs and play
parties, Vol. IV, religious songs, hymns, miscellaneous songs and
sentimental ballads. There are indices of titles, first lines,
contributors, and towns.

604. RANDOLPH, Vance. Ozark Folksongs. Edited and abridged by
     Norman Cohen. Urbana: University of Illinois Press,
     1982. 590 pp.

     Short form of previous and original work.

605. RANDOLPH, Vance, and EMBERSON, Frances. "The Collection of
     Folk Music in the Ozarks." Journal of American Folklore
     60-236 (Apr.-June 1947): 115-25.

     Chronological account of collecting in southern Missouri,
northern Arkansas, and eastern Oklahoma, with bibliography.

606. ROSENBAUM, Art. Folk Visions & Voices: Traditional Music
     and Song in North Georgia. Athens: University of Georgia
     Press, 1983. 240 pp.

A study based on about 100 examples from the author's collection of 2,000 items researched from 1977-1980, with some 81 musical examples by Bela Foltin, Jr. Based around 12 individuals or groups, both black and white, religious and secular, instrumental and vocal. Although not scholarly and having a focus on the songs, it is nonetheless a useful work. Some items were issued on Folkways FTS 31089 and Flyright (Sussex, England) 546.

607. SMITH, Reed. "The Traditional Ballad in the South." _Journal_ _of_ _American_ _Folklore_ 27-103 (Jan.-Mar. 1914): 55-66.

Important early article dealing with the ballad, its distribution, and textual content. The author offers ways to distinguish versions and variants, using statistics as one method.

608. SMITH, Reed. "The Traditional Ballad in the South During 1914." _Journal_ _of_ _American_ _Folklore_ 28-108 (Apr.-June 1915): 199-203.

Report of ballad discoveries in 1914 in the United States, but especially in the South.

Southwestern States

609. FINGER, Charles J. _Frontier_ _Ballads,_ _Heard_ _and_ _Gathered_ _by_ _the_ _Author._ Woodcuts by Paul Honore. Garden City, N.Y.: Doubleday, Page & Co., 1927. 181 pp.

Texts, some in dialect, collected from old singers, with discussion of the songs and their history. Mostly texts, but a few transcriptions of tunes.

610. MOORE, Ethel, and MOORE, Chauncey O. _Ballads_ _and_ _Folk_ _Songs_ _of_ _the_ _Southwest._ Norman: University of Oklahoma Press, 1964. 414 pp.

Background, texts, tunes, sources of 194 songs recorded in Oklahoma. Of British, Scottish, and American origins.

611. OWENS, William A. _Tell_ _Me_ _a_ _Story,_ _Sing_ _Me_ _a_ _Song:_ _a_ _Texas_ _Chronicle._ Austin: University of Texas Press, 1983. 328 pp. and 60' cassette tape.

Mix of biography, history, travel, and folk music from northeastern Texas. Covers a wide variety of topics: Mexican, black, Cajun, European; the tape emphasizes Anglo, Mexican, and black examples.

612. OWENS, William A. _Texas Folk Songs_. Publications of the Texas Folklore Society #23. Dallas: University Press of Dallas, 1950. 302 pp.

Originally a Ph.D. dissertation in English at the University of Iowa (1941), this study includes 120 songs transcribed from a larger collection actually made in Louisiana, Oklahoma, Missouri, and Texas. Variety includes British and American ballads and songs, children's songs and games, cowboy songs, Negro spirituals, play-parties, and miscellaneous songs.

613. RIENSTRA, Ellen Walker, and LINSLEY, Judith Walker. _Music in Texas-Frontier to 1900_. Beaumont, Tex.: Beaumont Historical Society, 1980. 28 pp.

Brief overview of the subject.

Western States

614. BLACK, Eleanora, and ROBERTSON, Sidney. _The Gold Rush Song Book_. San Francisco: Colt Press, 1940. 55 pp.

Twenty-five "authentic" ballads from 1849. Words, tunes, and sources given.

615. BOTKIN, Benjamin A. _A Treasury of Western Folklore_. New York: Crown, 1951. 806 pp.

Part 6, "Western Songs and Ballads" (pp. 728-92) includes an introduction and a collection of tunes and texts.

616. BRUNVAND, Jan Harold. "Folk Song Studies in Idaho." _Western Folklore_ 24-4 (Oct. 1965): 231-48.

A history of collecting and a review of literature, with textual examples.

617. BURT, Olive Woolley. "Murder Ballads of Mormondom."
     Western Folklore 18-2 (April 1959): 141-56.

     History of the Mormons through song as it pertains to
this grisly topic--words only.

618. CHENEY, Thomas E. Mormon Songs from the Rocky Mountains: a
     Compilation of Mormon Folksongs. Publications of the
     American Folklore Society, Memoir Series vol. 53.
     Austin: University of Texas Press, 1968. 221 pp.

     Ninety-nine texts and tunes, with documentation of field
collection, concerning Mormon history, religion, and social order.

619. COWELL, Sidney R. "The Recording of Folk Music in
     California." California Folklore Quarterly 1-1 (Jan.
     1942): 7-23.

     A history of the recording of "49er" songs done by
Charles F. Lummis, 1902-03, and discussion of his singers.

620. CULWELL, Gene Allen. "The English Language Songs in the
     Ben Gray Lumpkin Collection of Colorado Folklore." Ph.D.
     dissertation, University of Colorado (Boulder), 1976. 2
     vols. 96 pp., 205 pp.

     Outlines entire collection, discusses his informants, and
extensively describes and analyzes 13 representative songs.

621. DAUGHTERS OF UTAH PIONEERS. Pioneer Songs, Compiled by
     Daughters of Utah Pioneers. (Collection of Songs used by
     the Pioneers Enroute to and in the Early Settlement of
     the West; Also Songs Inspired and Composed by the
     Pioneers in Memory of their Experiences.) Salt Lake
     City: Daughters of Utah Pioneers, 1932; 2nd rev. ed.,
     1940. 6th ed., 1959. 324 pp.

     Hodge-podge of non-field collected songs arranged into
four-part harmony or with piano accompaniment by Alfred M. Durham,
including "Star Spangled Banner" and "Rock of Ages."

622. DAVIDSON, Levette J. "Mormon Songs." Journal of American
     Folklore 58-229 (July-Sept. 1945): 273-300. Reprinted in

GREENWAY, John. Folklore of the Great West. Palo Alto: American West Publishing Co., 1969, pp. 247-273.

Field collected under conditions made difficult by World War II. Texts for hymns, campaign songs, songs of migration, anti-federalism, gentile songs that ridicule Mormons, social, dream, and topical songs.

623. DAVIDSON, Levette J. "Songs of the Rocky Mountain Frontier." California Folklore Quarterly 2-2 (April 1943): 89-112.

Background information on songs brought by Mormon pioneers and collection of texts classified by type.

624. DWYER, Richard A., and LINGENFELTER, Richard E. The Songs of the Gold Rush. Berkeley and Los Angeles: University of California Press, 1965. 200 pp.

Brief introduction and collection of scantily documented songs, some composed, giving melody and guitar chords and words. Music arrangements by David Cohen.

625. FIFE, Austin E., and FIFE, Alta S. Ballads of the Great West. Palo Alto: American West Publishing Co., 1970. 272 pp.

Collection of "primitive" verse (no tunes) around topics of "human environment," "cowboy songs," "dramatic situations and events," "code of the cowboys." Also includes a lexicon.

626. FIFE, Austin E., and FIFE, Alta S. "Folk Songs of Mormon Inspiration." Western Folklore 6-1 (Jan. 1947): 42-52.

Texts and a little explanation for the first field recordings made in 1945 (on wire) and in 1946 (on disc).

627. HUBBARD, Lester. Ballads and Songs from Utah. Salt Lake City: University of Utah Press, 1961. 496 pp.

Classified and documented collection of 250 ballads and songs of nineteenth-century origin collected among Mormons, with music transcriptions by Kenly W. Whitelock.

628. HUBBARD, Lester A. "Variants of Utah Folksongs." Utah
Humanities Review 2-3 (July 1948): 241-58.

Text collection made in the field, singers identified.

629. HUBBARD, Lester A., and ROBERTSON, LeRoy J. "Traditional
Ballads from Utah." Journal of American Folklore 61-251
(Jan.-Mar. 1951): 37-54.

Series of ballads and variants, texts and tunes,
collected among the Mormons.

630. LINGENFELTER, Richard E., DWYER, Richard A., and COHEN,
David. Songs of the American West. Berkeley: University
of California Press, 1968. 595 pp.

Nearly 300 songs arranged with guitar with commentary on
historical conditions, role of parody, and lives of known
composers, with songs arranged by topic.

631. LUMPKIN, Ben Gray. Colorado Folksong Bulletin vols. 1-3
(1962-64) [Boulder: University of Colorado].

While there is an emphasis on Western folksong, these 178
items (tunes, texts, and headnotes) were gathered in 20 states and
four foreign countries.

632. LUMPKIN, Ben Gray. "Colorado Folk Songs." Western
Folklore 19-2 (April 1960): 77-97.

Provides background to the existence of folksongs in
Colorado, the types, when and how they came. Then follows a
series of examples with tunes and texts.

633. PLUMB, Margaret Lissold. "Folksongs of Wyoming." Ph.D.
dissertation, University of Wyoming, 1965. 170 pp.

No abstract available.

634. SILBER, Irwin. Songs of the Great American West. New
York: Macmillan, 1967. 400 pp.

With musical annotations and arrangements by Earl Robinson, this collection of 92 songs from Mexico, western Canada, and Alaska as well as the American West is organized by topic. Sections have short introductions and each song is documented in a headnote.

Occupational and Political Songs

Songs of the Cowboys

635. CARR, Robert. Cowboy Lyrics. Chicago: W. B. Conkey Co., 1908. 182 pp.

An anthology of cowboy poetry, some in dialect.

636. FIFE, Austin E., and FIFE, Alta S. Cowboy and Western Songs: a Comprehensive Anthology. New York: Clarkson N. Potter, 1969. 372 pp.

Headnotes, texts, and tunes with guitar chords (ed. by Mary Jo Schwab) for 128 topically classified songs.

637. LARKIN, Margaret. Singing Cowboy: a Book of Western Songs. New York: Alfred Knopf, 1931; reprint ed., New York: Oak, 1963 and New York: Da Capo, 1979. 176 pp.

Popular collection of songs arranged for piano and guitar, with minimal background information.

638. LEE, Katie. Ten Thousand Goddam Cattle: a History of the American Cowboy in Song, Story, and Verse. Flagstaff, Ariz.: Northland Press, 1976. 254 pp.

Text oriented study with some tunes of original cowboy songs, in addition to cowboy stories.

639. LOMAX, John A. Songs of the Cattle Trail and Cow Camp. New York: Macmillan, 1919; new ed., New York: Duell, Sloan, and Pierce, 1950. 189 pp.

Mostly a collection of texts with little introduction, an outgrowth of the following anthology.

640. LOMAX, John A., and LOMAX, Alan. Cowboy Songs and other
     Frontier Ballads. New York: Macmillan, 1910 (326 pp.),
     1916 (414 pp.), 1938 (431 pp.); rev. ed., 1950.

   Collected in the field early in the century, but newer
songs were added in later editions. Essentially a history of
cowboy and frontier life through over 200 topical songs presented
as text and tune. The original recordings are in the Library of
Congress, Archive of American Folk Song.

641. OHRLIN, Glenn. The Hell-Bound Train: a Cowboy Songbook.
     Urbana: University of Illinois Press, 1973. 290 pp.

   Collection of about 100 songs (texts and tunes
transcribed by Judith McCulloh) recorded by genuine cowboy-singer
Glenn Ohrlin who was discovered by folklorist Archie Green in 1963
and brought to the University of Illinois campus. Ohrlin became
well known as a singer during the 1960s folk revival. The biblio-
discography by Harlan Daniel (pp. 241-81) is especially valuable.
In 1964 the University of Illinois Folksong Club released a
recording of Ohrlin (CFC 301) which has been re-issued as Puritan
LP 5009.

642. ROTHEL, David. The Singing Cowboys. South Brunswick,
     N.J.: A. S. Barnes, 1978. 272 pp.

   Full of information but popular in orientation, this
collection of pictures and narrative covers the singing cowboys of
film, such as Gene Autry, Tex Ritter, and Roy Rogers.

643. SACKETT, Samuel J. Cowboys and the Songs They Sang. New
     York: W. R. Scott, 1967. 72 pp.

   Aimed at juvenile readers, this collection of photos,
texts, and arranged songs centers on the "standards," such as "The
Old Chisholm Trail" and "The Streets of Laredo."

644. SIRINGO, Charles A. The Song Companion of a Lone Star
     Cowboy: Old Favorite Cow-Camp Songs. Santa Fe, N.M.,
     n.p., 1919; reprint ed., Norwood, Pa.: Norwood Editions,
     1975. 42 pp.

   Collection of song texts and music.

645. THORP, N. Howard ("Jack"). Songs of the Cowboys. Boston: Houghton, Mifflin, 1908, 1921; reprint ed., 1948; rev. ed. by Austin E. and Alta S. FIFE. New York: Clarkson N. Potter, 1966. 346 pp.; reprint ed. of 1921. Lincoln: University of Nebraska Press, 1984.

Compiled from 1889-1890 and thereafter by a collector-composer-singer-publisher who spent 50 years on the range. The Fifes' revision adds commentary, variants, and a lexicon as well as transcriptions of 23 songs from later field recordings by music editor, Naunie Gardner.

646. TINSLEY, Jim Bob. He Was Singin' This Song: a Collection of Forty-eight Traditional Songs of the American Cowboy with Words, Music, Pictures, and Stories. Orlando: University Presses of Florida, 1981. 255 pp.

Written by an English teacher and performer of cowboy songs, this study provides stories of the songs, their texts and tunes along with guitar chords, and many pictures. From all this one can get the flavor of the genre.

647. WHITE, John I. Git Along, Little Dogies: Songs and Songmakers of the American West. Urbana: University of Illinois Press, 1975. 221 pp.

Compiled by an influential cowboy-singer from the 1930s who knew all the important singers. More personality oriented than on actual music, but good view of life in the West.

648. WILL, G. F. "Four Cowboy Songs." Journal of American Folklore 26-100 (Apr.-June 1913): 185-92.

Four texts collected in North Dakota.

Songs of the Lumberjacks and of the Shantyboy

649. BECK, Earl C. Songs of the Michigan Lumberjacks. Ann Arbor: University of Michigan Press, 1942; rev. ed. as Lore of the Lumbercamps, 1948. 295 pp.

Classified collection of 104 songs and ballads from the Michigan and French-Canadian areas. Eight-page introduction, headnotes, texts, and a few tunes.

650. FOWKE, Edith. <u>Lumbering</u> <u>Songs</u> <u>from</u> <u>the</u> <u>Northern</u> <u>Woods</u>.
American Folklore Society Memoir Series vol. 55. Austin:
University of Texas Press, 1970. 232 pp.

Although based on informants (former shantyboys) from
Ontario and Quebec, the songs include British-American ballads and
songs of American origin. The collection comprises 65 songs, 55
with melodies, with extensive documentation.

651. GRAY, Romand Palmer. <u>Songs</u> <u>and</u> <u>Ballads</u> <u>of</u> <u>the</u> <u>Maine</u>
<u>Lumberjacks</u>. Cambridge: Harvard University Press, 1924;
reprint ed., Detroit: Singing Tree Press, 1969. 191 pp.

Text and headnotes for 17 songs, 16 ballads, 12
historical songs and ballads and six broadsides.

652. IVES, Edward D. <u>Joe</u> <u>Scott</u>: <u>the</u> <u>Woodsman-Songmaker</u>.
Urbana: University of Illinois Press, 1978. 500 pp.

The songs of Joe Scott (1867-1918), which detail the life
and times of the Maine lumberjack, are here treated virtually as
art. Organized in chronological order, they have been transcribed
from later singers. The book is divided into three sections: The
Man, The Songs, The Tradition, and is a major resource.

653. RICKABY, Franz. <u>Ballads</u> <u>and</u> <u>Songs</u> <u>of</u> <u>the</u> <u>Shanty-Boy</u>.
Cambridge: Harvard University Press, 1926. 244 pp.

Ballads and songs collected in Michigan, Wisconsin, and
Minnesota, 1870-1900, among the shanty-boys or lumberjacks. Texts
and most tunes for 51 songs.

Songs of Miners

654. ADAMS, James Taylor. <u>Death</u> <u>in</u> <u>the</u> <u>Dark</u>; <u>a</u> <u>Collection</u> <u>of</u>
<u>Factual</u> <u>Ballads</u> <u>of</u> <u>American</u> <u>Mine</u> <u>Disasters</u>. Big Laurel
Va.: Adams-Mullins Press, 1941; reprint ed., Norwood,
Pa.: Norwood Editions, 1974; Philadelphia: Richard West,
1977. 119 pp.

Collection of texts without tunes on this unhappy topic.

655. EMRICH, Duncan. "Songs of the Western Miners." California
      Folklore Quarterly 1-3 (July 1942): 213-32.

      Examination of songs sung in 1942 in Montana area,
including texts, extensive notes, and some tunes. The first such
study in Montana.

656. GREEN, Archie. "A Discography of American Coal Miners'
      Songs." Labor History 2-1 (1961): 101-15.

      Written for non-folklorists, this historical introduction
to folksong with a bent to miners' songs is completed with a
discography on pp. 111-115, obviously now out of date.

657. GREEN, Archie. Only a Miner: Studies in Recorded Coal-
      Mining Songs. Urbana: University of Illinois Press, 1972.
      504 pp.

      Partly a study of songs as they portray the life of the
miner, partly case studies of selected songs recorded 1925-1970.
Comprehensive view of miner through topical songs, blues, ballads,
and other genres, with musical transcriptions by Judith McCulloh.

658. GREEN, Archie. "Recorded American Coal Mining Songs." Ph.D.
      dissertation, University of Pennsylvania, 1969. 522 pp.

      Examination of eight coal mining songs recorded between
1925 and 1969 from both hillbilly and race records. They portray
the life of the miner, his values. Drawn from ballad scholarship,
labor history, popular culture, and history. Songs studied are
"Only a Miner," "Dream of the Miner's Child," "Roll Down the
Line," "Coal Creek Troubles," "Death of Mother Jones," "Dark as a
Dungeon/Sixteen Tons," "Nine Pound Hammer," and "Coal Camp Blues."

659. HAND, Wayland, CUTTS, Charles, WYLDER, Robert C., and
      WYLDER, Betty. "Songs of the Butte Miners." Western
      Folklore 9-1 (Jan. 1950): 1-49.

      Collection of 30 songs recorded in Montana preceded by a
nine-page discussion of context. Texts, tunes, and notes provided
on each song, plus a classified list by origin.

660. KORSON, George G. _Black_ _Rock:_ _Mining_ _Folklore_ _of_ _the_
     Pennsylvania _Dutch._ Baltimore: Johns Hopkins Press, 1960.
     453 pp.

     The texts and some tunes of folksongs and ballads, with
background information, are treated pp. 348-402.

661. KORSON, George G. _Coal_ _Dust_ _on_ _the_ _Fiddle:_ _Songs_ _and_
     Stories _of_ _the_ _Bituminous_ _Industry._ Philadelphia:
     University of Pennsylvania Press, 1943; reprint ed.,
     Hatboro, Pa.: Folklore Associates, 1965. 460 pp.

     Background of coal camp life and the place of minstrelsy
in it, with many examples of song texts without tunes.

662. KORSON, George G. _Minstrels_ _of_ _the_ _Mine_ _Patch:_ _Songs_ _and_
     Stories _of_ _the_ _Anthracite_ _Industry._ Philadephia:
     University of Pennsylvania Press, 1938; reprint ed.,
     Hatboro, Pa.: Folklore Associates, 1964. 332 pp.

     Like the author's study of bituminous mining, this treats
ballads and songs within the context of life in the coal camps.

663. LE MON, Melvin William. "Pennsylvania Anthracite Miners'
     Folksongs." Ph.D. dissertation, University of Rochester
     (Eastman School of Music), 1942. 2 vols. (98 pp. of text
     and 107 pp. of music) and 15 phonograph records.

664. STEGNER, S. Page. "Protest Songs from the Butte Mines."
     Western _Folklore_ 26-3 (July 1967): 157-68.

     A study of texts and history based on a rare printed
booklet of 25 songs called "New Songs for Butte Mining Camp" which
included only the words, but alluded to well-known tunes.

Songs of Politics, Labor, and War

665. ALLAN, Francis D. _Allan's_ _Lone_ _Star_ _Ballads:_ _a_ _Collection_
     _of_ _Southern_ _Patriotic_ _Songs_ _made_ _during_ _Confederate_
     Times. [1874] New York: Burt Franklin, 1970. 199 pp.

     A collection of texts, sometimes with authors' names
given, and tune names indicated for some items.

666. BROWN, William W. The Anti-Slavery Harp: a Collection of Songs for Anti-Slavery Meetings. Boston: Bela Marsh, 1848; reprint ed., Philadelphia: Historic Publications, 1969. 48 pp.

Compiled by a fugitive slave, this collection of texts refers by name to the appropriate tunes.

667. CLEVELAND, Les. "Soldiers' Songs: the Folklore of the Powerless." New York Folklore 11-1/4 (1985): 79-98.

A study of song texts collected by the author during World War II while an infantryman. Proposes that soldiers are like miners, i.e., men working in hazardous conditions. This leads to a powerlessness which is dealt with in song. These are classified under humor, class struggle, secular prayer, cursing, etc. Not unexpectedly, this article is X-rated.

668. EGGLESTON, George Carey. American War Ballads & Lyrics: a Collection of the Songs and Ballads of the Colonial Wars, the Revolution, the War of 1812-15, the War with Mexico, and the Civil War. 2 vols. New York: G. P. Putnam's Songs, 1889. 226 pp. and 278 pp.

Collection of texts only.

669. FONER, Philip S. American Labor Songs of the Nineteenth Century. Urbana: University of Illinois Press, 1975. 373 pp. and soundsheet.

Comprehensive collection of 550 text examples either in full or in fragment, from Colonial and Revolutionary times to 1897 and the rise of socialism. Arranged in groups by period.

670. FOWKE, Edith, and GLAZER, Joe. Songs of Work and Freedom. Chicago: Roosevelt University, Labor Education Division, 1960; Garden City, N.Y.: Doubleday, 1961; reprint ed. as Songs of Work and Protest. New York: Dover, 1973. 211 pp.

Non-scholarly but practical collection of 100 harmonized songs organized by category (e.g., "Solidarity Forever," "Down in the Coal Mine") with some discussion.

671. GLASS, Paul. <u>Singing</u> <u>Soldiers</u> <u>(The</u> <u>Spirit</u> <u>of</u> <u>the</u> <u>Sixties):</u>
      <u>a</u> <u>History</u> <u>of</u> <u>the</u> <u>Civil</u> <u>War</u> <u>in</u> <u>Song</u>. New York: Grosset and
      Dunlap, 1968; reprint ed., New York: Dover, 1975. 300 pp.

      Collection of songs arranged for piano and/or guitar
accompaniment (by Louis C. Singer) with historical commentary.

672. GREEN, Archie. "A Discography (LP) of American Labor Union
      Songs." <u>New</u> <u>York</u> <u>Folklore</u> <u>Quarterly</u> 17-3 (Autumn, 1961):
      186-93.

      List of records with contents following a four-page intro-
duction giving some history of labor union songs and the earliest
known recordings. Distinguishes union songs from industrial songs.

673. GREENWAY, John. <u>American</u> <u>Folksongs</u> <u>of</u> <u>Protest</u>.
      Philadelphia: University of Pennsylvania Press, 1953;
      reprint ed., New York: Octagon Books, 1970. 348 pp.

      The social history of America through song, with emphasis
on the 19th and early 20th centuries. Texts, tunes, commentary,
and discography as well as biographies of ballad writers from Ella
May Wiggins to Woodie Guthrie.

674. HEAPS, Williard A., and HEAPS, Porter W. <u>The</u> <u>Singing</u>
      <u>Sixties:</u> <u>the</u> <u>Spirit</u> <u>of</u> <u>Civil</u> <u>War</u> <u>Days</u> <u>Drawn</u> <u>from</u> <u>Music</u> <u>of</u>
      <u>the</u> <u>Times</u>. Norman: University of Oklahoma Press, 1960.
      423 pp.

      A text oriented study of Civil War songs from both the
North and South, with a few tunes here and there.

675. HEFFNER, Susan R. "Labor and Industrial Folksongs: a Select
      Bibliography." Washington, D.C.: Library of Congress,
      Archive of Folk Song, 1978.

      Non-annotated list of 105 items.

676. LAWRENCE, Vera Brodsky. <u>Music</u> <u>for</u> <u>Patriots,</u> <u>Politicians,</u>
      <u>and</u> <u>Presidents:</u> <u>Harmonies</u> <u>and</u> <u>Discords</u> <u>of</u> <u>the</u> <u>First</u> <u>One</u>
      <u>Hundred</u> <u>Years</u>. New York: Macmillan, 1975. 480 pp.

Large format, coffee table type book emphasizing texts and context for the period 1764-1876. Included are some facsimiles and tunes as well as many illustrations, especially of broadsides.

677. NATHAN, Hans. "Two Inflation Songs of the Civil War." Musical Quarterly 29 (1943): 242-53.

Thorough study of New York minstrel show songs mocking the newly introduced "greenback dollars" of c.1863 and the war-time inflation that devalued the paper money. Tunes, sources, and texts included, with full documentation.

678. SILBER, Irwin. Songs America Voted By. Harrisburg: Stackpole Books, 1971. 320 pp.

Collection of songs used for presidential elections from 1788-1968. Includes tunes with chord symbols, words, and commentary. Some were topical words to standard tunes, others composed for the occasion.

679. STIMSON, Anna K. "Cries of Defiance and Derision and Rhythmic Chants of West Side, New York City, 1893-1902." Journal of American Folklore 58-228 (1945): 124-29.

Based on written sources, mostly a study of texts with a couple of tunes.

680. WELLMAN, Manly Wade, and WELLMAN, Frances. The Rebel Songster. Charlotte, N.C.: Heritage House, 1959. 53 pp.

Tunes, texts, and history of 21 "genuine" southern rebel songs such as "Yellow Rose of Texas," "Dixie," and "I'm Just a Rebel Soldier."

681. WILLIAMS, Alfred M. "Folk-Songs of the Civil War." Journal of American Folklore 5-19 (Oct.-Dec. 1892): 265-83.

Early study of texts from written sources.

FOLKSONGS AND BALLADS: OCCUPATIONAL

Songs of the Railroad

682. BOTKIN, Benjamin A., and HARLOW, Alvin F., eds. A Treasury
of Railroad Folklore. New York: Crown (Bonanza), 1953.
530 pp.

Part 5, "Blues, ballads, and worksongs" (pp. 434-66), has
an introduction and collection of tunes and texts, some from field
recordings.

683. COHEN, Norm. Long Steel Rail: the Railroad in American
Folksong. Urbana: University of Illinois Press, 1981.
733 pp.

Largely based on commercial recordings made 1920-1950, the
author recreates the history of American railroading through 85
songs (texts and tunes). Excellent bibliography and discography.

684. LYLE, Katie Letcher. Scalded to Death: Authentic Stories of
Railroad Disasters and the Ballads that were Written About
Them. Chapel Hill, N.C.: Algonquin, 1983. 212 pp.

Perhaps more for railroad buffs than folklorists, an
illustrated history of documented wrecks and the ballads about
them. Texts and tunes, with guitar chords.

Songs of the Sea

685. CAREY, George G. A Sailor's Songbag: an American Rebel in
an English Prison, 1777-1779. Amherst: University of
Massachusetts Press, 1976. 164 pp.

This study focuses on a manuscript of texts written by an
American privateersman who spent part of the Revolutionary War in
Forton Prison in Portsmouth. The original is in the Peabody
Museum, Salem, Massachusetts.

686. CARPENTER, James Madison. "Forecastle Songs and Chanties."
Ph.D. dissertation, Harvard University, 1929. 564 pp.

Field collected study providing texts and extensive
commentary for a great number of sea songs.

687. COLCORD, Joanna C. Roll and Go: Songs of American
     Sailormen. Indianapolis: Bobbs-Merrill, 1924. 118 pp.
     Rev. and enlarged as Songs of American Sailormen. New
     York: Bramhall House, 1938; reprint ed., New York: Oak,
     1964. 212 pp.

     Mostly texts, some tunes, in a popular-style survey.

688. DOERFLINGER, William Main. Shantymen and Shantyboys: Songs
     of the Sailor and Lumberman. New York: Macmillan, 1951;
     rev. ed. Songs of the Sailor and Lumberman, 1972. 374 pp.

     Field collected songs transcribed musically and textually
     with notes for each song in the back of the book.

689. HARLOW, Frederick Pease. Chanteying Aboard American Ships.
     Barre, Mass.: Barre Gazette, 1962. 250 pp.

     Collection of texts and tunes compiled by a retired sailor
     active in the 1870s (died in 1948) and edited by Ernest Dodge of
     the Peabody Museum in Salem, Massachusetts.

690. HUGILL, Stan. Shanties and Sailors' Songs. New York: E. P.
     Dutton, 1961; rev. ed., New York: Frederick A. Praeger,
     1969. 243 pp.

     Well-documented study, with 121-page introduction on
     historical background, the use of shanties, a study of collectors,
     books, and recordings. Forty shanties, with headnotes, texts, and
     tunes are included.

691. HUGILL, Stan. Songs of the Sea: the Tales and Tunes of
     Sailors and Sailing Ships. New York: McGraw-Hill, 1977.
     198 pp.

     This popular but attractive collection of 117 classified
     sea songs and shanties is preceded by an historical introduction
     on the age of sail, 1818-1920's. Included are the texts (written
     in long hand), tunes, commentary, and illustrations for song.

692. HUNTINGTON, Gale. Songs the Whalemen Sang. Barre, Mass.:
     Barre Publishers, 1964; reprint ed., New York: Dover,
     1970. 328 pp.

A collection of texts and monophonic tunes with a brief introduction.

693. HUTCHISON, Percy Adams. "Sailors' Chanties." Journal of American Folklore 19-72 (Jan.-Mar. 1906): 16-28.

Study of texts only.

694. MEAD, John Holstead. "Sea Shanties and Fo'c'sle Songs, 1768-1906, in the G. W. Blunt White Library, Mystic Seaport, Mystic, Connecticut." D.M.A. dissertation, University of Kentucky, 1973. 674 pp.

The author defines shanties as call and response songs sung to help coordinate work. They are divided into three categories depending on the length of the task. Because they have been so extensively studied, the author cross references and classifies them according to other sources. Fo'c'sle songs are songs sung off duty. The author examines their contents based on library collections.

695. ORING, Elliott. "Whalemen and their Songs: a Study of Folklore and Culture." New York Folklore Quarterly 27-1 (May 1971): 130-52.

Analysis of British and American song texts in relation to the culture of the occupation both in terms of literal and symbolic meanings. Seeks to answer two questions: 1) how is the culture of a particular folk group reflected in the songs, and 2) how do the songs function in the culture.

696. SHAY, Frank. American Sea Songs and Chanteys from the Days of Iron Men and Wooden Ships. New York: W. W. Norton, 1948; reprint ed., Freeport, N.Y.: Books for Libraries Press, 1969. 217 pp.

Collection of 78 songs with texts and tunes, and a brief introduction.

Play-Party Songs and Other Songs for Children

697. AMES, Mrs. L. D. "The Missouri Play-Party." Journal of American Folklore 24-94 (Oct.-Dec. 1911): 295-318.

Description of play-parties and a collection of both tunes and texts.

698. BACKUS, Emma M. "Song-Games from Connecticut." *Journal of American Folklore* 14-55 (Oct.-Dec. 1901): 295-99.

Collected in 1865 in Ashford and Eastford, this article presents five texts and four tunes.

699. BALL, Leona Nessly. "The Play Party in Idaho." *Journal of American Folklore* 44-171 (Jan.-Mar. 1931): 1-26.

Examples of texts and some tunes following a lengthy discussion of survival in Idaho.

700. BOTKIN, Benjamin Albert. *The American Play-Party Song; With a Collection of Oklahoma Texts and Tunes.* University of Nebraska University Studies, 37, nos. 1-4. Lincoln: University of Nebraska Press, 1937; reprint ed., New York: Frederick Ungar, 1963. 400 pp.

Originally the doctoral dissertation (1931) of one of America's most prolific folklorists, this massive study presents over 1,000 variants of 128 songs of both younger and older generations collected 1926-27 from teachers, students, and others. The author defines the play party as songs for children's games as well as mixers at square dances and for folk and country dances. The first part discusses the origins and usage of the genre, and the second part consists of texts and tunes.

701. BREWSTER, Paul G. "Game-Songs from Southern Indiana." *Journal of American Folklore* 49-193 (July-Sept. 1936): 243-62.

Based on recordings made 1935-6, the author presents 20 examples and variants, some with tunes.

702. BROOKS-BAHAM, Emma Sue. "A Model for Collecting Children's Singing Games for Use in Incorporating Movement in Elementary Music Instruction." D.M.A. dissertation, University of Washington, 1980. 116 pp.

Based on a study of black American children's games from Louisiana and Mississippi played by children aged 6-12, this study seeks a practical application of these materials into the classroom. There are both transcription and analysis of movements.

703. CASTAGNA, Barbara. "Some Rhymes, Games, and Songs from Children in the New Rochelle Area." New York Folklore Quarterly 25-3 (Sept. 1969): 221-37.

Collection of texts made in 1969, including jump rope rhymes, counting out songs, and songs for jeering and teasing.

704. COLLINS, Fletcher. Alamance Play-Party Songs and Singing Games. [A Collection of Forty-Five Songs from Alamance County, with Directions for their Performance. Contributed by a Cooperating Group of Teachers in the Schools of the County]. Elon, N.C.: Elon College, 1940; reprint ed., Norwood, Pa.: Norwood Editions, 1973.

705. DARBY, Loraine. "Ring-Games from Georgia." Journal of American Folklore 30-116 (Apr.-June 1917): 218-21.

Brief articles with two texts and tunes.

706. FOWKE, Edith Fulton. Sally Go Round the Sun: 300 Children's Songs, Rhymes, and Games. Music Arranged by Keith MacMillan. Garden City: Doubleday, 1969. 160 pp.

Collection of texts most of which include piano and guitar-chord accompaniment, with virtually no commentary.

707. GARDNER, Emelyn E. "Some Play-Party Games in Michigan." Journal of American Folklore 33-127 (Jan.-Mar. 1920): 91-133.

Descriptions of action and 51 examples, some with tunes.

708. HALL, Joseph S. "Some Play-Party Games of the Great Smokey Mountains." Journal of American Folklore 54-211/12 (Jan.-June 1941): 68-71.

Brief but interesting description of play-party songs in Cocke County, Tennessee, but without examples.

709. HAMILTON, Goldy M. "The Play-Party in Northeast Missouri."
     Journal _of_ _American_ _Folklore_ 27-105 (July-Sept. 1914):
     289-303.

     Inspired by Mrs. L. D. Ames' 1911 article, this study is
restricted to texts collected in northeastern Missouri.

710. HECK, Jean O. "Folk Poetry and Folk Criticism, as
     Illustrated by Cincinnati Children in their Singing
     Games." _Journal_ _of_ _American_ _Folklore_ 40-155 (Jan.-Mar.
     1927): 1-77.

     Survey of children's songs and a study of their tastes
and selection, with extensive examples.

711. HENRY, Mellinger E. "Nursery Rhymes and Game-Songs from
     Georgia." _Journal_ _of_ _American_ _Folklore_ 47-186 (Oct.-
     Dec. 1934): 334-40.

     Examples of 24 texts only.

712. HOWARD, Dorothy Mills. "The Rhythms of Ball-Bouncing and
     Ball Bouncing Rhymes." _Journal_ _of_ _American_ _Folklore_ 62-
     244 (Apr.-June 1949): 166-72.

     In spite of its title, a text-based study dividing the
songs into four categories, providing little rhythmic notation.

713. HULL, Myra E. "Kansas Play-Party Songs." _Kansas_
     Historical _Quarterly_ 7-3 (1938): 258-86.

     Description of the songs, texts, and some tunes.

714. McINTOSH, David S. _Folk_ _Songs_ _and_ _Singing_ _Games_ _of_ _the_
     Illinois _Ozarks._ Carbondale: Southern Illinois
     University Press, 1974. 136 pp.

     Collection of 52 songs and 32 rope skipping rhymes, many
with musical transcriptions by Dale Whiteside. The earlier
edition had two 7" 33 1/3 rpm discs, the later with a cassette
tape, but the examples recorded are not from the field.

715. MELAMED, Lanie. "The Play-Party Today." New York Folklore Quarterly 21-3 (Sept. 1965): 212-9.

A description of how the play-party was used when the article was written, based on a survey of 20 teachers and leaders around the country.

716. NEWELL, William Wells. Games and Songs of American Children Collected and Compared. New York: Harper, 1883; new and enlarged ed., New York and London: Harper and Bros., 1903; reprint ed. of 1903, New York: Dover, 1963. 289 pp.

Amazingly sensitive and thorough classic study of children's game song texts with some tunes with piano accompaniment.

717. OWENS, William A. Swing and Turn: Texas Play-Party Games. Dallas: Tardy Publishing Co., 1936. 117 pp.

Following a 33-page introduction is a collection of play party songs with descriptions, texts, and tunes.

718. PIPER, Edwin F. "Some Play-Party Games of the Middle West." Journal of American Folklore 28-109 (July-Sept. 1915): 262-89.

Based on research in Nebraska, Illinois, Montana, and Iowa, this article provides an excellent description of the play party and details its varying rates of survival and disappearance. Some textual examples included.

719. PORTER, Kenneth Wiggins. "Children's Songs and Rhymes of the Porter Family." Journal of American Folklore 54-213/214 (July-Dec. 1941): 167-75.

Texts collected from the writer's ancestors in Kansas.

720. RANDOLPH, Vance. "The Ozark Play Party." Journal of American Folklore 42-165 (July-Sept. 1929): 201-32.

Collection of 29 songs, most with tunes, field researched in Arkansas and Missouri.

721. RANDOLPH, Vance, and CLEMENS, Nancy. "Ozark Mountain
Party-Games." Journal of American Folklore 49-193 (July-
Sept. 1936): 199-206.

While this article is mostly about games, there are also
a number of songs, but no melodies.

722. SEEGER, Ruth Crawford. American Folk Songs for Children in
Home, School, and Nursery School. Garden City, N.Y.:
Doubleday, 1948. 190 pp.

Introduction on singing, improvising words, accompanying
with collection of classically arranged songs and texts. More
scholarly than many such collections.

723. VAN DOREN, Carl. "Some Play-Party Songs from Eastern
Illinois." Journal of American Folklore 32-126 (Oct.-
Dec. 1919): 486-96.

Collection of 25 texts (no tunes) made in 1907 in
Vermilion County, Illinois.

724. WARNICK, Florence. "Play-Party Songs in Western Maryland."
Journal of American Folklore 54-213/214 (July-Dec.
1941): 162-6.

Twelve texts from Garrett County, Maryland.

725. WEDGWOOD, Harriet L. "The Play-Party." Journal of
American Folklore 25-97 (July-Sept. 1912): 268-73.

Collection of seven texts from the Missouri area
stimulated by the article by Ames.

726. WOLFORD, Leah Jackson. The Play-Party in Indiana.
Indianapolis: Indiana Historical Commission, 1916. 120
pp.; edited and rev. by W. Edson RICHMOND and William
TILLSON, 1959 (Indiana Historical Society Publications
#20-2), 326 pp.; reprint ed., New York: Arno, 1976.

Instructions on how to perform play party songs, with
examples of texts and tunes.

727. YOFFIE, Leah Rachel Clara. "Three Generations of
Children's Singing Games in St. Louis." Journal of
American Folklore 60-235 (Jan.-Mar. 1947): 1-51.

Begins as a survey of singing games in existence when
author was a child and continues to the "present" to see which
have survived and how they have changed. In three sections: 1895-
1900 (with 47 song texts), to 1914, and to 1944.

Studies in Musical Analysis

728. ARMOUR, Eugene. "The Melodic and Rhythmic Characteristics
of the Music of the Traditional Ballad Variants Found in
the Southern Appalachians." Ph.D. dissertation, New York
University, 1961. 178 pp.

Investigation of both the melodic and rhythmic
characteristics found in the ballads printed by Sharp. First a
musical analysis of 187 ballad tunes, then a study of modal
classification in which 14 modes were isolated.

729. BAYARD, Samuel P. "Principal Versions of an International
Folk Tune." Journal of the International Folk Music
Council 3 (1951): 44-50.

A study of transcribed tunes used in singing Child 1 and 2.

730. BAYARD, Samuel P. "Prolegomena to a Study of the Principal
Melodic Families of British-American Folk Songs." Journal
of American Folklore 63-247 (Jan.-Mar. 1950): 1-44.

An effort to describe the nature and impact on our
tradition of extended tune-families, i.e., groups of versions or
derivatives presumably of a single tune composed and made current
at some unknown time in the past. Attempt also to delineate the
sorts of traditional re-creation the tunes' versions underwent.
(Annotation by author).

731. BOSWELL, George W. "Metrical Alternation in Folksinging."
Journal of American Folklore 85-337 (July-Sept. 1972):
248-59.

Technical article summarizing the results of analysis of
859 songs collected in Tennessee.

150

732. BOSWELL, George W. "Reciprocal Controls Exerted by Ballad
      Texts and Tunes." Journal of American Folklore 80-316
      (Apr.-June 1967): 169-74.

      Study of tune/text fit in terms of rhythm and meter in
series of ballads from the South.

733. BOSWELL, George W. "Shaping Controls of Ballad Tunes over
      their Texts." Tennessee Folklore Society Bulletin 17-1
      (March 1951): 9-18.

      Assumes that the text appeared before tune, but after
categorizing melody types, explores how melody might influence
text, especially in terms of accent.

734. BOSWELL, George W. "Stanza Form and Music-Imposed Scansion
      in Southern Ballads." Southern Folklore Quarterly 31-4
      (Dec. 1967): 320-31.

      Detailed study without introduction or conclusion that
examines rhythm and meter in ballads as they pertain to stanza
form. Lists and describes various forms.

735. BOSWELL, George W. "Text-Occasioned Ornamentation in
      Folksinging." Southern Folklore Quarterly 33-4 (Dec.
      1969): 333-8.

      Examination of slides and other melodic graces in
folksong to see whether they are related to poetic rhythm.
Concludes that while they influence the pattern, they are not the
sole determinants.

736. BRONSON, Bertrand Harris. The Ballad as Song. Berkeley:
      University of California Press, 1969. 324 pp.

      Collection of articles by Bronson concerning the ballads
studied by Child and Sharp. Emphasis is on the text/tune relationship, melodic analysis, and review of the work of previous writers.

737. BRONSON, Bertrand H. "The Interdependence of Ballad Tunes
      and Texts." California Folklore Quarterly 3-3 (July
      1944): 185-207.

Probably because previous ballad scholarship largely
ignored tunes, the author strongly recommends the study of tune as
well as text. Explores the implications of tunes in several
examples, showing how the two elements work together.

738. BRONSON, Bertrand H. "The Morphology of the Ballad-Tunes."
      Journal of American Folklore 67-263 (Jan.-Mar. 1954):
      1-13.

To counter-balance the studies of change, the author
focuses on variation, selection, and continuity. No examples.

739. BRONSON, Bertrand H. "The Music of the Ballads." Virginia
      Quarterly Review 34-3 (1958): 474-80.

A study of the Frank C. Brown Collection of North
Carolina Folklore and the difficulties of editing the music.

740. BRONSON, Bertrand H. "Professor Child's Ballad Tunes."
      California Folklore Quarterly 1-2 (April 1942): 185-200.

After bemoaning the loss of tunes, because few early
collectors bothered with them (or were trained to deal with them),
the author describes and discusses the tune appendix to Child's
monumental collection, the tunes being printed here.

741. BRONSON, Bertrand Harris. The Singing Tradition of Child's
      Popular Ballads. Princeton: Princeton University Press,
      1976. 530 pp.

An abridgement of the author's multi-volume study (The
Traditional Tunes of the Child Ballads), with emphasis on tune,
texts, background, and variants.

742. BRONSON, Bertrand H. "Toward the Comparative Analysis of
      British-American Folk Tunes." Journal of American
      Folklore 72-285 (July-Sept. 1959): 165-91.

Study of the use of the computer to aid in tune analysis,
with numerous transcriptions and tables.

743. BRONSON, Bertrand Harris. "Traditional Ballads Musically Considered." Critical Inquiry 2-1 (Fall, 1975): 29-42.

Article length overview of the musical aspects of ballads, the role of tune in stanzaic patterning, line length, refrain and chorus, etc. Also studies the modal character of tunes, their relationship to British-American folksong generally, range, phrase structure, and harmonic practice.

744. BRONSON, Bertrand Harris. The Traditional Tunes of the Child Ballads with their Texts, According to the Extant Records of Great Britain and America. 4 vols. Princeton: Princeton University Press, 1959-72.

Bronson's magnum opus, this monumental study does for ballad tunes what Child's collection did for ballad texts. Arranged in Child's order, the author provides texts, tunes, variants, extensive documentation and cross referencing for all that has been recorded, virtually all of Child's canon in this case. Bronson's musical theory, based on the church modes and gapped scales, is now being questioned, but the contribution stands on its own. What is perhaps missing is the human performance-practice element. Vol. 4 includes on pp. 437-513 an extensive bibliography of printed works and manuscripts.

745. CAZDEN, Norman. "A Simple Mode Classification for Traditional Anglo-American Song Titles." Yearbook of the International Folk Music Council 3 (1971): 45-78.

Extensively documented study which questions why we use the church modes in analysis, and not major and minor.

746. COFFIN, Tristram P. "Remarks Preliminary to a Study of Ballad Meter and Ballad Singing." Journal of American Folklore 78-308 (Apr.-June 1965): 149-53.

Argues that musicologists have unfairly attempted to establish priority for tunes in ballad research. Asserts that text dominates the tune, that poetry is foremost, while noting further that trained singers cannot sing ballads correctly.

747. COHEN, Anne and Norm. "Tune Evolution as an Indicator of Traditional Musical Norms." Journal of American Folklore 86-339 (Jan.-Mar. 1973): 37-47.

Study of evolution of tunes from folk traditions of the southeastern states to Tin Pan Alley. Appendix of tune sources.

748. COWDERY, James R. "A Fresh Look at the Concept of Tune Family." Ethnomusicology 28-3 (Sept. 1984): 495-504.

Reconsideration of the work of Bayard and Bronson as it relates to the study of tune families. Asserts that the ideas are not American in origin but permeate American ballad scholarship.

749. DINNEEN, William. "Early American Manuscript Music-Books." Musical Quarterly 30 (1944): 50-62.

Based on the study of four manuscript volumes compiled by amateurs, dated 1790-1800, the author describes a perceived influence of popular ballads on sheet music and songsters. Contents described in detail, and facsimiles as examples.

750. FOSS, George. "A Methodology for the Description and Classification of Anglo-American Traditional Tunes." Journal of the Folklore Institute 4-1 (June 1967): 102-26.

Technical and theoretical study about analysis of tunes.

751. GORDON, Philip. "The Music of the Ballads." Southern Folklore Quarterly 6-3 (Sept. 1942): 143-8.

Rather general study of church-mode interpretation.

752. HENDREN, J. W. A Study of Ballad Rhythm with Special Reference to Ballad Music. Princeton Studies in English #14. Princeton: Princeton University Press, 1936; reprint ed., New York: Gordian Press, 1966. 177 pp.

Systematic picture of variation of structure of ballad melodies and verse by an English professor concerned primarily with poetic rhythm. Technical and scholarly.

753. HORACEK, Leo. "The Relation of Mood and Melodic Pattern in Folk Songs." Ph.D. dissertation, University of Kansas, 1955. 141 pp.

Based on a study of about 100 folk songs from the Germans, French, English, and Southern Appalachians, the author examines modality, melodic patterns, and rhythmic structure, concluding that melodic pattern determines mood in the song.

754. JACKSON, George Pullen. "American Folksong and Musical Art." Southern Folklore Quarterly 17-2 (March 1953): 140-2.

Brief study of the use of folksong outside its original context, i.e., in "classical" arrangements.

755. JACKSON, George Pullen. "Stephen Foster's Debt to American Folk Song." Musical Quarterly 22 (1936): 154-69.

Study of the musical environment in which Foster grew up, the influences on him, and notes similarities to tunes found in singing school books. Further, there are 27 examples, and the assertion that Foster's songs are unrelated to Negro songs.

756. KOLINSKI, Mieczyslaw. "Barbara Allen: Tonal Versus Melodic Structure, Part I." Ethnomusicology 12-2 (1968): 208-18; "Part II." 13-1 (1969): 1-73.

Written for the theoretically adventurous, this extensive and highly technical study is based on an analysis system developed and used exclusively by the author.

757. LIST, George. "An Approach to the Indexing of Ballad Tunes." Folklore and Folk Music Archivist 6-1 (Spring, 1963): 7-16.

Shows that the tune for the first stanza of a ballad is usually the least stable, and recommends that one compare this stanza with all the others.

758. LIST, George. "Toward the Indexing of Ballad Texts." Journal of American Folklore 81-319 (Jan.-Mar. 1968): 44-61.

Suggests methods that could be applied to the classification and cataloguing of ballad texts.

759.   McCORMICK, Scott. "Scale and Structure in Ballads
        Collected by Cecil Sharp in the Southern Appalachian
        Mountains." Ph.D. dissertation, Northwestern University.
        In progress.

760.   McCULLOH, Judith Marie. "In the Pines: the Melodic-Textual
        Identity of an American Lyric Folksong Cluster." Ph.D.
        dissertation, Indiana University, 1970. 662 pp.

        Based on the premise that lyric folksongs are more
flexible and changeable than other types, the author suggests that
a close examination of both textual and musical elements can help
determine order in a folksong cluster. Using 153 variants, two
thirds from recordings, one third from written sources, of the song
"In the Pines" or "The Longest Train (I ever Saw)," the author
breaks down the song into couplets and demonstrates from these
building blocks how the song developed. Concludes that tunes are
more stable than texts.

761.   McCULLOH, Judith. "What is the Tune?" In Discourse in
        Ethnomusicology: Essays in Honor of George List, pp. 89-
        107. Edited by Caroline Card et al. Bloomington, Ind.:
        Ethnomusicology Publications Group, Archives of
        Traditional Music, 1978.

762.   MURPHY, William Robert. "Melodic Contour in White Anglo-
        American Traditional Narrative Song in North America."
        Ph.D. dissertation, University of Pennsylvania, 1969.
        345 pp.

        New approach to the study of ballad tunes inspired by
Alan Lomax's "Map of Song Style Areas in North America." Seeks a
Gestalt view of melody through the graphing of 664 tunes.

763.   NETTL, Bruno. "The Musical Style of the English Ballads
        Collected in Indiana." Acta Musicologica 27 (1955):77-84.

        Stylistic description, with emphasis on scale and
structure, of 27 tunes for Anglo-American balladry collected by
Lomax and Brewster in southern Indiana in 1938.

764.   SCHERRER, Deborah K., and SCHERRER, Philip H. "An
        Experiment in the Computer Measurement of Melodic

Variation in Folksong." Journal of American Folklore 84-332 (Apr.-June 1971): 230-41.

Highly technical study based on Child ballad tunes.

765. SEEGER, Charles. "Versions and Variants of 'Barbara Allen' in the Archive of American Folk Song in the Library of Congress." Selected Reports in Ethnomusicology, vol. 1, no. 1, pp. 120-67. Los Angeles: Institute of Ethnomusicology, University of California, 1966; reprinted as brochure for Library of Congress recording L54, 1966; reprinted in Studies in Musicology, 1935-1975. Berkeley: University of California Press, 1977, pp. 273-320.

One of the most important studies ever written on ballad tunes, variants of tunes, tune families, and the association of texts and tunes. Rather technical, but comprehensive.

766. SHAPIRO, Anne Dhu. "Regional Song Styles: the Scottish Connection." In Music and Context: Essays for John M. Ward, pp. 404-17. Edited by A. D. Shapiro. Cambridge: Harvard University, Department of Music, 1985.

Explores the melodic and rhythmic traits of Scottish style and its influence on American folksong based on the idea that one's singing style is derived from one's national origin.

767. SHAPIRO, Anne Dhu. "The Tune-Family Concept in British-American Folk-Song Scholarship." 2 vols. Ph.D. dissertation, Harvard University, 1975. 290 pp. of text and 104 pp. of music. (No abstract available)

768. WINKELMAN, Donald M. "Musicological Techniques of Ballad Analysis." Midwest Folklore 10-4 (Winter, 1960-1961): 197-205.

The author asserts that musical analysis had been neglected in ballad study up until then and therefore recommends that more be done. Asserts that tempo, harmony, phrasing, and pitch levels are all important aspects, citing many examples to justify his concerns.

769. WINKELMAN, Donald M. "Poetic/Rhythmic Stress in the Child
  Ballads." Keystone Folklore Quarterly 12-2 (Summer,
  1967): 103-17.

  Technical and analytical study of both poetic and musical
stresses in ballads.

770. WINKELMAN, Donald M. "Some Rhythmic Aspects of the Child
  Ballad." In New Voices in American Studies, pp. 151-66.
  Edited by Ray B. Browne, D. M. Winkelman, and Allan
  Hayman. Lafayette: Purdue University Studies, 1966.

  Sophisticated rhythmic analysis of ballad tunes based on
motives. The melodic and textual rhythms are also compared.

Studies of Individual Performers

771. ABRAHAMS, Roger D., ed. A Singer and her Songs: Almeda
  Riddle's Book of Ballads. Baton Rouge: Louisiana State
  University Press, 1970. 191 pp.

  Within a text that provides an autobiography of the
singer, who was born in 1898, is considerable information on
folklore of the Ozarks, the performance and transmission of songs,
and many songs.

772. BETHKE, Robert D. "Musical Tradition and Woodsmen Singer-
  Critics in Northwestern New York State." Ph.D.
  dissertation, University of Pennsylvania, 1973. 536 pp.

  Using informants of Anglo-Scots-Irish descent living in
Lawrence County, the author explores the ideas and values of
"native critics." The study also focuses on patterns in
traditional fiddling and singing, the types of songs and stories,
and the lives of individual singers.

773. BURTON, Thomas G. Some Ballad Folks. Boone, N.C.:
  Appalachian Consortium Press, 1978; reprint ed., 1981.
  108 pp.

  Biographies of five traditional singers, plus a
collection of Child ballads on pp. 62-105.

774. GREENE, Daniel W. "'Fiddle and I': The Story of Franz
     Rickaby." Journal of American Folklore 81-322 (Oct.-
     Dec. 1968): 316-36.

     A study of the life of Rickaby (d. 1925), an important
collector of woodsmen ballads (see #653) who was born in Arkansas,
grew up in the Midwest, and spent many years as a hitchhiker.

775. HIGH, Ellesa Clay. Past Titan Rock: Journeys Into an
     Appalachian Valley. Lexington: University Press of
     Kentucky, 1983. 192 pp.

     An account of musical life in the Red River Gorge area of
east central Kentucky through the life of singer and musician, Lily
May Ledford.

776. JONES, Loyal. "The Minstrel of the Appalachians: Bascom
     Lamar Lunsford at 91." JEMF Quarterly 9-29 (Spring,
     1973): 2-8.

     Lunsford (1882-1973), who founded the Mountain Dance and
Folk Festival in 1928 in Asheville, N.C., and recorded a vast
number of songs, discusses a variety of topics of concern to the
performer and festival organizer.

777. MULLEN, Patrick B. "Folk Songs and Family Traditions." In
     Observations & Reflections on Texas Folklore, pp. 49-64.
     Publications of the Texas Folklore Society, #37. Edited
     by Francis E. Abernethy. Austin: Encino Press, 1972.

     A folklorist discovers that his grandfather, Benjamin
Harrison Mullen, who had died 11 years earlier, had been a ballad
singer. Study based on a manuscript of 12 songs written in 1907.

778. RICHARDSON, Anna Davis. "Old Songs from Clarksburg, W.
     Va., 1918." Journal of American Folklore 32-126 (Oct.-
     Dec. 1919): 497-504.

     A brief study of an old singer from Upshur County, Mrs.
Rachel E. Fogg, and a report on her repertory. Included are five
texts and one melody.

779. SCHULMAN, Steven A. "Howess Dewey Winfrey: the Rejected
     Songmaker." Journal of American Folklore 87-343 (Jan.-
     Mar. 1974): 72-83.

     Unusual study of a Cumberland County, Kentucky, songmaker
who does satirical songs about his neighbors. Based on the texts,
the author seeks to explain why the songs are rejected.

Studies of Individual Ballads

780. "American Versions of the Ballad of the Elfin Knight."
     Journal of American Folklore 7-26 (July-Sept. 1894):
     228-32.

     Texts and analysis of three American versions from
Boston, Beverly, Mass., and western New York State, and one tune.

781. ANDERSON, George K. "Two Ballads from Nineteenth-Century
     Ohio." Journal of American Folklore 51-199 (Jan.-Mar.
     1938): 38-46.

     Texts and analysis of two "vulgar" ballads from the
author's grandfather's notebook, "Farmer Boy" and "Richard Guile,"
both from 1855.

782. BARRY, Phillips. "The Ballad of Lord Randall in New
     England." Journal of American Folklore 16-63 (Oct.-Dec.
     1903): 258-64.

     Texts and tunes for six versions from New England.

783. "A Brief List of Materials Relating to 'John Henry'."
     Washington, D.C.: Library of Congress, Archive of Folk
     Song, 1970. 3 pp. (32 items)

784. CAZDEN, Norman. "The Story of a Catskill Ballad." New
     York Folklore Quarterly 8-4 (Winter, 1952): 245-66.

     The study of a ballad theme, the tragedy of Yarrow, which
is found in Child 214 and 215.

785. COFFIN, Tristram P. "'Mary Hamilton' and the Anglo-
American Ballad as an Art Form." Journal of American
Folklore 70-277 (July-Sept. 1957): 208-14.

Assertion that ballad texts be seen as artistic.

786. COHEN, Norm. "'Casey Jones': at the Crossroads of Two
Ballad Traditions." Western Folklore 32-2 (April 1973):
77-103.

Historical study of the ballad tradition based on the
railroad death of John Luther "Casey" Jones on April 29, 1900, on
the Illinois Central, the song created nine years later by two
vaudevillians based on a black folk ballad, and the changes that
took place in this development. Extensively documented.

787. COHEN, Norm. "Robert W. Gordon and the Second Wreck of
'Old 97'." Journal of American Folklore 87-343 (Jan.-
Mar. 1974): 12-38.

This article reviews collected versions and studies of the
ballad, "Wreck of 'Old 97'" made in the 1920s by R. W. Gordon, the
first Archivist of the Archive of Folk Song.

788. COX, John Harrington. "'John Hardy'." Journal of American
Folklore 32-126 (Oct.-Dec. 1919): 505-20.

Study of the origin and history of this ballad from West
Virginia. Five text variants given.

789. DAVIS, Arthur Kyle, Jr. "'Far Fannil Town': a Ballad of
Mystery Examined." Southern Folklore Quarterly 36-1
(March 1972): 1-13.

A study of the roots of this particular ballad and its
relation to ballad literature generally. History of collecting of
it, its story, tune, and text.

790. GREENE, David Mason. "'The Lady and the Dragoon': a
Broadside Ballad in Oral Tradition." Journal of American
Folklore 70-277 (July-Sept. 1957): 221-30.

Demonstrates how the differences between the seventeenth century broadside version and that in oral tradition stem from a purposeful reshaping through concious imitation, rather than variation, of the Child type ballad.

791. IVES, Edward D. "'Ben Deane' and Joe Scott: a Ballad and its Probable Author." Journal of American Folklore 72-283 (Jan.-Mar. 1959): 53-66.

A study of a ballad in oral tradition in the Northeast, with text, tune, and variants, and discussion of its relationship to historical facts and to its probable author.

792. IVES, Edward D. "'The Teamster in Jack MacDonald's Crew': a Song in Context and its Singing." In Folklife Annual 1985. Washington, D.C.: American Folklife Center, 1985.

One of nine articles, this study is concerned with the origin of a lumber camp ballad and includes comments as well on poetry, art, and the singing of ballads.

793. KOUWENHOVEN, John A., and PATTEN, Lawton M. "New Light on 'The Star Spangled Banner'." Musical Quarterly 23 (1937): 198-200.

Basic history of Key's poem and questions about the tune. The study concludes that Key actually stood on the ship's deck on September 14, 1814, but had written the song nine years earlier.

794. LATHROP, Francis C. "Commercial Parlor Ballad to Folksong." Journal of American Folklore 70-277 (July-Sept. 1957): 240-6.

Technical study with many examples that shows how a commercial tune became the cowboy song, "O, Bury Me Not on the Lone Prairie."

795. LEMAY, J. A. Leo. "The American Origins of 'Yankee Doodle'." William and Mary Quarterly 33-3 (1976): 435-64.

A new study that questions, indeed refutes, the traditional wisdom on the song's origin and demonstrates that it had originated in America prior to 1740.

796. LUMPKIN, Ben Gray. "Tune for 'Baldy Green'." Southern Folklore Quarterly 34-1 (March 1970): 12-17.

"Baldy Green" had been studied as a text in earlier articles by Pound (same journal, vol. 6) and Alderson (vol. 9), but no tune was found until 1965 when the author discovered it in Colorado.

797. MORRIS, Alton C. "'The Rolling Stone': the Way of a Song." Southern Folklore Quarterly 37-4 (1973): 331-54.

Traces the history of an English ballad carried into the American West derived from "Since Times are so Bad," a song in Henry Purcell's The Comical History of Don Quixote, Part II, Act IV, Scene III. The original music is included (pp. 333-43).

798. SONNECK, Oscar George Theodore. Report on "The Star-Spangled Banner," "Hail Columbia," "America," and "Yankee Doodle." Washington, D.C.: U. S. Government Printing Office, 1909; reprint ed., New York: Dover, 1972. 203 pp.

A scholarly and historical study of four American patriotic songs, with extensive bibliography and examples.

799. TURNER, Martha Anne. The Yellow Rose of Texas: Her Saga and Her Song. Austin: Shoal Creek Publishers, 1976. 136 pp.

A study that traces this song from its folk origins to its commercial use.

800. WEST, John F. The Ballad of Tom Dula. Durham, N.C.: Moore, 1971. 212 pp.

A study of a ballad based on the murder in 1866 of Laura Foster by Tom Dula in Wilkes County, N.C. Besides giving the complete texts of traditional ballads on the subject, it provides the surviving court records of the murder trial.

801. WILGUS, D. K. "Fiddler's Farewell: the Legend of the Hanged Fiddler." Studia Musicologica 7-1/4 (1965): 195-209 (which is simultaneously Journal of the International Folk Music Council 17-2).

A study of a genre, the farewell songs of condemned men, focusing on the history of song about fiddlers both in the British Isles and the United States, giving both texts and transcriptions based on recordings.

802. WILGUS, D. K., and HURVITZ, Nathan. "'Little Mary Phagan': Further Notes on a Native American Ballad in Context." Journal of Country Music 4-1 (Spring, 1973): 17-30.

Examination of historical detail and various recordings of a ballad recounting the murder on April 26, 1913, of Mary Phagan and the trial of Leo Frank. Also a response to Saundra Keyes' article, "'Little Mary Phagan': a Native American Ballad in Context" in the same journal, vol. 3 (1972): 1-16.

803. WILGUS, D. K., and MONTELL, Lynwood. "Clure and Joe Williams: Legend and Blues Ballad." Journal of American Folklore 81-322 (Oct.-Dec. 1968): 295-315.

Texts, variants, tunes, history, and analysis of a ballad from south central Kentucky and northern Tennessee.

IV. LATER DEVELOPMENTS IN ANGLO-AMERICAN FOLK MUSIC

Section IV embraces three categories which might be thought
unusual or even controversial for a "folk music" bibliography. The
doubt is not so much that both country music and bluegrass have
folk roots, but whether, through their more-or-less commercial
dissemination and professional nature, they retain any of that
folkness. A stronger argument for the folkness of bluegrass can
perhaps be made than for country, because the former retains
acoustic instruments long used in Appalachia and performs some of
the same functions as the traditional string band.

Country music is less easy to defend. If _American_ music is
music which results from the unique circumstances found here, as
opposed to "music in America," which might well include unchanged
survivals from anywhere, including Laos and India, then there is no
doubt that country music is American music. While in some ways its
ballads are simply updated versions of the traditional folk song or
even a kind of white blues, the commercial success of country
music, its superstars, and its primary dissemination through the
media certainly make it different from, for example, lined hymns
sung by Primitive Baptists or lap dulcimers strummed by upland
Kentuckians. In selecting items listed here, there has been a
clear preference for both the scholarly and that pertaining to the
earlier forms of country music, but some of the "popular" types of
coffee-table books and other lighter fare have been included.

For purists, the Folk Revival is simply fake. Yet, it is a
significant part of our musical history. Users of this collection
who have trouble accepting this material can, of course, ignore it.
But it can be reasonably argued that a complete picture of American
folk music cannot be gotten without considering this phenomenon.

The association of the Folk Revival movement with protest
song, some of it of an extreme leftist orientation, may trouble
others. Part of the movement was indeed a people's movement,
although admittedly some of it might be seen as the work of a small
band of militants attempting to manipulate the masses through song.
In any case, significant research has already been done in this
area, especially by R. Serge Denisoff.

Naturally, the one sticky point is whether a given collection of songs ought to be included here or in Section III, where other collections of folksongs are to be found. Obviously, those collected in the field go in Section III and those written by "issues" singers, like the Carawans, or collected from written sources for use in sing-a-longs, belong here. A few might arguably belong in either location.

Bluegrass

804. ADLER, Thomas. "The Ballad in Bluegrass Music." Folklore Forum 7-1 (Jan. 1974): 3-47.

After a brief history of bluegrass, the author focuses on the use of traditional ballads in bluegrass music. The methodology is explained, followed by a list of 32 ballads, with their texts and relationships to previously known sources.

805. ADLER, Thomas A. "Manual Formulaic Composition: Innovation in Bluegrass Banjo Styles." Journal of Country Music 5-2 (Summer, 1974): 55-64. Reprinted in Banjo Newsletter 2-12 (October 1975): 4-8.

Discusses three types of picking: 1) Scruggs style, 2) chromatic, and 3) blues chromatic. Analysis in terms of functional and stereotypical formulas, with examples in both staff notation and tablature.

806. ARTIS, Bob. Bluegrass [From the Lonesome Wail of a Mountain Love Song to the Hammering Drive of the Scruggs-style Banjo, the Story of an American Musical Tradition]. New York: Hawthorn Books, 1975. 182 pp.

Relatively light history based around groups, both traditional and "newgrass," and the spread of the genre. There is also an appendix of bluegrass radio stations.

807. BAILEY, Mike. The Bluegrass Directory. Chattanooga: By the Author, 4005 Lara Lane, [37416], 1977.

808. BARTENSTEIN, Fred. "The Audience for Bluegrass: Muleskinner News Reader Survey." Journal of Country Music 4-3 (Fall, 1973): 74-105.

Scientific review of results of a ten-page questionnaire sent to some 304 readers, with 249 returned. Describes a cross section of people who enjoy bluegrass.

809. BASSHAM, Olan. Lester Flatt, Baron of Bluegrass. Summitville, Tenn., 1980. 44 pp.

Popular, illustrated biography of Flatt, one of the "founders" of bluegrass.

810. BRISLIN, Richard. "Old-Timey, Bluegrass, and Early Country and Western Music: a Selected Bibliography of Recent and Current Song Books." Washington, D.C.: Library of Congress, Archive of Folk Culture, 1979. 4 pp. (36 items)

811. CANTWELL, Robert. Bluegrass Breakdown: the Making of the Old Southern Sound. Urbana: University of Illinois Press, 1984. 309 pp.

Broad, non-technical study of how bluegrass results from the coming together of African and European traditions, its relationships to hillbilly, country, minstrel, folk revival, and jazz. Essentially a critical essay rather than a history.

812. CANTWELL, Robert. "Ten Thousand Acres of Bluegrass: Mimesis in Bill Monroe's Music." Journal of Popular Culture 13-2 (Fall, 1979): 209-20.

Concerned with the meaning of bluegrass and how it bridges the gap between the popular audience and the traditional string band.

813. CARNEY, George O. "Bluegrass Grows All 'Around: the Spatial Dimensions of a Country Music Style." Journal of Geography 73-4 (April 1974): 34-55.

Unusual study of musical geography, using maps to pinpoint the origin of bluegrass, its movement around the country, where it is performed live, and the steady increase in festivals. Also discusses place names in songs.

814. CLARKSON, Atelia, and MONTELL, W. Lynwood. "Letters to a
      Bluegrass DJ: Social Documents of Southern White Migrants
      in Southeastern Michigan 1964-74." Southern Folklore
      Quarterly 39-3 (Sept. 1975): 219-31.

      Based on eight A & P grocery sacks of letters received at
WNRS/WNRZ (Ann Arbor and Saline, Michigan) in response to a four-
hour bluegrass show, this article describes the musical tastes of
rural, white migrants in the urban north, with many excerpts.

815. DEAKINS, Betty. Bluegrass Directory: 1985-86. Murphys,
      Calif.: BD Products, 1986. 216 pp.

      Although "bluegrass" here denotes the genre in the
broadest sense, this useful reference tool lists 650 stores,
instrument makers and repairers, teachers, and organizations. The
second half of the work is a classified list of instruments, with
dealers, makers, and repairers, etc. under each heading, and lists
of instruction books, records, and other items of interest.

816. GREEN, James D., Jr. "A Musical Analysis of the Banjo
      Style of Earl Scruggs: an Examination of Country Music
      (Mercury [phonodisc] MG 20358." Journal of Country Music
      5-1 (Spring, 1974): 31-7.

      The recording in question, issued in the mid 1950's, is
one of the group's earliest. Brief but valuable analysis with
detailed transcriptions of melody, harmony, rhythm, and form.

817. HELT, Richard C. "A German Bluegrass Festival: the
      'Country-Boom' and some Notes on the History of American
      Popular Music in West Germany." Journal of Popular
      Culture 10-4 (Spring, 1977): 821-32.

      A history of German and European fascination with American
jazz, rock, country-western, and especially bluegrass.

818. HICKERSON, Joseph C. (Rev. by MacLEISH, Morellen, and SELBY,
      Hilary A.). "Bluegrass Music: a Select Bibliography."
      Washington, D.C.: Library of Congress, Archive of Folk
      Culture, 1977. 7 pp.

819. HILL, Fred. Grass Roots: Illustrated History of Bluegrass and Mountain Music. Rutland: Academy Books, 1980. 121 pp.

Lightweight illustrated history of bluegrass.

820. KOCHMAN, Marilyn, ed. The Big Book of Bluegrass: the Artists, the History, the Music. New York: Quill, 1984. 277 pp.

Illustrated, personality oriented history with instructions on how to play the five-string banjo, mandolin, guitar, fiddle, and dobro, plus list of instrument builders and a number of songs.

821. MARSHALL, Howard Wight. "'Keep on the Sunny Side of Life': Pattern and Religious Expression in Bluegrass Gospel Music." New York Folklore Quarterly 30-1 (March 1974): 3-43.

This article examines the historical climate and cultural and musical environments basic to an understanding of American evangelistic Protestant religion within which bluegrass gospel music thrives. The author also uses five familiar song texts to construct a pattern of commonplace themes which recur.

822. MARSHALL, Howard Wight. "'Open up them Pearly Gates': Pattern and Religious Expression in Bluegrass Gospel Music." Folklore Forum 4-5 (Sept. 1971): 92-112.

Studies how American evangelistic Protestantism relates to bluegrass gospel music based around five basic themes. There is also an alphabetical list of bluegrass gospel songs keyed to the five themes and a concordance of scriptural passages.

823. PRICE, Steven D. Old as the Hills: the Story of Bluegrass Music. New York: Viking Press, 1975. 110 pp.

After a general introduction, a lightweight history of bluegrass organized by groups.

824. ROSENBERG, Neil, comp. Bill Monroe and His Blue Grass Boys: an Illistrated Discography. Nashville: Country Music Foundation Press, 1974. 122 pp.

825. ROSENBERG, Neil V. Bluegrass: a History. Urbana and
     Chicago: University of Illinois Press, 1985. 447 pp.

    By far the best researched, most scholarly and complete
study of bluegrass, lavishly illustrated, but non-technical with
no musical examples. Chronological history from hillbilly origins
to Bill Monroe from 1938 onwards including chapters on the genre,
involvement with the folk revival, festivals, religion,
recordings, "newgrass," and the situation today. Massive
bibliography (pp. 377-405) and discography (pp. 406-20). In
addition, interviews, and song title index.

826. ROSENBERG, Neil V. "From Sound to Style: the Emergence of
     Bluegrass." Journal of American Folklore 80-316 (Apr.-
     June 1967): 143-50. Reprinted in GENTRY, Linnell. A
     History and Encyclopedia of Country, Western, and Gospel
     Music, 2nd ed. Nashville: Clairmont Corp., 1969, pp.
     309-18.

    Describes and evaluates the emergence of bluegrass as a
distinctive type of commerical country music.

827. RUTHERFORD, Doug. "A Partially Annotated Bibliography and
     Discography of the Bluegrass Music of Bill Monroe and His
     Blue Grass Boys, and Lester Flatt and Earl Scruggs and
     the Foggy Mountain Boys." Seattle Folklore Society
     Journal 5-2 (Dec. 1973): 14-24.

828. SCRUGGS, Earl. Earl Scruggs and the Five-String Banjo.
     New York: Peer International Corp., 1968. 156 pp.

    A cross between an autobiography and a self-instruction
book, for pp. 80-129 include songs and pp. 130-44 instruct on
building a banjo. Lastly, pp. 147-56 provide a bibliography.

829. SMITH, L. Mayne. "An Introduction to Bluegrass." Journal
     of American Folklore 78-309 (July-Sept., 1965): 245-56.

    Description of the most important musical and behavior
phenomena associated with bluegrass, including its stylistic
derivation and physical-cultural context.

830. WERNICK, Peter. Bluegrass Songbook. New York: Oak, 1976.
128 pp.

Over 130 old-time, traditional, "newgrass," gospel, and novelty bluegrass tunes presented in a new tablature for guitar or banjo, plus tips from the great players.

Country and Western Music

831. ALBERT, George, and HOFFMAN, Frank. The Cash Box Country Singles Charts, 1958-1982. Metuchen, N.J.: The Scarecrow Press, 1984. 596 pp.

A reference work listing all country music recordings listed in the Cash Box weekly charts during the years indicated. These varied from 20 listings when it began to 100 per week in the later years. The material is listed alphabetically, first by the artist's name, then by titles. Additional information is given.

832. ATKINS, John. The Carter Family. London: Old Time Music Booklet #1, 1973. 63 pp.

833. AVERILL, Patricia. "Folk and Popular Elements in Modern Country Music." Journal of Country Music 5-2 (Summer, 1974): 43-54.

Defines country music as vocal, male, accompanied by guitar. Asserting that it is neither folk nor popular, the author shows that it has traits of both and includes a list of them.

834. BARTHEL, Norma. Ernest Tubb Discography (1936-1969). Roland, Okla.: Norma Barthel, 1970. 36 pp.

835. BARTHEL, Norma. Ernest Tubb, the Original E. T. Roland, Okla.: Country Roads, 1984. 97 pp.

Ernest Tubb (b. 1914) is a well known country singer.

836. BRONNER, Simon J. "'I Kicked Three Slats Out of my Cradle First Time I heard That': Ken Kane, Country Music, and American Folklife." New York Folklore 3-1/4 (Summer-Winter, 1977): 53-82.

171

A case study of an old country musician from Hartwick, New York, with excerpts from interviews, his biography, career, and context. Also mentions other musicians of the group. Includes a number of photos.

837. BUSNAR, Gene. Superstars of Country Music. New York: Julian Messner, 1984. 239 pp.

Popularized collection of biographies aimed at high school age readers, focusing on the big names: e.g., Hank Williams, Willie Nelson, Charlie Pride, Dolly Parton, etc.

838. CARR, Patrick, and Editors of Country Music Magazine. The Illustrated History of Country Music. Garden City, N.Y.: Doubleday, 1979. 359 pp.

Traces history from folk origins to the studios, and to a multi-billion dollar industry, organized by genre. Many photos.

839. CASH, Johnny. Man in Black. Grand Rapids, Mich.: Zondervan, 1975. 244 pp.

An autobiography.

840. CHRISTIE, Keith G. Carter Family Discography. Nashville: Record's Associates, 1963. 28 pp.

841. COBB, James C. "From Muskogee to Luckenbach: Country Music and the 'Southernization' of America." Journal of Popular Culture 16-3 (Winter, 1982): 81-91.

A study that documents a change of attitude towards the South as seen in country music, comparing Merle Haggard's "Okie from Muskogee," which is seen as negative, to Waylon Jennings' "Luckenbach, Texas," which was seen as positive; they symbolize the change that took place.

842. COGSWELL, Robert. "Commercial Hillbilly Lyrics and the Folk Tradition." Journal of Country Music 3-3/4 (Fall-Winter, 1972-3): 65-106.

A study of the lyrics of hillbilly music, its general relationship to Anglo-American folk traditions, and an analysis of the elements thought typical of traditional art.

843. COHEN, Norm. "An Annotated Checklist of Published Hillbilly Discographies." JEMF Quarterly 3-1, no. 7 (Sept. 1967): 29-30; 3-2, no. 8 (Dec. 1967): 59-65; 4-1, no. 9 (March 1968): 28.

844. COHEN, Norman. "Computerized Hillbilly Discography: the Gennett Project." Western Folklore 30-3 (July 1971): 182-93.

Review of literature and assertion that compiling hillbilly discographies is both difficult and important. Introduction to project with Gennett records.

845. COHEN, Norman. "The Skillet Lickers: a Study of a Hillbilly String Band and its Repertoire." Journal of American Folklore 78-309 (July-Sept. 1965): 229-44.

Case study of one band, the Skillet Lickers who flourished in north Georgia in the 1920s and 1930s, and the development of hillbilly music generally.

846. CRUMP, George A. Write it Down: a History of Country Music in Hampton Roads. Norfolk: Donning, 1985. 142 pp.

847. CUMMINGS, Don G. Birth of Grand Ole Opry. Nashville: D. G. Cummings, 1964.

848. DANKER, Frederick E. "The Repertory and Style of a Country Singer: Johnny Cash." Journal of American Folklore 85-338 (Oct.-Dec. 1972): 309-29.

Describes performance style and organizes repertory by type, but provides no musical examples.

849. DELMORE, Alton. Truth is Stranger than Publicity: Alton Delmore's Autobiography. Nashville: Country Music Foundation Press, 1977. 188 pp.

Autobiography edited and introduced by Charles K. WOLFE. Includes a discography.

850. DENISOFF, R. Serge. _Waylon: a Biography_. Knoxville: University of Tennessee Press, 1983; reprint ed., New York: St. Martin's Press, 1984. 368 pp.

Concerns both the past 25 years of country music history, and especially the career of "outlaw" singer, Waylon Jennings, who cultivated an anti-Nashville-establishment image with aspects drawn from rock music culture. Includes an extensive discography for 1959-81 compiled by John L. Smith.

851. FABER, Charles F. _The Country Music Almanac, Volume One-- 1922-1943_. Lexington, Ken.: By the author, 3569 Cornwall Drive [40503], 1978. 106 pp.

Resource devoted to facts: a chronology of the 500 best recordings from the period, important performers, list of top songs, songwriters, members of groups, and other details.

852. GAILLARD, Frize. _Watermelon Wine: the Spirit of Country Music_. New York: St. Martin's Press, 1978. 236 pp.

Historical study that treats in chapters 1-3 the estrangement of country music from traditional music, and follows with a description of change in country music.

853. GENTRY, Linnell. _A History and Encyclopedia of Country, Western, and Gospel Music_. Nashville: Clairmont Corp., 1961; reprint ed., St. Clair Shores, Mich.: Scholarly Press, 1972. 380 pp.; 2nd ed., Nashville: Clairmont Corp., 1969. 598 pp.

Valuable resource which includes reprints of articles published between 1908 and 1968 (in 2nd edition, pp. 1-357) and biographies on pp. 358 to the end.

854. GREEN, Archie. "The Carter Family's 'Coal Miner's Blues'." _Southern Folklore Quarterly_ 25-4 (Dec. 1961): 226-37.

While this is a study of how the Carters came to sing white blues so early on, and focuses on one song in particular, it also serves as an obituary, biography, and discography for A. P. Carter, who had died one year earlier, in 1960.

855. GREEN, Archie. "Hillbilly Music: Source and Symbol." Journal of American Folklore 78-309 (July-Sept. 1965): 204-28.

    Concerned with the etymology of the word "hillbilly," the stereotypes, why this pejorative-humorous term was extended to traditional folk music, and what is hillbilly music. One of the most important articles listed here.

856. GREEN, Douglas B. Country Roots: the Origins of Country Music. New York: Hawthorn, 1976. 238 pp.

    An attempt at popularized history, but more illustrations than text with an 1877-1975 chronology on pp. 199-212.

857. GREENWAY, John. "Jimmie Rodgers--a Folksong Catalyst." Journal of American Folklore 70-277 (July-Sept. 1957): 231-34.

    Discussion of how Rodgers' songs came to be thought of as "folk" and represented as such. Also relationship to black song.

858. HAY, George D. A Story of the Grand Ole Opry. Nashville: George D. Hay, 1953. 62 pp.

    Light history of the radio program that made country music famous, written by an insider.

859. HURST, Jack. Nashville's Grand Ole Opry. New York: Harry N. Abrams, 1975. 404 pp.

    Useful but light book introduced by Roy Acuff, containing many color and black & white photos and some good material on history. Otherwise, in the "coffee table book" tradition.

860. JONES, Louis M. "Grandpa," with WOLFE, Charles K. Everybody's Grandpa: Fifty Years Behind the Mike. Knoxville: University of Tennessee Press, 1984. 288 pp.

The life of a country performer, with collection of 65 photos, many poems and songs, written by an insider and edited by the nation's leading authority on country music.

861.   KAHN, Ed. "Hillbilly Music: Source and Resource." _Journal of American Folklore_ 78-309 (July-Sept. 1965): 257-66.

Discusses the importance of the phonograph and how early recorded materials are an important resource, but asserts that there has been little work in the area.

862.   KRISHEF, Robert K. _The Grand Ole Opry_. Minneapolis: Lerner Publications, 1978.   71 pp.

Traces the origins and history of Grand Ole Opry and discusses the stars, locations, and the growth of country music.

863.   McCULLOH, Judith. "Hillbilly Records and Tune Transcriptions." _Western Folklore_ 26-4 (Oct. 1967): 225-44.

Asserting that commercial recordings of hillbilly music remained a neglected musical resource for both folklorists and ethnomusicologists, the author argues for their importance, especially as a source for transcriptions; cites examples.

864.   McCULLOH, Judith. "Some Child Ballads on Hillbilly Records." In _Folklore_ and _Society: Essays in Honor of Ben A. Botkin_, pp. 107-29.   Edited by Bruce Jackson. Hatboro, Pa.: Folklore Associates, 1966.

Transcriptions of eight hillbilly recordings of six Child ballads and a discussion of the problems raised by them.

865.   MALONE, Bill C. _Country Music, USA_. Memoir Series of the American Folklore Society #54.   Austin: University of Texas Press, 1968, 422 pp.; rev. ed., 1985, 562 pp.

Non-technical but scholarly study derived from the author's doctoral dissertation of the origins, early commercial success, and influence of country music on popular music.   Included are studies of important individuals and groups, from the Carter Family to Johnny Cash, and many more.

866. MALONE, Bill C. "Elvis, Country Music, and the South."
      Southern Quarterly 18-1 (Fall, 1979): 123-34.

      An exploration of the alleged roots that Elvis Presley
had in country music.

867. MALONE, Bill C. "From Folk to Hillbilly to Country: the
      Coming of Age of America's Rural Music." In Observations
      and Reflections on Texas Folklore, pp. 101-16. Edited by
      Francis E. Abernethy. Publications of the Texas Folklore
      Society #37. Austin: Encino Press, 1972.

      Study which puts the changes in country music from
tradition to commercialization to the establishment of an industry,
into perspective, with photos and drawings.

868. MALONE, Billy Charles. "A History of Commercial Country
      Music in the United States, 1920-1964." Ph.D. disser-
      tation, University of Texas at Austin, 1965. 515 pp.

      Traces how country music became both national and
commercial in the 1920s, how it absorbed non-white and non-country
influences, the "singing cowboys," and finally submits that country
music reflects the changes in society which produced it.

869. MALONE, Bill C. "Radio and Personal Appearances: Sources
      and Resources." Western Folklore 30-3 (July 1971):
      215-25.

      Asserting that recordings of country music give a one-
sided view of the genre, the author offers a study of context and
interaction in both radio and personal appearance formats. He also
provides a brief history of the use of country music in
advertising, medicine shows, and other such venues.

870. MALONE, Bill C., and McCULLOH, Judith, eds. Stars of
      Country Music: Uncle Dave Macon to Johnny Rodriguez.
      Urbana: University of Illinois Press, 1975; reprint ed.,
      New York: Avon Books, 1976. 488 pp.

      Surveys the lives and careers of 19 stars including the
Carter Family, Jimmie Rodgers, Bob Wills, Bill Monroe, etc. There
are also chapters on the early pioneers as well as country-western
since World War II.

871. MOORE, Thurston, ed. A Pictorial History of Country Music. 4 vols. Denver: Heather, 1969. [Vol. 1 is Pt. 6 of 1965 Who's Who in Country Music (Denver: Heather, 1965); Vol. 2 is Pt. 8 of 1966 Who's Who in Country Music (Denver: Heather, 1966); Vol. 3 is Pt. 7 of 1970 Who's Who in Country Music (New York: Record World, 1970); Vol. 4 is pp. G21-H64 in 1972 Who's Who in Country Music (Nashville: Record World, 1972). Vols. 1-2 also published separately.]

872. OERMANN, Robert K. The Listener's Guide to Country Music. New York: Facts on File, 1983. 137 pp.

Broad and light, covering old-time music, bluegrass, western swing, Cajun, country-rock, and others.

873. ORGILL, Michael. Anchored in Love: the Carter Family Story. Old Tappan, N.J.: Fleming H. Revell Co., 1975. 192 pp.

874. OTTO, John S., and BURNS, Augustus M. "Black and White Cultural Interaction in the Early Twentieth Century South: Race and Hillbilly Music." Phylon 35-4 (1974): 407-17.

Details one aspect of the acculturation process between Euro-American and Afro-American musics, where and how contacts took place, and asserts that musical interchange was easier than other kinds. Based on both primary and secondary sources.

875. PORTERFIELD, Nolan. Jimmie Rodgers: the Life and Times of America's Blue Yodeler. Urbana: University of Illinois Press, 1979. 512 pp.

Thorough study of one of country's greatest singers from the 1920s and 1930s, with bibliography and discography.

876. POULIOT, Les, and CHERRY, Hugh, eds. J. Thayer and Don Bruce Together Present the History of Country Music: a 36-Hour Radio Documentary. Memphis: J. Thayer and Don Bruce Together, 1970. 915 pp.

A vast collection of radio scripts.

877. PRICE, Steven D. Take Me Home: the Rise of Country and
      Western Music. New York: Praeger, 1974. 184 pp.

      Although the purpose is to provide a comprehensive
history of country music from its Anglo-American roots to the
present, the coverage is light and popular.

878. RODGERS, Carrie Cecil Williamson (Mrs. Jimmie). My Husband
      Jimmie Rodgers. San Antonio: Southern Literary
      Institute, 1935; reprint ed., Nashville: Country Music
      Foundation Press, 1975. 264 pp.

      The life of the singing brakeman and his courageous fight
against tuberculosis.

879. RODGERS, Jimmie. The Legendary Jimmie Rodgers Memorial
      Folio. 2 vols. New York: Peer International, 1967.

880. ROGERS, Jimmie N. The Country Music Message. Englewood
      Cliffs, N.J.: Prentice-Hall, 1983. 182 pp.

      Written by a professor of communication with a prophetic
name, this text-based study is concerned with the contents of
country songs, not its history or stars.

881. RORRER, Clifford Kinney. "Charlie Poole and the North
      Carolina Ramblers." Eden, N.C.: Tar Heel Printing, 1968.
      22 pp.

882. SHELDON, Ruth (Knowles). Hubbin' It: the Life of Bob
      Wills. Kingsport, Tenn.: Kingsport Press, 1938. 147 pp.

      Biography of one of the great early singers. May be
catalogued under KNOWLES.

883. SHELTON, Robert, and GOLDBLATT, Burt. The Country Music
      Story: a Picture History. Indianapolis: Bobbs-Merrill,
      1966; reprint ed., New Rochelle, N.Y.: Arlington House,
      1971. 256 pp.

      Popular history with many photos, including material on
the early history of country music.

884. SHESTACK, Melvin. _The Country Music Encyclopedia_. New
York: Thomas Y. Crowell, 1974. 410 pp.

Useful but popular type resource, organized from A to Z,
mostly on names. Includes a discography (pp. 325-75), list of
country radio stations in the United States, Canada, and Puerto
Rico (!), and a sampling of songs with words and chord symbols.

885. SHIELD, Renee Rose. "Country Corn: Performance in
Context." In _The Ethnography of Musical Performance_, pp.
105-22. Edited by Norma McLeod and Marcia Herndon.
Norwood, Pa.: Norwood Editions, 1980.

In order to illustrate some theoretical aspects of the
phenomenon of performance, this is a case study of dance events
with country music in an old-fashioned store in Helotes, Texas.

886. SIMIC, Andrei. "Country 'N' Western Yugoslav Style:
Contemporary Folk Music as a Mirror of Social Sentiment."
Journal of Popular Culture 10-1 (Summer, 1976): 156-66.

Not at all about country music in Yugoslavia but a
comparison of genres there which the author feels are parallel in
function to country music in the United States.

887. "Special Issue: Country Music: Tradition and the Individual
Talent." _Southern Quarterly_ 22-3 (Spring, 1984): 3-173.

Collection of 12 articles: "Introduction: We Were Country"
(Mark Royden Winchell), "Country Music Discography: Esoteric Art
and Humanistic Craft" (Nolan Porterfield), "A Brief History of
Western Swing" (Charles R. Townsend), "The Sons of the Pioneers"
(Douglas B. Green), "Bluegrass, Rock and Roll, and 'Blue Moon of
Kentucky'" (Neil V. Rosenberg), "Hillbilly Hipsters of the 1950s:
the Romance of Rockabilly" (Patrick B. Mullen), "Progressive
Country Music, 1972-1976: its Impact and Creative Highlights"
(Stephen R. Tucker), "Hollywood Barn Dance: a Brief Survey of
Country Music in Films" (Wade Austin), "Mother, Sister, Sweetheart,
Pal: Women in Old-Time Country Music" (Robert K. Oermann), "The
Feminist Sensibility in Post-War Country Music" (Mary Bufwack),
"Homemade Soap: the Sudsy Autobios of the Linsey Crowd" (Jac L.
Tharpe).

888. STAMBLER, Irwin, and LANDON, Grelun. Encyclopedia of Folk, Country and Western Music. New York: St. Martin's Press, 1969, 1982. 396 pp.; new ed., 1984. 902 pp.

A gold mine of information, mainly on names, contained in short entries focused around Country-western music.

889. STAMBLER, Irwin, and LANDON, Grelun. Golden Guitars: the Story of Country Music. New York: Four Winds Press, 1971. 186 pp.

Popular illustrated history of Country music, with focus on Nashville. Includes "Bluegrass Breakthrough," pp. 84-99.

890. STRIBLING, Cynthia D. "Black and White Elements in the Music of Jimmie Rodgers." Mississippi Folklore Register 101- (Spring, 1976): 41-53.

891. TASSIN, Myron, and HENDERSON, Jerry. Fifty Years at the Grand Ole Opry. Gretna, La.: Pelican, 1975; reprint ed., New York: Harcourt Brace, 1978. 112 pp.

Pictorial history of the Grand Ole Opry, the Nashville radio program.

892. TONACHEL, Ruth. "Country Music Before World War Two: a Selected Bibliography." Washington, D.C.: Library of Congress, Archive of Folk Song, 1978. 14 pp.

Lists 137 items and 3 journals.

893. TOSCHES, Nick. Country: the Biggest Music in America. New York: Stein and Day, 1977. 258 pp.

Colorful, non-scholarly book by free-lance writer on country, blues, and rock as well as the music industry. More a social history, but chocked full of details.

894. TOWNSEND, Charles. San Antonio Rose: the Life and Music of Bob Wills. Urbana: University of Illinois Press, 1976. 395 pp.

Biography of one of country's great stars.   Includes a
discography and filmography by Bob Pinson.

895.   TRIBE, Ivan M. Mountaineer Jamboree: Country Music in
       West Virginia. Lexington: University Press of Kentucky,
       1984.   256 pp.

A study of country music radio programming from 1926-
1950s in West Virginia, focusing on Wheeling's WMVA Jamboree,
which started in 1933, how it spawned more stations, and how
Nashville took over in the 1960s.

896.   TUCKER, Stephen R. "Pentecostalism and Popular Culture in
       the South: a Study of Four Musicians." Journal of Popular
       Culture 16-3 (Winter, 1982): 68-80.

A study of how religion has played an important role in
the lives of James Blackwood, Johnny Cash, Tammy Wynette, and Jerry
Lee Lewis.

897.   WILGUS, D. K. "Country-Western Music and the Urban
       Hillbilly." Journal of American Folklore 83-328 (April-
       June 1970): 157-84; reprinted in The Urban Experience
       and the Folk Tradition, pp. 137-64. Edited by Americo
       Paredes and Ellen J. Stekert. Austin: University of
       Texas Press, 1971.

A study of the development of folk music, urbanization,
and country music as an expression, with commentary and
discography by Judith McCulloh.

898.   WILGUS, D. K. "Current Hillbilly Recordings: a Review
       Article." Journal of American Folklore 78-309 (July-
       Sept. 1965): 267-86; reprinted in GENTRY, Linnell, A
       History and Encyclopedia of Country, Western, and Gospel
       Music, 2nd ed., pp. 168-91 (see #853f.

Attempt to deal with a backlog of 265 records sent to the
journal, but they illustrate the important developments going on.

899.   WILGUS, D. K. "An Introduction to the Study of Hillbilly
       Music." Journal of American Folklore 78-309 (July-Sept.
       1965): 195-203; reprinted in GENTRY, Linnell, A History

and Encyclopedia of Country, Western, and Gospel Music,
2nd ed., pp. 214-33 (see #853).

After refuting earlier and incorrect accounts, the author
explains what hillbilly music is and where it came from. An
important article for its clear definitions.

900. WILLIAMS, Roger M. Sing a Sad Song: the Life of Hank
     Williams. Garden City, N.Y.: Doubleday, 1970; 2nd ed.,
     Urbana: University of Illinois Press, 1981. 324 pp.

Biography of a great singer plus a comprehensive
discography by Bob Pinson.

901. WILLOUGHBY, Larry. Texas Rhythm, Texas Rhyme: a Pictorial
     History of Texas Music. Austin: Texas Monthly Press,
     1984. 144 pp.

Wide ranging study, generously illustrated, on nineteenth
century traditions, early country, singing cowboys, country blues,
western swing, jazz, rhythm 'n' blues, rock 'n' roll, country, and
the Austin legacy. Much information, though non-scholarly.

902. WOLFE, Charles K. The Grand Ole Opry: the Early Years,
     1925-35. Old Time Music Booklet #2. London: Old Time
     Music, 1975. 128 pp.

903. WOLFE, Charles K. "Nashville and Country Music, 1926-1930:
     Notes on Early Nashville Media and its Response to Old-
     Time Music." Journal of Country Music 4-1 (Spring,
     1973): 2-16.

Asserts that while there has been emphasis on individual
artists and the meanings of their songs, the history of the Grand
Ole Opry radio program in Nashville has been neglected; also an
attempt to account for the rise in popularity of country music.

904. WOLFE, Charles K. Tennessee Strings: the Story of Country
     Music in Tennessee. Knoxville: University of Tennessee
     Press, 1977. 118 pp.

Well researched history from its folk origins to today's
Nashville music industry.

Folksong Revival and Protest

The Folksong Revival

905. ALLEN, R. Raymond. "Old-Time Music and the Urban Folk
     Revival." New York Folklore 7-1/2 (Summer, 1981): 65-82.

   A history of the revival of "old time [instrumental]
music" starting in the late 1950s, this article focuses on fiddle
and banjo, noting personalities and the reasons for the revival.

906. BAYARD, Samuel P. "Decline and 'Revival' of Anglo-American
     Folk Music." In Folklore in Action and Essays for
     Discussion in Honor of MacEdward Leach, pp. 21-29.
     Edited by Horace P. Beck. Bibliographical and Special
     Series, vol. 14. Philadelphia: American Folklore
     Society, 1962; reprint ed., New York: Kraus, 1970.

   What kind of folk music came originally to this country,
how and why it declined, and how it changed in the revival.

907. BELZ, Carl I. "Popular Music and the Folk Tradition."
     Journal of American Folklore 80-316 (Apr.-June 1967):
     130-42.

   Discusses the relationship of folk music to rock 'n' roll
and proposes that the latter has assumed the function and
characteristics of traditional folksong.

908. BOTKIN, Benjamin A. "The Folksong Revival: a Symposium."
     New York Folklore Quarterly 19-2 (June 1963): 83-142.

   Transcript of a meeting moderated by Botkin on March 2,
1963, involving both scholars and performers. They are Willard
Rhodes, Oscar Brand, Mike Seeger, Alan Lomax, Israel Young, Irwin
Silber, Ellen Steckert, Lee Haring, Frank Warner, Ralph Rinzler,
and others. The central topic was culture as seen in folksong,
not the revival per se, but some of its central figures attended.

909. BRAND, Oscar. The Ballad Mongers: Rise of the Modern Folk
     Song. New York: Funk & Wagnalls, 1962; reprint ed.,
     Westport, Conn.: Greenwood, 1979. 240 pp.

Admittedly personal and subjective account by a Canadian writer and singer who describes the history and uses of folksong, its effect on the younger generation, and the main personalities of the folk music revival movement. Also deals with modern folk song industry and its practices.

910. "A Brief List of Material Relating to the Folksong Revival." Washington, D.C.: Library of Congress, Archive of Folk Song, 1969.

112 items, including many of an ephemeral nature, but important for someone thoroughly researching the period.

911. DENISOFF, R. S. "Folk Music and the American Life: a Generational-Ideological Comparison." British Journal of Sociology 20-4 (1969): 427-42.

A study of the sociological origins of folk consciousness in America and the revival of folk music. Also is concerned with the origin of the protest revival and its rejection of folk consciousness from the 1930s to the present.

912. DENISOFF, R. Serge. "Folk-Rock: Folk Music, Protest, or Commercialism?" Journal of Popular Culture 3-2 (Fall, 1969): 214-30.

Defines and traces the history of the relationship of rock and the folksong revival, including protest, and demonstrates how the revival was capitalized on.

913. DETURK, David A., and POULIN, A., Jr., eds. The American Folk Scene: Dimensions of the Folksong Revival. New York: Dell (Laurel), 1967. 334 pp.

Collection of articles by both performers (e.g., Pete Seeger) and scholars (e.g., B. A. Botkin) examining the folksong revival, topical protest songs, Woody Guthrie and his influence on other forms, and commercialism.

914. GRAFMAN, Howard, and MANNING, B. T. Folk Music USA. New York: Citadel, 1962. 144 pp.

Mostly organized as an illustrated (photos) alphabetical list of performers and groups from the folksong revival with brief articles, this popular collection also includes 15 songs (texts, tunes, guitar chords) and two articles: "The American Folk Music Revival" by Pete Seeger and "The Old Town School and Folk Music in Chicago" by Win Stracke.

915. JACKSON, Bruce. "The Folksong Revival." New York Folklore 11-1/4 (1985): 195-204.

Excellent historical introduction to the phenomenon, who was involved, and some of the reasons for it.

916. KNOTT, Sarah Gertrude. "The Folk Festival Movement in America." Southern Folklore Quarterly 17-2 (March 1953): 143-55.

While a number of festivals and their objectives are listed, this study concentrates on the National Folk Festival and describes three stages through which it has passed.

917. LUND, Jens, and DENISOFF, R. Serge. "The Folk Music Revival and the Counter Culture: Contributions and Contradictions." Journal of American Folklore 84-334 (Oct.-Dec. 1971): 394-405.

Historical study of the times which produced the counter culture, especially the beatniks, jazz, folkniks, and the music associated with them.

918. MOLIN, Sven Eric. "Lead Belly, Burl Ives, and Sam Hinton." Journal of American Folklore 71-279 (Jan.-Mar. 1958): 58-65.

As case histories involving social change, this article treats a record by Teresa Brewer, Lead Belly's career, Burl Ives' books and reviews of them, and a public confession by Sam Hinton. Includes replies by D. K. Wilgus, Charles Haywood, M. W. Tillson, and Sam Hinton.

919. MYRUS, Donald. Ballads, Blues, and the Big Beat. New York: Macmillan, 1966. 136 pp.

Lightweight survey organized around a number of personalities, including Dylan, Seeger, Baez, Odetta, as well as folk-
rock, hillbilly, Peter, Paul and Mary, and the folksong revival.

920. OKUN, Milton. Something to Sing About! The Personal
     Choices of America's Folk Singers. New York: Macmillan,
     1968. 241 pp.

     Combination of brief illustrated biographies of folksong
revival singers and songs from the 1950s.

921. PATTERSON, John S. "The Folksong Revival and Some Sources
     of the Popular Image of the Folksinger: 1920-1963." M.A.
     thesis, Indiana University, 1963. 97 pp.

     Although a master's thesis, it is listed because it was
written at the height of the movement and includes an excellent
bibliography (pp. 89-96). Available at Library of Congress.

922. PETERSEN, Karen. "Woman Sings her Song: an Investigation
     into Women-Identified Music." In Women and Music in
     Cross-Cultural Perspective. Edited by Ellen Koskoff.
     Westport, Conn.: Greenwood, at press.

     This article examines music written, produced, performed,
and, for the most part, marketed solely by women. Until now an
almost underground tradition, this music explores various
relationships between women. It also traces the growing involvement of women in all phases of the commercial music industry.

923. SCHMIDT, Eric von, and ROONEY, Jim. Baby, Let Me Follow
     You Down: the Illustrated Story of the Cambridge Folk
     Years. Garden City, N.Y.: Anchor, 1979. 315 pp.

     An illustrated history of the folk scene beginning in the
late 1950s in Cambridge and its movement throughout the U.S.

924. SHELTON, Robert. The Face of Folk Music. New York:
     Citadel, 1968. 372 pp.

     Memory book of the American folksong revival and its
origins, from blacks in Alabama to Joan Baez. Includes the
revival, blues, and protest. Photos by David Gahr.

925. SHEPARD, Sam. Rolling Thunder Logbook. New York: Viking, 1977. 184 pp.

Popular account of how Bob Dylan and Sam Shepard linked up to do a tour which was filmed as The Rolling Thunder Revue.

926. STEKERT, Ellen J. "Cents and Nonsense in the Urban Folksong Movement: 1930-1966." In Folklore and Society: Essays in Honor of Ben A. Botkin, pp. 153-68. Edited by Bruce Jackson. Hatboro, Pa.: Folklore Associates, 1966.

Traces the history of the folksong revival into popular culture, how it caught on and became lucrative. Also deals with use in protest, especially with Guthrie.

927. VASSAL, Jacques. Electric Children: Roots and Branches of Modern Folkrock. Translated by Paul Barnett. New York: Taplinger, 1976. 270 pp.

Originally published in France in 1971, this work discusses the influences on rock of blacks, Indians, whites, Guthrie and the urban folksong revival, Dylan, and the British.

The Advocacy of Social Change Through Folksong

928. DENISOFF, R. Serge. Great Day Coming: Folk Music and the American Left. Urbana: University of Illinois Press, 1971. 219 pp.

Scholarly study of the folksong revival and its political uses, the folk consciousness movement, People's Songs, Inc., and People's Artists, Inc. Also deals with ideology and includes an excellent discography.

929. DENISOFF, R. Serge. "Protest Movements: Class Consciousness and the Propaganda Song." Sociological Quarterly 9-2 (Spring, 1968): 228-47.

Important study which examines the relationship of propaganda songs to social movements, including the history of the phenomenon in the United States, the philosophical (and Marxist) foundations, and the important themes.

930. DENISOFF, R. Serge. "The Religious Roots of the American Song of Persuasion." Western Folklore 29-3 (July 1970): 175-84.

In this historical study, the author shows how both the contexts and the types of songs were similar in both religious revivals and social change movements.

931. DENISOFF, R. Serge. Sing a Song of Social Significance. Bowling Green, Oh.: Bowling Green University Popular Press, 1972, 227 pp.; rev. ed., 1983, 255 pp.

Derived from the author's 1968 master's thesis written at San Francisco State University, this is a well-documented history of protest song, from its origins and meanings in the American context to its influence and reactions. A history of texts, context, and history, not music per se.

932. DENISOFF, R. Serge. "Songs of Persuasion: a Sociological Analysis of Urban Propaganda." Journal of American Folklore 79-314 (Oct.-Dec., 1966): 581-89.

Probing article which analyzes the role of song in groups, movements, community, and society at large.

933. DENISOFF, R. Serge. Songs of Protest, War & Peace: a Bibliography & Discography. Santa Barbara, Calif.: ABC-Clio, 1973. 70 pp.

Published jointly with the California State University Center for the Study of Armament and Disarmament in Los Angeles. An unannotated listing, by category (e.g., books, periodicals, songbooks, communist, radical right, etc.) of items concerning the role of music in American anti-war movements from the Revolutionary War to the present.

934. DENISOFF, R. Serge, and PETERSON, Richard A., eds. The Sounds of Social Change: Studies in Popular Culture. Chicago: Rand McNally, 1972. 332 pp.

Collection of 25 articles in five sections: Music as Protest (3), Music in Social Movements (5), Rock (6), Changing Tastes (4), Music Industry and Epilogue (2). Mostly in the United States.

935. DUNAWAY, David King. "A Selected Bibliography: Protest
Song in the United States." Folklore Forum 10-2 (Fall,
1977): 8-25.

An unannotated list organized into categories, including
much of an emphemeral nature.

936. DUNAWAY, David King. "Unsung Songs of Protest: the
Composers Collective of New York." New York Folklore 5-
1/2 (Summer, 1979): 1-20.

The Composers Collective lasted from 1931-6 and sought
revolution through music and the creation of mass political songs.
Although coming from the extreme left, it represented the
beginning of the folksong revival. This article traces its
history, who was involved, why, what influences were at work, and
provides examples of texts.

937. DUNSON, Josh. Freedom in the Air: Song Movements of the
Sixties. New York: International Publishers, 1965;
reprint ed., Westport, Conn.: Greenwood, 1980. 127 pp.

Traces the history of protest song as it relates to the
civil rights movement, student songs, the growth of periodicals,
and the rise of singer-writers.

938. EWING, George W. The Well-Tempered Lyre: Songs and Verse
of the Temperance Movement. Bicentennial Series in
American Studies. Dallas: Southern Methodist University,
1977). 298 pp.

Well-documented study concerned with the use of songs in
the temperance movement and its songbooks, organized by topic,
with some illustrations of music, but emphasis is on the words.
Excellent bibliography of primary sources.

939. GREENWAY, John. American Folksongs of Protest. New York:
A. S. Barnes, 1960; reprint ed., New York: Octagon, 1970.
348 pp.

Derived from the author's dissertation entitled "American
Folksongs of Social and Economic Protest," University of
Pennsylvania, 1953, 348 pp. Treats songs of Afro-Americans,
textile workers, miners, migrant workers, farmers, and laborers.

Also includes chapter on "The Song Maker," which concerns Woody Guthrie, Joe Glazer, and others.

940. HALL, Covington. Battle Hymns of Toil. Oklahoma City: General Welfare Reporter, n.d. [1930s]. 119 pp.

941. HAMPTON, Wayne. Guerrilla Minstrels. Knoxville: University of Tennessee Press, 1986. 320 pp.

Organized around key personalities who typify an era, this history of protest song from World War I to the 1960s concentrates on John Lennon, Joe Hill, Woody Guthrie, and Bob Dylan. It shows how these musicians were part of a strategy whose goals included social harmony and the achievement of Utopian ideals. Available, August 1986.

942. REAGON, Bernice Johnson. "Songs of the Civil Rights Movement, 1955-65: a Study in Culture History." Ph.D. dissertation, Howard University, 1975. 235 pp.

The author divides songs into two categories: freedom songs composed by professional songwriters, and topical songs created by protesting groups. Provides insights into the motivations and aspirations of the groups.

943. REUSS, Richard A. "American Folksongs and Left-Wing Politics." Journal of the Folklore Institute 12-2/3 (1975): 89-111.

A history of the tension between the right, fearful of communism, and a denial of Communist Party involvement and leftist ideological influence in American folksongs during the period 1935-56, including those of Woody Guthrie. Includes a diagram showing the relationship of the Communist Party Folk Music Club to the party itself.

944. REUSS, Richard A. "The Roots of American Left-wing Interest in Folksong." Labor History 12-2 (Spring, 1971): 259-79.

Traces the history of protest folksong from its use by the Communist Party and the Socialists in the 1930s.

945. RODNITZKY, Jerome L. "The Decline of Contemporary Protest
     Music." Popular Culture and Society 1-1 (Fall, 1971):
     44-50.

     Traces the decline of protest song during the period
1965-1970 and offers reasons.

946. RODNITZKY, Jerome L. "The Evolution of the American
     Protest Song." Journal of Popular Culture 3-1 (Summer,
     1969): 35-45.

     An historical study from the turn of the century until
the present, with emphasis on the latter.

947. RODNITZKY, Jerome L. Minstrels of the Dawn: the Folk-
     Protest Singer as a Cultural Hero. Chicago: Nelson-Hall,
     1976. 192 pp.

     A social history of how folk revival and protest songs
came together and emphasis on the personalities involved, e.g.,
Guthrie, Seeger, Baez, Ochs, and Dylan.

948. ROSEN, David M. Protest Songs in America. Westlake
     Village, Calif.: Aware, 1972. 159 pp.

     Text study by a journalist surveying protest songs from
anti-British examples to the present.

949. SPECTOR, Bert. "The Weavers: a Case History in Show
     Blacklisting." Journal of American Culture 5-3 (Fall,
     1982): 113-20.

     The Weavers, which formed in 1948, included Pete Seeger
and Lee Hays. When the group began recording in 1950 an anti-
communist hysteria was sweeping the country. Because Seeger and
Hays had been identified with communist movements and sentiments
earlier, the group was blacklisted, and according to the author,
because of a few zealots, not because of mass feeling.

950. TRUZZI, Marcello. "The 100%-American Songbag: Conservative
     Folk Songs in America." Western Folklore 28 (Jan.
     1969): 27-40.

A study of the uses of folksong as propaganda for the conservative political movement.

951. WAFFEN, Les. "The Walls Came Tumbling Down: a Selective Discography of the Civil Rights Movement." Association for Recorded Sound Collections Journal 13-1 (1981): 43-8.

Reviews eight records, mostly issued by Folkways, giving each about one half page of commentary.

Personalities

952. BAEZ, Joan. Daybreak. New York: Dial, 1968. 159 pp.

Autobiography, but rather subjective, based on feelings about various incidents in her life.

953. COHEN, Edwin. "Woody Guthrie and the American Folk Song." Ph.D. dissertation, University of Southern California, 1971. 203 pp.

In order to put Guthrie's contributions in perspective, the author provides a history of folksong in the 1930s and 1940s, then divides Guthrie's songs into three groups: songs for special events and people close to him, protest songs, and songs in praise of the nation.

954. DENISOFF, R. Serge, and FANDRAY, David. "'Hey, Hey Woody Guthrie, I Wrote You a Song': the Political Side of Bob Dylan." Popular Music and Society 5-5 (1977): 31-42.

Traces the political side of protest folk song, with a focus on Dylan and Guthrie.

955. DILLSAVER, Joe Don. "Woody Guthrie's Depression: a Study of Situation." Ph.D. dissertation, University of Missouri-- Columbia, 1975. 153 pp.

Written by a speech-communication major, this text study describes how Guthrie conceived of the Depression and how he communicated it to audiences.

956. DUNAWAY, David King. <u>How</u> <u>Can</u> <u>I</u> <u>Keep</u> <u>from</u> <u>Singing</u>: <u>Peter</u> <u>Seeger</u>. New York: McGraw-Hill, 1981. 386 pp.

Biography of Pete Seeger.

957. ELIOT, Marc. <u>Death</u> <u>of</u> <u>a</u> <u>Rebel</u> <u>Starring</u> <u>Phil</u> <u>Ochs</u> <u>and</u> <u>a</u> <u>Small</u> <u>Circle</u> <u>of</u> <u>Friends</u>. New York: Anchor, 1979. 316 pp.

A biography of a promising protest folksinger who hanged himself on April 9, 1976, written by a professional writer friend. Also translated into French by Jacques Vassal as <u>Phil</u> <u>Ochs,</u> <u>vie</u> <u>et</u> <u>mort</u> <u>d'un</u> <u>rebelle</u> (Paris: Albin Michel, 1979).

958. GROSS, Michael, prod. <u>Bob</u> <u>Dylan:</u> <u>an</u> <u>Illustrated</u> <u>History</u>. New York: Grosset & Dunlap, 1965. 149 pp.

Although primarily a picture history, there is substantial text which explains why and how Dylan became famous.

959. GUTHRIE, Woody. <u>Bound</u> <u>for</u> <u>Glory</u>. Garden City, N.Y.: Doubleday, 1943; reprint ed., New York: E. P. Dutton, 1968, 1976. 430 pp.

Autobiography of America's most famous folksong singer, who lived from 1912 until 1967.

960. HERDMAN, John. <u>Voice</u> <u>Without</u> <u>Restraint:</u> <u>a</u> <u>Study</u> <u>of</u> <u>Bob</u> <u>Dylan's</u> <u>Lyrics</u> <u>and</u> <u>their</u> <u>Background</u>. New York: Delilah, 1981. 164 pp.

A scholarly study of Dylan's songs and their meanings.

961. IVES, Burl. <u>Wayfaring</u> <u>Stranger</u>. New York and Toronto: McGraw-Hill, 1948. 253 pp.

Lightweight autobiography of a well known-folk singer.

962. KLEIN, Joe. <u>Woody</u> <u>Guthrie:</u> <u>a</u> <u>Life</u>. New York: Knopf, 1980; New York: Ballantine, 1982. 475 pp.

The private life of Guthrie, especially his relationships with other people such as Will Geer, Alan Lomax, and the Almanac

Singers as well as his influence on such people as Pete Seeger, Bob
Dylan, and Arlo Guthrie, the latter being Woody Guthrie's son.

963. MARCHBANK, Pearce ("Miles"), ed. Bob Dylan in His Own
Words. New York: Quick Fox, 1978. 127 pp.

A popular illustrated history of Dylan with text mostly
from quotations and song texts.

964. MENIG, Harry. "Woody Guthrie: the Oklahoma Years, 1912-
1929." Chronicles of Oklahoma 53-2 (1975): 239-65.

This study, based on primary sources, details the
influences on Guthrie of his closely-knit family life, his small
town upbringing in Okemah, Oklahoma, his close relationship to the
black community and its influence on him through the blues, and
how he was affected by the Dust Bowl and Great Depression and
their impact on the common people.

965. PERRIS, Arnold. Music as Propaganda: Art to Persuade, Art
to Control. Contributions to the Study of Music and
Dance #8. Westport, Conn.: Greenwood, 1985.

Chapter 8, "The Decade of Protests: Popular Music in the
1960s," pp. 181-205, is a social history of protest music of the
period and the personalities, but it covers rock as well as "folk
revival" material. Discusses particular recordings and songs.

966. PRICE, Dan. "Bibliography of Bob Dylan." Popular Music
and Society 3-3 (1974): 227-41.

Extensive list of articles, books, and recordings.

967. REUSS, Richard A. "Folk Music and Social Conscience: the
Musical Odyssey of Charles Seeger." Western Folklore 38-
4 (Oct. 1979): 221-38.

Biography and career of one of America's most important
musical thinkers, who died February 7, 1979, at the age of 92.
This extensively researched study describes the influences that
shaped the career of composer/scholar Charles Seeger. These
include folk singer Aunt Molly Jackson and painter Thomas Hart
Benton as well as his association with the Marxist Composers

Collection, the Resettlement Administration, and the Federal Music Project of the Works Progress Administration. Seeger was also involved in classical composition and ethnomusicology.

968. REUSS, Richard A. "Woody Guthrie and His Folk Tradition." Journal of American Folklore 83-329 (July-Sept. 1970): 273-303.

The story of Guthrie's importance to folklorists based on his life and career. Also provides sources for his songs.

969. REUSS, Richard A. A Woody Guthrie Bibliography, 1912-1967. New York: Guthrie Children's Trust Fund, 1968. 95 pp.

A total of 501 annotated items published on the life and times of Guthrie, 100 of them by Guthrie, for the period 1912-67, including books, songbooks, newspaper columns, and record notes.

970. ROBBIN, Edward. Woody Guthrie and Me: an Intimate Reminiscence. Berkeley: Lancaster-Miller, 1979. 160 pp.

Personal biography by a close friend.

971. RODNITZKY, J. L. "The Mythology of Woody Guthrie." Popular Music and Society 2-3 (Spring, 1973): 227-43.

An appreciation of Guthrie and how he became a folk hero.

972. SCADUTO, Anthony. Bob Dylan: an Intimate Biography. New York: Grosset & Dunlap, 1971. 280 pp.

The private life of Dylan researched by a New York Post feature writer who interviewed friends and went to Dylan's home town. The manuscript was read and approved by Dylan.

973. SEEGER, Pete. The Incompleat Folksinger. Ed. by Jo Metcalf SCHWARTZ. New York: Simon and Schuster, 1972. 596 pp.

An autobiography with many illustrations, lists of songs, record companies, and folk music films, and information on the influence on Seeger of Guthrie, Jack Elliott, and Leadbelly.

974. SLOMAN, Larry. On the Road with Bob Dylan. New York:
Bantam, 1978. 412 pp.

A popular account of the tour of the Rolling Thunder
Revue in the fall of 1975 when Dylan came out of seclusion.

975. THOMPSON, Toby. Positively Main Street: an Unorthodox View
of Bob Dylan. New York: Coward-McCann, 1971. 188 pp.

A biography of the non-public Dylan, "the human behind
the mask." He was born Bobby Zimmerman and grew up in Hibbing,
Minnesota.

976. YURCHENCO, Henrietta. A Mighty Hard Road: the Woody
Guthrie Story. Assisted by Marjorie GUTHRIE. Intro. by
Arlo GUTHRIE. New York: McGraw-Hill, 1970. 159 pp.

A biography based on Guthrie's life in Oklahoma, Texas,
California, New York, and his last years. Includes photos and
discography, but is overall popular and undocumented.

Song Collections

977. CARAWAN, Guy and Candie. Freedom is a Constant Struggle:
Songs of the Freedom Movement. New York: Oak, 1968.
224 pp.

Tunes and texts for freedom songs since the 1963 civil
rights March on Washington by category, with commentary and photos.

978. CARAWAN, Guy and Candie. Voices from the Mountains. New
York: Knopf, 1975; reprint ed., Urbana: University of
Illinois Press, 1982. 256 pp.

The story of Appalachia through union songs, migration,
poverty, and protest, with music and texts.

979. CARAWAN, Guy and Candie. We Shall Overcome! Songs of the
Southern Freedom Movement. New York: Oak, 1963. 112 pp.

Brief headnotes, tunes, and texts for 46 songs under such
topics as "sit-ins," "freedom rides," and "voter registration,"
with photos for each.

980. COHEN, John, and SEEGER, Mike. The New Lost City Ramblers
      Song Book. New York: Oak, 1964. 256 pp.

      Brief headnotes, tunes with guitar chords, and words for
songs current in the 1920s and 1930s about love, for dance,
occupational hazards, blues, and other kinds.

981. GAMSE, Albert. The Best of Folk Music. New York: Lewis
      Music, 1968.

      Selection of folksongs and "folksongs" from various parts
of the world, including the United States. Tunes with chord
symbols and texts translated into English.

982. GLAZER, Tom. Songs of Peace, Freedom, and Protest. New
      York: David McKay, 1970; reprint ed., Greenwich, Conn.:
      Fawcett World Library, 1972. 357 pp.

      Vast collection in alphabetical order of melodies with
chords and texts (in "fakebook" style), with brief headnotes.

983. GUTHRIE, Arlo. This is the Arlo Guthrie Book. New York:
      Amsco Music Publishing Co., 1969. 96 pp.

984. HILLE, Waldemar. The People's Song Book. New York: Boni
      and Gaer, 1948, 1956, 1959, 1960; reprint ed., New York:
      Oak, 1961, 1966 etc. 128 pp.

      A collection of songs that "helped build America,"
including freedom songs, union songs, and other topical-political
songs, harmonized for piano accompaniment.

985. KREITZER, Jack, and BRAUNSTEIN, Susan. A Living Tradition:
      South Dakota Songwriter's Songbook. Sioux Falls, S.D.:
      George B. German Music Archives, 1983. 147 pp.

      A collection of 56 songs by 41 composers in chronological
order from the 1880s to the present, with emphasis on the latter
in styles from pop love ballads to rock and roll hits. Includes
protest songs.

986. LOMAX, Alan, GUTHRIE, Woody, and SEEGER, Pete. Hard
     Hitting Songs for Hard-Hit People. New York: Oak, 1967.
     368 pp.

     Tunes with chord symbols, texts, and commentaries on
nearly 200 songs of the working people, especially during the
Depression, classified as union songs, New Deal songs, songs of
evicted people, the down and out, etc.

987. [SEEGER, Pete.] American Favorite Ballads: Tunes and Songs
     as Sung by Pete Seeger. New York: Oak, 1961. 96 pp.

     Revival collection of favorite American songs, e.g.,
"Aunt Rhody" and "This Land is Your Land." Tunes with chord
symbols and words. Compiler asserts that we find belonging
through a common corpus of folk songs.

988. SILBER, Irwin. Lift Every Voice: the Second People's Song
     Book. New York: Oak, 1953, 1957. 96 pp.

     Songs of peace and of the struggle of common people, with
a forward by Paul Robeson. Tunes with harmonizations and texts.

989. SILBER, Irwin, ed. Reprints from the People's Songs
     Bulletin, 1946-1949. New York: Oak, 1961. 96 pp.

     A collection of unaccompanied melodies with texts.

990. SILBER, Irwin, and SILBER, Fred. Folksinger's Wordbook.
     New York: Oak, 1973; reprint ed., London: Music Sales,
     1975. 430 pp.

     Lyrics for over 1,000 songs, with chord symbols in the
texts. Classified into topics.

991. SILVERMAN, Jerry. Jerry Silverman's Folk Song
     Encyclopedia. 2 vols. New York: Chappell Music Co.,
     1975. 431 pp. each.

     Over 1,000 songs classified by type with melody and guitar
accompaniment, but without commentary.

992. SILVERMAN, Jerry. The Liberated Woman's Songbook. New
York: Macmillan, 1971. 153 pp.

A collection of 77 songs with tunes and texts, and brief
background to each illustrating the women's movement in history.
Types include songs of courting, marriage and home life, struggle,
and others.

993. STAVIS, Barrie, and HARMON, Frank, eds. The Songs of Joe
Hill. New York: People's Artists, 1955; reprint ed., New
York: Oak, 1960, 1967. 46 pp.

Labor songs of Joseph Hilltrom, 1879-1915, melody with
guitar chords and piano accompaniment.

V. TRADITIONAL INSTRUMENTS AND INSTRUMENTAL MUSIC

Musical instruments are usually among the easiest of musical phenomena to describe. They are objects, can be bought and sold, and can be played even by scholars. Their music is often more easily transcribed than vocal music and it can be played by anyone mastering the techniques. Further, because instruments are easily classified by type, if not individually, they are also easier to deal with in a bibliography.

In some ways the amount of published research on instruments and instrumental music is unexpectedly extensive, but in other ways it pales in comparison to both the depth and extent of work in, e.g., American Indian music or ballad/folksong. Most of it has only been accomplished in the last thirty years. The majority pertains to descriptions and history of instruments, with far less available on playing techniques or the literature.

The sub-categories were created according to the amount of literature on a given instrument. Not unexpectedly, those which have been most thoroughly studied are the banjo, the dulcimer (more so for the plucked type than the hammered variety), the fiddle, and the guitar. The most significant historical research has probably been lavished on the banjo, while the most extensive musical research has doubtless been expended on the fiddle, especially in the work of Linda C. Burman-Hall. Obviously, it was not possible to separate white and black instruments; the few that are exclusively played by blacks, e.g., the "diddly bow" or wall zither, are still included here rather than in Section VIII.

No attempt has been made to separate "authentic" traditions from "revival" traditions. Without doubt, revival-inspired "how-to-play" books dominate. Furthermore, they are nearly endless. A good number have been listed, especially those published by Oak, but a more complete list could be made from consulting some of the sources listed under "Reference Works" in Section I.

General Sources

994. BAINES, Anthony. European and American Musical Instruments. London: B. T. Batsford, 1966. 174 pp.

Although this exceptionally valuable resource includes
much on "classical" instruments of European origin, a goodly
number of American traditional fiddles, guitars, banjos, and
zithers are found as well, with photographic illustrations and
extensive commentary.

995. BAYARD, Samuel P. Dance to the Fiddle, March to the Fife:
Instrumental Folk Tunes in Pennsylvania. University Park
and London: Pennsylvania State University Press, 1982.
628 pp.

Vast array of 651 tunes and variants field collected
between 1928 and 1963 which amounts to everything the author
collected except those published separately in Hill Country Tunes
(below). Purpose is to provide a comprehensive view as well as
relate tunes here to versions found elsewhere in the Anglo-
American tradition. Transcriptions in rather rough manuscript.

996. BAYARD, Samuel Preston. Hill Country Tunes: Instrumental
Folk Music of Southwestern Pennsylvania. American Folklore Society Memoirs No. 39. Philadelphia: American
Folklore Society, 1944; reprint ed., New York: Kraus,
1970. 157 pp.

Close to 100 instrumental tunes, mostly for fiddle, field
collected by the author with commentary on their currency,
history, and related versions.

997. BAYARD, Samuel P. "A Miscellany of Tune Notes." In
Studies in Folklore: in Honor of Distinguished Service
Professor Stith Thompson, pp. 151-76. Edited by W. Edson
Richmond. Bloomington: Indiana University Press, 1957.

List of references to tune-versions (some scarce) found
in certain early instrumental and vocal collections of Anglo song.

998. DENSMORE, Frances. Handbook of the Collection of Musical
Instruments in the United States Museum. Smithsonian
Institution, United States National Museum Bulletin #136.

Washington, D.C.: U. S. Government Printing Office, 1927;
reprint ed., New York: Da Capo, 1971. 164 pp.

Catalogue of instruments with 49 plates and descriptions.
Scope is international, but includes many from North America.

999. DEPAUL, Andy. Makin' Your Own Country Instruments.
Willits, Calif.: Oliver Press, 1976. 206 pp.

Illustrated practical guide on making dulcimers,
mandolins, guitars, and fiddles. Also treats tools and instructs
in doing inlay decoration.

1000. FARRELL, Susan Caust. Directory of Contemporary American
Musical Instrument Makers. Columbia: University of
Missouri Press, 1981. 225 pp.

Major resource of information covering makers of all
types of instruments, both classical and folk. Entries include
name, address, whether full- or part-time, year started, number of
employees, and whether instruments are ready-made or custom-made.
Much of this is indicated by codes. Pages 1-154 comprise an
alphabetical list of makers, pp. 155-88 makers by instrument, and
pp. 189-208, makers by state. Also information on schools of
instrument making, professional societies and other groups, and a
list of books on instrument making.

1001. GOERTZEN, Chris. "Philander Seward's 'Musical Deposit' and
the History of American Instrumental Folk Music."
Ethnomusicology 26-1 (Jan. 1982): 1-10.

A study of a collection of "commonplace" musical material
(such as clippings) glued to the pages of a pre-existing bound
book by a rural New Yorker about 1807.

1002. GREEN, Douglas B., and GRUHN, George. Roy Acuff's Musical
Collection at Opryland. N.p.: WSM, Inc., 1982. 86 pp.

Good collection of photos, most in color, with sparse
text giving an overview of the history of stringed instrument
makers of Appalachia.

1003. IRWIN, John Rice. Musical Instruments of the Southern
      Appalachian Mountains. Exton, Pa.: Schiffler Publishing
      Company, 1979; 2nd ed., 1983. 104 pp.

      Mostly black and white pictures with captions but little
text covering fiddles, banjos, mouth bows, Appalachian dulcimers,
and some on guitars, mandolins, jews harps, and harmonicas.

1004. KELLER, Kate van Winkle, and SWEET, Ralph. A Choice
      Selection of American Country Dances of the Revolutionary
      Era, 1775-1795. New York: Country Dance and Song Society
      of America, 1975; 2nd rev. ed., 1976. 52 pp.

      Descriptions of dances with tunes provided; intended for
recreational dancers but carefully researched.

1005. Kicking Mule: Catalog of Records, Cassettes, Music Books, &
      Teaching Tapes for Acoustic Guitar, Banjo, Dulcimer,
      Fiddle, Harp, Autoharp, Harmonica, & Computer.
      Alderpoint, Calif.: 1985-6. 48 pp.

      A shop catalogue that lists much self-instruction
material for the instruments mentioned that is not listed in the
present work.

1006. LIBIN, Laurence. American Musical Instruments in the
      Metropolitan Museum of Art. New York: Metropolitan
      Museum and W. W. Norton, 1985. 224 pp.

      Lavishly illustrated, well-researched study of all kinds
of instruments, classical and folk. Well-researched text as well.

1007. LLOYD, Timothy. "Sam Boyles: the Traditional Musician in
      Rural and Urban Contexts." Journal of the Ohio Folklore
      Society (new series) 1-2 (Aug. 1972): 37-49.

      This is a case study of an Adams County man who played
early Country music (with much influence in style from Jimmie
Rodgers) on a variety of instruments, including guitar, fiddle,
banjo, dobro, and mandolin. The writer focuses on the differences
in his presentation at home and at festivals.

1008. MacLEOD, Bruce A. "The Musical Instruments of North
       American Slaves." _Mississippi_ _Folklore_ _Register_ 11-1
       (Spring, 1977): 34-49.

1009. McDONALD, James J. "Principal Influences on the Music of
       the Lilly Brothers of Clear Creek, W. Va." _Journal_ _of_
       American _Folklore_ 86-342 (Oct.-Dec. 1973): 331-44.
       Reprinted in _Goldenseal_ 1-1 (Apr.-June 1975): 27-36.

       Case study of a traditional string band active from 1938-
       1970, giving general context and specifics on the band.

1010. MARK, Jeffrey. "Recollections of Folk-Musicians." _Musical_
       Quarterly 16 (1930): 170-85.

       Reminiscences of Scottish musicians in Scotland and the
       United States and description of their music making.

1011. RAICHELSON, Richard. "The Social Context of Music
       Instruments within the Pennsylvania German Culture."
       Pennsylvania _Folklife_ 25-1 (Fall, 1975): 35-44.

       Illustrated study of context, how, when, and where
       instruments are used, both alone and for dancing. Includes a
       section on the views of the church and a useful bibliography.

1012. SHOEMAKER, Henry W. "The Music and Musical Instruments of
       the Pennsylvania Mountaineers." Altoona, Pa: Times
       Tribune Co., 1923. 9 pp.

       Pamphlet version of address given on October 20, 1923, to
       the Travelers Club of Smethport, McKean County, Pennsylvania.
       Lists instruments (Scottish pipes, hammered dulcimer, fiddles, and
       harp), but provides no illustrations. Rare.

1013. TOLMAN, Newton F. _Quick_ _Tunes_ _and_ _Good_ _Times:_ _a_ _Light-_
       Hearted _Guide_ _to_ _Jigs,_ _Reels,_ _Rants,_ _Planxtys,_ _and_ _other_
       Little-Known _New_ _England_ _Folk_ _Music._ Dublin, N.H.:
       William L. Bauhan, 1972. 109 pp.

       Personal reminiscences by an old New England square-dance
       bandsman and seven pages of tunes and definitions of dance types.

1014. TOLMAN, Newton F., and GILBERT, Kay. "The Nelson Music
Collection: Selected Authentic Square Dance Melodies."
Marlborough, N.H.: Newton F. Tolman, 1969. 23 pp.

1015. WARNER, Frank and Anne. "Frank Noah Proffitt: a Retrospec-
tive." Appalachian Journal 1-3 (Aug. 1973): 163-98.

Three articles on F. N. Proffitt (1913-1965) of Watauga
County, North Carolina, including his biography, music, and
career, with photos. One article is a sampling of his letters
while the final one is in the subject's own words.

The Banjo

1016. ADLER, Tom. "Physical Description of the Banjo." New York
Folklore Quarterly 28-3 (Sept. 1982): 187-208.

History and description of the banjo, especially the
changes and improvements. Also an eight-page list of patents.

1017. BAILEY, Jay. "Historical Origin and Stylistic Developments
of the Five-String Banjo." Journal of American Folklore
85-335 (Jan.-Mar. 1972): 58-65.

Rewriting the history of the banjo through a reexamina-
tion of previous sources, with descriptions of types and
techniques. Well documented but without illustrations.

1018. BLUESTEIN, Gene. "America's Folk Instrument: Notes on the
Five-String Banjo." Western Folklore 23-4 (Oct. 1964):
241-8; reprinted as "The Five-String Banjo--America's
Folk Instrument." In The Voice of the Folk: Folklore and
American Literary Theory, pp. 151-8. Amherst: University
of Massachusetts Press, 1972.

Introduction to the instrument, its origins, history, and
tunings.

1019. BROWN, J. C. Jr. "Five-String Banjo." In Carolina County
Reader, pp. 84-102. Edited by James A. Chaney. Durham,
N.C.: Moore Publishing Co., 1973.

1020. BURKE, John. John Burke's Book of Old Time Fiddle Tunes
for Banjo. New York: Amsco, 1968. 96 pp.

Collection of banjo music for practical performance.

1021. CLAYTON, Robert J. "A Bibliography of the History and
Playing Styles of the Five-String Banjo." Washington,
D.C.: Library of Congress, Archive of Folk Song. 10 pp.

1022. CONWAY, Cecilia. "The Afro-American Traditions of the Folk
Banjo." Ph.D. dissertation, University of North Carolina
at Chapel Hill, 1980. 243 pp.

History, playing styles, and song repertory of the banjo.

1023. COOLEN, Michael Theodore. "Senegambian Archetypes for the
American Folk Banjo." Western Folklore 43-2 (April
1984): 117-32.

About stringed instruments in Africa which may be
predecessors to the American banjo based on fieldwork in Senegal
and Gambia, 1973-6. Detailed descriptions of instruments, their
dimensions, tunings, and playing techniques, with drawings.

1024. EPSTEIN, Dena J. "The Folk Banjo: a Documentary History."
Ethnomusicology 19-3 (1975): 347-72.

Making a distinction between the folk and commercial
banjos, the author provides a wealth of information and five
illustrations. These include citations of nineteenth and
twentieth century documents, a chronological table of references,
and an extensive bibliography.

1025. HEATON, Cherrill P. "The 5-String Banjo in North
Carolina." Southern Folklore Quarterly 35-1 (Mar.
1971): 62-82.

History and description of the banjo, banjo makers,
playing styles, and important players, including Earl Scruggs.

1026. MARSHALL, John. "Earlie Botts." Kentucky Folklore Record
24-3/4 (1978): 81-8.

A case study of the career of Earlie Botts (1946-77) from Monroe County, Kentucky, "one of the few traditional 'standing hand' banjo players left in an area where that method of playing was once prevalent."

1027. NATHAN, Hans. "Early Banjo Tunes and American Syncopation." Musical Quarterly 42 (1956): 455-72.

Study of banjo tunes both in manuscripts and in methods dating from 1840s minstrel sources and the 1850s. Traces relationships of these tunes to those of blacks, Irish, and others. Includes 35 examples and all is well documented.

1028. PERLMAN, Ken. Clawhammer Style Banjo: a Complete Guide for Beginning & Advanced Players. Englewood Cliffs, N.J.: Prentice-Hall, 1983. 194 pp.

Popularized, but rather complete, self-instruction book.

1029. Ring the Banjar: the Banjo in American Folklore to Factory. Cambridge: M.I.T. Museum, 1984. 112 pp.

Catalogue of an exhibit from April 12 to September 29, 1984, with 37 plates (some in color), notes, bibliography and two essays: "Confidence and Admiration: the Enduring Ringing of the Banjo" by Robert Lloyd Webb, and "The Banjo Makers of Boston" by James F. Bollman. The first concerns history, the second concerns marketing.

1030. SANDBERG, Larry. Complete Banjo Repair. New York: Oak, 1979. 112 pp.

Technical manual with many illustrations.

1031. SCRUGGS, Louise (Mrs. Earl). "History of the 5-String Banjo." Tennessee Folklore Society Bulletin 27-1 (March 1961): 1-5; reprinted as "A History of America's Favorite Folk Instrument" in Sing Out 13-5 (Dec.-Jan. 1963-4): 26-29, and extracted in SCRUGGS, Earl. Earl Scruggs and the 5-String Banjo. New York: Peer International, 1968, 9-16.

Originally a paper read for the Tennessee Folklore
Society on November 12, 1960, this brief, non-scholarly and
somewhat unorthodox history cannot be taken as "gospel."

1032. SEEGER, Pete. How to Play the 5-String Banjo. 2nd ed.
      New York: Beacon, 1954. 40 pp. 3rd ed., 1961. 72 pp.
      Also by New York: Oak.

      A self-instruction book for beginners. Goes with
Folkways FM 8303, a 12 inch disc issued in 1954.

1033. SILVERMAN, Jerry. Beginning the Five-String Banjo. New
      York: Collier, 1974. 150 pp.

      Very basic instruction book for beginners.

1034. STAMM, Gus. Banjo Making--It's Easy. Evanston, Ill.:
      Musicraft Studios, 1962. 29 pp.

      Brief description with photos, including a "blueprint."

1035. STEWART, Samuel Swain. The Banjo! A Dissertation.
      Philadelphia: S. S. Stewart, 1888, 109 pp.; 2nd ed.,
      1894, 131 pp.

      This and three other items by Stewart are important for
their vintage, but they are evidently quite rare. They can be
found in the Library of Congress at least.

1036. STEWART, Samuel Swain. "The Banjo Philosophically: its
      Construction, its Capabilities, its Evolution, its Place
      as a Musical Instrument, its Possibilities and its
      Future: a Lecture." Philadelphia: S. S. Stewart, 1887;
      reprinted in Mugwumps 3-4 (July 1974): 11-13, 18-22.

1037. STEWART, Samuel Swain. S. S. Stewart's Banjo, Guitar and
      Mandolin Journal. Philadelphia: S. S. Stewart.

      Periodical published between May 1883, and April 1901.

1038.   [STEWART, S. S.].   S. S. Stewart's Extra Fine Banjos
        [company catalogue of 1896]; reprint ed., Silver Spring,
        Md.: Mugwumps Instrument Herald [12704 Barbara Rd.,
        Silver Spring, Md. 20906], 1973. 56 pp.

        Catalogue of individual banjos, mandolins, and guitars,
materials for orchestras, endorsements, and instructions for
putting the head on a banjo.

1039.   TALLMADGE, William H.   "The Folk Banjo and Clawhammer
        Performance Practice in the Upper South: s Study in
        Origins." In The Appalachian Experience: Proceedings of
        the Sixth Annual Appalachian Studies Conference, pp. 168-
        79.   Edited by Barry M. Buxton, et. al.   Boone, N.C.:
        Appalachian Consortium Press, 1983.

        Addresses two basic questions: 1) who transmitted banjo
playing in general and clawhammer style in particular to those
living in the Appalachians, and 2) when did it happen. Related to
this is the significance of Joel Walker Sweeney in this process.
The author concludes that blacks introduced the instrument through
contact connected with the salt industry in the early nineteenth
century, and that while Sweeney added a fifth string, he did not
add a drone string, which already existed by 1800.

1040.   WERNICK, Peter.   Bluegrass Banjo.   New York: Oak, 1975.
        143 pp. and phonodisc.

        A self-instruction book with music in tablature and a
list of records and groups on pp. 138-41.

1041.   WINANS, Robert B.   "The Black Banjo-Playing Tradition in
        Virginia and West Virginia." Journal of the Virginia
        Folklore Society 1 (1979): 7-30.

        Based on interviews with 13 living players in Virginia
and West Virginia, this study concentrates both on the history of
black banjo playing in Virginia and an examination of playing
styles, repertories, and interaction with whites.

1042.   WINANS, Robert B.   "The Folk, the Stage, and the Five-
        String Banjo in the Nineteenth-Century." Journal of
        American Folklore 89-354 (Oct.-Dec. 1976): 407-37.

Explores the relationships among black instruments, white mountain instruments, minstrel music, and the worlds of popular and classical musics.

Dulcimers, Both Hammered and Plucked

1043. ALVEY, R. Gerald. Dulcimer Maker: the Craft of Homer Ledford. Lexington: University Press of Kentucky, 1984. 186 pp.

Biography of noted maker from Winchester, Kentucky, and systematic description of how he makes his instruments. Also an appreciation of Ledford's work in its community context.

1044. ARONOW, Bethany. "A Bibliography of the Plucked (Appalachian or Mountain) Dulcimer and Related Instruments." Washington, D.C.: Library of Congress, Archive of Folk Culture, 1978. 10 pp.

A list of 110 items, including some in foreign languages. Many items are emphemeral in nature.

1045. BAILEY, John. Making an Appalachian Dulcimer. London: Cecil Sharp House, 1966. 50 pp.

Informal method book with excellent line drawings and plans as well as photos.

1046. BRYAN, Charles Faulkner. "American Folk Instruments: the Hammered Dulcimer." Tennessee Folklore Society Bulletin 18-2 (June 1952): 43-7.

Early appreciation of an instrument then coming to be known as "folk." Includes some history, comparison with the lap dulcimer, and some rather rough drawings.

1047. FOGEL, Rick, and MARGIN, N. A. Building a Hammered Dulcimer: Do-Kit-Yourself. Strongsville, Oh.: R. F. Printing Service, 1980. 35 pp.

1048. FORCE, Robert, and D'OSSCHE, Albert. In Search of the Wild
 Dulcimer. New York: Vintage, 1974; reprint ed., New
 York: Amsco, 1975. 109 pp.

 Self-instruction book in lap dulcimer playing.

1049. GAMSE, Albert. The Best Dulcimer Method Yet. Carlstadt,
 N.Y.: Lewis Music Publishing Co., 1974.

1050. GROCE, Nancy. The Hammered Dulcimer in America. Studies
 in History and Technology #44. Washington, D.C.:
 Smithsonian Institution, 1983. 99 pp.

 Central source that provides first a history of the
instrument in Europe and Asia, but concentrates on its development
and use in America based on both documents and field work.
Includes an appendix of dulcimer patents.

1051. HARRIS, Rodger. Notes on Dulcimer Making. Oklahoma City:
 Bois D'Arc, 1977. 54 pp.

 Systematic description of making the lap dulcimer by a
skilled builder, with many photos.

1052. HASTINGS, S. E. Jr. "Construction Techniques in an Old
 Appalachian Mountain Dulcimer." Journal of American
 Folklore 83-330 (Oct.-Dec. 1970): 462-68.

 Description, with careful drawings, of an hourglass
dulcimer from Kentucky, c. 1910.

1053. HINES, Chet. How to Make and Play the Dulcimore.
 Harrisburg: Stackpole, 1973. 159 pp.

 Written by a well-known maker and player, this non-
scholarly description provides history, photos, information on lap
dulcimer making, and how to play (primarily in number notation),
and includes a pattern for an instrument.

1054. HOLMES, Michael I., ed. The Hammer Dulcimer Compendium.
 Silver Spring, Md.: Mugwumps Magazine/MIH Publications,
 1977. 25 pp.

Bits of history, how to play, description, and photos, reprinted from Mugwumps.

1055. JOYNER, Charles W. "Dulcimer Making in Western North Carolina: Creativity in a Traditional Mountain Craft." Southern Folklore Quarterly 39 (1975): 341-61.

A study of the contrasting pulls of continuity and creativity with regard to the plucked dulcimer, organized by maker.

1056. KIMBALL, Dean. Constructing the Mountain Dulcimer. New York: McKay, 1975. 111 pp.

Fairly comprehensive description with photos and clear drawings for the lap type. One of the best books of its type.

1057. LEACH, John. "The Dulcimer." The Consort no. 25 (1968-9): 390-5.

Historical survey of the European version of the hammered dulcimer and its tunings. Valuable to an American researcher though not on the American instrument per se.

1058. McCUTCHEON, John. "Hammered Dulcimer Instruction Tapes." Woodstock, N.Y.: Homespun Tapes, 1982.

Set of six cassettes and one tablature booklet providing instruction and songs in six lessons. Order from Homespun Tapes, Box 694 F, Woodstock, N.Y. 12498.

1059. MASON, Phillip. "How to Tune & Play the Hammered Dulcimer." Bangor, Me.: by the author, RFD #2, Box 132 [04401]. 15 pp.

Practical, how-to book with four pages of tunes and a brief bibliography.

1060. MERCER, H. G. "The Zithers of the Pennsylvania Germans." A Collection of Papers Read Before the Bucks County Historical Society 5 (1927): 482-97.

Hard to find but probably valuable source.

213

1061. MITCHELL, Howie. How to Make and Play the Hammered
      Dulcimer. Sharon, Conn.: Folk Legacy Records, 1971.

      Self-instruction book with a record.

1062. MURPHY, Michael. The Appalachian Dulcimer Book. St.
      Clairsville, Oh.: The Folksay Press, 1976. 103 pp.

      Basic how-to book with examples in both staff and
tablature notations, as well as some history and photos.

1063. PEARSE, John. The Dulcimer Book. London: A.T.V. Kirshner
      Music and Welback Music Ltd., 1970. 72 pp.

      A book on how to make and play the lap dulcimer by an
innovative English fellow influenced by Jean Ritchie.

1064. PICKOW, Peter. Hammered Dulcimer. New York: Oak, 1979.
      111 pp.

      Beginning self-instruction book in "folk" style with
songs notated in both staff and tablature notations.

1065. PUTNAM, John F. The Mountain Dulcimer of the Southern
      Mountains. Berea, Ken.: Council of the Southern
      Mountains, 1957; rev. ed. as The Plucked Dulcimer and How
      to Play It, 1961. 29 pp.

      Brief, practical self-instruction book.

1066. PYLE, Paul W. The Appalachian Mountain Dulcimer Book.
      Tullahoma, Tenn.: Paul Pyle Studios, 1976.

1067. PYLE, Paul W. "To Build a Dulcimer: a Simplified,
      Economical Demonstration in the Construction, Tuning and
      Playing of the Dulcimer." Tullahoma, Tenn.: Paul Pyle
      Studios, 1972. 14 pp.

1068. RITCHIE, Jean. The Dulcimer Book. New York: Oak, 1963,
      1974. 45 pp.

The history, making, and playing of the lap dulcimer with many songs by one of America's foremost folk singer/players.

1069. [RITCHIE, Jean]. Jean Ritchie's Dulcimer People. New York: Oak, 1975. 128 pp.

Personal and informal discussion of lap dulcimers in Europe, players past and present in both Europe and America, how to play and make the instrument, with many photos.

1070. SACKETT, S. J. "The Hammered Dulcimer in Ellis County, Kansas." Journal of the International Folk Music Council 14 (1962): 61-4.

Brief description with background and tunings of the instrument and who played it.

1071. SEEGER, Charles. "The Appalachian Dulcimer." Journal of American Folklore 71-279 (Jan.-March 1958): 40-51; reprinted in SEEGER, Charles. Studies in Musicology, (see #105, pp. 252-72).

Description, tunings, playing styles, and especially history and origin by a noted scholar. Indeed, this is probably the most carefully researched article on the lap dulcimer.

1072. SMITH, L. Allen. "The Appalachian Dulcimer to 1940: a Census and Typology of Pre-Revival Eighteenth- and Early Twentieth-Century Fretted Zithers in the Upland South of the United States, with an Analysis of Their Musical Intervals." Ph.D. dissertation, University of Leeds, Institute of Dialect and Folk Life Studies, 1979. 800 pp.

No abstract is available of this hard-to-find, but obviously valuable, work, but its title says it well.

1073. SMITH, L. Allen. A Catalogue of Pre-Revival Appalachian Dulcimers. Columbia: University of Missouri Press, 1983. 160 pp.

Apparently a revision of the previous item, this study classifies lap dulcimers into five types, lists known dulcimer makers, and provides detailed photos. There is also an historical

survey and photographic record. Obviously, the best of the book-
length studies of this instrument.

1074. SMITH, L. Allen. "Toward a Reconstruction of the
Development of the Appalachian Dulcimer: What the
Instruments Suggest." Journal of American Folklore 93-
370 (Oct.-Dec. 1980): 385-96.

Presents a theory of development and lists five types of
lap dulcimers based on a census of pre-1940 instruments, including
those of the Pennsylvania Germans.

Fiddles

1075. AHRENS, Pat J. Union Grove: the First Fifty Years. Union
Grove, N.C.: Union Grove Old Time Fiddlers' Convention,
1975. 244 pp.

A history of the convention, with extensive bibliography
(pp. 136-43) and discography (pp. 150-9).

1076. ARTLEY, Malvin Newton. "The West Virginia Country Fiddler:
an Aspect of the Folk Music Tradition in the United
States." D.F.A. dissertation, Chicago Musical College,
1955. 119 pp.

A "scientific" study that is rather technical, but
apparently not based on field work with individuals.

1077. BAYARD, Samuel P. "Scales and Ranges in Anglo-American
Fiddle Tunes: Report on a Desultory Experiment." In Two
Penny Ballads and Four Dollar Whiskey: a Pennsylvania
Folklore Miscellany, pp. 51-60. Ed. Kenneth S. Goldstein
and Robert H. Byington. Hatboro, Pa.: Folklore
Associates, 1966.

A study of fiddle tunes and their scales and usual ranges
and the possible influence on them of fifer's tunes.

1078. BAYARD, Samuel P. "Some Folk Fiddlers' Habits and Styles
in Western Pennsylvania." Journal of the International
Folk Music Council 8 (1956): 15-18.

Based on a paper presented in Oslo, Norway, this study focuses on different ways of playing by local fiddlers.

1079. BETHKE, Robert D. "Old-Time Fiddling and Social Dance in Central St. Lawrence Country." New York Folklore Quarterly 30-3 (Sept. 1974): 163-84.

Survey of traditional music and history in the St. Lawrence river valley in the western Adirondacks. Non-technical and without examples.

1080. BLACK, Ann McMurry. "Old-Timey Fiddler." Appalachian Journal 5-2 (1978): 256-67.

A study of the fiddling of James "Buster" Russell, of Claiborne County, Tennessee, and thoughts on the origins of Appalachian music in the Renaissance and in British and French country music.

1081. BLAUSTEIN, Richard. "Traditional Music and Social Change: the Old Time Fiddlers Association Movement in the United States." Ph.D. dissertation, Indiana University, 1975. 185 pp.

A study of the (then) 25 Old Time Fiddler Associations with about 11,000 members, their importance in encouraging and preserving fiddling through contests, festivals, recordings, and the fiddler's art.

1082. BURMAN, Linda C. "The Technique of Variation in an American Fiddle Tune." Ethnomusicology 12-1 (Jan. 1968): 49-71.

A concentrated and technical study of a 1926 performance of "Sail Away Lady" recorded for Columbia Records by Uncle Bunt Stephens. An analysis of seven melodico-harmonic variations in order to discover the performer's concept of the basic tune.

1083. BURMAN-HALL, Linda C. "American Traditional Fiddling: Performance Contexts and Techniques." In Performance Practice: Ethnomusicological Perspectives, pp. 149-221. Edited by Gerard Behague. Westport, Conn.: Greenwood, 1984.

217

A study of the performance practices of American fiddlers, including excellent bibliography, discography, and chronology of sources.

1084. BURMAN-HALL, Linda C. "Southern American Folk Fiddle Styles." Ethnomusicology 19-1 (Jan. 1975): 47-66.

Overview of traditional and regional fiddling dialects, performance practices, and tunes. The author differentiates three styles: Blue Ridge, Southern Appalachian, and Western Style.

1085. BURMAN-HALL, Linda C. "Southern American Folk Fiddling: Context and Style." Ph.D. dissertation, Princeton University, 1974. 362 pp.

Comprehensive study of fiddling in the United States, beginning with its origins in Britain and Europe. Defines the sub-cultures within the Anglo-American tradition, presents 42 transcriptions to compare versions, and examines these according to 15 stylistic variables. Four fiddling dialects are defined: Blue Ridge, Southern Appalachian, Ozark, and Western Style.

1086. BURMAN-HALL, Linda C. "Tune Identity and Performance Style: the Case of 'Bonaparte's Retreat'." Selected Reports in Ethnomusicology III-1, pp. 77-98. Los Angeles: University of California, 1978.

Shenkerian analysis applied to a traditional fiddle tune. Many examples together delineate regional styles. Discography.

1087. BURRISON, John A. "Fiddlers in the Alley: Atlanta as an Early Country Music Center." Atlanta Historical Bulletin 21-2 (Summer, 1977): 59-87.

1088. CHRISTESON, R. P., ed. and comp. The Old-Time Fiddler's Repertory: 245 Traditional Tunes. Columbia: University of Missouri Press, 1973. 224 pp. Two-record set.

After a short introduction, there are 245 tunes by 33 fiddlers from nine states organized into categories (breakdowns, quadrilles, pieces, waltzes, and accompaniments for a second fiddle), and an index of tunes. Tunes collected over a 30 year period from recordings and notes dating from the 1920s-1940s.

1089. CHRISTESON, R. P., ed. and comp. The Old-Time Fiddler's
      Repertory, Volume 2. Columbia: University of Missouri
      Press, 1985. 208 pp.

      Additional collection (see preceding entry) of more than
200 tunes, mostly from Missouri, with some information on the
fiddlers. Organized by types similar to the above.

1090. COPPAGE, Noel. "Fights, Fiddles, and Foxhunts." Kentucky
      Folklore Record 7-1 (1961): 1-14.

      Collection of vignettes, including one on a fiddler, by
an amateur folklorist from Ohio County, Kentucky.

1091. DE RYKE, Delores. "So Hell is Full of Fiddlers--Bet it
      Won't be Crowded!" Western Folklore 23-3 (1964): 181-6.

      A study of the fiddler as a person (as opposed to being
only a musician), with three pages of direct quotes of fiddlers
about themselves.

1092. FEINTUCH, Burt. "Examining Musical Motivation: Why Does
      Sammie Play the Fiddle"? Western Folklore 42-3 (July
      1983): 208-14.

      Seeks to answer two questions with regard to a fiddler
named Sammie in south central Kentucky who has been playing for 60
years--1) why did he start playing, and 2) why did he keep at it
for so long? Provides both biography and description of playing
contexts.

1093. FEINTUCH, Burt. "The Fiddle in the United States: an
      Historical Overview." Kentucky Folklore Record 29-1/2
      (Jan.-June 1983): 30-8.

      Overview of the advent of fiddles, who played them, for
what purposes, early recordings, and current uses.

1094. FEINTUCH, Burt. "Pop Ziegler, Fiddler: a Study of
      Folkloric Performance." Ph.D. dissertation, University
      of Pennsylvania, 1975. 284 pp.

Although centered around Earl "Pop" Ziegler of Bucks
County, Pennsylvania, this is a study of the customary knowledge
and behavior of fiddlers to shed light on the regularities of performance, plus an analysis of Ziegler's style.

1095. GUNTHARP, Matthew G. Learning the Fiddler's Ways.
University Park: Pennsylvania State University Press,
1980. 159 pp.

Written from the viewpoint of an old-time and bluegrass
fiddler from the Buffalo Valley of Union County, Pennsylvania,
this practical study concentrates on technique, ornamentation, and
includes transcriptions of the author's favorite tunes.

1096. HICKERSON, Joseph C., and HOLTZBERG, Maggie, comps. "A
Bibliography of Fiddling, Fiddle Tunes, and Related Dance
Tune Collections in North America: Including
representative materials from the British Isles and
Scandinavia." Washington, D.C.: Library of Congress,
Archive of Folk Culture, 1974. 28 pp.

A list of 322 sources, including methods, some of them
quite old, plus many tune collections.

1097. LOWINGER, Gene. Bluegrass Fiddle [a Guide to Bluegrass and
Country Style Fiddling; Right Hand Techniques, Double-
stops, Slurs, and Slides]. New York: Oak, 1974. 64 pp.

Self-instruction book for experienced players.

1098. OSBORNE, Lettie. "Fiddle-Tunes from Orange County, New
York." New York Folklore Quarterly 8-3 (1952): 211-15.

Light but interesting article based on a 1930s student-
written report. The collector recorded 59 tunes, which are
listed, and wrote a brief essay on fiddles.

1099. PHILLIPS, Stacy, and KOSEK, Kenny. Bluegrass Fiddle
Styles. New York: Oak, 1978. 112 pp.

Although an instruction book for experienced players, it
also includes some 70 tunes transcribed from 25 major players
explored in some depth.

1100. SILVERMAN, Jerry. Play Old-Time Country Fiddle: 75
Traditional Fiddle Tunes Arranged with Words & Chords.
Radnor, Pa.: Chilton, 1975. 134 pp.

A collection of exactly notated tunes with words, some
quite challenging. Also a brief introduction.

1101. SPIELMAN, Earl V. "Fiddling Traditions of Cape Breton and
Texas: a Study in Parallels and Contrasts." Yearbook for
Inter-American Music Research 8 (1972): 39-48.

Using 14 stylistic variables, the author describes
parallel and contrasting elements in this short study.

1102. SPIELMAN, Earl V. "Traditional North American Fiddling: a
Methodology for the Historical and Comparative Analytical
Style Study of Instrumental Musical Traditions." Ph.D.
dissertation, University of Wisconsin, 1975. 619 pp.

Pilot project to determine a method for broad study using
both descriptive and contextual data. Further, it provides a
history of traditional fiddling in North America and profiles
various traditions in the United States.

1103. THEDE, Marion. The Fiddle Book. New York: Oak, 1967.
160 pp.

After an 18-page introduction, various technical matters,
e.g., bowing and tuning, are discussed, followed by transcriptions,
many in scordatura tunings, of music collected in Oklahoma from
1928 to 1958. Also, information on fiddlers, singing, and texts.

1104. THEDE, Marion Unger. "Traditional Fiddling." Ethnomusicology 6-1 (Jan. 1962): 19-24.

A brief overview of the tradition based on incomplete
results from a questionnaire.

1105. TOELKEN, Barre. "Traditional Fiddling in Idaho." Western
Folklore 24-4 (Oct. 1965): 259-62.

A history and description of the National Oldtime
Fiddlers' Contest and Folk Music Festival in Weiser, Idaho.

1106. WIGGINTON, Eliot, ed. "Fiddle Making" in Foxfire 4, pp. 106-25. Garden City, N.Y.: Anchor, 1977.

Case studies of three makers: Harley Thomas of Macon County, Georgia, Garrett Arwood, and Clarence Rathbone.

1107. ZENGER, Dixie Robison. "Violin Techniques and Traditions Useful in Identifying and Playing North American Fiddle Styles." D.M.A. dissertation, Stanford, 1980. 75 pp.

The purpose of this grand tour of fiddle styles (Cajun, French-Canadian, Irish, New England, Scottish-Canadian, Southeastern Mountain, and Texas) is to identify the characteristics needed by a "traditional violinist," based on comparing and analyzing these styles.

Guitar

1108. BROSNAC, Donald. The Steel String Guitar: its Construction, Origin and Design. San Francisco: Panjandrum Press, 1973. 94 pp.

While the history portion is light, the systematic description of how to build a guitar is better. Provides schematics and a list of where to buy materials.

1109. GARWOOD, Donald. Masters of Instrumental Blues Guitar. Laguna Beach, Calif.: Traditional Stringed Instruments, 1967; reprint ed., New York: Oak, 1968. 78 pp.

Analytical instructional method for blues guitar.

1110. GROSSMAN, Stefan. Delta Blues Guitar. New York: Oak, 1969, 1972. 136 pp.

Detailed analysis and transcriptions (in both staff and tablature notations) of the personal guitar styles of legendary greats of the Mississippi Delta region.

1111. The Guitar Player Book, rev. ed. Cupertino, Calif.: Guitar Player Books, and New York: Grove Press, 1979. 403 pp.

Compiled by the Editors of Guitar Player Magazine, this
lightweight but extensive collection of information is mainly
devoted to personalities (pp. 3-256), with additional information
on the guitar in contemporary society, guitars and accessories,
maintenance, and major manufacturers, both electric and acoustic.

1112. IVEY, William. The 1921 Gibson Catalog. Historical
      Instrument Series #1. Nashville: Country Music Foundation
      Press, 1973. 120 pp.

More than just a catalog of the Gibson Mandolin-Guitar
Company of Kalamazoo, Michigan, there are many photos and much text
describing groups, instruments, parts, playing tips, and
endorsements.

1113. KAMIMOTO, Hideo. Complete Guitar Repair. New York: Oak,
      1975. 174 pp.

A technical manual for both electric and acoustic guitars,
illustrated with photos and drawings.

1114. LESTER, Julius, and SEEGER, Pete. The 12-String Guitar as
      Played by Leadbelly: an Instruction Manual. New York:
      Oak, 1965. 79 pp.

More a book on how to play a style, that of Huddie
Leadbetter, than a beginner's manual, for it assumes quite a bit of
skill from the start.

1115. LONGWORTH, Mike. Martin Guitars: a History. Cedar Knolls,
      N.J.: Colonial Press, 1975; 2nd ed., Nazareth, Pa.: M.
      Longworth, 1980. 247 pp.

History of a family and a company, with descriptions of
all their styles of guitars, mandolins, ukeleles, tiples, etc.
Extensive detail with lists, prices, and photos.

1116. MARTIN, Will. The Guitar Owner's Manual. Santa Fe: John
      Muir Publishers, 1983. 107 pp.

Basic book covering such subjects as choosing an instrument, maintenance, tuning, changing strings, adjustments, repairs,
mostly for acoustic guitars.

1117. SEEGER, Pete, and SILVERMAN, Jerry. The Folksinger's Guitar Guide. 2 vols. New York: Oak, 1962. 80 and 96 pp.

Vol. 1 is rather basic and presents songs in both staff and tablature notations. Vol. 2, entitled An Advanced Instruction Manual and written by Silverman, treats such topics as chromatic bass runs, melody and accompaniment, four-finger picking, special effects, the circle of fifths, Greek 7/8 time, etc.

1118. SILVERMAN, Jerry. The Art of the Folk-Blues Guitar: an Instruction Manual. New York: Oak, 1964. 71 pp.

A treatment of the styles of Josh White, Leadbelly, Big Bill Broonzy, and others, especially their variation techniques, with notation in tablature and staff.

1119. SILVERMAN, Jerry. Beginning Folk Guitar. New York: Oak, 1964. 96 pages and 2 disc recordings.

Basic book covering the usual topics such as keys, runs, arpeggios, transposing, with a selection of songs.

1120. SILVERMAN, Jerry. Jerry Silverman's Folk Guitar Method. New York: Grossett and Dunlap, 1974. 199 pp.

Self-instruction manual for beginning guitar.

1121. SLOANE, Irving. Steel-String Guitar Construction. New York: E. P. Dutton, 1975. 127 pp.

Systematic how-to manual with many illustrations by a New York City maker.

1122. WHEELER, Tom. American Guitars: an Illustrated History. New York: Harper & Row, 1982. 370 pp.

A one-volume encyclopedia of names and companies with entries of various lengths, some 1/2 page, others (e.g., "Gibson") nearly 100 pages long. A major resource.

1123. YOUNG, David Russell. The Steel String Guitar: Construction & Repair. Radnor, Pa.: Chilton Book Co., 1975. 159 pp.

A manual on the construction, painting, and repair of acoustic guitars written by a self-taught luthier who had earned a degree in psychology from U.C.L.A.

Miscellaneous Stringed Instruments

1124. AHRENS, Pat J. "A History of the Musical Careers of Dewitt "Snuffy" Jenkins, Banjoist, and Homer "Pappy" Sherrill, Fiddler." West Columbia, S.C.: Wentworth Corp., 1970. 24 pp.

Brief biographies of two elderly string-band players, Jenkins born in 1908 and Sherrill in 1915, both in North Carolina. Also a discography and bibliography.

1125. AULDRIDGE, Mike. Bluegrass Dobro. Saratoga, Calif.: Guitar Player Productions, 1975. 72 pp.

Written with the help of Bob Lawrence, this is a self-instruction book with music.

1126. BELLSON, Julius. The Gibson Story: from 1894 Through Year After Tomorrow. N.p.: n.p., 1973. 96 pp.

The history of a factory and the people who created it, with many valuable pictures.

1127. BLACKLEY, Becky. The Autoharp Book. Brisbane, Calif.: i.a.d. Publications, 1983. 256 pp.

The ultimate book on the autoharp, with an extensive bibliography of articles, books, and instruction books, as well as history. Also explores the models for the autoharp, and related instruments, and provides some 500 photos of instruments, color ads, and patents as well as a discography, list of events, and companies providing autoharp materials.

1128. COHEN, Norman. "The Skillet Lickers: a Study of a Hillbilly String Band and its Repertoire." Journal of American Folklore 78-309 (July-Sept. 1965): 229-44.

The story of a hillbilly string band active in north Georgia in the 1920s and 1930s, including some of their songs.

1129. EVANS, David. "Afro-American One-Stringed Instruments."
Western Folklore 29-4 (Oct. 1970): 229-46.

A detailed study of the "jitterbug" or "diddlybow," a one-
stringed zither usually attached to the wall and used with singing.
Based on 13 informants, the author describes how it is played, the
African connection, its relationship to guitar, especially slide
techniques, and the etymology of the words. Includes two photos.

1130. HAMBLY, Scott. "Mandolins in the United States since 1880:
an Industrial and Sociocultural History of Form." Ph.D.
dissertation, University of Pennsylvania, 1977. 602 pp.

Study of why and how the mandolin became popular and its
offshoots, with a focus on the University of Pennsylvania Mandolin
Club, which flourished from 1890-1920. Part I is sociocultural and
Part II is a formal history. Little on musical literature, but
much on American makers. Extensive bibliography, pp. 577-602.

1131. HORWITZ, Elinor Lander. Mountain People, Mountain Crafts.
Philadelphia: J. B. Lippincott, 1974.

The section entitled "Dulcimers, Banjors and Fiddles," pp.
20-33, is lightweight and focuses on several makers. Photos.

1132. MAGUIRE, Marsha. "The Autoharp: a Select Listing of Instruction Books and Articles." Washington, D.C.: Library of
Congress, Archive of Folk Song, 1979. 4 pp. (39 items)

1133. MOORE, A. Doyle. "The Autoharp: its Origin and Development
from a Popular to a Folk Instrument." New York Folklore
Quarterly 19-4 (Dec. 1963): 261-74; reprinted in Mugwumps
2-1 (Jan. 1973): 1-14.

Well-documented illustrated history from the autoharp's
invention in 1881 by Charles F. Zimmermann, with further
discussions of companies, improvements, and early recordings.

1134. SIMINOFF, Roger H. Constructing a Bluegrass Mandolin: a
Complete Technical Guide. Winona, Minn.: Hal Leonard
Publishing Co., 1981. 54 pp. and 17 blueprint drawings.

Illustrated practical guide.

1135. WIGGINTON, Eliot, ed. "Banjos and Dulcimers" in Foxfire 3,
      pp. 121-207. Garden City, N.Y.: Anchor Press, 1975.

      Introduction and articles on eight individual makers, with
photos and drawings (some technical). Much of the text is in the
words of the makers.

1136. WIGGINTON, Eliot, ed. "Gourd Banjos and Songbows" in
      Foxfire 6, pp. 54-92 [gourd banjos, pp. 54-83; songbows,
      pp. 84-92]. Garden City, N.Y.: Anchor, 1980.

      Each article centers around one maker, Leonard Webb in the
case of the gourd banjo, and Babe Henson in the case of the
songbow. Description of how to make them with photos.

Miscellaneous Non-Stringed Instruments

1137. BLAUSTEIN, Richard. "Jugs, Washboards and Spoons; Why
      Improvised Instruments Make us Laugh." Tennessee Folklore
      Society Bulletin 67 (June 1981): 76-79.

1138. GAMSE, Albert. The Best Harmonica Method Yet. Carlstadt,
      N.J.: Lewis Music Publishing Co., 1971. 97 pp.

      Method for both diatonic and chromatic types.

1139. GLOVER, Tony ("Little Son") I. Edited by Kristin White.
      Blues Harp: an Instruction Method for Playing the Blues
      Harmonica. New York: Oak, 1965, 1973. 72 pp.

      Self-instruction book for harmonica with two 7-inch
records.

1140. HOWARD, Joseph H. Drums in the Americas. New York: Oak,
      1967. 319 pp.

      Scholarly study of drums of several origins: Amerindian,
European-American, African, and Afro-American. Also studies
Asiatic and Oceanic influences as well as drums in North, Central,
and South America, including "slit drums." Numerous excellent
photos and line drawings, and a bibliography on pp. 294-311.

INSTRUMENTS: MISCELLANEOUS

1141. LICHT, Michael S. "Harmonica Magic: Virtuoso Display in
American Folk Music." Ethnomusicology 24-2 (May 1980):
211-21.

Sociological approach to the development of solo harmonica
playing in the United States. Author asserts that Africa influence is greater than European, but that changes in society (e.g.,
industrialization) are symbolized in such pieces as "locomotive"
and man's conflict with nature in such pieces as "fox chase."

1142. MacLEOD, Bruce A. "Quills, Fifes, and Flutes Before the
Civil War." Southern Folklore Quarterly 42 (1978): 201-8.

A survey of early sources that mention these instruments
[quills are pan pipes] and references to early recordings.

1143. PIERCE, Edwin H. "On Some Old Bugle-Calls of the U. S.
Navy." Musical Quarterly 18 (1932): 134-9.

A study of the bugle tunes found in a c.1830 Station Book
from Concord, N.H., for a unit commanded by Matthew C. Perry.
Illustrated with drawings.

1144. SCHULZ, Russell Eugene. "The Reed Organ in Nineteenth-
Century America." Ph.D. dissertation, University of Texas
at Austin, 1974. 194 pp.

A sociological study of the instrument and its literature,
its history, how it operated, and the instruction books (especially
Kimball's of 1872). Explores the attitudes by Americans based on a
questionnaire given to older people. The bibliography includes
method books and catalogues.

1145. VARELIA, Donald, and MacLEOD, Peter R. The United States
Bicentennial Collection of Bagpipe Music. 2 vols.
Pontiac, Mich.: Piping, 1976. 165 pp.

VI.   AMERICAN PSALMODY AND HYMNODY

The study of hymns provides a particular challenge to the
question of folkness, for except in cases where hymns are
transmitted entirely by oral tradition, some written source is
involved.   Minimally, this is a "hymnal," i.e., a collection of
texts.   In this case, the tunes are orally transmitted and often
the performance practices are those basic to folk music.   In other
cases the tunes are written out.   This is especially true of early
psalmody and more recently of gospel hymnody.   Admittedly, then, a
certain number of entries in this section pertain to types of
hymnody that are close to the written tradition.

On the other hand, hymnody outside mainline churches, where it
tends to be regulated by a denominational hymnal and an organist,
is essentially "of the people."   Although gospel hymns have always
been transmitted, at least at the beginning, by written means, they
constitute a musical expression of common people and as such could
easily be described as part of the larger folk picture.

One of the earliest writers to call attention to the existence
of folk hymnody was George Pullen Jackson, although his collections
of "folk hymns" were taken entirely from written sources--shape-
note singing school books--rather than from field recordings.   It
is only in more recent years that scholars, and only a few at that,
have taken an interest in folk hymnody on its own terms.   Folk
hymnody remains a rich but little worked field, and one which
cannot be said to be dying, like certain other kinds of folk music.
Furthermore, church services, being more or less public events,
permit observation by interested scholars.

After sections devoted to folk hymnody, gospel hymnody, and
the inevitible "miscellaneous studies," there are also brief
sections for Mormon and Shaker hymns.   The former, however, came to
include other material concerning Mormon songs as well.   The latter
(Shaker) is primarily the work of one scholar, Daniel Patterson.
Again, Shaker hymnody has many elements associated with folk
traditions while being largely written down in musical notation.

General and Miscellaneous Studies

1146. APPEL, Richard G. The Music of the Bay Psalm Book: 9th
Edition (1698). I.S.A.M. Monographs #5. New York:
Institute for Studies in American Music, 1975. 43 pp.

Historical introduction to The Whole Booke of Psalmes
commonly known as the "Bay Psalm Book" and in particular to the
ninth edition, the first to include music notation. Includes all
13 tunes both in facsimile and transcription, and texts.

1147. BAKER, Paul. Why Should the Devil Have All the Good Music?
Jesus Music--Where it Began, Where it is, Where it is
Going. Waco: Word Books, 1979. 235 pp.

Written by an insider, this focuses on the influence of
"folk" and rock musics, especially the latter, on contemporary
religious music. Personal, but well done.

1148. CAMPBELL, John C. The Southern Highlander and His
Homeland. New York: Russell Sage Foundation, 1921;
reprint ed., Lexington: University Press of Kentucky,
1969; Spartanburg, S.C.: Reprint Co., 1973. 405 pp.

Not on music per se, this book provides valuable
background information on Appalachian religions, especially
chapter 8, "The Growth of Denominationalism in the Highlands" (pp.
152-75) and chapter 9, "The Religious Life of the Rural Highlands"
(pp. 176-94). The latter includes some tunes and descriptions of
practices.

1149. COVEY, Cyclone. "Religion and Music in Colonial America."
Ph.D. dissertation, Stanford University, 1949. 224 pp.

1150. ELLINWOOD, Leonard, and LOCKWOOD, Elizabeth. Bibliography
of American Hymnals. New York: University Music Editions
for the Hymn Society of America, 1983. 27 microfiche.

An index of 7,500 hymnals for 140 religious bodies
published between 1640 and 1978 in both North and South America
based on the holdings of 82 libraries. Extensive information is
given regarding each item. This project, the equivalent of 1,500
pages of data, was the basis of the following item.

1151. ELLINWOOD, Leonard, and LOCKWOOD, Elizabeth. The Dictionary
       of American Hymnology: First Line Index. New York:
       University Music Editions, 1984. 179 microfilm reels, 16
       mm. negative film.

       This mind-boggling first-line index of all hymns in 7,500
hymnals from 1640-1978 (see previous item) totals some 1 million
entries. A 118-page User's Guide explains the organization and
use of the Index.

1152. ELLINWOOD, Leonard. "Religious Music in America." In
       Religious Perspectives in American Culture, pp. 289-359.
       Edited by Will Herberg. Princeton: Princeton University
       Press, 1961.

       Broad descriptive survey of the development of religious
music in America, including American Indians, early groups (e.g.,
Franciscans and Moravians), Negro spirituals, gospel songs, early
psalmody, and performance practices.

1153. FOOTE, Henry Wilder. An Account of the Bay Psalm Book.
       Papers of the Hymn Society of America, Vol. 7. N.p.:
       Hymn Society of America, 1940; reprint ed., n.d., [c.
       1980]. 18 pp.

       A brief history of the Bay Psalm Book with more emphasis
on the translations of the psalms than on the music.

1154. GILLESPIE, Paul F., ed. Foxfire 7. Garden City, N.Y.:
       Anchor Press/Doubleday, 1982. 510 pp.

       Primarily a collection of studies of particular Appalach-
ian denominations (Baptists, Roman Catholic, Church of Christ,
Episcopal, Jehovahs Witnesses, Methodists, Pentecostals,
Presbyterians, Camp Meetings), but does include articles on shaped
notes and Gospel shaped notes as well as baptism, foot washing,
and snake handling. While not on folk hymnody per se, it is a
valuable foundation for that study.

1155. HILL, Double E. "A Study of Tastes in American Church
       Music as Reflected in the Music of the Methodist
       Episcopal Church to 1900." Ph.D. dissertation, Univer-
       sity of Illinois at Urbana-Champaign, 1962. 900 pp.

Based on a close examination of 70 hymn books from 1765-1878 including their prefaces, this study seeks to compare the tastes in church music of the nineteenth century to the present through the Methodist Church's usage. It also examines Wesley's preferences in hymnody and the types of tunes used.

1156. HINKS, Donald R. Brethren Hymn Books and Hymnals, 1720-1884. Gettysburg, Pa.: Brethren Heritage Press, 1986. 205 pp.

Description of hymn books and hymnals used by the Brethren Church during their first 176 years. They pertain to all five branches: Church of the Brethren, The Fellowship of Grace Brethren Churches, The Brethren Church (Ashland), The Old German Baptist Brethren Church, and The Dunkard Brethren. This extremely thorough study in 10 chapters includes photographs of each of the 50 important collections, and concludes with 15 appendices.

1157. INSERRA, Lorraine, and HITCHCOCK, H. Wiley. The Music of Henry Ainsworth's Psalter (Amsterdam, 1612). I.S.A.M. Monograph #15. New York: Institute for Studies in American Music, 1981. 126 pp.

Scholarly study of this important psalter of European origin, including its history, sources, plus all 39 tunes and texts with bibliography and discography.

1158. LAWLESS, Elaine J. "Making a Joyful Noise: an Ethnography of Communication in the Pentecostal Religious Service." Southern Folklore Quarterly 44 (1980): 1-22.

This is a detailed description of services at Johnson Creek Church, a Oneness Pentecostal congregation south of Bloomington, Indiana. Music plays a major role in the services, and its place is described. This research was in preparation for a 58' TV documentary entitled Joy Unspeakable filmed at the Sixteenth Street Pentecostal Assembly in Bloomington and available from Indiana University's Audio-Visual Services.

1159. LIPPINCOTT, Peter. Psalm Singing of the Covenanters. [University City, Mo.: Prairie Schooner Records, 1977 ?]. 96 pp. and recording, Prairie Schooner PSI 102.

A musical history of the Reformed Presbyterian Church in America, including its doctrines and psalmody, by several authorities. It is illustrated by a disc field recorded in church services and family worship in various parts of the Midwest.

1160. McCARROLL, Jesse Cornelius. "Black Influence on Southern White Protestant Church Music during Slavery." Ed.D. dissertation, Columbia University, 1972. 176 pp.

1161. MacDOUGALL, Hamilton C. Early New England Psalmody: an Historical Appreciation, 1620-1820. Brattleboro, Vt.: Stephen Daye Press, 1940; reprint ed., New York: Da Capo, 1969. 187 pp.

An important early survey of the coming of psalmody in America from Europe and England, the influence of the compilers (especially T. Rosencroft, John Playford, Tate and Brady), and the American collections done by John Tufts, William Billings, and Lowell Mason. Also studies the singing school tradition, notations, and the use of instruments.

1162. MARTIN, Raymond Jones. "The Transition from Psalmody to Hymnody in Southern Presbyterianism, 1753-1901." S.M.D. dissertation, Union Theological Seminary, 1963. 173 pp.

Although psalmody was at first the only accepted form of singing, Samuel Davies first introduced psalm paraphrases by Watts, then hymns, which supplemented the psalms. The author traces these changes through the official hymnals of the church.

1163. PATTERSON, Daniel W. "Word, Song, and Motion: Instruments of Celebration among Protestant Radicals in Early Nineteenth-Century America." In Celebrations: Studies in Festivity and Ritual, pp. 220-30. Edited by Victor Turner. Washington, D.C.: Smithsonian Institution, 1982.

Fascinating introduction to the musical practices of the radical protestant sects, especially the Baptists and Shakers.

1164. PRATT, Waldo Selden. The Music of the Pilgrims: a Description of the Psalm Book Brought to Plymouth in 1620. Boston: Oliver Ditson, 1921; reprint ed., New York: Russell & Russell, 1971. 80 pp.

A study of the earliest psalm singing in America, the books they brought and the tunes used, with examples given.

1165. SCHOLES, Percy A. "The Truth About the New England Pilgrims and Music." Musical Quarterly 19 (1933): 1-17.

Seeks to correct the view that the Puritans hated music by showing from original sources exactly what kind of music making was going on. Includes many quotations from primary sources.

1166. SMEETON, Donald D. "Holiness Hymns and Pentecostal Power." The Hymn 31 (July 1980): 183-5.

This brief essay begins by making the important but often overlooked distinction between the terms "holiness" and "pentecostal." The author then proceeds to describe the texts and underlying messages of four early holiness and pentecostal hymns.

1167. STEVENSON, Arthur Linwood. The Story of Southern Hymnology. Roanoke, Va.: Stone Printing and Manufacturing Co., 1931. 193 pp.

Survey of Baptist, Presbyterian, and Methodist hymn singing and hymnals from the South, including Moravian influence, the coming of Gospel and revival hymns, and other matters.

1168. TALLMADGE, William. "Folk Organum: a Study of Origins." American Music 2-3 (Fall, 1984): 47-65.

For the author, organum means polyphony. This study is based on five operational definitions of polyphony derived from Reese's 1940 Music of the Middle Ages, three of which he finds in southern Appalachia. Numerous examples are drawn from folk hymnody. Also studied are heterophonic texture, drone, call and response, and the quartal harmony of the singing school books.

1169. TITON, Jeff Todd. "Stance, Role, and Identity in Fieldwork among Folk Baptists and Pentecostals." American Music 3-1 (Spring, 1985): 16-24.

Based on the author's experiences, this is a discussion of the role of the researcher in the context of religious services and the difficulties of establishing and maintaining an appro-

priate identity vis-a-vis that desired by the host members.
Discusses the dilemma between who the researcher is and what
he/she believes (especially difficult for atheists and agnostics)
and what he/she wants the informants to think about him/her.

1170. TUCKER, Stephen R. "Pentecostalism and Popular Culture in
       the South: a Study of Four Musicians." Journal of
       Popular Culture 16-3 (Winter, 1982): 68-80.

       Discusses the influence of pentecostalism on Southern
culture in general and music in particular, as seen in the lives
of James Blackwood, Johnny Cash, Tammy Wynette, and Jerry Lee
Lewis

1171. YOUNG, Robert H. "The History of Baptist Hymnody in
       England from 1612 to 1800." D.M.A. dissertation,
       University of Southern California, 1959. 252 pp.

       A study of the attitudes of Baptist church founders in
England towards hymnody and the spread of hymns and tunes both in
England and in America.

Traditional and Camp-Meeting Hymnody

1172. ASBURY, Samuel E., and MEYER, Henry E. "Old-Time White
       Camp-Meeting Spirituals." Austin: Texas Folklore
       Society, 1932. 17 pp.

       A small collection of camp-meeting spirituals in
arrangements by Meyer, with an accompanying text by Asbury in
which he describes camp meeting singing as he heard it in South
Carolina in the 1880s.

1173. ASHBY, Rickie Zayne. "The Brush Arbor Revival." Kentucky
       Folklore Record 21 (Jan.-Mar. 1975): 15-17.

       A brief description of brush arbor revival services held
by Holiness churches in eastern Kentucky. Includes an oral
tradition song performed at a revival.

1174. BRUCE, Dickson Davies, Jr. And They All Sang Hallelujah.
       Knoxville: University of Tennessee Press, 1974. 155 pp.

This book, based on the author's dissertation, discusses the theology, symbolism and music of the American frontier camp-meeting movement, 1800-1845. The camp-meeting spirituals are studied in light of the three basic symbols which they include-- heaven, Jesus, and the church. In form, the hymns are then related to the conversional theology of the movement.

1175. BUCHANAN, Annabel Morris. Folk Hymns of America. New York: J. Fischer and Bros., 1938. 94 pp.

Although there is a seven-page introduction, the bulk consists of 50 arranged folk hymns and headnotes for each. Not done in style, but an early appreciation of the genre.

1176. CLEMENTS, William M. "The American Folk Church." Ph.D. dissertation, Indiana University, 1974. 457 pp.

An attempt to define and describe the folk level of American religion, which is seen as that body of belief and ritual which has no direct association with a given community's secular power structure. With this definition in mind, a number of folk religious events were observed at Baptist and Pentecostal churches, and interviews with participants conducted. The traits delineated are: general orientation towards the past, scriptural literalism, consciousness of providence, emphasis on evangelism, informality, emotionalism, moral rigorism, sectarianism, egalitarianism, and relative physical isolation of church plants. Not about folk hymnody, but the most significant study yet on its context.

1177. CLEMENTS, William M. "The American Folk Church in Northeast Arkansas." Journal of the Folklore Institute 15-2 (May-Aug. 1978): 161-80.

An overview of the folk church and its elements. Essential to understanding the context of folk hymnody.

1178. DOWNEY, James C. "The Music of American Revivalism." Ph.D. dissertation, Tulane University, 1968. 223 pp.

The purpose of this study was to isolate and categorize the music influenced by revivalistic religion in the period 1740-1800 and to define the relationships existing between this musical practice and the forces of social and religious change.

1179. EDDY, Mary O. "Twenty Folk Hymns." Midwest Folklore 3-1
       (Spring, 1953): 35-44.

A collection of secular tunes from printed songsters such
as the Sacred Harp with religious words added to them, as well as
some discussion.

1180. FIFE, Austin E., and FIFE, Alta S. Heaven on Horseback;
       Revivalist Songs and Verse in the Cowboy Idiom. Western
       Texts Society, Series Vol. 1, No. 1. Logan: Utah State
       University Press, 1970. 114 pp.

A treatment of all aspects of religious expression in the
cowboy idiom and its relationship to both sacred and secular life
in the American West. There are 49 songs, each with headnotes,
texts, and sometimes the tune.

1181. GARRISON, Webb B. "Salem Camp Meeting: Symbol of an Era."
       Georgia Review 5 (Winter, 1951): 445-52. Reprinted in
       Music in Georgia, pp. 163-70. Edited by Frank W.
       Hoogerwerf. New York: Da Capo, 1984.

Non-technical, historical background of one particular
camp meeting.

1182. GREEN, Archie. "Hear These Beautiful Sacred Selections."
       In 1970 Yearbook of the International Folk Music Council,
       pp. 28-50. Edited by Alexander L. Ringer.

A study of commercially recorded sacred folk and folk-
like songs, and an attempt to explain why G. P. Jackson omitted
this material in his studies on folk hymnody.

1183. HORN, Dorothy D. "A Study of the Folk Hymns of
       Southeastern America." Ph.D. dissertation, University
       of Rochester, Eastman School of Music, 1953. 252 pp.

A dissertation written in music theory which examines the
folk hymns of the singing school books in analytical detail.

1184. HULAN, Richard Huffman. "Camp-Meeting Spiritual Folksongs:
       Legacy of the 'Great Revival in the West'." Ph.D. diss-
       ertation, University of Texas at Austin, 1978. 279 pp.

This work describes a unique genre of publication, the camp-meeting songster. Furthermore, it distinguishes such books both from denominational hymnals and from singing school books. The author's approach isolates the earlier body of camp-meeting hymnody, 1800-1805, and examines it from the perspective of hymnology rather than that of musicology.

1185. JACKSON, Bruce. "Glory Songs of the Lord." In Our Living Traditions: an Introduction to American Folklore, pp. 103-19. Edited by Tristram Potter Coffin. New York: Basic Books, 1968.

Distillation of important research relating to the "spiritual." Three kinds are distinguished: 1) those sung by the Pennsylvania Dutch, 2) those sung by whites, and 3) those sung by blacks. Examples of each are given and research summarized.

1186. JACKSON, George Pullen. Another Sheaf of White Spirituals. Gainesville, University of Florida Press, 1952. 233 pp.

Jackson's final collection of rural white religious folk-songs contains 363 tunes and texts arranged in nine groups and ob-tained from living singers, printed sources, and unpublished coll-ections. Each has a headnote with background information. This volume also contains a comprehensive index to all of Jackson's books on white and black spirituals--titles, first lines, refrains, and choruses.

1187. JACKSON, George Pullen. Down-East Spirituals and Others. Locust Valley, N.Y.: J. J. Augustine, 1941; 2nd ed., 1953; reprint ed., New York: Da Capo, 1975. 296 pp.

A supplement to Spiritual Folk-Songs. . . ., this collection includes 300 songs from printed singing school books, 60 of them religious ballads, 152 folk hymns, and 88 revival spiritual songs. Additionally Jackson provides the tune, text, source and composer (when known). About 100 of them are from New England, the region from which the white spiritual is alleged to have originated.

1188. JACKSON, George Pullen. Spiritual Folk-Songs of Early America [(250 Tunes and Texts)]. New York: J. J. Augus-tine, 1937; reprint ed., New York: Dover, 1964. 254 pp.

The collection of 250 songs is preceded by an introduction, cross references, and a now-discredited tune analysis based on modes and gapped scales.

1189. JACKSON, George Pullen. White and Negro Spirituals: their Life Span and Kinship. Locust Valley, N.Y.: J. J. Augustine, 1943; reprint ed., New York: Da Capo, 1975. 349 pp.

This controversial study of the origins of white and black spiritual folk songs begins with "a review and reinterpretation of the nineteenth-century heydey and decline of religious folk song among the white people" from the Great Awakening on, and continues with a survey of publications of black spirituals. A "tune comparative list" pairs 116 white spiritual melodies with an equal number of "Negro-sung variants," demonstrating the huge percentage of close melodic relationships. For Jackson, this was sufficient proof that the Negro spiritual was an adaptation of the white spiritual, a view no longer accepted by most scholars.

1190. JOHNSON, Charles Albert. The Frontier Camp Meeting: Religion's Harvest Time. Dallas: Southern Methodist University Press, 1955. 325 pp.

A scholarly study of the camp meeting in frontier America (especially Kentucky) between 1800 and 1840, this book contains much that is relevant to the religious folk music of both whites and blacks. In addition to describing the development of this form of worship, Johnson gives a detailed portrait of the characteristics of frontier revivalism in which references to singing are common. Chapter 10 is entirely devoted to camp-meeting hymns.

1191. LORENZ, Ellen Jane. Glory Hallelujah! The Story of the Campmeeting Spiritual. Nashville: Abingdon Press, 1980. 144 pp.

Written in popular style, this book examines the camp-meeting movement on the American frontier in the early nineteenth century. Special attention is given to the music and its history from the inception to the present, including continued use. The book also includes an annotated list of 48 camp-meeting spirituals, a glossary, and a brief bibliography.

1192. McDOWELL, Lucien L., comp. Songs of the Old Camp Ground:
      Genuine Religious Folk Songs of the Tennessee Hill
      Country. Ann Arbor, Mich.: Edwards Brothers, 1937. 85 pp.

      Tunes and texts for 44 white religious folk songs from a
remote area of Tennessee by a compiler imbued with the knowledge
and spirit of the tradition. Songs are given as recollected by
the compiler and his friends, organized into three groups, with
brief notes for each.

1193. MILLER, Terry E. "Voices From the Past: the Singing and
      Preaching at Otter Creek Church." Journal of American
      Folklore 88-349 (July-Sept. 1975): 266-82.

      A description of the singing and preaching at Otter Creek
Regular Predestinarian Baptist Church in Putnam County, Indiana.
After a brief historical summary of the conservative branches of
the Baptist faith, the author describes in some detail his field
observations, focusing on the oral tradition hymns sung. Although
lining out no longer occurs, the heterophonic texture associated
with it does. Several transcriptions are included along with a
repertory and source list for the church.

1194. PATTERSON, Daniel W. "The Bible and the American Folk
      Arts." In The Bible in American Arts and Letters, pp.
      187-217. Edited by Giles Gunn. Philadelphia: Fortress
      Press, 1983.

      A discussion of black, white camp-meeting, and Shaker
spirituals as well as the New Mexican alabados.

1195. PATTERSON, Daniel W. "Hunting for the American White
      Spiritual: a Survey of Scholarship, with Discography."
      Journal of the Association for Recorded Sound Collections
      3-1 (Winter, 1970-71): 7-18.

      Review of G. P. Jackson's work and its stimulation of
research and collecting, a review of records with shape-note
singing, and discussion of what singing remains today. Includes
materials on Shaker spirituals.

1196. PORTER, Ellen Jane Lorenz. "A Treasure of Campmeeting
      Spirituals." Ph.D. dissertation, Union Graduate School
      [Ohio], 1978. 458 pp.

This is a study of the camp-meeting spiritual as it appears in northern hymnbooks, especially The Revivalist of 1868. There are descriptions of the camp meetings of the early nineteenth century, analyses of the characteristic forms and themes of the songs, and an account of the songs' early appearances in print. The northern spirituals are compared with the southern, the Negro, and the Pennsylvania Dutch spirituals.

1197. RALSTON, Jack L. "Come Thou Fount of Every Blessing." The Hymn 16-1 (Jan., 1965): 5-12.

Study of one particular hymn, with emphasis on text, use in later sources, and history, including tune settings used.

1198. SALTZMAN, Herbert. "A Historical Study of the Function of Music Among the Brethren in Christ." D.M.A. dissertation, University of Southern California, 1964. 338 pp.

A study of the Original River Brethren, a German-origin sect started in the late eighteenth century. It centers around their unaccompanied hymnody, hymnals, writers, composers, social life, singing schools, domestic hymnody, and change.

1199. SASSON, Diane Hyde. "'The Stone': Versions of a Camp-Meeting Song Collected in North Carolina." Southern Folklore Quarterly 42-4 (1978): 375-84.

A comparison of three versions of an old camp-meeting hymn found in oral tradition in the piedmont area of North Carolina, based on full transcriptions.

1200. SIMS, John Norman. "The Hymnody of the Camp-Meeting Tradition." Ph.D. dissertation, Union Theological Seminary, 1960. 181 pp.

1201. SMITH, Timothy Alan. "The Southern Folk-Hymn, 1800-1860: Notes on Performance Practice." Choral Journal 24 (March 1983): 23-9.

An examination of performance suggestions found in the introductions of early tunebooks. Topics include sources of information, theoretical and notational idiosyncrasies, pedagogy, ensemble singing, tempi, and ornamentation.

1202.   SUTTON, Brett, and HARTMAN, Pete. Primitive Baptist Hymns
        of the Blue Ridge. Chapel Hill: University of North
        Carolina Press, 1982. One 12" LP disc and 27 pp. booklet
        by Sutton.

        A study of oral tradition hymnody among both white and
black Primitive Baptists in Virginia recorded in 1976, many of
which are lined out and sung heterophonically. Interestingly, a
number of them are pairs, sung first by blacks, then by whites.
The booklet provides extensive information about the history and
doctrine of the Primitive Baptists, notes on the selections,
examples of musical notation, and professional photos.

1203.   TALLMADGE, William H. "Baptist Monophonic and Heterophonic
        Hymnody in Southern Appalachia." Yearbook of Inter-
        American Musical Research 11 (1975): 106-36.

        Good description of the oral-tradition hymnody of the Old
Regular Baptists of Kentucky. Additionally, pp. 118-26 are melodic
transcriptions, and pp. 128-36 are a list of 302 song titles with
cross references to eight sources and nine types of songs.

1204.   TALLMADGE, William H. "The Nomenclature of Folk Hymnody."
        The Hymn 30 (Oct. 1979): 240-2.

        A brief attempt to sort out and define five terms used in
reference to American religious music: folk hymn, white spiritual,
spiritual, spiritual folk song, and revival spiritual.

1205.   TEMPERLEY, Nicholas. "The Old Way of Singing: its Origin
        and Development." Journal of the American Musicological
        Society 34-3 (1981): 511-44.

        Scholarly and significant, this thoroughly documented
article traces the development of lined, heterophonic psalm and
hymn singing from the British Isles to America, with numerous
musical examples and quotations from primary sources.

1206.   THOMAS, Dwight. "A Brief Introduction to the Hymnody and
        Musical Life of the Old Order River Brethren of Central
        Pennsylvania." The Hymn 35-2 (April 1984): 107-15.

        After a brief introduction to the history of the Old Order
River Brethren, the author describes the hymnals used and

performance practices associated with hymn singing. These include
the non-use of accompaniment, the use of simple harmony, and
extensive ornamentation. Two transcriptions are included.

1207. TITON, Jeff Todd. "Hymnody at the Fellowship Independent
Baptist Church, Stanley, Virginia." Appalachian Journal
(in press)

Affect, interpretation, intention, and evaluation of
hymns from the church members' point of view, as revealed in
conversation with the author.

1208. TITON, Jeff Todd. "Some Recent Pentecostal Revivals."
Georgia Review 32 (Fall, 1978): 579-606.

This essay is based on the author's field research in two
Pentecostal revivals during the spring and summer of 1977.
Included are musical transcriptions and verbatim transcripts of a
message in tongues and its interpretation. Fifteen pages of
photographs follow the text.

1209. TITON, Jeff Todd. "A Song from the Holy Spirit."
Ethnomusicology 24 (May 1980): 223-31.

This article, which includes verbatim transcripts of an
interview taped during the field work, documents the way in which
a white, fundamentalist Baptist lay preacher composed a song under
the influence of the Holy Spirit. Includes transcriptions of the
tune and text.

1210. TITON, Jeff Todd, and GEORGE, Kenneth M. Powerhouse for
God: Sacred Speech, Chant, and Song in an Appalachian
Baptist Church. Chapel Hill: University of North Carolina
Press, 1982. 2 12" LP recordings and 24 pp. booklet.

Recorded 1977 and 1978 at the Fellowship Independent
Baptist Church, Stanley, Virginia, by Titon and George, this is
more than just an anthology of congregational and small group
hymns, an excerpt of Sunday School, preaching, and the life story
of the leader, John Sherfey. The booklet traces the history and
doctrine of the congregation and provides extensive commentary,
photos, and musical examples for each selection, including a
transcription of the speaking.

1211. WICKS, Sammie Ann. "Life and Meaning: Singing, Praying, and the Word among the Old Regular Baptists of Eastern Kentucky." Ph.D. dissertation, University of Texas at Austin, 1983. 182 pp.

This study deals essentially with the universe of the people, an ethnography which looks at the expressive and symbolic aspects of hymnody. Treats the religious heritage of the sect, its history, styles of hymnody, lining out, and demonstrates its continued existence.

1212. YORK, Terry. "Lining-out in Congregational Singing." The Hymn 28 (July 1977): 110-17.

This article traces the historical development of lining-out from the British Isles to the American colonies and concludes with survivals among rural Baptists today. Includes a transcription of a hymn sung by Elder Walter Evans of a Primitive Baptist church in Sparta, North Carolina.

Gospel Hymnody (White)

1213. ANDERSON, Robert, and NORTH, Gail. Gospel Music Encyclopedia. New York: Sterling, 1979. 320 pp.

Popular-style alphabetical list of singers, each including biography and a picture. Also, information on the Gospel Hall of Fame, radio and TV stations, plus a photo album and a series of musical selections.

1214. AVERILL, Patricia. "Media Review: the Anglo-Protestant Traditions." Journal of the Ohio Folklore Society 1 (Dec. 1972): 57-64.

A discussion of Gospel music in Ohio.

1215. BAXTER, Mrs. T. R. (Ma), and POLK, Videt. Gospel Song Writers Biography. Dallas: Stamps-Baxter, 1971. 386 pp.

Biographical portraits of 102 white gospel song composers, a few from the nineteenth century (e.g., Bliss, Sankey, Mason, and Fanny Crosby), but most of southern composers from the present century. The style is more "human interest" than scholarly. Each entry includes a photo as well.

1216. BLACKWELL, Lois S. The Wings of the Dove: the Story of
Gospel Music in America. Norfolk: Donning, 1978. 173 pp.

Although an attempt at a serious history of southern,
white Gospel music, and full of much valuable and scarce
information, it is not scholarly. It is more or less a collection
of personal impressions, anecdotes, and biographical sketches.

1217. BROBSTON, Stanley Heard. "A Brief History of White Southern Gospel Music and a Study of Selected Amateur Family
Gospel Music Singing Groups in Rural Georgia." Ph.D.
dissertation, New York University, 1977. 2 vols., 614 pp.

A history of Gospel music, especially the white southern
tradition, but founded on a history of hymnody from the camp
meeting and singing schools. Chapter 9 details the distinctions
among the three types of southern religious musical institutions:
Sacred Harp singing conventions, Gospel singing conventions, and
Gospel sings. In addition, the author traces the commercial
growth of Gospel music. The second part of the study deals with
the author's field research among amateurs in rural Georgia.

1218. BURT, Jesse, and ALLEN, Duane. The History of Gospel
Music. Nashville: K & S Press, 1971. 205 pp.

Non-scholarly, but an insider's gold mine of information
on white Gospel. Includes 84 pages of biographies, since the book
focuses on groups and individuals.

1219. CRAWFORD, David. "Gospel Songs in Court: From Rural Music
to Urban Industry in the 1950's." Journal of Popular
Culture 11-3 (Winter, 1977): 551-67.

This article documents an extended court case involving
an anti-trust suit over the licensing of performance rights with
the repertory associated with what is now the Gospel Music
Association in Nashville. The evidence submitted during the 1957
trial, recounted here, is of relevance because the legal issues
had to include defining Gospel music, including the shape-note
variety. There is much historical and descriptive material
relating to southern, white Gospel not found elsewhere in print.

1220. DOWNEY, James C. "Mississippi Music: That Gospel Sound."
Southern Quarterly 17-3/4 (Spring-Summer, 1979): 216-23.

A description of the powerful impact of white Gospel
music in the South. The rise of the male quartet and the all-
night singing are examined, as are the publishing companies whose
influence helped bring Gospel music to its level of prominence.

1221. DOWNEY, James C. "Revivalism, the Gospel Songs, and
      Social Reform." Ethnomusicology 9-2 (May 1965): 115-25.

A study of the background and context of Revival and
Gospel song with several complete examples.

1222. KAATRUD, Paul G. "Revivalism and the Popular Spiritual
      Song in Mid-Nineteenth Century America: 1830-1870."
      Ph.D. dissertation, University of Minnesota, 1977. 2
      vols., 183 pp. and 186 pp.

The first three chapters deal with revivalism: its
underlying philosophy, inner nature, and socio-religious
manifestations. The remaining portion is devoted to the three
major strands of popular spiritual song: 1) the traditional
revival song, 2) the American hymn tune, and 3) the Gospel song.
The first is seen as an inheritance from the folk culture, the
second--as personified in Lowell Mason--is seen as an innovation,
and the third is seen as a synthesis of the first two in addition
to a number of popular secular song types.

1223. PIERCE, Edwin H. "'Gospel Hymns' and Their Tunes."
      Musical Quarterly 26 (1940); 355-64.

Wide-ranging article centered on Sankey's hymns but based
on personal experience. More of an essay than a scholarly study.

1224. PORTER, Ellen Jane. "William B. Bradbury, the Campmeeting
      Spiritual, and the Gospel Song." The Hymn 34-1 (1983):
      34-39.

A study of Bradbury and the sources of his song style,
especially in relation to the two genres in the title.

1225. SANKEY, Ira D., McGRANAHAN, James, STEBBINS, George C., and
      BLISS, Philip P. Gospel Hymns Nos. 1 to 6 Complete.
      Chicago: Biglow & Main Co., 1895; reprint ed., New York:
      Da Capo, 1972. 512 pp.

Extensive collection of Gospel hymns in round-note notation on two staves.

1226. SCHEIPS, Paul J. Hold the Fort! The Story of a Song from the Sawdust Trail to the Picket Line. Smithsonian Studies in History and Technology, #91. Washington, D.C.: Smithsonian Institution Press, 1971. 57 pp.

History of a Gospel song that was based on a Civil War battle at Allatoona (near Atlanta, Georgia) on October 5, 1864. Discusses the context, Civil War history, but little on music.

1227. SIZER, Sandra S. Gospel Hymns and Social Religion: the Rhetoric of Nineteenth-Century Revivalism. Philadelphia: Temple University, 1978. 222 pp.

A study of the meaning of Gospel hymns from the time of Sankey to the present, but the emphasis is on text, not tune. It focuses on the images, how they have influenced society, and how they were influenced by society.

1228. STEWART, T. H. "Psalms, Hymns and Spiritual Songs: Geneses of Gospel Song Poems." Tennessee Folklore Society Bulletin 46 (1980): 68-72.

This article discusses the roots, development and perpetuations of the Gospel song. Especially interesting is the author's discussion of the striking similarities between the white spiritual "Jesus, Hold my Hand" and Thomas A. Dorsey's "Precious Lord, Take my Hand." Other similar borrowings are pointed out.

1229. WILHOIT, Melvin Ross. "A Guide to the Principal Authors and Composers of Gospel Song in the Nineteenth Century." D.M.A. dissertation, Southern Baptist Theological Seminary, 1982. 367 pp.

The purpose of the research project was to develop a practical reference tool or guide to the principal authors and composers of Gospel song. The unique nature of the guide was its compilation of widely scattered and often unavailable literature of both a published and unpublished nature.

1230. WOLFE, Charles. "'Gospel Boogie': White Southern Gospel
    Music in Transition, 1945-55." Popular Music 1 (1981):
    73-82.

    This article documents the commercialization and rapid
rise in popularity of southern Gospel music after World War II.
Special attention is focused on the Homeland Harmony Quartet and
their recording of Le Roy Abernethy's "Gospel Boogie" which helped
lead the transition.

1231. WOLFE, Charles. "Presley and the Gospel Tradition."
    Southern Quarterly 18-1 (Fall, 1979): 135-50.

    An exploration of the "ignored" influence on Presley of
white Gospel.

Songs and Hymnody of the Mormons

1232. CHENEY, Thomas E. Mormon Songs from the Rocky Mountains: a
    Compilation of Mormon Folk Song. Austin: University of
    Texas Press, 1968. 221 pp.

    Based on both oral tradition and texts preserved in
writing by "early folksingers," this collection includes both
secular and sacred texts. The bibliography includes much obscure
material on Mormon folk song.

1233. DAVIDSON, Levette J. "Mormon Songs." Journal of American
    Folklore 58-230 (Oct.-Dec. 1945): 273-300.

    Textually oriented, this collection divides songs into
hymns, campaign songs, migration songs, social songs, etc.

1234. PURDY, William Earl. "Music in Mormon Culture, 1830-1876."
    Ph.D. dissertation, Northwestern University, 1960. 384 pp.

    A comprehensive view of music in Mormon life, this study
treats music in education, theater, military and community bands,
folksong, hymns and religious songs.

1235. "A Selected List of References on Mormon Folklore and
    Folksong." Washington, D.C. Library of Congress, Archive
    of Folk Song, 1970. 4 pp. (47 items).

1236. SLAUGHTER, Jay L. "The Role of Music in the Mormon Church, School, and Life." Mus.Ed.D. dissertation, Indiana University, 1964. 414 pp.

In order to identify the ideologies of music and music education in the Mormon Church, the author traces the history of music education in the Church, studies its practices and procedures and the music used.

1237. WEIGHT, Newell Bryan. "An Historical Study of the Origin and Character of Indigenous Hymn Tunes of the Latter Day Saints." D.M.A. dissertation, University of Southern California, 1961. 465 pp.

Traces the development of hymnody from the first tuneless hymnal of c. 1832 to the first collection with tunes in 1857, then to the present. The emphasis is on indigenous hymnody.

Religious Song of the Shakers

1238. ANDREWS, Edward D. The Gift to be Simple: Songs, Dances, and Rituals of the American Shakers. New York: J. J. Augustine, 1940; reprint ed., New York: Dover, 1962. 170 pp.

Important and careful study of music among the Shakers, including 79 songs, songs in ritual, tunes and music, notations, and dances.

1239. ANDREWS, Edward D. "Shaker Songs." Musical Quarterly 23 (1937): 491-508.

Describes how songs were received, how used in marches and dances, and presents selected songs derived from manuscripts.

1240. A Collection of Millennial Hymns Adapted to the Present Order of the Church (Shakers). Canterbury, N.H.: United Society, 1847; reprint ed., New York: AMS Press, 1975. 200 pp.

1241. COOK, Harold E. Shaker Music: a Manifestation of American Folk Culture. Lewisburg, Pa.: Bucknell University Press, 1973. 312 pp.

Based on the author's 1947 dissertation written at Western Reserve University, this comprehensive study encompasses the social milieu and history of the Shakers, their hymnals (including a 41-page list of manuscript hymnals and a 2-page list of printed hymnals), music theory, performance practices, and provides musical analysis. One of two major sources.

1242. EVANS, Frederick William, comp., Shaker Music. Inspirational Hymns and Melodies Illustrative of the Resurrection Life and Testimony of the Shakers. Albany: Weed, Parsons and Co., 1875; reprint ed., New York: AMS Press, 1974. 67 pp.

Shaker songs in 2-4 parts, on 2 staves in round notes, apparently reprinted from various sources. Brief singing tutor at the end by John Howard.

1243. GRIMES, Anne. "Possible Relationship Between 'Jump Jim Crow' and Shaker Songs." Midwest Folklore 3-1 (Spring, 1953): 47-57.

More a study of a particular song, who was Jim Crow, how did the song pass into the minstrel tradition and undergo transformations around the world? The author then attempts to prove melodic relationships with certain Shaker songs.

1244. HALL, Roger L., ed. A Western Shaker Music Sampler. Cleveland: Western Reserve Historical Society, 1976. 40 pp.

While there is a bit of introductory history, primarily a collection of songs and texts.

1245. PATTERSON, Daniel W. "Authority and Inspiration in the Development of the Shaker Spiritual." In Folklore Studies in Honor of Arthur Palmer Hudson [doubles as North Carolina Folklore 13], pp. 111-20. Edited by D. W. Patterson. Chapel Hill: The North Carolina Folklore Society, 1965.

1246. PATTERSON, Daniel W. "'Bearing for the Dead': a Shaker Belief and its Impress on the Shaker Spiritual." The Shaker Quarterly 8 (Winter, 1968): 116-28.

Examination of a folk belief that spirits cause illness and death and how these beliefs are reflected in the songs.

1247. PATTERSON, Daniel W. "Early Shaker Spirituals Sung by Sister R. Mildred Barker . . . and other Members of the United Society of Shakers, Sabbathday Lake, Maine." Sommerville, Mass.: Rounder Records 0078, 1976. One 12" 33 1/3 rpm disc.

This recording includes an extensive booklet documenting the material recorded. The singer on this recording is one of the few remaining living Shakers.

1248. PATTERSON, Daniel W. Nine Shaker Spirituals with a Brief Account of Early Shaker Song. Old Chatham, N.Y.: The Quaker Museum Foundation, 1964. 34 pp.

1249. PATTERSON, Daniel W. The Shaker Spiritual. Princeton: Princeton University Press, 1979. 562 pp.

This comprehensive and scholarly study delves into the history and beliefs of the community and its notations, but the primary strength is to provide over 300 spirituals and classify and discuss them. The categories include songs of the gospel parents, solemn songs, laboring songs, ballads, hymns, extra songs, occasional songs, anthems, and gift songs. Also the author provides an extensive list of manuscript sources and locations.

1250. RHODES, Willard. "Music of the North American Indian Shaker Religion." In Festschrift to Ernst Emsheimer on the Occasion of his 70th Birthday, January 15th, 1974, pp. 180-4. Studia instrumentorum musicae popularis III. Stockholm: Nordiska Musikforlaget, 1974.

Arguably not the same Shakers as in the other entries, but similar nonetheless. A study of American Indians of the northwest coast whose religion synthesizes elements of Christian symbolism and practices of the indigenous guardian-spirit religion. As in the case of many Shakers, they receive their songs in dreams.

1251. TERRI, Salli. "The Gift of Shaker Music." Music Educators' Journal 62-1 (1975): 22-35.

Attractive, non-technical survey article covering Shaker history, the place of singing in the community, dance, and includes many illustrations and transcriptions of songs.

1252.   THOMASON, Jean Healan. Shaker Manuscript Hymnals from
        South Union, Kentucky. Kentucky Folklore Series #3.
        Bowling Green, Ken.: Kentucky Folklore Society, 1967.
        56 pp.

        Brief study of Shaker texts, songs, and notations.

VII. THE SINGING SCHOOL AND SHAPE-NOTE TRADITION

The singing school tradition in the United States both represents an ideal kind of "folk music" and its antithesis. In support of the former contention, it can be asserted that the singing school is a musical activity of common people, especially of rural areas, of people making their own music and requiring a minimum of expertise. The tradition is more than two hundred years old, and today, without consciously trying to be so, it is little changed from the way it was in the late eighteenth century. Shape-note singing--the later and more usual form--is recognized as part of the authentic American folk tradition by the Library of Congress and the National Council for Traditional Arts.

On the other hand, the very purpose for the establishment of singing schools was to stamp out oral-tradition hymnody and replace it with a relatively sophisticated part-music dependent on musical literacy and printed songbooks. Indeed, many of the compilers of early singing school books comprise the first generation of native-born American composers. Best known is William Billings.

It could also be pointed out that while the preceding points are valid, they are valid only in a relative sense. As America's musical life became yet more sophisticated by the end of the eighteenth century with the arrival of increasing numbers of European- and British-trained musicians, the singing school masters were more and more seen as country bumpkins associated both with a compositional idiom seen as unlettered and with a stratum of people seen as old-fashioned and "folksy." After the Revolutionary War when people began migrating in large numbers to the "South and West," the singing masters went too, and from that point onwards--and to the present day--the tradition has been associated with unsophisticated, rural people, both black and white, whose music is outside the mainstream and mostly unknown to "cultivated" musicians. The addition of unorthodox notations--shape notes, numerals, letters, and other configurations--in the nineteenth century only added to the tradition's negative reputation among learned musicians who rejected such notations as gimmicks.

253

The pioneering work was George Pullen Jackson's 1933 White Spirituals in the Southern Uplands. Although his work has been superceded by research published by younger scholars, few could deny the importance of Jackson's book, in spite of its weaknesses. Since that time numerous scholars have made further contributions, but none of them have had the scope of Jackson's original work.

Four sub-headings beyond "General and Miscellaneous" seemed appropriate: 1) materials dealing with singing schools, 2) items dealing with specific individuals, 3) bibliographies, and 4) facsimile editions. Of all the individuals, the one most heavily studied is William Billings (1746-1800). In a way, he is atypical of the tradition, for he published only his own works. Still, Billings has become America's best-known composer for the period preceding Stephen Foster and Louis Moreau Gottschalk.

Because the tradition is based on printed books, bibliographies are naturally important. Similarly, a number of facsimile editions of early collections are available, some for singers who maintain the tradition, others for scholars and libraries.

Shape-note singing, whether in the context of singing schools or recreational singings, is an authentic living tradition which maintains itself on its own interest. Because it is performed by a group of people who need not be specialists, it is open to outsiders. Consequently, this music can be enjoyed by anyone able to read the notation and "carry a tune." As such it is certainly one of America's most significant "folk" traditions.

General and Miscellaneous Studies

1253. BEARY, Shirley Lorraine. "The Stamps-Baxter Music and Printing Company: a Continuing American Tradition, 1926-1976." D.M.A. dissertation, Southwestern Baptist Theological Seminary, 1977.

1254. BEARY, Shirley. "Stylistic Traits of Southern Shape-Note Gospel Songs." The Hymn 30 (Jan. 1979): 26-33.

Discussion of musical characteristics--melodic, rhythmic, and harmonic--as well as texts of southern, white Gospel music. Special attention is given the Stamps-Baxter Co. of Dallas.

1255. BOSWELL, George W. "Verse and Music in the Sacred Harp." Southern Folklore Quarterly 34-1 (March 1970): 53-61.

A statistical analysis of the 300 non-fuging tunes in the
Original Sacred Harp. Several methods were used to analyze their
employment of texts and tunes and to compare them both to secular
folksongs and to standard composed hymns. Aspects analyzed were
verse structure, musical and poetic meters, mode, range, and form.

1256. BRITTON, Allen Perdue. "Theoretical Introductions in
      American Tune-Books to 1800." Ph.D. dissertation,
      University of Michigan, 1950. 697 pp.

Examination of introductions to tune books, with emphasis
on history, theory, and the implications of American psalmody.
Part II is an annotated bibliography of tune books, sermons and
pamphlets relating to music, English tune books and other foreign
works, and secondary sources including other bibliographies.

1257. COBB, Buell E., Jr. The Sacred Harp: a Tradition and its
      Music. Athens: University of Georgia Press, 1978.
      245 pp.

Written by an English professor and not especially on the
music (in spite of its title), this valuable work provides the
complete history of the book, its revisions, performance practice
variants, and lists singings and conventions.

1258. CRAWFORD, Richard, ed. The Core Repertory of Early Ameri-
      can Psalmody. Recent Researches in American Music, Vols.
      11 & 12. Madison, Wis.: A-R Editions, 1984. 165 pp.

The second half consists of 101 psalm tunes in 3 or 4
voices on separate staves with words. The first half is an introduction to this material--eighteenth century American harmonized
psalm tunes--and notes on editing, history, and tables.

1259. CRAWFORD, Richard. "Watts for Singing: Metrical Poetry in
      American Sacred Tunebooks, 1761-1785." Early American
      Literature 11-2 (Fall, 1976): 139-46.

Introductory survey of poetry used in tunebooks, its
value, what was selected, and the general nature of the early
oblong collections.

1260. CRAWFORD, Richard, and MCKAY, David P. "Music in
       Manuscript: a Massachusetts Tune-book of 1782." American
       Antiquarian Society Proceedings 84 (Apr. 1974): 43-64;
       also separately, Worcester, Mass.: American Antiquarian
       Society, 1974.

       Study of an eighteenth-century collection made by "Sukey"
Heath, which includes a small repertory of mostly unpublished and
previously unknown American psalm tunes.

1261. DANIEL, Ralph T. The Anthem in New England Before 1800.
       Evanston: Northwestern University Press, 1966; reprint
       ed., New York: Da Capo, 1979. 282 pp.

       Although the anthem was the least "folkish" of the
American singing school repertory, this study is the most
scholarly to date on this still important aspect. After an
extensive introduction, there is a musical supplement of examples
nearly one hundred pages in length.

1262. DAVIDSON, Donald. "The Sacred Harp in the Land of Eden."
       Virginia Quarterly Review 10 (Apr. 1934): 203-17;
       Reprinted in Music in Georgia, pp. 1-16. Edited by Frank
       W. Hoogerwerf. New York: Da Capo, 1984.

       Neither scholarly nor technical, this is a general
introduction to Sacred Harp singing.

1263. "The Eighteenth-Century Hymn Tune." Inter-American Music
       Review 2-1 (Fall, 1979): 1-33.

       Paper read in Los Angeles in 1977 during which live
examples were used, but the author's name was omitted in publication. Focuses on tunes, names, sources, and authors with illustrations from early singing school books. Extensive bibliography
provided which is strong in English sources as well.

1264. ELLINGTON, Charles Linwood. "The Sacred Harp Tradition of
       the South: its Origin and Evolution." Ph.D. disserta-
       tion, The Florida State University, 1969. 172 pp.

       A history of the Sacred Harp and its use among singing
groups, with emphasis on five aspects: 1) relation of this book to
the tradition of the early nineteenth century, 2) the compilation

of the first edition by B. F. White and his role in establishing a
singing movement, 3) the "typical" Sacred Harp song, 4) the
successive editions and revisions and the singing practices which
attended them, 5) the nature and extent of the movement today.

1265. ELLIS, Howard. "Lowell Mason and the Manual of the Boston
      Academy of Music." Journal of Research in Music
      Education 3-1 (Spring, 1955): 3-10.

Lowell Mason's Manual was extremely influential, having
gone through eight editions from 1834 to 1861, and claimed to be
Pestalozzian, but the author attempts to show two things: 1) that
Mason was more an editor than the author, 2) that the book is not
essentially Pestalozzian.

1266. ENGELKE, Hans. "A Study of Ornaments in American Tune
      Books, 1760-1800." Ph.D. dissertation, University of
      Southern California, 1960. 217 pp.

Systematic investigation of ornaments in books from the
indicated period and the correct performance practice of them
based on all tunebooks having such material in introductions.

1267. ESKEW, Harry B. "Joseph Funk's 'Allgemein nützliche
      Choral-Music' (1816)." In Thirty-Second Report, pp. 38-
      46. Baltimore: Society for the History of the Germans in
      Maryland, 1966.

An introduction to this German-American shape-note
tunebook of the Shenandoah Valley which contains several American
folk hymns to German texts.

1268. ESKEW, Harry B. "Shape-Note Hymnody in the Shenandoah
      Valley, 1816-1860." Ph.D. dissertation, Tulane
      University, 1966. 182 pp.

This study is an historical treatment of shape-note
hymnody in the Shenandoah Valley from its beginnings to the Civil
War. It examines two series of thirteen singing-school tunebooks
in shape notation published in 31 known editions, beginning with
Ananias Davisson's Kentucky Harmony (1816) and closing with the
tenth edition of Joseph Funk's Harmonia Sacra (1860).

1269. ESKEW, Harry B. "Using Early American Hymnals and
Tunebooks." Music Library Association Notes 27-1 (Sept.
1970): 19-23.

Brief article for the music librarian describing tunebooks, telling how to acquire them, and what the best reference
works on the subject are.

1270. FINNEY, Theodore M. "The Third Edition of Tuft's
Introduction to the Art of Singing Psalm Tunes." Journal
of Research in Music Education 14 (Fall, 1966): 163-70.

Describes a heretofore·unknown copy of the third edition
of 1723 found in the Pittsburgh Theological Seminary Library.

1271. FISHER, William Arms. Notes on Music in Old Boston.
Boston: Oliver Ditson, 1918; reprint ed., New York: AMS
Press, 1976. 105 pp.

Although much is on classical music, there is some
material on psalm singing and early singing schools, musical life,
and early publications.

1272. GILMAN, Samuel. Memoirs of a New England Village Choir.
Boston, 1829; reprint ed., New York: Da Capo, 1984. 150
pp.

Fictional account of the musical and social life around
1800 of a village church written by a clergyman. Describes the
role of the church choir in both worship and social life.

1273. GILSON, F. "The History of Shaped or Character Notes, with
Specimens." Boston: F. H. Gilson, 1889. 6 pp.

Essay attacking the monopoly of Jesse Aikin's "patent
notes" within the shape-note tradition. A photocopy exists in the
Library of Congress of this very rare pamphlet.

1274. GOULD, Nathaniel D. Church Music in America, Comprising
its History and its Peculiarities of Different Periods
with Cursory Remarks. . . . Boston: A. N. Johnson, 1853;
reprint ed., New York: AMS Press, 1972. 240 pp.

Although the author attempts a comprehensive history of music and aesthetics, this part is of far less importance than his history of psalmody, singing schools, composers, and description of exactly how the schools worked. Written by an insider.

1275. HALL, Paul M. "The Musical Million: a Study and Analysis of the Periodical Promoting Music Reading Through Shape-Notes in North America from 1870 to 1914." D.M.A. dissertation, The Catholic University of America, 1970. 148 pp.

The periodical was published monthly by Ruebush-Kieffer Company of Singer's Glen and Dayton, Virginia. Its primary function was the promotion of shape-notes as the best method of teaching the masses of America to read music. Besides analyzing the contents of all 540 issues, it also describes the schemes used to promote circulation, measures its influence, and offers reasons for its demise.

1276. HALL, Paul M. "The Shape-Note Hymnals and Tune Books of the Ruebush-Kieffer Company." The Hymn 22-3 (July 1971): 69-76.

An historical account of the Virginia family whose publishing enterprises led to the spread of shape-note songbooks throughout the southern United States. Lists many of the books published between 1870 and 1912 and provides a chart comparing five different types of shape-note notation used.

1277. HAMM, Charles. "Patent Notes in Cincinnati." Historical and Philosophical Society of Ohio Bulletin 16-1 (Oct. 1958): 293-310.

Cincinnati was an important place in the history of shape notes, not because they were especially widely used there, but because Cincinnati publishers printed a high percentage of the important collections of the nineteenth century. This article traces the history of these publications as well as the counter movement against shape notes.

1278. HOOD, George. A History of Music in New England: with Biographical Sketches of Reformers and Psalmists. Boston: Wilkins, Carter, & Co., 1846; reprint ed., New York: Johnson Reprint Corp., 1970. 252 pp.

The history of church music generally and psalmody in
particular in seventeenth and eighteenth century New England, as
well as the early singing schools, the work of reformers and
especially Billings. Extensive quotations from primary sources,
biographies, and a bibliography of early publications.

1279. HORN, Dorothy D. Sing to Me of Heaven: a Study of Folk and
        Early American Materials in Three Old Harp Books.
        Gainesville: University of Florida Press, 1970. 212 pp.

A collection of articles mostly previously published
dealing with the music and musical style found in nineteenth-
century singing school books, especially Southern Harmony,
Original Sacred Harp, and New Harp of Columbia. Good bibliography.

1280. JACKSON, George Pullen. "Buckwheat Notes." Musical
        Quarterly 19 (1933): 393-400.

Early, brief, and superficial study of the phenomenon of
shape notes and singing schools, in 1933 still mostly unknown.

1281. JACKSON, George Pullen. The Story of the Sacred Harp, 1844-
        1944. Nashville: Vanderbilt University Press, 1944, 46
        pp.; reprinted in Preface to facsimile edition of White,
        B. F. and King, E. J. The Sacred Harp, 3rd ed., pp. v-xx.
        Philadelphia: S. C. Collins, 1860 [1859]; reprint ed.,
        Nashville: Broadman Press, 1968.

The first comprehensive history of the Sacred Harp, its
compilers, the editions, and its use today. Also includes a
history of the singing school up to the appearance of this collection in 1844 in Georgia. Valuable in spite of its age.

1282. JACKSON, George Pullen. White Spirituals in the Southern
        Uplands. Chapel Hill: University of North Carolina Press,
        1933; reprint ed., Hatboro, Pa.: Folklore Associates, 1964
        [Forward by Don Yoder]; New York: Dover, 1965. 444 pp.

The first important and pioneering study of singing
schools and shape notes of the nineteenth and twentieth centuries.
Although much further work has been done on individual aspects,
Jackson's study stimulated most of it. Besides the basic southern
tradition, it also includes material on notations besides shape
notes, their use in the North and South, and later developments in

Gospel hymnody. Still valuable reading, for much was based on first-hand experience and conversations with people who could remember practices back to the turn of the century.

1283. JAMES, Joseph S. "A Brief History of the Sacred Harp and its Author, B. F. White, Sr., and Contributors." Douglasville, Ga.: New South Book and Job Print, 1904.

Written by the Chairman of the 1911 Revision Committee of the Sacred Harp, which produced the "James Revision" (which was the basis of the currently-used "Denson Revision"), this was the first attempt to write a history of what became America's most famous shape-note book.

1284. KELTON, Mai Hogan. "An Analysis of the Music Curriculum of Sacred Harp (American Tune-Book, 1971 Edition) and its Continuing Tradition." Ed.D. dissertation, University of Alabama, 1985. 343 pp.

No abstract yet available.

1285. KEMP, Father [Robert H.]. A History of the Old Folks' Concerts. Boston: by the author, 1868; reprint ed., New York: Da Capo, 1984. 254 pp.

An account of the musical activities of Robert H. Kemp (1820-1897), who, in the late 1850s began a series of concerts that included humor, impersonations, history, and a revival of the use of eighteenth-century singing school repertory.

1286. KROEGER, Karl Douglas. "'The Worcester Collection of Sacred Harmony' and Sacred Music in America, 1786-1803." Ph.D. dissertation, Brown University, 1976. 708 pp.

The author uses the above collection, published in eight editions between 1786 and 1803, by Isaiah Thomas of Worcester, Massachusetts, as a mirror of popular taste of the day, especially as the repertory changed from one edition to the next. Also provides background data, analyzes the repertory and the ideas in the tunebook's theoretical introduction.

1287. KROHN, Ernst C. Missouri Music. N.p.: Missouri Historical Society, 1924; reprint ed., New York: Da Capo, 1971. 380 pp.

261

Although much of this book is devoted to classical music, pp. 189-99 comprise a study of The Missouri Harmony, a shape-note tunebook that first appeared in 1820, and pp. 200-28 are a checklist of editions.

1288. KROHN, Ernst C. Music Publishing in the Middle Western States Before the Civil War. Detroit Studies in Music Bibliography #23. Detroit: Information Coordinators, 1972. 44 pp.

Well-documented study of publishing, with some data on early singing school books.

1289. KYME, George H. "An Experiment in Teaching Children to Read Music with Shape Notes." Journal of Research in Music Education 8 (1960): 3-8.

Description of a controlled experiment in sight singing done in 1955-6 with 183 fourth and fifth graders from the San Francisco area. The experimental group was taught to sing using Aikin's seven shape notes while the control groups used ordinary notation. It was concluded that the experimental group could sight sing better at the end of the experiment.

1290. LINDSLEY, Charles Edward. "Scoring and Placement of the 'Air' in Early American Tunebooks." Musical Quarterly 58 (1972): 365-82.

Detailed study of who sang which part in the early tunebooks, both round and shape, especially who sang the tune.

1291. LOCKE, Theresa Ann. "The Forgotten Sacred Harp." Negro History Bulletin 39 (Sept.-Oct. 1976): 619-21.

Although brief, this article is one of few to deal with Judge Jackson's The Colored Sacred Harp, a four-shape book in the Sacred Harp tradition but having its origin in the twentieth century among Alabama blacks. Includes illustrations.

1292. LOWENS, Irving. Music and Musicians in Early America. New York: W. W. Norton, 1964. 328 pp.

Collection of important articles by Lowens, who was an important figure in the Library of Congress, Music Division. Subjects are mainly on eighteenth-century composers, compilers, and collections. Includes the text of Tuft's important tutor and a list of editions of the Easy Instructor, the first shape-note collection. More concerned with bibliography than music.

1293. METCALF, Frank J. "'The Easy Instructor': a Bibliographical Study." Musical Quarterly 23 (1937): 89-97.

Careful examination of the publishing history of this important first shape-note collection, each of the editions, the numbers of pages, and other differences.

1294. MUSIC, David W. "The Meyer Manuscript: an 18th-Century American Tunebook." Current Musicology 29 (1980): 31-40.

A study of a manuscript probably from New England, 1750-1800, found in the Southwestern Baptist Theological Seminary Library in Ft. Worth, Texas. The music is in three voices like that of Walter's collection.

1295. OSTERHOUT, Paul Ragatz. "Music in Northampton, Massachusetts to 1820." Ph.D. dissertation, University of Michigan, 1978. 405 pp.

Iconoclastic study that challenges many previously-held assumptions concerning the development of music in early Massachusetts. Discusses local meanings of such terms as "regular singing," demonstrates different rates of development according to area, and generally deals with the issue of musical reform in the churches.

1296. OSTERHOUT, Paul R. "Note Reading and Regular Singing in Eighteenth-Century New England." American Music 4-2 (Summer, 1986): 125-44.

Based on early eighteenth-century church records, the author asserts that the term "Regular Singing," which is usually understood to mean singing by note, meant something less than this in the rural areas of Connecticut and Massachusetts. Here it meant singing in unison, and in a manner thought more civilized than the "Usual Way," with its heterophony.

1297. PERRIN, Phil D. "Systems of Scale Notation in Nineteenth
      Century American Tune Books." Journal of Research in
      Music Education 18-3 (Fall, 1970): 257-64.

      Brief survey of notations in American tunebooks, from
standard staff notation to shape notes (four and seven), letter
notation, and numeral notation.

1298. PERRIN, Phil D. "Theoretical Introductions in American
      Tune Books from 1801 to 1860." Ph.D. dissertation,
      Southwestern Baptist Theological Seminary, 1968. 203 pp.

      No abstract available.

1299. PICHIERRI, Louis. Music in New Hampshire, 1623-1800. New
      York: Columbia University Press, 1960. 297 pp.

      Although concerned mostly with classical music, there is
valuable information on psalm singing, singing schools, and early
publications from New Hampshire.

1300. PIERCE, Edwin H. "The Rise and Fall of the 'Fugue-Tune' in
      America." Musical Quarterly 16 (1930): 214-28.

      After defining the fugue-tune, the author traces its rise
and fall during a 75-year period, from Tufts and Walter through
Billings, with many examples.

1301. RALSTON, Jack L. "Russia." The Hymn 15-4 (Oct. 1964):
      115-22.

      A study of one of Daniel Read's fugue tunes first
published in Amos Doolittle's The American Musical Magazine, 1786-
7. Examines its use in later collections and includes facsimiles.

1302. ROGERS, Samuel Kirby. "The Social and Pedagogical Function
      of 'The Worcester Collection', 'The Village Harmony', and
      'The Easy Instructor' in the Early American Singing
      School." Ph.D. dissertation, The Florida State
      University, 1969. 219 pp.

      Rather broad study of several important collections and
their pedagogical functions in relation to singing schools.

1303. SEEGER, Charles. "Contrapuntal Style in the Three-Voice
       Shape-Note Hymns." Musical Quarterly 26-4 (1940):483-93;
       reprinted in Studies in Musicology, 1935-1975, pp. 237-
       51. Berkeley: University of California Press, 1977.

       First attempt to describe the unique style of writing
found in the shape-note tunebooks. Technical with many examples,
some being facsimiles of the originals.

1304. SIMMS, L. Moody, Jr. "Aldine S. Kieffer and the Musical
       Million." Journal of Popular Culture 3-2 (Fall, 1969):
       281-6.

       Light treatment of this important shape-note periodical
published in Virginia from 1870-1915 by Kieffer and E. Ruebush,
describing their attitudes, goals, and type of music.

1305. SLUDER, Claude K. "The Ketcham Tune-Book: Examples of
       18th-Century Hymnody in Indiana." Current Musicology 23
       (1977): 79-89.

       Description of a manuscript tunebook located in the Music
Library of Indiana University from c. 1802 which includes singing
school repertory partly in regular notation, partly in four-shape
notation. There are 78 pieces, six of them anthems, the rest
hymns, mostly in three-voice settings.

1306. STANISLAW, Richard John. "Choral Performance Practice in
       the Four-Shape Literature of American Frontier Singing
       Schools." Ph.D. dissertation, University of Illinois,
       1976. 479 pp.

       Concerned with creating authentic modern performance of
the early nineteenth-century four-shape literature. After an
introduction, the author concentrates on specific problems of
performance, such as who sings what part, ornamentation, mode
changes, time beating, and so forth.

1307. STEEL, David Warren. "Sacred Music in Early Winchester."
       Connecticut Historical Society Bulletin 45-2 (Apr.
       1980): 33-44.

       An historical case study of how sacred music developed in
a small town in northwestern Connecticut based on local records.

265

The author traces changes from lined psalmody to the singing school and mixed choirs and comments on the continuing importance of psalmody in rural New England.

1308. STEINBERG, Judith T. "Old Folks Concerts and the Revival of New England Psalmody." Musical Quarterly 59 (1973): 602-19.

As the eighteenth-century singing school music (anthems, psalms, and fuging tunes) fell out of favor and was replaced in the next century by refined, "correct" music, a longing developed in the 1850s in New England for the old music, which was satisfied by the Old Folks Concerts, but these vanished by the century's end.

1309. SUTTON, Brett. "Shape-Note Tune Books and Primitive Hymns." Ethnomusicology 26 (Jan. 1982): 11-26.

This is a discussion of the relationship between the many published American tunebooks of the nineteenth century and the orally-transmitted hymnody of the rural South, with special emphasis on the practices of the Primitive Baptists.

1310. TEMPERLEY, Nicholas, and MANNS, Charles G. Fuging Tunes in the Eighteenth Century. Detroit Studies in Music Bibliography #49. Detroit: Information Coordinators, 1983. 493 pp.

Following a 51-page introduction on the history and development of the fuging tune in both Britain and America based on recent research is a census (or theme dictionary) of virtually all fuging tunes. Using numbers to indicate solmization syllable (do = 1, re = 2, etc.), the first 15 notes of each tenor part are given. Also indices of texts, tune names, persons, modern editions, and in each cover is an explanation of how to use the book.

1311. THOMPSON, James William. "Music and Musical Activities in New England, 1800-1838." Ph.D. dissertation, George Peabody College for Teachers, 1962. 672 pp.

An historical study of musical activity in New England up to the introduction of musical education around 1838 under Lowell Mason. Most information is about singing schools and choirs.

1312. URKOWITZ, Steven, and BENNETT, Lawrence. "Early American Vocal Music." Journal of Popular Culture 12-1 (Summer, 1978): 5-10.

Very light historical survey of singing school music.

1313. VAUGHAN, Stella B. "A Heritage to Keep: History of the James D. Vaughan Music, Publisher." Cleveland, Tenn.: James D. Vaughan, Music Publisher, n.d. [c. 1980]. 8 pp.

Brief history of a company which produces southern Gospel songbooks in seven-shape notation written in 1964 and updated by then Editor-in-Chief, Connor B. Hall.

1314. WOLF, Irving. "The Sacred Harp in Mississippi." Journal of American Folklore 81-322 (Oct.-Dec. 1968): 337-41.

An informative article on white Mississippi singers who use the Denson Revision of the Sacred Harp, but sing it to the seven-shape solmization after Walker's Christian Harmony.

1315. WORST, John William. "New England Psalmody, 1760-1810: Analysis of an American Idiom." Ph.D. dissertation, University of Michigan, 1974. 564 pp.

A study of 174 metrical, rhymed psalm tunes, 37 of them considered the core. The analysis shows that linear, not vertical, considerations took precedence. In addition, they are edited for modern performance.

The Singing School Itself

1316. ABERNETHY, Francis E. "Singing All Day and Dinner on the Grounds." In Observations and Reflections on Texas Folkore, pp. 131-40. Publications of the Texas Folklore Society #37. Austin: Encino Press, 1972.

Description of the one hundredth annual all-day singing and dinner on the grounds at Harris Chapel church near Marshall, Texas. It is particularly interesting because the author is an outsider, an English professor, and his descriptions of the singers, the music, and the Sacred Harp tradition are insightful, wistful, and at times, humorous. Illustrated with photos.

1317. BLUM, Beula Blanche Eisenstadt. "Solmization in Nineteenth-Century American Sight Singing Instruction." Ed.D. dissertation, University of Michigan, 1968. 273 pp.

A history of solmization and its introduction into America using both the four and seven syllable systems and fixed do. Also a study of its use in instruction materials in shape-notes, numerals, and tonic sol-fa.

1318. BOTTOMS, Jack S. "The Singing School in Texas: 1971." Ph.D. dissertation, University of Colorado, 1972. 173 pp.

This study was done to ascertain the number and types of singing schools in Texas, to identify the philosophical ideas which make the singing school important to the rural population, to examine the teaching techniques and materials employed by the teachers of singing schools, to investigate performance practices, and to examine the compositional techniques used by composers in writing music for the singing school and singing convention.

1319. BOYD, Joe Dan. "Negro Sacred Harp Songsters in Mississippi." Mississippi Folklore Register 5 (Fall, 1971): 60-83.

In this excellent article, the author writes about the black Sacred Harp singers in north central Mississippi who use the Denson Revision of the Sacred Harp.

1320. BUECHNER, Alan C. "Yankee Singing Schools and the Golden Age of Choral Music in New England, 1760-1800." Ph.D. dissertation, Harvard University, 1960.

No abstract available.

1321. CARD, Edith B. "'Saints Bound for Heaven': the Singing School Lives On." The Southern Quarterly 15-3 (Oct. 1976): 75-88.

Description of the historical roots of the shape-note singing school as well as the living tradition as it exists today in the mountains of western North Carolina. Emphasis is placed on the continuing use of William Walker's Christian Harmony.

1322. CHEEK, Curtis Leo. "The Singing School and Shaped Note Tradition Residuals in Twentieth-Century American Hymnody." D.M.A. dissertation, University of Southern California, 1968. 306 pp.

Traces the history of psalmody from Europe to the United States, the advent of "Regular Singing," and the singing school to the present day. Basic information and breaks no new ground.

1323. Directory and Minutes of Annual Sacred Harp Singings. Bremen, Ga.: Sacred Harp Publishing Co., [current year].

Since at least the 1960s, the Sacred Harp Publishing Company has published each year a list of singings using the Denson Revision, i.e., The Original Sacred Harp, organized according to "annual" singings and monthly singings. The bulk of the work, however, is the Minutes of each singing from the previous year. Besides listing officers for each singing, the minutes include which songs were sung and by whom they were led.

1324. FOUTS, Gordon E. "Music Instruction in America to Around 1830 as Suggested by the Hartzler Collection of Early Protestant American Tune Books." Ph.D. dissertation, University of Iowa, 1968. 352 pp.

The Hartzler Collection, kept at Goshen College, Goshen, Indiana, consists of about 120 books pre-dating the year 1831. This dissertation is a study of these books, especially their introductory singing tutors.

1325. GRAHAM, John R. "Early Twentieth-Century Singing Schools in Kentucky Appalachia." Journal of Research in Music Education 19 (Spring, 1971): 77-84.

An historical survey of shape-note schools and teachers using this methodology in Kentucky in the early part of this century. Special attention is given to organization of the schools and pedagogical practices of the teachers.

1326. JACKSON, Karen Luke. "The Royal Singing Convention, 1893-1931: Shape Note Singing Tradition in Irwin County, Georgia." Georgia Historical Quarterly 56 (Winter, 1972): 495-509. Reprinted in Music in Georgia, pp. 289-304. Edited by Frank Hoogerwerf. New York: Da Capo, 1984.

History of a particular seven-shape convention and its place in the history of shaped notes.

1327. KOUWENHOVEN, John Atlee. "Some Unfamiliar Aspects of Singing in New England, 1620-1810." New England Quarterly 6-3 (Sept. 1933): 567-88.

An ambitious history of the changes in singing practices from lined psalms to "Regular Singing" and singing schools, but at least it is well documented and highly detailed.

1328. LOESSEL, Earl Oliver. "The Use of Character Notes and Other Unorthodox Notations in Teaching the Reading of Music in Northern United States during the Nineteenth Century." Ph.D. dissertation, University of Michigan, 1959. 556 pp.

The value of this work is in part its historical coverage of singing school books in general, and a variety of notations in particular (four-shape, seven-shape, numeral, and others) but mainly because of the extensive quotations from the primary sources as well as numerous illustrations and facsimiles. Additionally, there are extensive lists of collections, but because it emphasizes the North, is not comprehensive in a national sense.

1329. MARTIN, Katherine Rosser. "The Cumberland County Singing Convention." Kentucky Folklore Record 20 (Apr.-June 1974): 29-32.

Brief but first-hand description of the above Convention which has been held on the fourth Sunday of each month since 1946. The author lists three basic functions of these singings: 1) as a social outlet, 2) as a reinforcement of religious beliefs, 3) as a provider of entertainment. There is also discussion of change.

1330. MILLER, Terry E. "Old-Time Shape-Note Singing Schools in Eastern Kentucky." The Southern Quarterly 20-1 (Fall, 1981): 35-45.

An oral history of seven-shape-note singing in eastern Kentucky in the Pikeville-Virgie area and career biography of the informant, Francis Marion Tackett, who has been teaching singing schools since 1922. Additionally, the author observed and described an on-going class and the pedagogical methodology used in this singing school from late 1977 led by Mr. Tackett in Virgie at a Freewill Baptist Church.

1331. MOSER, Mabel Y. "Christian Harmony Singing at Etowah." Appalachian Journal 1 (Spring, 1974): 263-70.

Description of the first Sunday singings held at the Etowah Baptist Church in Transylvania County, North Carolina with additional details about other Christian Harmony singings elsewhere in western North Carolina.

1332. ORR, S. H. "Country Singing Schools and Social Functions." A Collection of Papers Proposed for the Historical Society of Montgomery County, Pennsylvania 6 (1929): 390-7.

1333. RICHARDSON, Thomas J. "Daddy's Shaped Notes: a Review of Sacred Harp Traditions." Mississippi Folklore Register 13 (Spring, 1979): 45-51.

1334. SCHOLTEN, James W. "Fa-Sol-La or Do-Re-Mi: a Diary of Shape-Note Singings, Summer 1978." The Hymn 30 (April, 1979): 119-21, 127.

A survey of the variety of shape-note books (four-shape and seven-shape) used in the southeastern United States.

1335. STANLEY, David H. "The Gospel Singing Convention in South Georgia." Journal of American Folklore 95-375 (Jan.-Mar. 1982): 1-32.

A discussion of the musical and social ramifications of the 85th Annual Royal Singing Convention held in Irwin County, Georgia. The article traces the development of Gospel shape-note singing schools and conventions in the South in general and describes the Royal Convention in detail. Excellent introduction.

1336. TADLOCK, Paula. "Shape-Note Singing in Mississippi." In Discourse in Ethnomusicology: Essays in Honor of George List, pp. 191-207. Edited by Caroline Card, et al. Bloomington: Indiana University Press, 1978.

Survey of shape-note singing conventions, black and white, old and new styles, from the 1860s to the present, with emphasis on continuity and change and social implications.

1337. WORK, John W. "Plantation Meistersinger." *Musical Quarterly* 27 (1941): 97-106.

A study of black shape-note singers in Dale County, Alabama, where the Cooper Revision of the *Sacred Harp* is used. Written by an eye-witness in the style of a diary.

Individual Composers and Compilers

1338. ANDERSON, Gillian B. "Eighteenth-Century Evaluations of William Billings: a Reappraisal." *Quarterly Journal of the Library of Congress* 35-1 (Jan. 1978): 48-58.

Billings' career is discussed within the late eighteenth-century milieu, its attitudes towards music in general and Billings in particular based on both British and American primary sources.

1339. BARBOUR, J. Murray. *The Church Music of William Billings.* East Lansing: Michigan State University Press, 1960; reprint ed., New York: Da Capo, 1972. 167 pp.

Technical study that analyzes the various aspects of Billings' music—texts, rhythm, meter, melody, counterpoint, harmony, modality and tonality, texture, and form.

1340. BOYD, Joe Dan. "Judge Jackson: Black Giant of White Spirituals." *Journal of American Folklore* 83-330 (Oct.-Dec. 1970): 446-51.

A discussion of acculturation of Sacred Harp music by black singers, with special attention to Judge Jackson, author and compiler of *The Colored Sacred Harp* first published in 1931 in Ozark, Alabama, and still used today.

1341. CLARKE, Garry E. *Essays on American Music.* Westport, Conn.: Greenwood Press, 1977. 259 pp.

Pertinent here is chapter 1, "The Yankee Tunesmiths," pp. 3-16, which includes musical examples as well.

1342. CRAWFORD, Richard. Andrew Law, American Psalmodist.
Evanston: Northwestern University Press, 1968; reprint
ed., New York: Da Capo, 1981. 424 pp.

Thorough scholarly biography of Law (1749-1821), an early
musical pioneer, his musical style, publications, sources, and
provides indices of tunes, composers, and a bibliography. From the
author's doctoral dissertation, "Andrew Law (1749-1821), the Career
of an American Musician," University of Michigan, 1965. 473 pp.

1343. CRAWFORD, Richard, and HITCHCOCK, H. Wiley. "The Papers of
Andrew Law in the William L. Clements Library." Bulletin
#68. Ann Arbor: William L. Clements Library, 1961. 13 pp.

Brief description of the 1,900 items held by the library,
including 500 letters, 700 accounts, etc., 368 examples of music,
350 memoranda, and 35 lists of students, plus his works.

1344. CRAWFORD, Richard, and McKAY, David P. "The Performance
of William Billings' Music." Journal of Research in
Music Education 21-4 (Winter, 1973): 318-30.

Cautioning that this material does not necessarily apply
to Billings' contemporaries, the author explains Billings' comments
on performance practices, especially regarding who sang which
parts, vocal production, ornamentation, tempo, and accompaniment
(whether or not there was accompaniment, and if so, what).

1345. CROUSE, David Lee. "The Work of Allen D. Carden and
Associates in the Shape-Note Tunebooks, The Missouri
Harmony, Western Harmony, and United States Harmony."
D.M.A. dissertation, Southern Baptist Theological
Seminary, 1972. 204 pp.

The Missouri Harmony (1820), Western Harmony (1824), and
U.S. Harmony (1829) were all important collections initiated by
Carden (1792-1859), who lived in Tennessee. This work provides
biographies of Carden and others, describes the changes in the
various editions, their importance as an influence on others, and
lists 117 extant copies of the Missouri Harmony.

1346. DOOLEY, James Edward. "Thomas Hastings, American Church
Musician." Ph.D. dissertation, The Florida State
University, 1963. 278 pp.

The biography of a teacher, lecturer, author, and compiler who spent 50 years and created 50 published works, many with Lowell Mason and William Bradbury, to the end that "bad" music and performance be replaced with enlightened music. Hastings, who composed the well-known "Toplady" (tune for "Rock of Ages"), was oriented towards "correct" European music and against shape-notes.

1347. EDDY, Mary O. "Three Early Hymn Writers." Southern
    Folklore Quarterly 10 (1946): 177-82.

    Brief biographies of Amzi Chapin (1768-1835), Samuel Wakefield (1799-1895), and Amos Sutton Hayden (1813-1880), all compilers of singing school books or composers in the nineteenth century.

1348. ESKEW, Harry B. "William Walker, 1809-1875: Popular
    Southern Hymnist." The Hymn 15-1 (Jan. 1964): 5-13.

    A brief summary of the author's master's thesis ("The Life and Work of William Walker," New Orleans Baptist Seminary School of Church Music, 1960) in which Walker's life and activities are introduced.

1349. FLEMING, Jo Lee. "James D. Vaughan, Music Publisher."
    S.M.D. dissertation, Union Theological Seminary, 1972.
    182 pp.

    A study of the prolific and influential publisher of seven-shape Gospel songbooks. Discusses the Vaughan Company's role in the rise of the male Gospel quartet. This is the major scholarly work on the post-1920 Gospel music period.

1350. GARRETT, Allen. "The Works of William Billings." Ph.D.
    dissertation, University of North Carolina, 1952. 215 pp.

    No abstract available.

1351. GENUCHI, Marvin Charles. "The Life and Music of Jacob
    French (1754-1817), Colonial American Composer." Vol. 1:
    "Background Biography, Style Study." Vol. 2: "Music
    Supplement of Anthems, Psalm Tunes, and Hymn Tunes."
    Ph.D. dissertation, University of Iowa, 1964. 307 pp.

French, of Stoughton, Massachusetts, was an important New England composer of psalmody who was influenced by Billings.

1352. HAMM, Charles. "The Chapins and Sacred Music in the South and West." Journal of Research in Music Education 8-2 (Fall, 1960): 91-8.

One of the first studies to attempt an identification of the Chapins--Amzi and Lucius--as well as others who were important composers in the singing school tradition.

1353. HAMMOND, Paul G. "Jesse B. Aikin and The Christian Minstrel." American Music 3-4 (Winter, 1985): 442-51.

Reviews Aikin's life, his publishing activities, and especially the important Christian Minstrel of 1846 which went through at least 171 printings by 1873. Aikin's seven shape notes eventually became the standard of the publishing industry. Reviews the milieu of the contents, borrowings, and discusses the editions.

1354. HARLEY, Rachel Augusta. "Ananias Davisson: Southern Tunebook Compiler." Ph.D. dissertation, University of Michigan, 1972. 320 pp.

A study of the first shape-note publisher who worked in the Shenandoah Valley, with special attention to the influence of Davisson's tunebooks on later Southern collections. Included in the Appendix are 24 sets of transcriptions, each containing a melody claimed by Davisson and additional versions of the same melody as claimed by other musicians, these illustrating the pervasiveness of the oral tradition.

1355. HIGGINSON, J. Vincent. "Andrew Law, American Psalmodist." The Hymn 20-2 (April 1969): 53-7.

Brief introduction to the life and publications of Law, whose The Art of Singing was probably the second shape-note book published, but using a different arrangement of shapes from those of Little and Smith.

1356. HORST, Irvin B. "Joseph Funk, Early Mennonite Printer and Publisher." Mennonite Quarterly Review 31-4 (Oct. 1957): 260-77.

Biography of the German-descended shape-note printer and teacher from the Shenandoah Valley, Joseph Funk (1778-1862). The article treats the subject as a writer, printer, publisher, and bookbinder. Of considerable value is a bibliography of secondary sources and a 49-item annotated bibliography of all known writings by Funk with indications of which libraries hold the items.

1357. JOHNSON, H. Earle. "George K. Jackson, Doctor of Music (1745-1822)." Musical Quarterly 29 (1943): 113-21.

Jackson came from England to America in 1796 and became the first Ph.D. in Music in the United States. While he was classically oriented, he also published singing school books containing only "correct" European style music.

1358. KLOCKO, David Grover. "Jeremiah Ingall's The Christian Harmony, or, Songster's Companion (1805)." Ph.D. dissertation, University of Michigan, 1978. 3 vols. 1,332 pp.

This thorough and scholarly work delves deeply into Ingalls and his collection, the latter important for its primary and extensive use of spiritual folk songs. Part I reproduces all references to the compiler and the book, Part II deals with text related issues and textual sources, Part III concerns the sources of Ingalls' melodies, some having been borrowed, others composed by him, and Part IV deals with the publication and reception of the main collection and later reprintings of songs.

1359. KROEGER, Karl. "William Billing's Music in Manuscript Copy and Some Notes on Variant Versions of his Pieces." Music Library Association Notes 39-2 (Dec. 1982): 316-45.

A study of the variants of Billings' music found in manuscript, particularly at the ends of tunebook copies where students copied them.

1360. KROEGER, Karl. "A Yankee Tunebook from the Old South: Amos Pilsbury's The United States Sacred Harmony." The Hymn 32-3 (1981): 154-62.

The life of Pilsbury from Charleston and the contents of his collection, with examples.

1361. LINDSTROM, Carl E. "William Billings and His Times."
Musical Quarterly 25 (1939): 479-97.

Detailed early study of Billings' biography, the context
of his musical life. Includes many contemporary quotes as well as
the views of later historians.

1362. McCORMICK, David W. "Oliver Holden, Composer and
Anthologist." D.S.M. dissertation, Union Theological
Seminary, 1963. 501 pp.

The definitive biography of Holden, the composer of the
well-known hymn tune "Coronation." Traces his stylistic
development and determines the authorship of a number of works
usually ascribed to him.

1363. McKAY, David, and CRAWFORD, Richard. William Billings of
Boston. Princeton: Princeton University Press, 1975.
303 pp.

Perhaps the best study of Billings to date, this work
includes his biography, a study of the performance of his works, a
complete list of works, and an extensive bibliography.

1364. METCALF, Frank J. American Writers and Compilers of Sacred
Music. New York: Abingdon, 1925; reprint ed., New York:
Russell and Russell, 1967. 373 pp.

Biographies of important singing school composers and
others from the seventeenth to nineteenth centuries. Although
much new data has come to light since this was written, it was
exceptionally well done for its time.

1365. MILLER, Terry E. "Alexander Auld, 1816-1898: Early Ohio
Musician." The Cincinnati Historical Society Bulletin
33-4 (Winter, 1975): 245-60.

Derived from the author's master's thesis (Indiana
University, 1971), this is a biography of Ohio's most famous
shape-note singing master and composer who in 1847 printed The
Ohio Harmonist in which he used his own seven shapes. Auld, from
Deersville (Harrison County), was active as a teacher and compiler
of three further collections, until near the end of the century.

1366. MURRAY, Sterling E. "Timothy Swan and Yankee Psalmody."
Musical Quarterly 61 (1975): 433-63.

Based on the author's 1969 master's thesis (University of
Michigan), this is a study of Swan's life, music, and relationships to his fellow professional singing teachers. It includes a
list of Swan's compilations.

1367. OWEN, Earl McLain, Jr. "The Life and Music of Supply
Belcher (1751-1836), 'Handel of Maine'." D.M.A.
dissertation, Southern Baptist Theological Seminary,
1969. 2 vols. 152 pp. (text) and 204 pp. (music).

Belcher, known for his Harmony of Maine, is treated
thoroughly in this work, in terms of both his life and music.
There is an exceptionally lengthy review by Sterling E. Murray in
Current Musicology 12 (1971): 102-8.

1368. PATTERSON, Relford. "Three American 'Primitives': a Study
of the Musical Style of Hans Gram, Oliver Holden, and
Samuel Holyoke." Ph.D. dissertation, Washington
University, 1963. 268 pp.

Using the word "primitive" as art historians do, to
denote simple, direct, self-taught, and even crude art, the author
studies three men who jointly compiled in the late eighteenth
century The Massachusetts Compiler, which was a European-oriented
"correct" music collection done in reaction against the "inferior"
style of people like Billings.

1369. SCANLON, Mary Browning. "Thomas Hastings." Musical
Quarterly 32 (1946): 265-77.

Although superceded by James E. Dooley's dissertation
(see #1346), this article presented what was then known of
Hasting's life, his views on music, publications, and other musical
activities.

1370. SCHOLTEN, James W. "Amzi Chapin: Frontier Singing Master
and Folk-Hymn Composer." Journal of Research in Music
Education 23 (Summer, 1975): 109-19.

This article, as well as #1372 on Lucius Chapin, are
derived from the author's doctoral dissertation (#1373) which

studied two brothers who were New England singing school masters
and composers. They migrated west of the Alleghenies in the late
eighteenth century and took with them the styles from their home
region. Their compositions were published widely, especially in
Wyeth's Repository of Sacred Music, Part II and Patterson's Church
Music. While they promoted the music of Andrew Law, their own
composition styles differed from Law's.

1371. SCHOLTEN, James W. "The Chapins: a Study of Men and Sacred
      Music West of the Alleghenies, 1795-1842." Ed.D.
      dissertation, University of Michigan, 1972. 167 pp.

      See previous annotation.

1372. SCHOLTEN, James W. "Lucius Chapin: a New England Singing
      Master on the Frontier." Contributions to Music
      Education 4 (1976): 64-76.

      See previous annotation.

1373. SONNECK, Oscar George Theodore. Francis Hopkinson, the
      First American Poet-Composer (1737-1791) and James Lyon,
      Patriot, Preacher, Psalmodist (1735-1789). Washington,
      D.C., 1905; reprint ed., New York: Da Capo, 1966. 213 pp.

      Of greater interest is James Lyon, compiler of Urania,
the first oblong singing-school book published in America (1761).
The reprint edition includes an introduction by Richard Crawford.

1374. STEEL, David Warren. "Stephen Jenks (1772-1856): American
      Composer and Tunebook Compiler (New England)." Ph.D.
      dissertation, University of Michigan, 1982. 487 pp.

      Jenks, a compiler and composer from New England, wrote
125 compositions and issued ten collections of sacred and two of
secular music between 1799 and 1818. He moved to Ohio in 1829 and
continued composing until 1850, writing fuging tunes. His works
appear in a number of singing school collections.

1375. STEEL, David Warren. "Truman S. Wetmore of Winchester and
      his Republican Harmony." Connecticut Historical Society
      Bulletin 45-3 (July 1980): 75-89.

Wetmore (1774-1861), a physician professionally, taught singing schools and composed psalmody at least until 1810 in his home town of Winchester, Connecticut. This article is a study of a manuscript tunebook containing both his own compositions and those of others in the vicinity.

1376. TEAL, Mary D. "Letters of Thomas Hastings." Music Library Association Notes 34-2 (Dec. 1977): 303-18.

While the letters are mostly a reflection of Hastings' life, some offer observations on the folk performance of church music of the early nineteenth century.

1377. WAYLAND, John W. "Joseph Funk, Father of Song in Northern Virginia." Penn Germania; a Popular Journal of German History and Ideals in the United States 10 (1911).

1378. WEBB, Guy Bedford. "Timothy Swan: Yankee Tunesmith." D.M.A. dissertation, University of Illinois at Urbana-Champaign, 1972. 210 pp.

Swan (1758-1842), who made hats for a living in both Massachusetts and Connecticut, partly through lack of training in music, partly from individuality, created a style of composing quite his own, especially with regard to modulation and accidentals. Some of his works, found in 27 tunebooks, two of his own, are still sung today in the South. This work includes an index of tunes by Swan published in collections before 1800 and a performing edition of his set pieces and anthems.

1379. WILGUS, D. K. "Andrew Jenkins, Folk Composer: an Overview." Lore and Language 3 (Jan.-July 1981): 109-28.

Bibliographies and Discographies

1380. BRITTON, Allen P., and LOWENS, Irving. "Daniel Bayley's The American Harmony: a Bibliographical Study." Papers of the Bibliographical Society of America 49 (4th Quarter, 1955): 340-54.

Traces the lineage and editions of this important early tunebook published between 1769 and 1774.

1381. BRITTON, Allen P., and LOWENS, Irving. "Unlocated Titles
in Early Sacred American Music." Music Library
Association Notes 11 (Dec. 1953): 33-48.

Descriptions of earlier bibliographies and list (title
page information) of 82 items not yet located but known through
other sources, such as copyright announcements.

1382. BRITTON, Allen P., LOWENS, Irving, and CRAWFORD, Richard.
A Bibliography of American Sacred Music Imprints, 1698-
1810. Worcester: American Antiquarian Society, in press.

1383. BROCKWAY, Duncan. "More American Temperance Song-Books."
The Hymn 22-2 (April 1971): 54-6.

Thirty titles in addition to those by Rogal (see #1397)
of material dating from 1839 to 1916.

1384. BROCKWAY, Duncan. "More American Temperance Song-Books."
The Hymn 25-3 (July 1974): 82-4.

Similar to the previous item, this adds some 25 sources
from 1867 to 1971.

1385. CRAWFORD, Richard. "Connecticut Sacred Music Imprints,
1778-1810." Music Library Association Notes 27-3 (Mar.
1971): 445-52; 27-4 (June 1971): 671-9.

A checklist of tunebooks published in Connecticut with
annotations. Especially useful for Andrew Law and Daniel Read.

1386. DANIEL, Harlan. "78 RPM Recordings of Sacred Harp Songs."
JEMF Quarterly 6 (Spring, 1970): 6-16.

1387. KROHN, Ernst C. "The Missouri Harmony: a Study in Early
American Psalmody." Missouri Historical Society Bulletin
6-1 (Oct. 1949): 25-33.

1388. KROHN, Ernst C. "A Check List of Editions of 'The Missouri
Harmony'." Missouri Historical Society Bulletin 6-3
(April 1950): 374-99.

1389. LINDSLEY, Charles Edward. "Early Nineteenth-Century
    American Collections of Sacred Choral Music, 1800-1810."
    Part I: "A Historical Survey of Tune-book Production to
    1810." Part II: "An Annotated Bibliography of Tune
    Books, 1800-1810." Ph.D. dissertation, The University of
    Iowa, 1968. 283 pp.

    In Part I the author seeks to demonstrate that tunebook
production in the period 1800-10 is stylistically a continuation
of the late eighteenth century. Part II is an annotated
bibliography of all known sacred tunebooks from 1800-10.

1390. LINDSLEY, Charles Edward. "An Important Tunebook
    Collection in California." Music Library Association
    Notes 29-4 (June 1973): 671-5.

    A description of the holdings of the Honnold Library of
Claremont College where the Robert G. McCutchan Collection of
Hymns and Hymnology contains 3,810 volumes of which 650 are
American tunebooks of the eighteenth and nineteenth centuries.

1391. LOWENS, Irving. A Bibliography of Songsters Printed in
    America Before 1821. Worcester: American Antiquarian
    Society, 1976. 229 pp.

    A songster is a collection of secular lyrics without
musical notation, although some refer to specific tunes. After a
20-page introduction, history, definitions of terms, and origins,
there is a list of libraries, a bibliography of bibliographies,
and a list of 649 songsters from 1734 to 1820 giving title page
information, cross references, libraries which hold the item, and
materials on other editions.

1392. METCALF, Frank J. American Psalmody, or, Titles of Books
    Containing Tunes Printed in America from 1721 to 1820.
    New York, 1917; reprint ed., New York: Da Capo, 1968.
    54 pp.

    Useful but now out-of-date list of tunebooks and
editions, with some facsimiles of title pages, based on James
Warrington's Short Titles (see #1401).

1393. NATHAN, Hans. "William Billings: a Bibliography." Music
    Library Association Notes 29-4 (June 1973): 658-70.

Annotated list of 25 items published by Billings, mostly songbooks.

1394. NATHAN, Hans. William Billings: Data and Documents.
Bibliographies in American Music #2. Detroit:
Information Coordinators, 1976. 69 pp.

Brief biography of Billings and bibliography of tunebooks, compositions, manuscripts, etc., with numerous illustrations.

1395. RALSTON, Jack L. "A Bibliography of Currently Available
Early American Tunebook Reprints." The Hymn 33-4 (1982):
212-4.

A fairly complete list of books with publishers' addresses.

1396. REVITT, Paul J., ed. The George Pullen Jackson Collection
of Southern Hymnody: a Bibliography. Los Angeles:
University of California Library, 1964. 26 pp.

After an eight-page introduction and description of the collection, there is a list of its contents, many with short annotations.

1397. ROGAL, Samuel J. "A Sampling of American Temperance Song
Books." The Hymn 21-4 (Oct. 1970): 112-5.

A list of 23 entries for books from 1845 to 1964 preceded by a brief discussion of temperance songbooks.

1398. SHOWALTER, Grace I. The Music Books of Ruebush & Kieffer,
1866-1942: a Bibliography. Richmond: Virginia State
Library, 1975. 40 pp.

A list of more than 200 titles in chronological order with descriptions and notes on later editions. Further and undated materials are listed by type, including charts and periodicals.

1399.   STANISLAW, Richard J. A Checklist of Four-Shape Shape-Note
        Tunebooks. I.S.A.M. Monographs #10. New York: Institute
        for Studies in American Music, 1978. 61 pp.

        Alphabetical list of more than 305 tunebooks (including
        multiple editions of the same item) giving basic publication
        information, some with annotations, and a list of libraries
        holding each item. An addendum adds 14 items and deletes seven,
        for a total of 312.

1400.   TEMPERLEY, Nicholas, et al. Hymn Tune Index. Urbana:
        University of Illinois Press, (forthcoming).

        An example of how modern technology will change biblio-
        graphic research, this item will be an on-line computer data base.

1401.   WARRINGTON, James. Short Titles of Books, Relating to or
        Illustrating the History and Practice of Psalmody in the
        United States, 1620-1820. Edited by Theodore Finney.
        Philadelphia: private, 1898; reprint ed., Pittsburgh:
        Pittsburgh Theological Seminary [Tripotamopolitana #1],
        1970; New York: Burt Franklin, 1971. 98 pp.

        An early bibliography of material relating to psalmody,
        meant as a preliminary checklist for the longer work, History of
        Psalmody in the United States, 1620-1820. Material covered runs
        from 1538 to 1898 including foreign publications for the earlier
        years and American after 1700.

Facsimile Editions of Tunebooks

1402.   BELCHER, Supply. The Harmony of Maine. Boston: Isaiah
        Thomas and Ebenezer Andrews, 1794; reprint ed., New York:
        Da Capo, 1972. 104 pp.

        Belcher, called "The Handel of Maine," compiled this
        collection of his own compositions, especially anthems, in the
        usual format of the time.

1403.   [BILLINGS, William]. NATHAN, Hans, gen. ed. The Complete
        Works of William Billings. 2 vols. Boston: AMS Press
        and Colonial Society of Massachusetts, distributed by
        University of Virginia Press, 1977-present. Vol. 1: New
        England Psalm Singer [1770], ed. by Karl Kroeger; Vol. 2:

Singing Masters Assistant [1778] and Music in Miniature
[1779], ed. by Hans Nathan. [Projected. Vol. 3: Psalm
Singer's Amusement {1781} and Suffolk Harmony {1786} and
occasional works. Vol. 4: Continental Harmony {1794}.]

Vol. 1 includes a 68-page introduction. The volumes
include both the facsimile of the original and a modern version.

1404. BILLINGS, William. The Continental Harmony. Boston:
Isaiah Thomas and Ebenezer T. Andrews, 1794; reprint ed.,
Cambridge: Belknap Press of Harvard University Press,
1961. 201 pp. [Introduction by Hans Nathan].

1405. BILLINGS, William. Psalm Singer's Amusement. Boston: by
the author, 1781; reprint ed., New York: Da Capo, 1974.
104 pp.

This crudely engraved book includes Billings' famous
"Modern Music," nine anthems, and 15 tunes.

1406. BRUNK, J. D. Church & Sunday School Hymnal: a Collection
of Hymns and Sacred Songs. Scottdale, Pa.: Herald Press,
1902; Supplement, 1911 edition; reprint ed., Scottdale,
Pa.: Mennonite Publishing House, 1972, 1976. 413 pp.

A collection of 532 hymns, 50 of them in German, written
on two staves in round notes.

1407. CAYCE, Elder C. H. The Good Old Songs, The Cream of the
Old Music. [1913]. Thornton, Ark.: Cayce Publishing
Co., 1980. 444 pp.

The editor has taken many of these songs from the earlier
oblong tunebooks, rearranged them on two staves with tune in the
soprano part, and printed them in Aikin's seven-shape notes.

1408. CHENEY, Simeon Pease. The American Singing Book of Sacred
and Secular Music. Boston: White, 1879; reprint ed., New
York: Da Capo, 1980. 320 pp.

Besides the collection of songs, there are 40 biographies
of leading composers and compilers from Billings to Woodbury, pp.
168-213, in a section charmingly called "Biographical Department."

285

1409. DAVISSON, A[nanias]. <u>Kentucky</u> <u>Harmony</u>, <u>or</u>, <u>a</u> <u>Choice</u>
<u>Collection</u> <u>of</u> <u>Psalm</u> <u>Tunes</u>, <u>Hymns</u>, <u>and</u> <u>Anthems</u> <u>in</u> <u>Three</u>
<u>Parts</u>. Harrisonburg, Va., 1816; reprint ed.,
Minneapolis: Augsburg, 1976. 160 pp.

Introduction by Irving Lowens. One of the most important
early four-shape-note collections because of its influence on
later compilations. Includes the eighteenth-century repertory of
psalms, hymns, anthems, and fuging tunes, but also the newly
appearing genre of folk hymns. Music is in four-part harmony.

1410. ECKHARD, Jacob. <u>Jacob</u> <u>Eckhard's</u> <u>Choirmaster's</u> <u>Book</u> <u>of</u>
<u>1809</u>. [Manuscript of 1809]. Tricentennial edition #2.
Facsimile ed., Columbia, S.C.: University of South
Carolina Press, 1971. 124 pp.

Introduction and notes by George W. Williams. Eckhard
came to America from Germany in 1776 and settled in Charleston
where he lived until his death in 1833. The manuscript included
songs from diverse sources, some of them American. The editor has
provided annotations for each song and a bibliography.

1411. FUNK, Joseph, and Sons. <u>New</u> <u>Harmonia</u> <u>Sacra</u>: <u>a</u> <u>Compilation</u>
<u>of</u> <u>Genuine</u> <u>Church</u> <u>Music</u>. 22nd ed. Harrisonburg, Va.: H.
A. Brunk, 1959 [364 pp. in oblong format with Funk's
shape notes]; Sesquicentennial ed. Broadway, Va.:
Trissels Mennonite Church, 1972 [370 pp. in oblong format
with Funk's shape notes]; 24th or Legacy ed. Dayton,
Va.: Legacy Book Publishers, 1980 [378 pp. in upright
form using Aikin's shape notes].

Introduction by H. A. Brunk in 22nd ed. This is the
modern version of Joseph Funk's <u>Harmonia</u> <u>Sacra</u>, a Shenandoah Valley
tunebook that went through 17 editions between 1832 and 1877 and
used Funk's seven shape notes. The present volumes, however, have
for the most part a totally different repertory from the original
collection, being almost entirely nineteenth-century hymns in four
voices. Various editions of this book are still used in singings
held at various locations in the Shenandoah Valley.

1412. HAYDEN, Amos S. <u>The</u> <u>Sacred</u> <u>Melodeon</u>. Cincinnati: Moore,
Wilstach, Keys, & Co., 1848 and later; facsimile edition
from microfilm, Ann Arbor: University Microfilms, 1978.
304 pp.

Hayden's important collection, compiled by a minister from Euclid, Ohio, copied the format of Jesse Aikin's Christian Minstrel, the first book with seven shape-notes, but the repertory is old-fashioned, consisting of psalms, hymns, folk hymns, anthems, fuging tunes, as well as some later compositions. A number of the harmonizations are quite unusual.

1413. INGALLS, Jeremiah. The Christian Harmony; or, Songster's Companion. Exeter, N.H.: Henry Ranlet for the compiler, 1805; reprint ed., New York: Da Capo, 1981. 200 pp.

Introduction by David Klocko. Although printed in standard notation, the number of parts are only three and the contents include the first appearances of folk hymns. Because of its influence on later compilations, the importance of this book cannot be overestimated.

1414. JACKSON, Judge. The Colored Sacred Harp. Ozark, Ala.: J. Jackson, 1934; rev. ed., Montgomery, Ala.: Paragon Press, 1973. 96 pp.

Probably the last four-shape collection published, other than the new editions of the Sacred Harp, this oblong book containing mostly compositions by Jackson represents a black continuation of the Sacred Harp tradition in southern Alabama. The book is available from Mr. H. J. Jackson, 27 Willa St., Ozark, Ala. 36360.

1415. LYON, James. Urania. Philadelphia, 1761; reprint ed., New York: Da Capo, 1974. 198 pp.

Preface by Richard Crawford. This hand-engraved collection was the first American oblong tunebook and contained compositions mostly of English origin with, however, at least one thought to be American. Published in four voices in regular notation.

1416. McCURRY, John G. The Social Harp. Philadelphia: T. K. Collins, 1855; reprint ed., Athens: University of Georgia Press, 1973. 268 pp.

Introduction by Daniel Patterson and John F. Garst (18 pp.). Although published three times (1855, 1859, 1868), this extremely rare tunebook was once widely used in the Hart County,

Georgia, area. Its contents, in three voices using four-shape
notation, are typical of its time and provenance--psalms, hymns,
folk hymns, anthems, and fuging tunes.

1417. [MASON, Lowell]. The Boston Handel and Haydn Society
      Collection of Church Music. Boston: Richardson and Lord,
      1822; reprint ed., New York: Da Capo, 1973. 323 pp.

      Although Mason is best known for his dislike of tradi-
tional singing school music and shape notes and advocacy of
Europeanized "scientific" music and pedagogy, this tunebook is
still representative of one part of the American singing school
family. The music, however, is printed in regular notation on
four staves with figured bass numbers beneath and consists
primarily of urban and European style hymns and set pieces.

1418. MASON, Lowell, and WEBB, George J. The Boston Glee Book,
      Consisting of an Extensive Collection of Glees,
      Madrigals, and Rounds. Boston: J. H. Wilkins, R. B.
      Carter, and Jenks and Palmer, 1844; reprint ed., New
      York: Da Capo, 1977. 264 pp.

      Like the above collection, this one consists of
"scientific" or Europeanized music in four-part harmony.
Certainly the music is not folk, but the oblong form of the book
is traditional.

1419. ORR, James L. Grange Melodies. Philadelphia: George S.
      Ferguson Co., 1917 [original edition, 1891]; reprint ed.,
      New York: Arno Press, 1975. 200 pp.

      Edited by Dan C. McCurry and Richard E. Rubenstein. This
short oblong book consists of social music for grange activities
printed mostly on two staves in ordinary notation. Apparently it
was not used in singing schools but for recreational sings.

1420. The Stoughton Musical Society's Centennial Collection of
      Sacred Music. Boston and New York: Oliver Ditson, 1878;
      reprint ed., New York: Da Capo, 1980. 304 pp.

      New introduction by Roger L. Hall.

1421. SWAN, M. L. New Harp of Columbia. [Originally Phila-
delphia, 1867]. Nashville: Publishing House of the M. E.
Church, South, and Smith & Lamar, 1919; reprint ed.,
Knoxville: University of Tennessee Press, 1978. 226 pp.

Introduction by Dorothy Horn, Ron Peterson, and Candra
Phillips. Using Swan's set of seven shape notes, which are unique
to this collection, the New Harp of Columbia is in three and four
voices and is still used in the mountains near Knoxville for an
occasional singing. The contents are traditional singing school
fare, such as fuging tunes, anthems, as well as hymns and psalms.

1422. WALKER, William. The Christian Harmony: in the Seven-
Syllable Character Note System of Music. Philadelphia,
1866; rev. ed. by John H. DEASON and O. A. PARRIS. Mobile,
Ala.: Henry M. Deason [161 Poydras Ave.], 1958; reprint
ed. of 1873 ed., Greenville, S.C.: A Press, 1979. 390 pp.

Although Walker had become quite famous for his 1835
Southern Harmony, which used the four-shape notation, his
Christian Harmony was printed with seven notes, in a set unique to
Walker. His justification: "Would any parents having seven
children ever think of calling them by only four names?" The
contents are more heavily hymns than was true of his earlier
publication. Christian Harmony sings are still held today. In
essence, these new editions were made for practical rather than
scholarly use. The 1873 reprint is available from Brent H.
Holcomb, Box 21766, Columbia, S.C. 29221.

1423. WALKER, William. Southern Harmony, and Musical Companion.
[1835]. Rev. ed. Philadelphia: E. W. Miller, 1854; reprint ed., Los Angeles: Pro Musicamericana, 1966. 336 pp.

Walker's first collection is still considered one of the
most important of the four-shape tunebooks, though it is only used
once a year at a singing in Benton, Kentucky. It contains the old
repertory of hymns, psalms, folk hymns, fuging tunes, and anthems.
Now available from Glenn C. Wilcox, Pro Musicamericana, Box 649,
Murray, Kentucky 42071.

1424. WALTER, Thomas. The Grounds and Rules of Musick Explained:
Or, an Introduction to the Art of Singing by Note.
Fitted to the Meanest Capacities. Boston: Benjamin
Mecom, 1721; facsimile ed. from microfilm, Ann Arbor:
University Microfilms, 1978. 58 pp.

Walter's singing tutor was, along with Tuft's, of the first generation of American singing school books. There are 20 pages of tunes printed on three staves using standard (diamond shaped) notes. Preceding these is a 25-page introduction in which Walter rails against the prevailing practices of the times in psalm singing, namely, lining out (i.e., the Old Way of Singing) and the heterophonic performance of the tune. This facsimile also includes 13 pages of staff manuscript with tunes added in the nineteenth century.

1425. WARREN, J. S., Jr. Warren's Minstrel Containing a Plain and Concise Introduction to Sacred Music. [1856]. 2nd ed. Columbus, Ohio: J. H. Riley, for the author, 1857; reprint ed., Athens: Ohio University Press, 1984. 153 pp.

Edited and 36-page introduction by John Lawrence Brasher. Warren, an obscure composer, compiler, and singing school teacher from South Olive, Noble County, Ohio, used the seven shape notes designed by Alexander Auld of Deersville, Ohio, who first used them in 1846 in his Ohio Harmonist. The repertory includes psalms, hymns, fuging tunes, and anthems. Hymns by Warren are harmonized in an extremely unusual and dissonant manner.

1426. WHITE, B. F., and KING, E. J. The Sacred Harp. [1844]. 3rd ed. Philadelphia: S. C. Collins, 1860 [1859]; reprint ed., Nashville: Broadman Press, 1968. 432 pp.

The Sacred Harp remains the most famous of all four-shape tunebooks because of its widespread use today in revised editions (below). Compiled in Georgia in 1844 for the Southern Musical Convention, it was revised in 1850, 1859, and 1869. The repertory includes all the usual types: psalms, hymns, folk hymns, fuging tunes, and anthems. Because of its widespread use, it influenced other compilations, even while having been built on the foundation of earlier models, especially Walker's Southern Harmony. The introduction includes George Pullen Jackson's article "The Story of the Sacred Harp, 1844-1944" (see #1281).

1427. WHITE, Benjamin Frank [and E. J. King]. The B. F. White Sacred Harp Revised and Improved by W. M. Cooper and Others. [1902]. Troy, Ala.: Sacred Harp Book Co., 1960. 577 pp.

Available from Sacred Harp Book Co., 300 W. Fairview St., Troy, Alabama 36081. This was the first important and lasting revision of the Sacred Harp, and one which is still used today, especially in southern Alabama by both whites and blacks. While it kept much of the original repertory, the editor added alto lines as well as a number of "up-to-date" Gospel type hymns.

1428. [WHITE, B. F., and KING, E. J.]. "Original Sacred Harp" (Denson Revision). [1935]. Cullman, Ala.: Sacred Harp Publishing Co., 1971. 586 pp.

Obviously this version is not the "original" Sacred Harp, but the revisers wished to assert its primacy over the Cooper revision (#1427). The Denson revision is based on the 1911 James revision, which bore the same title. Like the Cooper revision, alto lines were added, but the newer repertory was similar in style to the earlier types, including fuging tunes that continue to be written up to the present time. The Denson revision is widely used in the South today for hundreds of one-, two-, and three-day singings. With an organization led by Mr. Hugh McGraw, Sacred Harp singing has become nationally known through recordings and appearances of singers at major folk festivals.

1429. WHITTEN, A. N. Harp of Ages, Containing a Special Collection of Sacred Songs Adapted for Use in Singing Schools, Singing Conventions and in the Church and Home. [1925]. Muleshoe, Tex.: Harp of Ages, Inc., 1973.

1430. WYETH, John. Wyeth's Repository of Sacred Music. [1810]. 5th ed. Harrisburg, Pa.: J. Wyeth, 1820; reprint ed., New York: Da Capo, 1974. 132 pp.

Introduction by Irving Lowens. Wyeth's first compilation was more similar to the eighteenth-century tunebooks than was his more important second collection (see below), for it did not yet include any folk hymns. Published in four-shape notation.

1431. WYETH, John. Wyeth's Repository of Sacred Music, Part Second. [1813]. 2nd ed. Harrisburg, Pa.: J. Wyeth, 1820; reprint ed., New York: Da Capo, 1964. 132 pp.

Introduction by Irving Lowens. As noted above, this was the more important of Wyeth's two four-shape tunebooks because it included folk hymns.

VIII. AFRO-AMERICAN MUSIC

Afro-American music is a world within a world. As will be
noted, substantial bibliographies have been published previously
which exceed by far the coverage provided in the following pages.
These sources, however, also include a number of genres not covered
here, including jazz, rhythm and blues, and soul, as well as items
of less interest to scholars.

In attempting to delimit Afro-American "folk music," two basic
areas have required inclusion--blues and religious music. Admittedly, making a distinction between blues (included) and rhythm and
blues (excluded) might seem arbitrary. Certainly both R&B and soul
have deep roots in folk-type music, especially religious music.
Both are also genres which today are primarily disseminated through
the media, whereas blues was originally a live, orally transmitted
phenomenon, especially the down-home or country blues. The
inclusion of jazz was deemed unwise for two reasons: 1) its
performance requires a fairly advanced degree of specialization,
and 2) it would require a separate volume in and of itself. Few
people usually place jazz under the "folk" heading in common usage.

The author is aware, however, that the inclusion of black
Gospel may cause trouble for some, since this genre is widely heard
on records and stylistically relates more to the "popular" genres
than to the down-home types like the spiritual. True, Gospel is
widely transmitted through the media, but Gospel began as a religious expression of the Sanctified churches, of street preachers
and street singers, and today is widely heard in all kinds of black
churches. It is transmitted orally, reinterpreted by each choir
director, and is a sincere expression of ordinary people who need
not be specialists. Indeed, many of the recordings are of amateur
choirs with or without an amateur or semi-professional soloist.

The kinds of Afro-American religious music that are closest to
the "folk" definition are the spiritual and the lined hymn. A
greater amount of research has been published on the spiritual than
on the lined hymn, whose roots are in Anglo-Protestant hymnody.
But research generally in Afro-American religious music has
blossomed in the past twenty years.

292

Research, if we use the word generously, in Afro-American music began in the late nineteenth century, but until relatively recently, much of it was published by white Americans who displayed various degrees of sensitivity. Most of the spirituals that came to be so popular with white audiences were of the arranged variety. This Section includes many of these earlier publications, but one must use them judiciously. In more recent years periodicals devoted to black music have begun (e.g., The Black Perspective in Music), although most of these publications include all kinds of black music, including composed "classical" music.

The list of materials pertaining to the blues is certainly impressive as far as length is concerned. Two aspects of this body of literature may seem surprising, at least to myself, an ethnomusicologist. Firstly, very little has been written that has anything to do with the blues musically. Aside from the work of Jeff Todd Titon, which is rather recent, one might be hard-pressed to think of other authors. The bulk of the writing concerns the blues singer and his/her life and/or the meaning of the words and what they say about black culture in America. Certainly, one has to be impressed with the work of Michael Taft, whose collection of blues texts along with the even more impressive concordance, show a devotion to a genre rarely encountered in other kinds of American folk music. Secondly, it is striking how many of the writers, or at least publishers, are British. As an American I remain uncertain why the blues have so fascinated our friends in the United Kingdom.

A number of extensive bibliographies on Afro-American music have previously appeared and are listed here. Most impressive of them is De Lerma's three-volume set. But other significant items are those by Floyd and Reisser, Jackson, Szwed and Abrahams, the Tudors, and Skowronski. In the realm of discography, one can only marvel at the dedication, if not obsession, exhibited in the many works of Michel Ruppli, whose books providing the complete contents of the offerings of five black record companies unsettle the mind of even the most diligent researcher.

Bibliographies and Discographies

1432. BROWN, Rae Linda. Music, Printed and Manuscript, in the James Weldon Johnson Memorial Collection of Negro Arts and Letters, Yale University: an Annotated Catalog. Critical Studies on Black Life and Culture #23; Garland Reference Library of the Humanities #277. New York: Garland, 1981. 322 pp.

Catalogue of 1,067 entries from the 1850s to the present, including composed materials by such men as W. C. Handy, Harry T. Burleigh, and William Grant Still. Collection also includes much material on Afro-American cultural life.

1433. De LERMA, Dominique-Rene. Bibliography of Black Music. 4 vols. Westport, Conn.: Greenwood, 1981-4.

A truly massive undertaking, this bibliography covers black musics throughout the world, though especially in the Americas. Unfortunately, entries lack annotations, making it difficult to distinguish important items from ephemera. Evidently, further volumes are planned in this series which is expected eventually to include about 88,000 entries.

Vol. 1. Reference Materials. 1980. 124 pp.

Organized in 14 categories and many subcategories based on those used in RILM, there are some 2,800 entries in the following areas: libraries, museums, collections, encyclopedias, lexicons, etymologies, bibliographies of the music, bibliographies of the literature, discographies, iconographies, directories and organization news, dissertations and theses, and periodicals.

Vol. 2. Afro-American Idioms. 1981. 220 pp.

Organized according to types, such as general histories, minstrelsy, songsters, spirituals, ragtime, musical theater, concert music, band music, blues, gospel, rhythm and blues, and jazz.

Vol. 3. Geographical Studies. 1982. 284 pp.

Entries are classified by broad areas (Africa, the Caribbean, South America, and North America) under which there are subcategories for countries and states. In the case of Africa, there is an index of African ethnic groups.

Vol. 4. Theory, Education, and Related Studies. 1984. 254 pp.

Since most of these entries relate to composed music, they are of less interest to the folk music scholar.

1434. De LERMA, Dominique-Rene. Concert Music and Spirituals: a Selective Discography. Nashville: Fisk University Institute for Research in Black American Music, 1981. 44 pp.

1435. FERRIS, William R., Jr. Mississippi Black Folklore: a
Research Bibliography and Discography. Hattiesburg:
University and College Press of Mississippi, 1971. 61 pp.

Although a portion of this compilation concerns folklore
generally, pp. 24-48 are a bibliography of black song and the
blues while pp. 49-60 are a discography of traditional singers,
blues singers, and gospel singers, and p. 61 is a filmography.

1436. FLOYD, Samuel, Jr., and REISSER, Marsha J. Black Music in
the United States: an Annotated Bibliography of Selected
Reference and Research Material. Millwood, N.Y.: Kraus
International Publishers, 1983. 234 pp.

A list of 388 items plus 23 in the appendix organized in
these categories: general guides, dictionary catalogues, bibliographies of bibliographies, bibliographies, discographies, periodical indices, dictionaries and encyclopedias, topical studies,
collective biographies, iconographies, pedagogy, anthologies,
records and record collecting, and repositories and archives.
Indexed by subject, name, and title.

1437. GEORGE, Zelma Watson. "A Guide to Negro Music: an
Annotated Bibliography of Negro Folk Music and Art Music
by Negro Composers or Based on Negro Thematic Material."
Ed.D. dissertation, New York University, 1953. 302 pp.

Part I is a bibliography of 12,163 titles on Negro music
at the Howard University Library. Part II attempts to define
Negro music, provides a critical overview of material on the
subject, and describes the contents of the above collection.

1438. Index to Negro Spirituals. Cleveland: Cleveland Public
Library, 1937. 146 pp.

A title index to 30 collections of arranged spirituals.

1439. JACKSON, Irene V. Afro-American Religious Music: a
Bibliography and a Catalogue of Gospel Music. Westport,
Conn.: Greenwood, 1979. 210 pp.

In spite of its title, this unannotated and only briefly
introduced bibliography includes much material on Afro-American
folklore and dance as well as on religion. Its range, however,

covers the Caribbean as well as North America. Pages 61-184 comprise a catalogue of compositions of Afro-American gospel composers from 1938 to 1965.

1440. JOHNSON, James Peter. "Bibliographic Guide to the Study of Afro-American Music." Washington, D.C.: Howard University Libraries, 1973. 24 pp.

This unannotated bibliography covers folk and popular styles.

1441. MAULTSBY, Portia K. "Selective Bibliography: United States Black Music." Ethnomusicology 19-3 (1975): 421-49.

Non-annotated list under these headings: general, origin and acculturation, religious and secular music (ante-bellum), minstrels and musicals, blues, jazz, gospel, urban popular music, "art" music of black composers. Obviously, this list is highly selective since the potential material is much greater.

1442. MAULTSBY, Portia K. "Sources of Films, Video-Tapes, Dissertations, and Field Recordings for Afro-American Music." Musical Library Association Newsletter 14 (Sept.-Oct. 1973): 4-5.

A rather minimal list of 23 items but with addresses.

1443. MEADOWS, Eddie S. "Theses and Dissertations on Black American Music." Beverly Hills, Cal.: Theodore Front Musical Literature, 1980. 19 pp.

1444. RUPPLI, Michel. Atlantic Records. 4 vols. Westport, Conn.: Greenwood, 1979.

As will be seen in this item and those that follow, Ruppli is one of the most amazing discographers of our time, for he has indexed in detail the entire output, or virtually so, of several record companies that specialized in Afro-American music. This resource indexes Atlantic Records from 1947-1978. Vol. 1: (404 pp.) covers blues and jazz, 1947-66; Vol. 2: (394 pp.) covers rhythm and blues, gospel, jazz, and pop for 1966-1970s; Vol. 3: (382 pp.) covers rhythm and blues, jazz, and pop for 1970-1974; Vol. 4: (273 pp.) covers the same for 1974-1978.

1445. RUPPLI, Michel. The Chess Labels: a Discography. 2 vols.
Westport, Conn.: Greenwood, 1983. 733 pp.

Chess records and its subsidiaries produced material on
blues, rhythm and blues, gospel, and spirituals starting in 1947.

1446. RUPPLI, Michel. The King Labels: a Discography. 2 vols.
Westport, Conn.: Greenwood, 1985. 944 pp.

Complete listing of all records made by King and its
subsidiaries, including foreign issues, for material on country-
western, gospel, blues, and rhythm and blues from 1943 to 1973.

1447. RUPPLI, Michel. The Prestige Label: a Discography.
Westport, Conn.: Greenwood, 1980. 377 pp.

Complete listing of all records by Prestige, 1949-1979,
which specialized in jazz and other non-folk styles, but included
some folk genres.

1448. RUPPLI, Michel. The Savoy Label: a Discography. Westport,
Conn.: Greenwood, 1980. 442 pp.

Savoy specialized in religious genres, but also produced
hillbilly, classical, ethnic, swing, gospel, and blues, starting
in 1942.

1449. SKOWRONSKI, JoAnn. Black Music in America: a Bibliography.
Metuchen, N.J.: Scarecrow Press, 1981. 723 pp.

An unannotated listing of 14,319 items, including general
reference, periodicals and magazines, but the bulk is on
particular musicians and singers. This work covers all Afro-
American genres, some folk, some not.

1450. SZWED, John F., and ABRAHAMS, Roger D. Afro-American Folk
Culture: an Annotated Bibliography of Materials from
North, Central, and South America and the West Indies.
2 vols. Philadelphia: Institute for the Study of Human
Issues, 1978. 814 pp. and 814 pp.

Volume 1 covers North America with 3,331 items. Items
are fully indexed, but annotations are mostly brief.

1451. TUDOR, Dean, and TUDOR, Nancy. Black Music. Littleton, Colo.: Libraries Unlimited, 1979. 262 pp.

Discography of blues, rhythm and blues, gospel, soul, and reggae musics.

General and Miscellaneous Studies

1452. ALLEN, William Francis, WARE, Charles Pickard, and GARRISON, Lucy McKim. Slave Songs of the United States. New York: A. Simpson & Co., 1867; reprint ed., New York: Peter Smith, 1951. 115 pp. Popular edition, New York: Oak, 1965. 176 pp.

These songs, collected in the South, have only tune and text in the original, but in Oak's popular edition, accompaniments have been added. This was one of the earliest collections of Afro-American folk songs, but the notation lacks the nuances that make the style distinctive.

1453. AMES, Russell. "Art in Negro Folksong." Journal of American Folklore 56-222 (Oct.-Dec. 1943): 241-54.

An assertion of artistic merit for Afro-American folksong, but focused on texts.

1454. BANE, Michael. White Boy Singin' the Blues. Middlesex, England: Penguin, 1982. 269 pp.

A social history of the black influence on white music, especially rock, which the author considers white blues.

1455. BARAKA, Imamu Amiri [JONES, LeRoi]. Black Music. New York: Morrow, 1967; reprint ed., Westport, Conn.: Greenwood, 1980. 221 pp.

A social study of black music and of protest expressed through it.

1456. BASS, Robert Duncan. "Negro Songs from Pedee Country." Journal of American Folklore 44-174 (Oct.-Dec. 1931): 418-36.

Texts and some tunes for 64 songs from South Carolina, with cross references to other printed versions.

1457. BEASLEY, Cecily Reeves. "Creole and Afro-Creole Music of Louisiana: its Origin and Influence." D.M. dissertation, The Florida State University, 1976.

No abstract available.

1458. Black Music Research Journal. Nashville: Fisk University, Institute for Research in Black Music. 1980--.

Although apparently a journal, this once-a-year publication is a collection of invited articles on various kinds of black musics, including gospel, rhythm and blues, musical behavior, etc., by leading black writers and researchers.

1459. BROOKS, Tilford. America's Black Musical Heritage. Englewood Cliffs, N.J.: Prentice-Hall, 1984. 336 pp.

A comprehensive survey of Afro-American music, its roots, history up to 1900, ragtime, jazz, rhythm and blues, gospel, and musicians, including classical composers and performers. Some analysis of selected works. This is an excellent introduction.

1460. BROWNE, Ray B. "Some Notes on the Southern 'Holler'." Journal of American Folklore 67-263 (Jan.-Mar. 1954): 73-98.

Defines the "holler," and describes field work done in 1952 with Mr. Richard Sullivan of Bluff, Alabama, the original purpose and context of the genre, and provides three examples.

1461. BUCKLEY, Bruce R. "'Uncle' Ira Cephas--a Negro Folk Singer in Ohio." Midwest Folklore 3-1 (Spring, 1953): 5-18.

Cephas was born in Madison County, Kentucky, but later lived in Scioto County, Ohio. Based on research from 1951-2, the author provides a biography and appreciation of the singer, along with a collection of tales, songs, and blues (texts only), the original material being in the Archive of Ohio Folklore and Music.

1462. BURLIN, Natalie Curtis. "Negro Music at Birth." Musical
    Quarterly 5 (1919): 86-9.

    A revealing essay giving the reaction of a white observer
encountering the "real" black folk music in Alabama for the first
time.

1463. CLARK, Edgar Rogie. "Negro Folk Music in America." Jour-
    nal of American Folklore 64-253 (July-Sept. 1951): 281-7.

    Discussion of the problems relating to the study of this
subject.

1464. COURLANDER, Harold. Negro Folk Music U.S.A.. New York:
    Columbia University Press, 1963. 324 pp.

    Comprehensive study of black folk music, by genre,
including calls, work songs, blues, ring games, creole songs,
ballads and minstrels, dances, and instrumental music. Includes
64 pp. of songs, a bibliography and discography.

1465. COURLANDER, Harold. Negro Songs from Alabama. New York:
    Courlander, 1960 [76 pp.]; rev. and enl. ed., New York:
    Oak, 1963. 112 pp.

    A collection of 66 songs transcribed by John Benson
Brook, including 32 religious songs (prayers, anthems, and
spirituals), nine work songs, five calls, two lullabies, and 18
children's game songs.

1466. CRAY, Ed. "An Acculturative Continuum for Negro Folk Song
    in the United States." Ethnomusicology 5-1 (Jan. 1961):
    10-15.

    Attempt to formulate a Gestalt view of Negro folksong,
partly through explanation, partly through a chart.

1467. CUNEY-HARE, Maud. Negro Musicians and their Music.
    Washington, D.C.: Associated Publishers, 1936; reprint
    ed., New York: Da Capo, 1974. 451 pp.

    While the emphasis is on classical in this comprehensive
survey of Afro-American music, its roots, and types, folksong

predominates on pp. 1-156, especially pp. 61-112. This area includes spirituals and the blues, with emphasis on text.

1468. DENNISON, Sam. Scandalize My Name: Black Imagery in American Popular Music. New York: Garland, 1982. 594 pp.

Although neither about black music or folk music, this study of blacks in music from the eighteenth century to the present is valuable as an adjunct to any study of black music.

1469. DRAPER, David Elliott. "The Mardi Gras Indians: the Ethnomusicology of Black Associations in New Orleans." Ph.D. dissertation, Tulane University, 1973. 638 pp.

This is an anthropological study of the phenomenon of blacks masking as Indians in New Orleans, but performing dances and songs with African roots. Part 1 is an ethnology of black associations, and Part 2 is a study of their musical repertories.

1470. EPSTEIN, Dena. "African Music in British and French America." Musical Quarterly 59 (1973): 61-91.

Fascinating and well-documented study in which three questions are attempted: 1) what music was brought from Africa, 2) how long did it last, and 3) how was it transformed. Documentation includes many contemporary quotations.

1471. EPSTEIN, Dena J. "Documenting the History of Black Folk Music in the United States: a Librarian's Odyssey." Fontes Artis Musical 23-4 (Oct.-Dec. 1976): 151-7.

A study of the kinds of sources available for documenting early Afro-American musical history and a discussion of the problems involved with such sources.

1472. EPSTEIN, Dena J. "Lucy McKim Garrison, American Musician." New York Public Library Bulletin 67 (Oct. 1963): 529-46.

The biography of one of the three editors of the 1867 Slave Songs of the United States, her publications, views on blacks and black song.

301

1473. EPSTEIN, Dena J. Sinful Tunes and Spirituals: Black Folk
    Music to the Civil War. Music in American Life. Urbana:
    University of Illinois Press, 1977. 433 pp.

    Thoroughly researched and documented history of Afro-
American folk music from about 1640 to the publication of Slave
Songs of the United States in 1867. Beginning with the African
heritage and what is known about the role of music in relation to
the slave trade, the author traces both secular and sacred genres
and instrumental music to 1867 and beyond. Included is a
significant bibliography.

1474. EPSTEIN, Dena J. "Slave Music in the United States Before
    1860: a Survey of Sources." Music Library Association
    Notes 20 (Spring-Summer, 1963): 195-212, 377-90.

    Basically a review of early literature organized in two
sections, "Before 1800" and "After 1800." It covers the spiritual,
corn songs, boat songs, patting juba, ring shouts, music of Place
Congo, and restrictions on singing.

1475. FISHER, Miles Mark. Negro Slave Songs of the United
    States. Ithaca: Cornell University Press for American
    Historical Association, 1953; reprint ed., London and New
    York: Russel and Russel, 1968. 223 pp.

    A rewritten 1949 University of Chicago dissertation ("The
Evolution of Slave Songs of the United States") in church history,
this work focuses on the spiritual but seeks to show that Negro
folk songs are indeed folk music.

1476. HANDY, W. C. Unsung Americans Sung. New York: W. C. Handy
    Co., 1944. 236 pp.

    A collection of black songs arranged for four-part chorus
and piano accompaniment whose purpose is to bolster the courage of
and broaden the outlook of blacks. Includes some pictures and
commentary on the songs.

1477. HENRY, Mellinger E. "Negro Songs from Georgia." Journal
    of American Folklore 44-124 (Oct.-Dec. 1931): 437-47.

    A collection of 14 texts without tunes.

1478. HOLZKNECHT, K. J. "Some Negro Song Variants from
Louisville." Journal of American Folklore 41-162 (Oct.-
Dec. 1928): 558-78.

Religious and secular song texts obtained from black
teachers in Louisville.

1479. HURSTON, Zora N. Mules and Men. Philadelphia: Lippincott,
1935; reprint ed., London: Kegan Paul, 1936; New York:
Negro Universities Press, 1969; New York: Harper and Row,
1970; Westport, Conn.: Greenwood, 1970; Bloomington:
Indiana University Press, 1978. 342 pp.

Hurston, perhaps America's most famous and important
black anthropologist and folklorist, who died in 1960, included
the study of music in her research. In this particular book one
section is devoted to "Negro Songs with Music," pp. 309-31, giving
texts and harmonized arrangements of "John Henry," "East Coast
Blues," and others.

1480. JACKSON, Bruce. "Prison Worksongs: the Composer in
Negatives." Western Folklore 26-4 (Oct. 1967): 245-68.

A study of worksongs based on the melody of one
particular cotton song with 130 stanzas sung by J. B. Smith of the
Texas Prison system. Includes texts, tunes, commentary, and
explanations of certain words.

1481. JACKSON, Bruce. Wake Up Dead Man: Afro-American Worksongs
from Texas Prisons. Cambridge: Harvard University Press,
1972. 326 pp.

A total of 65 texts and commentaries with tunes
transcribed by Judith McCulloh and Norman Cazden with commentary
on context, some in the form of the informant's own words. They
are organized as: cotton and cane songs (solo and group), axe
songs--cross cutting, axe songs--logging, and flatweeding.

1482. JACKSON, Clyde Owen. The Songs of our Years: a Study of
Negro Folk Music. New York: Exposition Press, 1968.
54 pp.

A rather dated survey inspired by Antonin Dvorak's
comments on black music, organized as "Before the Dvorak

Statement" and "After the Dvorak Statement." The survey ends
around the 1940s.

1483. JACKSON, Irene V., ed. More than Dancing: Essays on Afro-
American Music and Musicians. Contributions in Afro-
American and African Studies, #83. Westport, Conn.:
Greenwood, 1985. 281 pp.

A collection of 11 essays by leading authorities on
various aspects of Afro-American music, including Portia Maultsby
(African retentions), George L. Starks, Jr. (S. Carolina Sea Island
songs), Horace Clarence Boyer (Gospel music), and Mellonee Burnim
(gospel music). Also treats aesthetics and the blues.

1484. JAMES, Willis Lawrence. "The Romance of the Negro Folk Cry
in America." Phylon 16 (March 1955): 15-30.

The "cry is instant reminder of the primitive. It is the
oldest form of vocal expression." This work emphasizes the cry
among blacks, but also compares them with white cries, providing
examples as well.

1485. JOHNSON, Guy B. John Henry: Tracking Down a Negro Legend.
Chapel Hill: University of North Carolina Press, 1929.
155 pp.

Comprehensive study of the origin and history of a legend
and the ballads that resulted, with texts and some musical
examples.

1486. JOHNSON, Guy Benton. "A Study of the Musical Talent of the
American Negro." Ph.D. dissertation, University of North
Carolina, 1927.

The author administered the Seashore Test to 3,500 blacks
in North Carolina, South Carolina, and Virginia, and found no
appreciable differences in aptitude between whites and blacks.

1487. JOHNSON, Guy B., and ODUM, Howard W. The Negro and His
Songs: a Study of Typical Negro Songs in the South.
Chapel Hill: University of North Carolina Press, 1925;
reprint ed., Hatboro, Pa.: Folklore Associates, 1964; New
York: Negro Universities Press, 1968, 1972. 306 pp.

This is primarily a collection of about 200 song texts organized into three categories: religious, social, and work. The goal of the authors is not to preserve Negro song but to explain the character of the Negro through his songs. The authors also reacted strongly to what they considered obscenity in the texts and carefully cleaned them up.

1488. JONES, Bessie, [and STEWART, John]. For the Ancestors: Autogiographical Memories. Urbana: University of Illinois Press, 1983. 203 pp.

This is an oral history of Georgia Sea Island folksinger, Bessie Jones, her birth, life, and performing career, with emphasis on the game songs.

1489. JONES, Bessie, and HAWES, Bess Lomax. Step it Down: Games, Plays, Songs, and Stories from the Afro-American Heritage. New York: Harper & Row, 1972. 233 pp.

The words and tunes of 70 songs from the Georgia Sea Islands transmitted to Hawes via folksinger Bessie Jones, with introductory material on them.

1490. JONES, Hettie. Big Star Fallin' Mama; Five Women in Black Music. New York: Viking Press, 1974. 150 pp.

Brief biographies of Ma Rainey, Bessie Smith, Mahalia Jackson, Billie Holiday, and Aretha Franklin.

1491. JOYNER, Charles W. Down by the Riverside: a South Carolina Slave Community. Urbana: University of Illinois Press, 1984. 345 pp.

An attempt, based on interviews with former slaves, to reconstruct the life of a slave community in All Saints Parish, Georgetown District, South Carolina. The words for a number of spirituals are included on pp. 163-9.

1492. KATZ, Bernard, ed. The Social Implications of Early Negro Music in the United States [With Over One Hundred Fifty of the Songs, Many of Them with their Music]. New York: Arno Press, The New York Times Book Co., 1969. 188 pp.

A valuable collection of reprints of ten early articles and three prefaces on Negro music, such as that of Slave Songs of the United States (1867) and W. E. B. DuBois' 1903 article, "On the Sorrow Songs."

1493. KIRBY, Percival R. "A Study of Negro Harmony." Musical Quarterly 16 (1930): 404-14.

A short description of African style music based on secondary sources followed by an examination of the harmony for eight arranged spirituals.

1494. KMEN, Henry A. "Old Corn Meal: a Forgotten Urban Negro Folksinger." Journal of American Folklore 75-295 (Jan.-Mar. 1962): 29-34.

Interesting history of "Old Corn Meal," a black corn vendor who was discovered and put on stage in New Orleans c. 1837.

1495. KMEN, Henry A. "The Roots of Jazz and the Dance in Place Congo: a Reappraisal." Yearbook for Inter-American Musical Research 8 (1972): 5-16.

A re-examination and questioning of jazz history literature that assumes jazz originated at Place Congo. The author cites the known facts and quotes from contemporary documents up to 1835 and beyond. Concludes by strongly questioning whether Place Congo had anything at all to do with the origin of jazz.

1496. KREHBIEL, Henry Edward. Afro-American Folksongs: a Study in Racial and National Music. New York: G. Schirmer, 1913; reprint ed., New York: Frederick Ungar, 1962; Portland: M. E. Longwood, 1976. 176 pp.

A presentation of and argument for Negro music as "fit material for artistic treatment." Seeks to define it as folksong, show what elements are African, and disprove the idea that Afro-Americans only imitated other styles. Most examples are provided in arrangements.

1497. LaBREW, Arthur R. Black Musicians of the Colonial Period, 1700-1800. Detroit: by the author, 1977. 183 pp.

A book about the author's search for individual black
musicians in history, with biographies of those who were found.
The documentation is sometimes uncertain, however.

1498. LADNER, Robert A., Jr. "Folk Music, Pholk Music, and the
        Angry Children of Malcolm X." Southern Folklore
        Quarterly 34-2 (June 1970): 131-45.

        A seemingly unnecessary defense of the idea that blacks
have their own musical style and a study of black protest song
with examples.

1499. LAUBENSTEIN, Paul Fritz. "Race Values in Aframerican
        Music." Musical Quarterly 16 (1930): 378-403.

        A cultural study of African consciousness by an outsider
to the tradition with a concern for its preservation. He treats
African religion, the adoption of white religion, and compares the
significance of call and response in Africa and the United States.

1500. LEVINE, Lawrence W. "Slave Songs and Slave Consciousness:
        an Exploration in Neglected Sources." In Anonymous
        Americans: Explorations in Nineteenth-Century Social
        History, pp. 99-130. Edited by Tamara K. Hareven.
        Englewood Cliffs, N.J.: Prentice-Hall, 1971.

        The author proposes to explore black consciousness
through the (neglected) sources of songs and sermons, which if
ignored would allegedly leave blacks mute.

1501. LOCKE, Alain. The Negro and His Music. Washington, D.C.:
        The Associates in Negro Folk Education, 1936; reprint
        ed., Port Washington, N.Y.: Kennikat, 1968. 142 pp.
        Also reprinted in Negro Art, Past and Present. New York:
        Arno Press, 1969. 282 pp.

        General history of Negro music in America and its place
in contemporary life written by the first black Rhodes Scholar.

1502. LOMAX, Alan. "The Homogeneity of African-Afro-American
        Musical Style." In Afro-American Anthropology, pp. 181-
        201. Edited by Norman E. Whitten, Jr., and John F.
        Szwed. New York: Free Press, 1970.

Seeks to demonstrate through the author's Cantometrics system that Afro-American music is part of the larger African music system, albeit somewhat affected by European style. It includes Cantometrics worksheets.

1503. LOMAX, John A. "'Sinful Songs' of the Southern Negro." _Musical Quarterly_ 21 (1934): 177-87.

Interesting report by Lomax written after a summer of field recording in the South for the Library of Congress while in search of "uncorrupted" Negro songs.

1504. LOMAX, John A., and LOMAX, Alan. _The Leadbelly Legend: a Collection of World-Famous Songs by Huddie Ledbetter._ Rev. ed. New York: TRO Folkways Music, 1965. 96 pp.

A collection of Leadbelly's songs, with music edited by Hally Wood.

1505. LOMAX, John A., and LOMAX, Alan. _Negro Folk Songs as Sung by Lead Belly: "King of the Twelve-String Guitar Players of the World."_ New York: Macmillan, 1936. 242 pp.

A collection of texts, tunes, and commentary on them by a famous and long-time convict of the Texas and Louisiana prison systems preceded by a 64-page introduction. The notation attempts to capture the nuances of style typical of Lead Belly and therefore its details are explained. The songs include reels, work songs, hollers, blues, talkin' blues, ballads, and others.

1506. LONGINI, Muriel Davis. "Folk Songs of Chicago Negroes." _Journal of American Folklore_ 52-302 (Jan.-Mar. 1939): 96-111.

The history and background of blacks in Chicago at this time and a collection of song texts.

1507. MARKS, Morton Allen. "Performance Rules and Ritual Structures in Afro-American Music." Ph.D. dissertation, University of California, Berkeley, 1972.

No abstract available.

1508. MAULTSBY, Portia K. "Influences and Retentions of West
       African Musical Concepts in U.S. Black Music." The
       Western Journal of Black Studies 3 (Fall, 1979): 197-215.

       Well-documented historical survey and discussion of
African influences in Afro-American music, in the church, on
Gospel music, and on other types.

1509. METFESSEL, Milton. Phonophotography in Folk Music:
       American Negro Songs in New Notation. Chapel Hill:
       University of North Carolina Press, 1928. 181 pp.

       An early scientific examination of black musical style in
graphic notation produced through a photographic technique in
response to recorded sounds.

1510. MOTEN, R. R. "Negro Folk Songs." Southern Workman 24
       (Feb., 1895): 30-2; reprinted in Black Perspective in
       Music 4-2 (1976): 145-51.

       An early account of research into black corn songs,
giving examples of texts and a description of style.

1511. NELSON, Ella Joy. "Black American Folk Song: an Analytical
       Study with Implications for Music Education." D.M.A.
       dissertation, Stanford University, 1981. 113 pp.

       Asserts that the Kodaly method favors Anglo-American folk
song and ignores the musics of other ethnic groups. The author is
concerned with defining a "musical mother tongue" for black
American children and using it in relation to Kodaly's
methodology. Also analyzes several black folk songs.

1512. NILES, John J. "Shout, Coon, Shout!" Musical Quarterly 16
       (1930): 516-30.

       A study of both sacred and secular shouts based on
personal experience, with examples of texts. Some of these have
been used in jazz and other genres.

1513. NILES, John J. Singing Soldiers. New York: Charles
       Scribner's Sons, 1927. 171 pp.

A personal and unsystematic account of the author's experience during World War I trying to collect the songs of white American soldiers. Finding that they sang only composed songs, especially of the Broadway type, he turned to black soldiers whom he found singing their own songs. He therefore collected them and published a number of them here with piano accompaniment.

1514. NILES, John Jacob. "White Pioneers and Black." Musical Quarterly 18 (1932): 60-75.

The story of the coming of the Africans to America and the relationship of black song texts to white. Told in the engaging style of a story teller.

1515. ODUM, Howard W. "Folk-Song and Folk-Poetry as Found in the Secular Songs of the Southern Negroes." Journal of American Folklore 24-93 (July-Sept. 1911): 255-94; 24-94 (Oct.-Dec. 1911): 351-96.

Extensive study of texts from numerous examples and an extensive bibliography of early materials.

1516. ODUM, Howard W. "Religious Folk-Songs of the Southern Negroes." American Journal of Religious Psychology and Education 3-3 (July 1909): 265-365.

The author, a psychologist, asserts that one can know a person's soul through his music. This article, therefore, is study of the words, especially in religious song, with many text examples.

1517. ODUM, Howard W., and JOHNSON, Guy B. The Negro and His Songs: a Study of Typical Negro Songs in the South. Chapel Hill: University of North Carolina Press, 1925; reprint ed., Hatboro, Pa.: Folklore Associates, 1964; New York: Negro Universities Press, 1968, 1972. 306 pp.

The story of black Americans as told by their songs, with texts organized by topic.

1518. ODUM, Howard W., and JOHNSON, Guy B. Negro Workaday Songs. Chapel Hill: University of North Carolina Press, 1926; reprint ed., New York: Negro Universities Press, 1969; Westport, Conn.: Greenwood, 1977. 278 pp.

Although much of this work is a study of the texts of
blues, ballads, work songs, social songs, and religious songs, the
authors also attempt a description of musical style (pp. 241-64),
especially melody, towards elucidating the peculiarities of black
song style.

1519. OLIVER, Paul. Songsters and Saints: Vocal Traditions on
      Race Records. New York: Cambridge University Press,
      1984. 300 pp.

The author asserts that a traditional emphasis on blues
research has blinded us to other types, which are treated here:
southern rural dance music, comic and social songs, ballads from
the medicine shows, and travelling entertainment songs.

1520. PARRISH, Lydia. Slave Songs of the Georgia Sea Islands.
      New York: Creative Age Press, 1942; reprint ed.,
      Hatboro, Pa.: Folklore Associates, 1965. 256 pp.

Songs compiled by a white Quaker from New Jersey who grew
up without music and first heard black songs in Georgia in 1909.
After an extensive introduction, the songs include text,
commentary, and tune (and polyphony when present) organized under
a number of categories: African survivals, Afro-American shout
songs, ring-play, religious and work songs. Music transcribed by
Creighton Churchhill and Robert MacGimsey.

1521. PASTEUR, Alfred B., and TOLDSON, Ivory L. Roots of Soul;
      the Psychology of Black Expressiveness. Garden City,
      N.Y.: Anchor, 1982. 324 pp.

A study, not so much of black music, but black
expressiveness through music, a holistic view by a psychologist
concerned with "black folk expressions in the enrichment of life."
Examines emotionalism, spontaneity, and rhythm.

1522. PEABODY, Charles. "Notes on Negro Music." Journal of
      American Folklore 16-62 (July-Sept. 1903): 148-52.

Examples of texts, tunes, and commentary on black song
written by a non-specialist who observed the music being performed
in Coahoma County, Mississippi, in 1901-2.

1523. PING, Nancy R. "Black Musical Activities in Antebellum
Wilmington, North Carolina." Black Perspective in Music
8-2 (Fall, 1980): 139-60.

A study of blacks in the musical life of eighteenth and
nineteenth century Wilmington, with emphasis on festivals,
including the "John Canoe" Christmas celebration. Also includes
mention of singing schools, revivals, and camp meetings and black
participation in other facets of musical life, such as bands.

1524. RAMSEY, Frederic, Jr. Been Here and Gone. New Brunswick,
N.J.: Rutgers University Press, 1960. 177 pp.

Popular account of the author's trips to collect music
throughout the South during the years 1951-7, with reminiscences,
excerpts of interviews, and photos.

1525. ROACH, Hildred. Black American Music: Past and Present.
Boston: Crescendo Publishing Co., 1973. 199 pp.

A survey of black American music from colonial and slave
times to the present, including folk songs and spirituals,
minstrel songs, and jazz. Much material on composed music as
well. Somewhat technical.

1526. RUBLOWSKY, John. Black Music in America. New York: Basic
Books, 1971. 150 pp.

Comprehensive but light historical survey of black music
from Africa to jazz and classical by a popular culture writer.

1527. SAMPSON, Henry T. Blacks in Blackface: a Source Book on
Early Black Musical Shows. Metuchen, N.J.: Scarecrow
Press, 1980. 552 pp.

Partly to be read, partly a goldmine of data, this is a
history of the times, of minstrel shows, theatres, comedy shows,
and biographies of individuals. Includes a list of shows produced
from 1900-40 and a list of black newspapers for the same period.

1528. SCARBOROUGH, Dorothy. On the Trail of Negro Folk-Songs.
Cambridge: Harvard University Press, 1925; reprint ed.,
Hatboro, Pa.: Folklore Associates, 1963. 289 pp.

A collection of song texts, with a few tunes, that together portray the life of southern blacks and the social history of the South. The songs are organized by topics: ballads, dance songs, game songs, lullabies, work songs, and blues. The reprint edition includes a foreword by Roger D. Abrahams telling of the author's work in Texas.

1529. SOUTHERN, Eileen. Biographical Dictionary of Afro-American and African Musicians. Westport, Conn.: Greenwood, 1982. 478 pp.

Short biographies of all kinds of people, from all aspects of Afro-American music, with entries organized by period, place of birth, occupation. The approximately 1,500 entries range from Sebastian Rodriguez (born c. 1642) to the generation of musicians like Donna Summer (born 1948). Forty subjects were born in Africa. There is also a bibliography.

1530. SOUTHERN, Eileen. The Music of Black Americans: a History. New York: W. W. Norton, 1971, 552 pp.; 2nd ed., 1983. 622 pp.

Not the first comprehensive history, but certainly the best, tracing the story from Africa to the New World, from Colonial times to the present based on written documentation, excerpts of which are cited. The author also provides the social and historical contexts for the music. Organized chronologically, with many different genres studied within a given period. The new edition was redone in a number of ways, including organization.

1531. SOUTHERN, Eileen. Readings in Black American Music. New York: W. W. Norton, 1971, 302 pp.; 2nd ed., 1983. 350 pp.

Meant to be used in conjunction with the previous item, this book consists of selected readings starting the African era and covers slave life, religious music, plantation culture, city life, and the time of freedom from slavery. Sources include early newspapers, letters, mission reports, travelogues, etc.

1532. SPIVEY, Donald. Union and the Black Musician: the Narrative of William Everett Samuels and Chicago. Lanham, Md.: University Press of America, 1984. 158 pp.

An oral history based on the life of William Everett Samuels, a black professional musician who joined Local 208 of the oldest union of black musicians in 1918. Discusses the union struggles in the 1920s and 1930s, the Depression, and noted musicians of the time. While not on folk music per se, based to some extent on a folk experience.

1533. STARKS, George Leroy, Jr. "Black Music in the Sea Islands of South Carolina: its Cultural Context--Continuity and Change." Ph.D. dissertation, Wesleyan University, 1973.

Researched during 1972-3 on James, Johns, Yonges, Edisto, St. Helena, and Daufuski Islands and at Red Top, North Carolina. Nearly half of the work is concerned with background information (cultural context), providing geographical setting, history, language, African retentions, and then treats both religious and secular music.

1534. SZWED, John F. "Afro-American Musical Adaptation." In Afro-American Anthropology, pp. 219-30. Edited by Norman E. Whitten, Jr. and J. F. Szwed. New York: Free Press, 1970.

A re-examination of how scholars have hitherto viewed the alleged African origin of Afro-American music, with focus on preaching and blues.

1535. SZWED, John F. "Musical Adaptation among Afro-Americans." Journal of American Folklore 82-324 (Apr.-June 1969): 112-21.

This article is concerned with change in Afro-American music, and its thesis is "Song forms and performances are themselves models of social behavior. . . ."

1536. TALLEY, Thomas W. Negro Folk Rhymes. New York: Macmillan, 1922; reprint ed., Port Washington, N.Y.: Kennikat Press, 1968; Folcroft, Pa.: Folcroft Library Editions, 1980. 347 pp.

Field collected song texts with commentary, but from a condescending view.

1537. TALLMADGE, William H. "Afro-American Music." Rev. ed.
Buffalo: State University College Bookstore, 1969. 16 pp.

Revised from an article originally published in Music
Educator's Journal for Sept.-Oct. 1957. Very brief overview and
a chart showing relationships among musics, including jazz, and a
jazz chronology.

1538. THOMAS, Will H. "Some Current Folk-Songs of the Negro."
Austin: Texas Folklore Society, 1936. 13 pp.

A study of texts, originally done as a paper in 1912.

1539. TITON, Jeff Todd. "North America/Black Music." In Worlds
of Music: an Introduction to the Music of the World's
Peoples, pp. 105-65. Edited by J. T. Titon. New York:
Schirmer Books, 1984.

One part of a collection intended for students taking a
survey of world musics, Titon's article surveys religious music,
work songs, play songs, and the blues, using many excellent
photographs, musical examples, and an accompanying cassette tape.

1540. WALDO, Terry. This is Ragtime. New York: Hawthorn Books,
1976; reprint ed., New York: Da Capo, 1984. 244 pp.

The history of ragtime from its folk roots to its arrival
on the popular stage in the 1970s, written by a protégé of Eubie
Blake.

1541. WALTON, Ortiz. Music: Black, White & Blue. New York:
William Morrow, 1972. 180 pp.

Concerned with the social and cultural matrix into which
Afro-American music is created, this sociological study examines
slave music, blues, jazz, and music in the modern period.

1542. WATERMAN, Richard Alan. "African Influence on the Music of
the Americas." In Acculturation in the Americas, Pro-
ceedings and Selected Papers of the XXIXth International
Congress of Americanists, pp. 207-18. Edited by Sol Tax.
Chicago: University of Chicago Press, 1952; reprint ed.,
New York: Cooper Square, 1967.

A non-technical discussion of stylistic features held in
common by African and Afro-American musics, written by an
associate of Herskovits.

1543. WHARTON, Linda F. "Black American Children's Singing
       Games: a Structural Analysis." Ph.D. dissertation,
       University of Pittsburgh, 1979. 502 pp.

An examination of children's singing games in general,
how they are used world-wide, their meaning, and combining of the
physical, mental, and emotional aspects of play, with emphasis on
these games within black American culture.

1544. WHITE, Newman I. American Negro Folk-Songs. Cambridge:
       Harvard University Press, 1928; reprint ed., Hatboro,
       Pa.: Folklore Associates, 1965. 501 pp.

Compiled in order to counter what the author considers an
over-interest in the blues, this study of black song texts,
organized by topic, still assumes white influence. Includes 15
tune samples as well.

1545. WORK, John W. American Negro Songs: a Comprehensive
       Collection of 230 Folksongs, Religious and Secular. New
       York: Howell, Soskin & Co., 1940; reprint ed., New York:
       Bonanza Book, 1976. 266 pp.

Partly a history of Negro folksongs from African times to
the present, including the spiritual, the blues, worksongs, and
social songs, partly a collection of 200 songs in four-part
harmony and 30 more with single line melody.

1546. WORK, John Wesley. Folk Song of the American Negro.
       Nashville: Fisk University, 1915; reprint ed., Westport,
       Conn.: Negro Universities Press, 1969. 131 pp.

Written by a member of the board for the 1871 tour of the
Jubilee Singers, this early description of Afro-American music
divides texts into two categories: African heritage and American
heritage, and by type. It is partly a history of the fostering of
black American music and partly the story of the Jubilee Singers.

1547. WRIGHT, Josephine, and SOUTHERN, Eileen. "On Folk Music."
Black Perspective in Music 4-Special Issue #2 (1976):
132-55.

A collection of reprints from nineteenth-century
newspapers that describe black music, including the yodel,
religious songs, and folk songs.

1548. YIZAR, Terrye Barron. "Afro-American Music in North
America Before 1865: a Study of 'The First of August
Celebration' in the United States." Ph.D. dissertation,
University of California, Berkeley, 1984. 322 pp.

Written by a student of Speech-Communication, this work
focuses on celebrations in parts of New England that commemorate
the freeing on August 1, 1834, of 800,000 slaves in the British
West Indies. Afro-American music was performed at these. The
study concentrates on festivals in Providence, Rhode Island.

1549. ZUR HEIDE, Karl Gert. Deep South Piano: the Story of
Little Brother Montgomery. London: Studio Vista, 1970.
112 pp.

Non-technical but carefully researched biography of a
black musician and pianist, with many illustrations.

Religious Music (Including Spirituals) Except Gospel

1550. BAER, Hans A. "Introduction: an Overview of Ritual, Oratory
and Music in Southern Black Religion." Southern Quarterly
23-3 (Spring, 1985): 5-14.

The introduction to a special issue of the Southern
Quarterly entitled "Black Church Ritual and Aesthetics" in which
the editor reviews the articles included.

1551. BAILEY, Ben E. "The Lined-Hymn Tradition in Black
Mississippi Churches." The Black Perspective in Music 6-1
(Spring, 1978): 3-17.

A good but brief introduction to traditional lined hymns
(pp. 3-9) with eight tunes and words included as examples.

1552. BARTON, William E. Old Plantation Hymns. Boston: Lamson,
       Wolffe and Co., 1899; reprint ed., New York: AMS Press,
       1972. 45 pp.

       Compiled by a writer who lived in the South from 1880-7
and collected a series of texts and melodies. Organized under
headings such as "old plantation hymns" and "slave and freedman
hymns."

1553. BOGGS, Beverly. "Some Aspects of Worship in a Holiness
       Church." New York Folklore 3 (Summer-Winter, 1977):29-44.

       Excellent study based on the author's observations of
services at Mt. Nebo Church of God in Christ in Binghamton, New
York, from 1971-4. It includes interview excerpts, transcriptions
of services, and a discussion of the musical style employed.

1554. BOYER, Horace Clarence. "An Analysis of Black Church Music
       with Examples Drawn from Services in Rochester, New York."
       Ph.D. dissertation, University of Rochester (Eastman
       School of Music), 1973. 266 pp.

       Based on 20 taped services in various churches, 15 of
which were transcribed and analyzed, this survey of black church
music includes historical and theoretical perspectives on service
music as well as a study of melody, rhythm, harmony, performance
practices, and a statement on the nature of the musical expression.
Organized around fringe denominations, Methodists, Baptists,
Holiness churches, and the music of special services. Lined hymns
are described on pp. 137-43.

1555. BROWN, Marian Tally. "A Resource Manual on the Music of the
       Southern Fundamentalist Black Church." Ed.D.
       dissertation, Indiana University, 1974. 180 pp.

       Teaching materials on and description of Southern
fundamentalist church music for use in junior college humanities
classes. Before submitting the dissertation, the author
experimented with the material at Florida Junior College in
Jacksonville, and the results are given.

1556. COHEN, Lily Young. Lost Spirituals [With Thirty-Six
       Illustrations by Kenneth K. Pointer, and 41 Plates of
       Musical Compositions as Composed by Negroes and Set Down

in Music by the Author]. New York: Walter Neale, 1928;
reprint ed., Freeport, N.Y.: Books for Libraries Press,
1972. 143 pp.

A narrative of folklore and folklife written by an
inquisitive white, with texts in black dialect (Gullah).

1557. CONE, James H. The Spirituals and the Blues: an
Interpretation. New York: Seabury Press, 1972; reprint
ed., Westport, Conn.: Greenwood, 1980. 152 pp.

More of a theological study than a musical one, with
interpretation of the words most important. Treatment of the
spiritual dominates the book (pp. 8-107), while the blues is
treated less thoroughly (pp. 108-42. Chapter 6, "The Blues: a
Secular Spiritual," attempts an interpretation of the two.

1558. DARGAN, William Thomas. "Congregational Gospel Songs in a
Black Holiness Church: a Musical and Textual Analysis."
Ph.D. dissertation, Wesleyan University, 1983. 421 pp.

Based on extensive field work in a single congregation,
the New Born Church (no location given), the author examines what
songs were actually sung, what their significance was in terms of
musical and ritual forms, and how these are interrelated. The
author found fairly consistent musical traits associated with
certain theological ones, but suggests that further study in
churches different from this one be undertaken. A major goal was
also to determine the relationship of this music to Gospel music.

1559. DETT, R. Nathaniel. Religious Folk-Songs of the Negro as
Sung at Hampton Institute. Hampton, Va.: Hampton
Institute Press, 1927. 276 pp.

This book consists of 165 "cabin and plantation songs"
(spirituals) arranged for unaccompanied chorus and organized by
topic, by an important early black composer, preceded by a
description of singing practices in Southern black churches.

1560. DIXON, Christa K. Negro Spirituals: From Bible to Folk
Songs. Philadelphia: Fortress Press, 1976. 117 pp.

An examination of spiritual texts, especially in terms of
their Biblical origins.

1561. DIXON, Christa K. "Negro Spirituals, Wesen und Wandel
       geistlicher Volkslieder" [Negro spirituals, essence and
       evolution of spiritual folk songs]. Ph.D. dissertation,
       Rheinische Friedrich-Wilhelm University [Bonn], 1965;
       Wuppertal: Jugenddienst, 1967. 333 pp.

       This important, but apparently untranslated, work in
English philology is entirely oriented to text and its interpretation, but quite valuable to anyone doing research in spirituals.
In three parts: 1: cultural, historical, religious matrix, 2: 282
texts and variants arranged by topic and compared, 3: indices.

1562. DJEDJE, Jacqueline Cogdell. American Black Spiritual and
       Gospel Songs from Southeast Georgia: a Comparative Study.
       Monograph series #7. Los Angeles: Center for Afro-
       American Studies, University of California, 1978. 105 pp.

1563. DYEN, Doris Jane. "The Role of Shape Note Singing in the
       Musical Culture of Black Communities in Southeast
       Alabama." Ph.D. dissertation, University of Illinois,
       1977. 407 pp.

       Introduced by an extensive ethnographic study of the
population involved and the place of shape note singing in the
society, this work concentrates on the singing from four-shape
notation books, especially the Cooper Revision of the Sacred Harp
(#1427) and Judge Jackson's 1934 Colored Sacred Harp (#1414).
Much attention is given to repertory and performance practices,
especially how they differ from white shape-note singing. Some
attention is also given to the parallel tradition of lined hymns.

1564. EPSTEIN, Dena J. "A White Origin for the Black Spiritual?
       An Invalid Theory and How it Grew." American Music 1
       (Summer, 1983): 53-9.

       A careful review of all the literature asserting that
black spirituals had a white origin, and the conclusion that the
idea is specious.

1565. EVANS, Arthur Lee. "The Development of the Negro Spiritual
       as Choral Art Music by Afro-American Composers, with an
       Annotated Guide to the Performance of Selected
       Spirituals." D.M.A. dissertation, University of Miami,
       1972. 264 pp.

While the author seeks answers to questions of African influence on the spiritual and how to define what the spiritual is, most of this study deals with the development of the genre into "art music," how this trend affected style, and who the prime movers were. Composers/arrangers include Burleigh, Dett, Dawson, and Work, Jr.

1566. FERRIS, William R. Jr. "The Rose Hill Service." Mississippi Folklore Register 6 (1972): 37-56.

A first-hand account of an oral tradition folk service at the Rose Hill Church in Warren County, Mississippi. "Dr. Watts" hymns are discussed and special attention is given to the chanted sermon with which the congregation actively interacts with sung response. Transcriptions and photographs are included.

1567. GREEN, Archie. "Hear These Beautiful Sacred Selections." Yearbook of the International Folk Music Council 2 (1970): 28-50.

While predominantly a description of surviving wax cylinder recordings of spirituals, additional but general information on the spiritual is also given.

1568. GRISSOM, Mary Allen. The Negro Sings a New Heaven. Chapel Hill: University of North Carolina Press, 1930. 101 pp.

Classified collection of 45 songs (songs of death, of heaven and resurrection, Bible stories in song, of exhortation, of service and personal experience, shouting and triumph songs) from Louisville, Kentucky, and Adair County.

1569. HURSTON, Zora Neale. The Sanctified Church. Berkeley, Calif.: Turtle Island, 1981, 1983. 107 pp.

Published posthumously, this book is a study of the entire church and not just its music, but includes valuable material on spirituals, preaching, and shouting.

1570. JOHNSON, Guy B. "The Negro Spiritual: a Problem in Anthropology." American Anthropologist 33-2 (Apr.-June 1931): 157-71.

Interesting but strongly questioned article which explores the effects of blacks coming into contact with Europeans and their music. The author argues that the spiritual is based on white music rather than African, but admits to not knowing much about African musical style.

1571. JOHNSON, James Weldon, and JOHNSON, J. Rosamond. The Books of American Negro Spirituals. 2 vols. New York: Viking Press, 1925/1926; reprint ed., 1940; reprint in 1 vol., New York: Da Capo, 1969.

A genuine attempt to appreciate spirituals on black terms, giving a survey of origin and history and a description of group singing practices, responsorial form, and rhythm. Volume 1 includes a 39-page introduction followed by 187 arranged (voices and piano) spirituals, while volume 2 has a shorter introduction and 189 additional spirituals. "The arrangers have striven to give the characteristic harmonies that would be used in spontaneous group singing." (1:37)

1572. KLEBER, Helen Lida Phillips. "Raising Spirit: a Comparative Analysis of Three Black Religious Rituals." Ph.D. dissertation, University of North Carolina, 1973.

No abstract available.

1573. LOVELL, John, Jr. Black Song: the Forge and the Flame. New York: Macmillan, 1972. 686 pp.

Subtitled "The story of how the Afro-American Spiritual was Hammered Out." A non-technical study of context and meaning, origin and diffusion of the spiritual. Part I is based on answering a series of questions (e.g., How much of Africa?). Part II comprises an analysis of meaning to the community and of the texts. Part III describes the diffusion of the spiritual and its influence.

1574. McCARTHY, S. Margaret W. "The Afro-American Sermon and the Blues: Some Parallels." Black Perspective in Music 4-3 (1976): 269-77.

An examination of how the sermon and blues have many parallels in terms of vocabulary, delivery, and meaning, based entirely on textual samples, which are compared side by side.

1575. McINTYRE, Paul. Black Pentecostal Music in Windsor.
Ottawa: National Museums of Canada, 1976. 124 pp.

Although the venue is Canada, this is a study of black
pentecostal music in the Church of God in Christ, an American
denomination. The author's work is carefully detailed and based on
extensive field work in this city lying near Detroit.

1576. MAPSON, Jesse Wendell. "Some Guidelines for the Use of
Music in the Black Church." D.Min. dissertation, Eastern
Baptist Theological Seminary, 1983. 178 pp.

A conservative statement and survey intended to help
ministers become aware of the issues of modern black religious
music. Although it is part survey, it also includes assertions
that the music has become overly commercialized and no longer has a
place in the church, indeed having become an end unto itself.

1577. MARSH, J. B. T. The Story of the Jubilee Singers, with
their Songs. London: Hodder and Stoughton, 1875 and many
other editions; Cleveland: Cleveland Printing and
Publishing Co., 1892; reprint ed. of 1885, New York:
Negro Universities Press, 1969. 265 pp.

A contemporary history of Fisk University's famous
touring choir formed by George L. White to raise money for the
Nashville institution and sent on a six-year world-wide tour
led by F. J. Loudin during which their greatest success came from
singing arranged spirituals. The author also provides biographies
of the singers and a description of the tour to Britain and
Europe. The book also includes 128 jubilee songs in four-part
harmony as sung by the group. The 1892 edition includes a
supplement by F. J. Loudin.

1578. MAULTSBY, Portia K. "Africanisms Retained in the Spiritual
Tradition." Report of the Twelfth Congress--
International Musicological Society, pp. 75-82. Kassel:
Barenreiter, 1981.

1579. MAULTSBY, Portia K. "Afro-American Religious Music: 1619-
1861. Part 1: Historical Development, Part 2: Computer
Analysis of One Hundred Spirituals." Ph.D. dissertation,
University of Wisconsin, 1974. 480 pp.

In Part 1 the author seeks to redress a perceived lack of musical information, e.g., concerning style and performance practices, regarding pre-Civil War period spirituals. She defines the circumstances in which the music flourished, the West African retentions and the European influences, and defined the black characteristics in their religious music. In Part II she analyzes 100 spirituals by parameter—scale, range, phrase, etc.

1580.   MAULTSBY, Portia K. "Afro-American Religious Music: a Study in Musical Diversity." Papers of the Hymn Society of America #35. Springfield, Ohio: Hymn Society of America, [1981]. 19 pp.

Introductory essay and survey of black religious music, documented, but not detailed.

1581.   MAULTSBY, Portia K. "Black Spirituals: an Analysis of Textual Forms and Structures." Black Perspective in Music 4-1 (1976): 54-69.

A detailed analysis of textual and musical form in 100 songs from Slave Songs of the United States (#1452) and The Story of the Jubilee Singers (#1577).

1582.   MAULTSBY, Portia K. "Music of Northern Independent Black Churches During the Ante-Bellum Period." Ethnomusicology 19-3 (1975): 401-20.

This article traces the development of a distinct black religious style during the late eighteenth century, although one influenced by European style. After the Revolutionary War blacks in the North had their own churches and therefore their own music.

1583.   MAULTSBY, Portia K. "The Origin of Black Spirituals: a Summary and Analysis of Theories." Internationale Arbeitsgemeinschaft für Hymnologie Bulletin 2 (Mei, 1983): 118-24.

1584.   MITCHELL, Henry W. Black Preaching. Philadelphia: Lippincott, 1970; reprint ed., New York: Harper & Row, 1979. 248 pp.

Black sermons often assume a musical delivery, even to the point of being accompanied by instruments. This book traces the history and context of black preaching, with discussions of the "black Bible," black English, style, and examples. A cassette tape of this title was produced at the Princeton Theological Seminary Speech Studio in 1969.

1585. PAUL, June Dolores Brooks. "Music in Culture: Black Sacred Song Style in Slidell, Louisiana, and Chicago, Illinois." Ph.D. dissertation, Northwestern University, 1973. 465 pp.

Based on field work among four congregations, two each in Louisiana and Chicago, all made up of people either in or from the South, this study emphasizes the historical, sociological, and religious interrelationships of black sacred song.

1586. PERKINS, A. E. "Negro Spirituals from the Far South." Journal of American Folklore 35-137 (July-Sept. 1922): 223-49.

A collection of 48 texts, without information on sources, made by someone presumably from the "far North."

1587. PIKE, Gustavus D. The Singing Campaign for Ten Thousand Pounds. London: Hodder and Stoughton, 1874 [202 pp.]; rev. ed., New York: American Missionary Association, 1875; reprint ed. of rev. ed., Freeport, N.Y.: Books for Libraries Press, 1971. 273 pp.

Similar to the Marsh book (#1577) in many ways, this is the story of the Fisk University Jubilee Singers' tour of Great Britain, and includes an appendix of their songs.

1588. PINKSTON, Alfred Adolphus. "Lined Hymns, Spirituals, and the Associated Lifestyle of Rural Black People in the United States." Ph.D. dissertation, University of Miami, 1975. 246 pp.

This work is partly description of the cultural context of Southern religious music among black people, based on written documentation and interviews, and partly description of musical style, especially of the spiritual. He found that both hymns and spirituals tend to the anhemitonic pentatonic scale and emphasize

325

the use of the major 2nd, major 3rd, and minor 3rd. Most spirituals were found to be in 4/4 time and to have four phrases.

1589. RAICHELSON, Richard M. "Black Religious Folksong: a Study in Generic and Social Change." Ph.D. dissertation, University of Pennsylvania, 1975. 566 pp.

This investigation attempts to understand how sociocultural and historical transformations have affected the development and scope of the genre. Types studied include psalms, hymns, folk-hymns, anthems, spirituals, jubilee songs, Gosepl songs, Sacred Harp, and religious ballads. Performance practices discussed include lining-out, the song-sermon, the ring-shout, spiritual singing, Gospel singing, and Sacred Harp singing.

1590. RICKS, George Robinson. Some Aspects of the Religious Music of the United States Negro. New York: Arno Press, 1977. 418 pp.

An unrevised doctoral dissertation (Northwestern University, 1960), this study attempts first to define and describe gospel music and its historical and stylistic antecedents, but concentrates on musical analysis through more than half the work. Many transcriptions, including some from the author's field work in Chicago, appear in this section.

1591. ROSENBERG, Bruce A. The Art of the American Folk Preacher. New York: Oxford University Press, 1970. 265 pp.

An insightful look at the content, structure, musical elements, and process of the "spiritual sermon." Stress is placed on the formulaic quality of the chanted sermon and comparison is made with Lord's study of the epic singers of Yugoslavia. Chapter 4, "Chanting," is of special interest because of its emphasis on the musical structure of chanted sermons, and includes several transcriptions. Part 2 is devoted to transcripts of 13 oral traditional sermons, some in two versions.

1592. ROSENBERG, Bruce A. "The Formulaic Quality of Spontaneous Sermons." Journal of American Folklore 83-327 (Jan.-Mar. 1970): 3-20.

Modeled after the Yugoslav folk epic studies of Lord and Parry, the author submits that black preachers compose their

sermons like the Yugoslav guslar. Examples are given, some in
musical notation, and texts are analyzed.

1593. ROSENBERG, Bruce A. "The Genre of the Folk Sermon." Genre
      4 (June 1971): 189-211.

      Well-documented history of chanted sermons, black and
white, and a comparison with the Yugoslav guslar. Includes
historical descriptions of chanted sermons and contemporary
transcriptions.

1594. SIMPSON, Robert. "The Shout and Shouting in the Slave
      Religion of the United States." Southern Quarterly 23-3
      (Spring, 1985): 34-48.

      Definitions and descriptions of both individual and group
shouting, the latter being the "ring shout."

1595. SINGER, Merrill. "'Now I Know What the Song Mean!':
      Traditional Black Music in a Contemporary Black Sect."
      Southern Quarterly 23-3 (Spring, 1985): 125-40.

      Study of meaning in the words of the songs of Black Jews.

1596. SMITH, Carl Henry. "The Religious Music of Logan County,
      Kentucky Blacks During the Second Awakening Period
      Between 1780-1830: an Ethnomusicological Study." Ph.D.
      dissertation, University of Pittsburgh, in progress.

1597. SMITH, Therese. "Chanted Prayer in Southern Black
      Churches." Southern Quarterly 23-3 (Spring, 1985): 70-82.

      Written by a participant-observer at the Congdon Street
Baptist Church, Providence, R.I., and the Annual Convocation of
the Oxford-Tallahatchie Missionary Baptist Church in northern
Mississippi. Defines chanted prayers, places them in context and
provides examples of texts and melodic patterns. Attempts to
explain why the phenomenon occurs.

1598. STONE, Sara M. "The Choir as Congregation: Harmonic Song
      in the Church of God and Saints of Christ." The Hymn 35-
      4 (Oct. 1984): 233-9.

After a brief history of the Church of God and Saints of Christ, founded 1896 by William Saunders Crowdy of Guthrie, Oklahoma, there is a discussion of the service (held on Saturday), the use of singing in the service, the lack of congregational song but extensive use of the choir, and the composition and transmission of the songs, which originate within the denomination.

1599. STONE, Sara M. "Song Composition, Transmission, and Performance Practice in an Urban Black Denomination, the Church of God and Saints of Christ." Ph.D. dissertation, Kent State University, 1985. 439 pp.

The denomination was founded in 1896 by William Saunders Crowdy, an ex-slave living in Guthrie, Oklahoma, who began hearing voices telling him to found a church. Basing many of its practices on Old Testament, even Jewish, models, the denomination meets on Saturdays. Central to the service is the choir, which sings unaccompanied, in many parts, and without notation. All songs have been orally composed or arranged by members or leaders of the choirs and stylistically can be described as having complex, chromatic harmonies, a characteristic rhythm, and a multi-sectional formal structure based on the texts, many of which come directly from the Bible. Songs are performed throughout the service, and especially during elaborate marches throughout the tabernacle. The church split in 1909, the Christian and original group having its headquarters in Cleveland, Ohio, and the Jewish group having its headquarters in Bellville, Virginia, and now called Temple Beth El.

1600. TALLMADGE, William H. "The Black in Jackson's White Spirituals." The Black Perspective in Music 9-2 (1981): 139-60.

The author poses the questions, did the structure of camp-meeting hymns arise among white singers resulting from their own creation or from a natural process of growth as G. P. Jackson claims? After presenting evidence, the author concludes that the identifying characteristic of the camp-meeting song, the structure, was a black contribution, and therefore refutes Jackson's claim of a white source for the spiritual tunes.

1601. TALLMADGE, William H. "Dr. Watts and Mahalia Jackson--the Development, Decline, and Survival of a Folk Style in America." Ethnomusicology 5-2 (May 1961): 95-9.

This article traces the development of and describes lined hymns among black singers, especially the Baptists, a genre called "Dr. Watts." The author asserts that the ornamentation characteristic of the genre may have influenced both Gospel singer Mahalia Jackson and early rock-'n'-roll.

1602. TAYLOR, John E. "Somethin' on my Mind: a Cultural and Historical Interpretation of Spiritual Texts." Ethnomusicology 19-3 (Sept. 1975): 387-99.

A study of spiritual texts in which the author shows that while the language and images derive from the Judeo-Christian tradition, the meanings to the slaves were often different and helped to maintain courage and strength in times of trouble.

1603. THURMAN, Howard. Deep River and the Negro Spiritual Speaks of Life and Death. Richmond, Ind.: Friends United Press, 1975. 136 pp.

Originally written in 1945 and 1947, respectively, these articles concentrate on the meanings to blacks of spiritual texts.

1604. TURNER, Lucile Price. "Negro Spirituals in the Making." Musical Quarterly 17 (1931): 480-5.

A misguided article by a northerner who went to live in Arkansas and hired a "darky" named Tom who was a member of "The Church of Christ in God." This article, which describes what they sang, is so ethnocentric and elitist that it is interesting.

1605. TYLER, Mary Ann Lancaster. "The Music of Charles Henry Pace and its Relationship to the Afro-American Church Experience." Ph.D. dissertation, University of Pittsburgh, 1980. 235 pp.

Pace (1886-1963) composed 104 church songs and eight spiritual medleys in Pittsburgh. The author examines Pace as a composer, his recordings, performances, organizations, and compares his style to traditional Afro-American and African music.

1606. WALKER, Wyatt Tee. "Somebody's Calling My Name": Black Sacred Music and Social Change. Valley Forge, Pa.: Judson Press, 1979. 208 pp.

Described by the writer as a "general, socio-historico
introduction," and revised from his 1975 Colgate University
dissertation, this study treats both the origin of black sacred
music and the broad continuum. Specific topics covered include
pentecostal music, possession, African roots, the transmission of
oral traditions to the present, the spiritual, improvised hymns,
gospel, and "black meter music," i.e., Dr. Watts style hymns.

1607. WASHINGTON, Joseph R., Jr. "Negro Spirituals." The Hymn
      15-4 (Oct. 1964): 101-10.

    Primarily a study of religion and the spiritual texts
used in worship along with their meanings. No musical examples.

1608. WILLIAMS, Robert. "Preservation of the Oral Tradition of
      Singing Hymns in Negro Religious Music." Ph.D. disser-
      tation, The Florida State University, 1973. 123 pp.

    Based on field recordings made in Florida and Georgia,
this study of black hymnody, whose aim is to encourage its
preservation and allow for performance by outsiders, seeks to
describe its most salient characteristics. It was concluded that
texts were most commonly in short meter, short particular meter,
common meter, and long meter. The performance techniques
described were called "lining out a hymn," "raising a hymn,"
"singing a hymn," and "moaning a hymn."

1609. WORK, John W. "Changing Patterns in Negro Folk Songs."
      Journal of American Folklore 62-244 (Apr.-June 1949):
      136-44.

    Valuable study of change and acculturation in religious
music, the introduction of instruments, and early Gospel.

Black Gospel Music

1610. BAKER, Barbara Wesley. "Black Gospel Music." In Univer-
      sals in Music. Edited by Shelby G. Davis and Karl Sig-
      nell. College Park, Md.: University of Maryland, 1977.

1611. BAKER, Barbara Wesley. "Black Gospel Music Styles, 1942-
      1979: Analysis and Implications for Music Education."
      Ph.D. dissertation, University of Maryland, 1978.

A study of styles and style changes in Gospel music since 1942 and exploration of how Gospel song could be used in secondary education and for teacher training. Includes cassette tapes documenting the music.

1612. BOYER, Horace Clarence. "Charles Albert Tindley: Progenitor of Black-American Gospel Music." The Black Perspective in Music 11 (Fall, 1983): 103-32.

An expanded version of a paper read at the Colloquium on Charles A. Tindley, 7-9 May 1982, at the Smithsonian Institution, this article provides a biography of the subject and a discussion of the development of Gospel music. Subsequent sections discuss the publication and arrangements of Tindley's songs, including an in-depth analysis of his best-known works, with several pages of musical examples included. Finally, there is a chronological listing of Tindley's compositions.

1613. BOYER, Horace Clarence. "Contemporary Gospel Music. I: Sacred or Secular; II: Characteristics and Style." The Black Perspective in Music 7-1 (Spring, 1979): 5-58.

Part I is a history of Gospel music from 1945 into the 1970s with attention to a number of composers and performers: Mahalia Jackson, James Cleveland, Mother Katie Bell, Rosetta Thorpe, Clara Ward, and The Staple Singers. Part II is a study of Gospel music stylistic features, defined as both a kind of song and a way of playing the piano. Transcriptions of "Amazing Grace" and "Surely, God is Able" by Mahalia Jackson and Clara Ward, respectively, are added.

1614. BOYER, Horace Clarence. "Thomas A. Dorsey: 'Father of Gospel Music'." Black World 23 (July 1974): 20-3.

This analysis of Dorsey's contributions begins with his visit to a Billy Sunday crusade at Atlanta in 1911 and traces his subsequent career as a teacher, composer, and publisher. Additionally, Dorsey's influence on later compositions and performers is documented. There is also a selective discography.

1615. BROUGHTON, Viv. Black Gospel: an Illustrated History of the Gospel Sound. Poole, Dorset, England: Blandford Press, 1985. 160 pp.

1616. BURNIM, Mellonee Victoria. "The Black Gospel Music
       Tradition: Symbol of Ethnicity." Ph.D. dissertation,
       Indiana University, 1980. 327 pp.

       Submitting that Gospel is part of black identity, not
just for the church alone, the author concentrates on Gospel as an
expression of all black people and more than a musical genre. Her
field work was done at two black churches in Indiana.

1617. BURNIM, Mellonee. "Culture Bearer and Tradition Bearer: an
       Ethnomusicologist's Research on Gospel Music." Ethno-
       musicology 29-3 (Fall, 1985): 432-47.

       An examination first of the premise common among ethno-
musicologists that one studies a tradition different from one's
own in order to maintain objectivity. The author then discusses
her work in two black churches, one each in Bloomington and
Indianapolis, Indiana, her experiences, the advantages of being a
culture bearer and tradition bearer. The article is therefore
partly about Gospel music and partly about the phenomenon of doing
research within one's own culture group.

1618. BURNIM, Mellonee. "Gospel Music Research." Black Music
       Research Journal 1 (1980): 63-70.

       A review of literature and a 23-item bibliography.

1619. DJEDJE, Jacqueline Cogdell. "Change and Differentiation:
       The Adoption of Black American Gospel Music in the
       Catholic Church." Ethnomusicology 30-2 (Spring-Summer,
       1986): 223-52.

       Based on field work in seven Los Angeles Roman Catholic
Churches, the author traces the history of black parishes and the
gradual changes in musical style permitted. Essentially, the
changes amounted to gradually permitting black style to penetrate
into the otherwise European-oriented service which has now
culminated in the admission of Gospel music, which had its origin
in black sanctified churches where emotionalism was expected.
Includes three transcriptions, extensive notes, and bibliography.

1620. DORSEY, Thomas A. "Gospel Music." In Reflections on Afro-
       American Music, pp. 189-95. Edited by Dominique Rene
       De Lerma. Kent, Oh.: Kent State University Press, 1973.

Based on an interview with Dorsey, a retelling of Dorsey's life and answers to questions concerning his opinions, activities, etc.

1621. FEINTUCH, Burt. "A Noncommercial Black Gospel Group in Context: We Live the Life We Sing About." Black Music Research Journal 1 (1980): 37-50.

A study of the Cross Family of Russellville, Logan County, Kentucky, from the perspective of a folklorist. Descriptive of what they do, where they perform, for what occasions. This study is significant because very few noncommercial Gospel groups have yet been investigated.

1622. FRANKLIN, Marion Joseph. "The Relationship of Black Preaching to Black Gospel Music." D.Min. dissertation, Drew University, 1982. 178 pp.

This study provides a model and teaching plan for the educating of black ministers to maintain the black oral traditions of lined hymns, prayers, and moaning, and encourages the finding of balance between meaning and showiness in black Gospel music.

1623. GOREAU, Laurraine. Just Mahalia, Baby. Waco, Tex.: Word Books, 1975. 611 pp.

Because Jackson felt that so much in print about her was inaccurate, she authorized this biography, which is comprehensive, well-researched, and probably the ultimate work on the subject.

1624. HARRIS, Michael Wesley. "The Advent of Gospel Blues in Black Old-Line Churches in Chicago, 1932-33 as Seen Through the Life and Mind of Thomas Andrew Dorsey." Ph.D. dissertation, Harvard University, 1982. 356 pp.

Although Gospel music permeates black worship today, it was not always so. The author first describes the musical practices of the major, mainline black churches of Chicago up to 1932. He then traces the infusion of Gospel blues style music into these churches via a new choral movement. The prime mover of this movement was Thomas A. Dorsey, a versatile blues guitarist and pianist active in the late 1920s. It was he who brought together blues style and religious texts to create a music that symbolizes not just black Christianity but black Americans generally.

1625. HEILBUT, Tony. The Gospel Sound: Good News and Bad Times.
      New York: Simon and Schuster, 1971. 350 pp.

      Although there is introductory material on the
development of black Gospel music, much of the book is devoted to
individual performers, such as Mahalia Jackson and The Soul
Stirrers, as well as Gospel music in the holiness churches and in
black life generally.

1626. JACKSON, Irene Viola. "Afro-American Gospel Music and its
      Social Setting with Special Attention to Roberta Martin."
      Ph.D. dissertation, Wesleyan University, 1974. 361 pp.

      Both an historical introduction to Gospel music and a
discussion of the place of Roberta Martin in that development.
Martin was a singer, composer, arranger, accompanist, and began
her own publishing company.

1627. JACKSON, Mahalia, with Evan McLeod WYLIE. Movin' on Up.
      New York: Hawthorn Books, 1966. 212 pp.

      An autobiography with discography.

1628. LORNELL, Christopher. "Happy in the Service of the Lord:
      Afro-American Gospel Quartets in Memphis, Tennessee." Ph.
      D. dissertation, Memphis State University, 1983. 259 pp.

      This is a history of Afro-American Gospel quartets from
the 1890s to the present, both in general and through a case study
of Memphis, Tennessee. Quartets had a number of influences,
including minstrel songs, jubilee songs, spirituals, and
"barbershop" quartet songs. Their heyday was the 1930s and 1940s,
having been eclipsed by new developments in black music after World
War II. This work is to be used with Highwater Records LP-1002 of
the same title.

1629. SITOLE, E. M. T. "The Role of Gospel Music in Black
      Churches in Chicago." Ph.D. dissertation, Belfast
      [Ireland] University, 1976.

      No abstract available.

1630. TALLMADGE, William H. "The Responsorial and Antiphonal
Practice in Gospel Song." Ethnomusicology 12 (May
1968): 219-38.

Three patterns of antiphony or response style in Gospel
music are examined. The source of the practice is traced to the
anthems, motets, and secular pieces of the early nineteenth
century composers whose works appeared in American song books.

1631. WARRICK, Mancel, HILLSMAN, Joan R., and MANNO, Anthony.
The Progress of Gospel Music: from Spiritual to
Contemporary Gospel. New York: Vantage, 1977. 99 pp.

Popular introduction intended for classroom use on
spirituals and Gospel music and their offshoots, with some
examples given and directions for classroom use.

1632. WATERMAN, Richard. "Gospel Hymns of a Negro Church in
Chicago." International Folk Music Journal 3 (1951): 87-
93.

In part a survey of black sacred musical genres, but
mainly a description of the structure of services in a Chicago-
area black church.

1633. WILLIAMS-JONES, Pearl. "Afro-American Gospel Music: a
Brief Historical and Analytical Survey (1930-1970)." In
The Development of Materials for a One Year Course in
African Music for the General Undergraduate Student, pp.
199-219. Edited by Vada Butcher, et al. Washington,
D.C.: Howard University, Center for Ethnic Music, 1970.

A history of Gospel, definitions, a comparison with
spirituals, and description of practices along with examples to
illustrate the earlier styles. Unfortunately, this valuable study
is part of a mimeographed collection that is rather rare.

1634. WILLIAMS-JONES, Pearl. "Afro-American Gospel Music: a
Crystallization of the Black Aesthetic." Ethnomusicology 19-3 (1975): 373-86.

An article which attempts to convey what Gospel music
means to a black musician and how it typifies the black identity.
The author further submits that Gospel is African derived.

335

The Blues

1635. ALBERTSON, Chris. Bessie. New York: Stein and Day, 1972.
253 pp.

Well-researched, comprehensive, factual, and illustrated
biography of Bessie Smith (c.1894-1937), probably the most
important of all the female blues singers. Although there is
comparatively little information on Smith's earlier years, there
is a wealth of detail about her career years, including those
aspects of her life which do little to enhance her reputation.

1636. ALBERTSON, Chris. Bessie Smith: Empress of the Blues. New
York: Walter Kane, 1975. 144 pp.

In part the life of Bessie Smith with many illustrations,
but mostly a collection of her songs arranged with piano
accompaniment and two pages of commentary on her singing style by
Gunther Schuller.

1637. BARNIE, John. "Formulaic Lines and Stanzas in the Country
Blues." Ethnomusicology 22-3 (Sept. 1978): 457-74.

Using Milman Parry's classic study of Yugoslavian epics as
the model, the author demonstrates how bluesmen use formulaic lines
in ways that are both similar and dissimilar to Parry's subjects.
The author shows that the habit of using formulas, especially in
the typical three-line stanza, predates the 1930s from which time
it has been assumed that formulaicness started.

1638. BARNIE, John. "Oral Formulas in the Country Blues."
Southern Folklore Quarterly 42-1 (1978): 39-52.

Similar to the previous article by the same author, but
includes an appendix with five pages of text examples.

1639. BASTIN, Bruce. Crying for the Carolines. London: Studio
Vista, 1971. 112 pp.

Partly based on documents and recordings, but largely
based on fieldwork in South Carolina, northern Georgia, and
Virginia, this is a study of the "Piedmont blues," a regional
variation within the greater blues family. After a chapter on
Blind Boy Fuller, there is a geographical survey of blues centers,

including Durham, Atlanta, Spartanburg, Greenville, and Charlotte. There is also information on Brownie McGhee and Sonny Terry.

1640. BEYER, Jimmy. Baton Rouge Blues. Baton Rouge, La.: Arts and Humanities Council, 1980. 48 pp.

This small book is actually a resource of information about local bluesmen, both downhome and urban. It includes oral histories and 18 biographical-musical portraits of some of the local musicians.

1641. BIRD, Brian. Skiffle: the Story of Folk-Song with a Jazz Beat. London: Robert Hale, 1958. 125 pp.

1642. BOGAERT, Karel. Blues Lexicon: Blues, Cajun, Boogie Woogie, Gospel. Antwerp: Standaard Uitgeverij, 1972. 480 pp.

Although unfortunately in Flemish--though having an English introduction by John Godrich--this is an otherwise valuable biographical dictionary (not terms as the title implies) of singers in several fields, but especially the blues. Much information was obtained through questionnaires to the artists themselves.

1643. BRADFORD, Perry. Born With the Blues: the True Story of the Pioneering Blues Singers and Musicians in the Early Days of Jazz. New York: Oak, 1965. 175 pp.

Bradford (1895-1970) was an important early bluesman and jazz performer who wrote the earliest blues recorded, in 1920, "That Thing Called Love" and "Crazy Blues," recordings which first allowed blacks into the white recording industry. Since this work is an autobiography, not all is objective.

1644. BROOKS, Edward. The Bessie Smith Companion: a Critical and Detailed Appreciation of the Recordings. Herts, England: Cavendish, 1982; New York: Da Capo, 1982. 244 pp.

A comprehensive study of 159 recordings of Bessie Smith (1898?-1937), with biographical data, musical analysis, chronology, and discography.

1645. BROONZY, William. Big Bill Blues: William Broonzy's Story
as Told to Yannick Bruynoghe. London: Cassell, 1955;
rev. ed., New York: Oak, 1964. 176 pp.

The biography of Big Bill Broonzy and an extensive
discography.

1646. CHARTERS, Samuel Barclay. The Bluesmen; the Story and the
Music of the Men Who Made the Blues. New York: Oak,
1967.

Prefaced by information on the African roots of the
blues, this book offers a broad view of musicians living in
Mississippi, Alabama, and Texas up to World War II. This book
became Vol. 1 of a two-volume set called The Bluesmen, the second
of which is Sweet as the Showers of Rain (#1651).

1647. CHARTERS, Samuel Barclay. The Country Blues. New York:
Rinehart, 1959; reprint ed., New York: Da Capo, 1975.
288 pp.

Emphasizing the early history of the downhome blues, the
author focuses on the times, the lives, and the recordings of the
early blues artists, with little on the music itself.

1648. CHARTERS, Samuel B. The Legacy of the Blues: a Glimpse into
the Art and the Lives of Twelve Great Bluesmen: an Informal
Study. London: Calder & Boyars, 1975; reprint ed., New
York: Da Capo, 1977; New York: Plenum, 1978. 192 pp.

1649. CHARTERS, Samuel B. The Poetry of the Blues. New York:
Oak, 1963; reprint ed., New York: Avon, 1970. 173 pp.

Using poetry excerpts and commentary, the author loosely
strings together a portrait of the blues musician and his world.

1650. CHARTERS, Samuel Barclay. The Roots of the Blues: an
African Search. Boston: M. Boyars, 1981. 151 pp.

Rather personal account of the author's search for the
roots of the blues in West Africa among the griots or praise
singers. In some ways this is more a description of African music
than of the blues, but the relationship is more or less shown.

1651. CHARTERS, Samuel B. Sweet as the Showers of Rain (The Bluesmen, Vol. II). New York: Oak, 1977. 178 pp.

This book concentrates on the regional blues of the pre-World War II period, including Memphis jug bands, and individuals such as Fuzzy Lewis, Sleepy John Estes, Peg Leg Howell, and Blind Blake.

1652. CLAR, Mimi. "Folk Belief and Custom in the Blues." Western Folklore 19-3 (July 1960): 173-89.

An examination of the verbal aspects of the blues, the poetry, themes, and meanings.

1653. CLARK, R. Douglas. "Pitch Structures in Vocal Blues Melody." Southern Folklore Quarterly 42-1 (1978): 17-30.

An attempt to define a cross-stylistic grammar of blues melodies, especially in post-1935 blues. Treats tune, mode, and harmony and provides seven pages of transcriptions.

1654. COOK, Bruce. Listen to the Blues. London: Robson Books, 1975. 263 pp.

Personal reminiscences more than scholarship by a musician who is inclined towards the jazz blues.

1655. COOPER, David Edwin. International Bibliography of Discographies. Classical Music and Jazz & Blues, 1962-1972. Keys to Music Bibliography #2. Littleton, Colo.: Libraries Unlimited, 1975. 272 pp.

A buyer's guide, Part II covers jazz and the blues. The latter is treated in pp. 145-52 while in a section on performers there are 62 additional items.

1656. DANKER, Frederick E. "Towards an Intrinsic Study of the Blues Ballads: 'Casey Jones' and 'Louis Collins'." Southern Folklore Quarterly 34-2 (June 1970): 90-103.

A detailed examination of performances of these two ballads by Mississippi John Hurt.

1657. DIXON, Robert M. W., and GODRICH, John. Recording the
      Blues. New York: Stein and Day, 1970. 112 pp.

      A book about the recording industry, the companies, and
the artists who recorded from 1920 to 1945, organized by period.
Many illustrations make this a fascinating book.

1658. EVANS, David. Big Road Blues: Tradition and Creativity in
      the Folk Blues. Berkeley: University of California
      Press, 1982. 329 pp.

      One of the relatively few scholarly studies of the
country blues. It concentrates on process in the tradition,
especially composition. Included is an extensive bibliography.

1659. EVANS, David. "Field Work with Blues Singers: the
      Unintentionally Induced Natural Context." Southern
      Folklore Quarterly 42-1 (1978): 9-16.

      A report on the author's nine field trips, 1965-76, to
Louisiana and Mississippi where he recorded some 700 blues
performances by 80 artists. His interest is in stability, change,
and transmission.

1660. EVANS, David. "Techniques of Blues Composition among Black
      Folksingers." Journal of American Folklore 87-345 (July-
      Sept. 1974): 240-9.

      A comparison of how black and white singers learn and
compose songs. Two approaches are seen according to differences
in backgrounds, attitudes, and audiences.

1661. EVANS, David Huhn, Jr. "Tradition and Creativity in the
      Blues." Ph.D. dissertation, University of California,
      Los Angeles, 1976. 610 pp.

      Based on field recordings and other materials made 1964-
1973 in Mississippi (and elsewhere to a lesser extent), the author
examines how traditional blues singers handle transmission,
learning, composition, recomposition, and repertory.

1662. FAHEY, John. Charley Patton. London: Studio Vista, 1970.
      112 pp.

Biographical and musical study of a Yazoo Delta guitar player and blues singer who recorded 52 sides between 1929 and 1934. The author examines 46 of these in order to describe style, explore texts, and transmutations. A discography is included too.

1663. FEATHER, Leonard G. A History of the Blues. New York: Hansen, 1972. 200 pp.

After a lightweight introduction, the compiler presents about 60 mostly urban blues in arrangements for piano and guitar.

1664. FERRIS, William R., Jr. Blues from the Delta. London: Studio Vista, 1971; rev. ed., Garden City, N.Y.: Anchor Press/Doubleday, 1978; reprint ed., New York: Da Capo, 1984 (of 1978). 226 pp.

While the book is organized to trace blues roots, blues composition, and the blues home party, its main emphasis is the new generation of blues performers (1967-76) who are reshaping the tradition today.

1665. FERRIS, William R., Jr. "Racial Repertoires Among Blues Performers." Ethnomusicology 14-3 (Sept. 1970): 439-49.

A fascinating study of how black blues singers from Mississippi alter their repertories according to the audience. When performing for a white audience, protest and obscenity are avoided and blues that sound similar to hillbilly music are chosen.

1666. FERRIS, William R., Jr. "Records and the Delta Blues Tradition." Keystone Folklore Quarterly 14-4 (Winter, 1969): 158-65.

This article deals with the changing tastes of young blacks who often do not prefer blues, saying that blues appeal to people who grew up before the civil rights movement, for blues tend to express resignation to the way things are.

1667. GARON, Paul. Blues & the Poetic Spirit. London: Eddison Press, 1975; reprint ed., New York: Da Capo, 1978. 178 pp.

A study of blues texts and a search for meaning, but different in its approach from other similar studies.

1668. GODRICH, John, and DIXON, Robert M. W. Blues & Gospel Records, 1902-1942. N.p.: n.p, 1963 [765 pp.]; rev. ed., Essex, England: Storyville Publications, 1969 (912 pp.); 3rd ed. Blues & Gospel Records, 1902-1943. London: Storyville, 1982. 900 pp.

Compiled by people who obviously are deeply committed to this music, this reference work attempts to list all Afro-American recordings made up to 1942 (or 1943 in the later edition). The alphabetical list of individuals and groups, whose entries provide a wealth of detail, is preceded by a history of the record companies involved and their recording trips.

1669. GOMBOSI, Otto. "The Pedigree of the Blues." Proceedings of the Music Teacher's National Association 40th series, 70th year (1946): 382-9.

An attempt by a musicologist to define the blues musically, but without musical examples.

1670. GROOM, Bob. The Blues Revival. London: Studio Vista, 1971. 112 pp.

A study of the popularity of blues among whites, from the discovery of artists such as Leadbelly to blues influence on white popular music.

1671. HANDY, William Christopher, ed. Blues; an Anthology. Complete Words and Music of 53 Great Songs. New York: Albert and Chas. Boni, 1926 (181 pp.); rev. ed. by Jerry SILVERMAN. New York: Macmillan, 1972. 224 pp. Also revised as A Treasury of the Blues with an historical and critical introduction by Abbe NILES. New York: Charles Boni, 1949. 258 pp.

A collection of blues for performance with piano accompaniment, with words in black dialect.

1672. HANDY, William Christopher. Father of the Blues; an Autobiography. Ed. by Arna Bontemps. New York:

Macmillan, 1941; reprint ed., New York: Collier Books,
1970. 317 pp.

Handy (1873-1958), often called the "Father of the
Blues," was a black composer, arranger, bandmaster, and publisher
from Alabama who published the "Memphis Blues" in 1912 and the
"St. Louis Blues" in 1914, the first blues to come to the
attention of white America. This new style competed with the
popularity of ragtime, and eventually brought the public to
recognize and appreciate the genuine country blues.

1673. HARALAMBOS, Michael. Right On: From Blues to Soul in Black
America. London: Eddison, 1974; New York: Drake, 1975.
187 pp.

A popular style study of the changes in blues as they
moved from the countryside to the cities and eventually became
soul music. Many illustrations.

1674. HARALAMBOS, Michael. "Soul Music and Blues: Their Meaning
and Relevance in Northern United States Black Ghettos."
In Afro-American Anthropology, pp. 367-84. Edited by
Norman E. Whitten, Jr. and John F. Szwed. New York: Free
Press, 1970.

Examines the range of expressive meaning in music of
northern U.S. ghettos. The author finds that soul music is far
more relevant than blues, which is seen as traditional.

1675. HARRIS, Sheldon. Blues Who's Who: a Biographical Dictionary
of Blues Singers. New Rochelle, N.Y.: Arlington House,
1979. 775 pp.

A goldmine of information, this extensive work provides
names, photos, and biographies of blues singers from film, radio,
television, theatre, and records as well as lists of songs that
influenced the blues and songs influenced by the blues, with cross
referencing.

1676. HAYAKAWA, S. I. "Popular Songs vs. the Facts of Life."
Etc.: a Review of General Semantics 12-2 (Winter, 1955):
83-95; reprinted in Mass Culture: the Popular Arts in
America, pp. 393-403. Edited by Bernard Rosenburg and
David Manny White. Glencoe, N.Y.: Free Press, 1957; in

Our Language and Our World, pp. 279-92. Edited by S. I.
Hayakawa. New York: Harper and Bros., 1959; in The Use
and Misuse of Language, pp. 150-63. Edited by S. I.
Hayakawa. Greenwich, Conn.: Fawcett Publications, 1962.

Written from a semantics point of view, the author
examines whether reality is portrayed in the language of blues
(especially jazz blues). Finding instead Idealization,
Frustration, and Demoralization, he criticizes the blues and asks
that a greater degree of reality be communicated in them.

1677. HICKERSON, Joseph C. "A Bibliography of the Blues."
Washington, D.C.: Library of Congress, Archive of Folk
Culture, 1971. 16 pp.

An unannotated bibliography that includes five blues
periodicals and many articles from magazines generally about the
blues.

1678. JARRETT, Dennis. "The Singer and the Bluesman:
Formulations of Personality in the Lyrics of the Blues."
Southern Folklore Quarterly 42-1 (1978): 31-7.

Assesses the extent to which blues are truly autobiographical and to what extent formulaic.

1679. JEFFERSON, Lemon. Blind Lemon Jefferson. Ed. by Bob
Groom. Knutsford, Cheshire, England: Blues World, 1970.
35 pp.

A collection of texts by Blind Lemon Jefferson, the early
bluesman, transcribed from his recordings.

1680. JOHNSON, Guy B. "Double Meaning in the Popular Negro
Blues." Journal of Abnormal and Social Psychology 22-1
(April-June 1927): 12-20.

Early treatment of symbols in blues texts, especially the
double meanings associated with sex.

1681. JOHNSON, Robert. Robert Johnson. Lyrics Transcribed by
Bob Groom and Bob Yates. 4th ed. Knutsford, Cheshire,
England: Blues World, 1969. 28 pp.

1682. JONES, LeRoi [BARAKA, Imamu Amiri]. Blues People: the
Negro Experience in White America and the Music that
Developed from It. New York: W. Morrow, 1963; reprint ed.
of 1967 ed. under BARAKA, Westport, Conn.: Greenwood,
1980. 244 pp.

This is a cultural history of blacks by a militant
writer. He includes chapters on Christian music, slave music, and
both the rural and urban blues as well as jazz.

1683. KEIL, Charles. Urban Blues. Chicago: University of
Chicago Press, 1966. 231 pp.

Written more from the viewpoint of an anthropologist than
of a musicologist, this study focuses on the urban blues and its
background, and especially its context.

1684. KIRBY, Edward "Prince Gabe." Memories of Beale Street.
Memphis: Penny Pincher Sales, 1979. 73 pp.

The personal reminiscences of a jazz musician who came to
Memphis' Beale Street in 1943, with many illustrations.

1685. LEADBITTER, Mike. Delta Country Blues. Bexhill-on-Sea,
England: Blues Unlimited, 1968. 47 pp.

1686. LEADBITTER, Mike. Nothing but the Blues: an Illustrated
Documentary. London: Hanover Books, 1971. 278 pp.

A collection of materials from early issues of Blues
Unlimited from 1963 onwards. Much is biographical. There is an
index, but no table of contents.

1687. LEADBITTER, Mike, and SLAVEN, Neil. Blues Records, January,
1943 to December, 1966. London: Hanover, 1968. 381 pp.

An alphabetical list by artist.

1688. LEHMANN, Theo. Blues and Trouble. Berlin: Henschelverlag,
1966. 192 pp.

Besides an historical survey and treatment of textual meaning and form, this book includes 41 blues texts in both English and German.

1689. LIEB, Sandra. Mother of the Blues: a Study of Ma Rainey. Amherst: University of Massachusetts Press, 1981. 248 pp.

Divided into three parts, this work covers Rainey's life and career in Part I, provides musical and textual analyses of her songs, especially those of her own composition, in Part II, and includes a classified discography in Part III. The author further notes the particular expression of women's concerns in Rainey.

1690. McCUTCHEON, Lynn Ellis. Rhythm and Blues: an Experience and Adventure in its Origin and Development. Arlington, Pa.: Beatty, 1971. 305 pp.

1691. McKEE, Margaret, and CHISENHALL, Fred. Beale Black & Blue: Life and Music on Black America's Main Street. Baton Rouge, La.: Louisiana State University Press, 1981. 265 pp.

An oral history of the blues written by two journalists. The study of bluesmen who worked on Beale St. in Memphis, Tenn.

1692. MIDDLETON, Richard. Pop Music and the Blues: a Study of Relationship and its Significance. London: Victor Gollancz, 1972. 271 pp.

A slightly technical history of the blues, especially the city blues, and how they evolved into rhythm and blues and then into rock-'n'-roll.

1693. MITCHELL, George. Blow My Blues Away. Baton Rouge, La.: Louisiana State University Press, 1971; reprint ed., New York: Da Capo, 1984. 208 pp.

Report of research, which emphasized the social aspects of the genre, on country blues in the Mississippi Delta region, with numerous illustrations.

1694. MOORE, Carman. Somebody's Angel Child: the Story of Bessie Smith. New York: Thomas Y. Crowell, 1969. 121 pp.

A juvenile biography of Bessie Smith.

1695. MURRAY, Albert. Stomping the Blues. New York: McGraw-Hill, 1976. 264 pp.

Popular history of the city blues with many illustrations.

1696. NAPIER, Simon, comp. Back Woods Blues. Bexhill-on-Sea, England: Blues Unlimited, 1968. 55 pp.

A collection of reprints from Blues Unlimited and other magazines published in Britain.

1697. NARVAEZ, Peter. "Afro-American and Mexican Street Singers: an Ethnohistorical Hypothesis." Southern Folklore Quarterly 42-1 (1978): 73-84.

A study of the alleged relationships between and influences from Mexican-American street singers and bluesmen, especially in terms of the instruments, performance rituals, and life style. This article is primarily historical in that it documents contact between the two groups.

1698. NEFF, Robert, and CONNOR, Anthony. Blues. Boston: David R. Godine, 1975. 141 pp.

Based on two years of field work in the American South, this "mingling of the voices of scores of blues musicians" combines stories, often in their own words, with blues texts.

1699. OAKLEY, Giles. The Devil's Music: a History of the Blues. London: BBC, 1976; New York: Taplinger, 1977. 289 pp.

Comprehensive but popular survey of the blues and their cultural context, from slavery to the present, with numerous illustrations.

1700. OLIVER, Paul. Bessie Smith. Kings of Jazz #3. London: Cassel, 1959; New York: A. S. Barnes, 1961. 82 pp.

The biography of a fascinating person, with a discography and a list of her songs.

1701. OLIVER, Paul. Blues Fell This Morning; the Meaning of the Blues. London: Cassell, 1960; New York: Horizon Press, 1961. 355 pp. Republished as The Meaning of the Blues. New York: Collier, 1963. 383 pp.

A study of text and meaning in the popular blues, with sections organized around individuals.

1702. OLIVER, Paul. Conversation with the Blues. New York: Horizon Press, 1965. 217 pp.

Based on field interviews in the American South during the summer of 1960, this work is mostly quotations from living bluesmen about the blues and its meaning in their lives.

1703. OLIVER, Paul. Savannah Syncopators: African Retentions in the Blues. London: Studio Vista, 1970; New York: Stein and Day, 1970. 112 pp.

Based on field work in West Africa, the author explores the relationships between African and Afro-American musics, especially the blues.

1704. OLIVER, Paul. Screening the Blues: Aspects of the Blues Tradition. London: Cassell, 1968; reprinted as Aspects of the Blues Tradition. New York: Oak, 1970. 294 pp.

A text-based study which seeks to go beyond the apparent meaning of the blues to a deeper meaning. The author further submits that recorded blues tend to distort the tradition because certain kinds of texts were avoided or part eliminated, and much of what remained was misunderstood.

1705. OLIVER, Paul. The Story of the Blues. London: Carrie & Rockliff, 1969; Radnor, Pa.: Chilton Book Co., 1969, 1982. 176 pp.

A general history of the blues, with numerous illustrations.

1706. OLSSON, Bengt. Memphis Blues and Jug Bands. London:
Studio Vista, 1970. 112 pp.

Popular illustrated story of jug bands and their blues,
with a collection of texts taken from early recordings.

1707. OSTER, Harry. Living Country Blues. Detroit: Folklore
Associates, 1969. 464 pp.

A text-oriented popular-style study of the cultural
context, history, themes, and poetry of the blues, with some
transcriptions.

1708. OTTENHEIMER, Harriet J. "Catharsis, Communication, and
Evocation: Alternative Views of the Sociopsychological
Functions of Blues Singing." Ethnomusicology 23-1 (Jan.
1979): 75-86.

An article that seeks to correct the assumed view that
the singer releases emotions through the blues. Based on research
in New Orleans, 1966-67, especially with singers Jewell "Babe"
Stovall and Pleasant "Cousin Joe" Joseph, this study attempts to
show that singers seek to evoke, intensify, and match the moods of
the listeners, and using language held in common between blues and
speech, to communicate more forcefully.

1709. OTTO, John Solomon, and BURNS, Augustus M. "'Tough Times':
Downhome Blues Recordings as Folk History." Southern
Quarterly 21-3 (Spring, 1983): 27-43.

An exploration of blues themes from a literary
standpoint.

1710. OTTO, John, and BURNS, Augustus M. "Welfare Store Blues--
Blues Recordings and the Great Depression." Popular Music
and Society 7-2 (1980): 95-102.

A brief analysis of blues texts that were stimulated by
the Great Depression.

1711. PALMER, Robert. Deep Blues. New York: Viking Press, 1981.
310 pp.

Diary-like, personal and sociological study of the Delta blues, the lives of the musicians, and the meaning of the blues in expressing their lives.

1712. PEARSON, Barry Lee. "The Life Story of the Blues Musician: an Analysis of the Tradition of Oral Self-Portrayal." Ph.D. dissertation, Indiana University, 1977. 293 pp.

The study of how individuals blend themselves into a tradition, based on field work in Mississippi. Deals with the confluence of personal experience and stereotypical images that are traditional among blues musicians.

1713. PEARSON, Barry Lee. "Sounds So Good to Me": the Bluesman's Story. Philadelphia: University of Pennsylvania Press, 1984. 175 pp.

Scholarly collection of biographies of bluesmen based on field interviews and previously published autobiographies detailing the lives, careers, community context, and process of transmission of the blues.

1714. ROWE, Mike. Chicago Breakdown. Eddison Blues Book #1. London: Eddison, 1973; reprint ed., New York: Drake, 1975; reprinted as Chicago Blues: the City & the Music. New York: Da Capo, 1979. 226 pp.

A well-done social history of the blues in Chicago by a British writer.

1715. RUSSELL, Tony. Blacks Whites and Blues. London: Studio Vista, 1970; New York: Stein and Day, 1970. 112 pp.

A fairly detailed but poorly documented comparison of Afro-American and Anglo-American musical traditions, differences in song topics, goals of the singers, and preferences of the audiences.

1716. SACKHEIM, Eric, and SHAHN, Jonathan. The Blues Line: a Collection of Blues Lyrics. New York: Grossman, 1969. 499 pp.

A topically organized collection of blues texts with little further information on them. Shahn was illustrator and Sackheim was compiler.

1717. SCARBOROUGH, Dorothy. "The 'Blues' as Folk-Songs." Publications of the Texas Folklore Society #2, 1923; reprinted in Coffee in the Gourd, pp. 52-66. Edited by J. Frank Dobie. Dallas: Texas Folklore Society, 1935; reprint ed., Dallas: Southern Methodist University Press, 1969.

Based in part on an interview with W. C. Handy, this surprisingly unenlightened and unsympathetic study of the blues, which are described as "barbaric," attempts to trace its origin and includes examples of texts and one musical transcription.

1718. SCHRODT, Helen, and WILKINSON, Bailey. "Sam Lindsey and Milton Roby: Memphis Blues Musicians." Tennessee Folklore Society Bulletin 30-2 (June 1964): 52-6.

Brief biographies of the lives and careers of two men active in the early Memphis skiffle or jug bands.

1719. SHAW, Arnold. Honkers and Shouters: the Golden Age of Rhythm and Blues. New York: Macmillan, 1978. 555 pp.

A popular but thorough history of both the era and the genre, with a focus on the roots of rhythm and blues, personalities and record companies, all organized by region.

1720. SHIRLEY, Kay, and DRIGGS, Frank. The Book of the Blues. New York: Leeds Music and MCA, 1963. 301 pp.

Collection of blues melodies with guitar chord symbols. Annotations by Frank Driggs, record research by Joy Graeme, and music research by Bob Hartsell.

1721. SILVERMAN, Jerry. 100 American Folk Blues. New York: Macmillan, 1970.

1722. SPRINGER, Robert. "The Regulatory Function of the Blues." Black Perspective in Music 4-3 (1976): 278-88.

While showing that there were African precedents for the same function, the author demonstrates how blues helped Afro-Americans release tension as a group during the period when survival in an often hostile society was paramount.

1723. STEWART-BAXTER, Derrick. Ma Rainey and the Classic Blues Singers. London: Studio Vista; New York: Stein and Day, 1970. 112 pp.

Biographies and related material on the great women blues singers, such as Ma Rainey, Bessie Smith, Mamie Smith, and Lucille Hegamin.

1724. STRACHWITZ, Chris. "Blues from Coast to Coast." American Folk Music Occasional 1 (1964): 20-37.

1725. TAFT, Michael. Blues Lyric Poetry: an Anthology. Garland Reference Library of the Humanities, Vol. 361. New York: Garland, 1983. 379 pp.

The complete texts for over 2,000 blues songs recorded from 1920 to 1942 by more than 350 singers. Each entry provides the name of the singer, title, place and date of recording, record number, and the text. This collection provides the complete poems which are examined word-for-word in the author's companion work, Blues Lyric Poetry: a Concordance (see next entry).

1726. TAFT, Michael. Blues Lyric Poetry: a Concordance. 3 vols. Garland Reference Library of the Humanities. New York: Garland, 1983. 3,150 pp.

The result of 15 years of work, much with the aid of a computer, and meant to be used in conjunction with the previous entry, Blues Lyric Poetry: an Anthology, this extraordinary resource breaks down the lines of poetry ("deconstruction") into individual words and phrases in order to get at the matter of formulaic structure. It is thoroughly indexed by word, which makes it possible to find all lines using a given phrase. Symbols refer the reader to the complete poems in the companion anthology.

1727. TAFT, Michael. "Willie McTell's Rules of Rhyme: a Brief Excursion into Blues Phonetics." Southern Folklore Quarterly 42-1 (1978): 53-72.

Citing statements made by various bluesmen about rhyme, the author focuses on Willie McTell, who recorded between 1927 and 1956. From this he formulates 14 rules.

1728. TALLMADGE, William H. "Blue Notes and Blue Tonality." The Black Perspective in Music 12-2 (1984): 155-65.

An examination of selected writings on blue notes and blue tonality, together with melodic and harmonic analysis of a number of blues performances, establish that blue notes exist only in conjunction with a harmonic substructure, and the total sonority (blue tonality) is created by means of an Afro-American polychordal practice initiated in North America. It follows that all ascriptions of blue notes or blue tonality to non-Western musics are in error, as these musics do not possess a European harmonic substructure. (author)

1729. TITON, Jeff Todd. Downhome Blues Lyrics: an Anthology from the Post-World War II Era. Twayne Music Series. Boston: G. K. Hall & Co., 1981. 214 pp.

Offered as poetry because the compiler/transcriber feels they have literary merit, this collection of 125 blues lyrics were taken from commercial recordings from 1946 to 1964 aimed at the black communities.

1730. TITON, Jeff Todd. Early Downhome Blues: a Musical and Cultural Analysis. Urbana: University of Illinois Press, 1977. 296 pp.

Perhaps the best overall study of the downhome, or country, blues to date, for it treats not only the cultural context and meaning of the blues, the formulaicness of the texts, but also the structure of the musical elements. From some 50 texts and tunes transcribed from early recordings, the author is able to construct a musical grammar of the blue melody and describe the process of improvisation. An appendix offers additional information about blues recordings and the public's buying habits.

1731. TITON, Jeff Todd. "Ethnomusicology of Downhome Blues Phonograph Records, 1926-1930." Ph.D. dissertation, University of Minnesota, 1971. 314 pp.

This work includes both an analysis of blues style, behavior, and beliefs as well as close examination of three groups concerned with blues: the artists, the record companies, and the record buyers. Record sales reached their peak from 1926-30.

1732. TITON, Jeff Todd. "Every Day I Have the Blues: Improvisation and Daily Life." Southern Folklore Quarterly 42-1 (1978): 1-7, 85-98.

The author asserts that improvisation in music is not as mysterious as it seems when we realize we engage in such behavior daily. The author distinguishes between memorized musical performance, variation, and improvisation, the latter defined as creation at the moment of performance. Improvisation usually proceeds by higher-level groupings of roughly-shaped and stored note-sequences called preforms. (author)

1733. TITON, Jeff Todd, ed. "From Blues to Pop: the Autobiography of Leonard 'Baby Doo' Caston." Los Angeles: John Edwards Memorial Foundation, Special Series, No. 4, 1974. 29 pp.

Caston, a singer-pianist and guitarist, had a career as a blues singer in the South in the 1920s and 1930s. Then as he "improved" as a musician, he sang in various uptown blues groups in Chicago in the 1940s and eventually became a cocktail pianist, supporting himself and a large family wholly from his musical income. In this spoken autobiography, he reviews his life, his motives, and his career. (author)

1734. TITON, Jeff Todd. "Thematic Pattern in Downhome Blues Lyrics: the Evidence on Commercial Phonograph Records Since World War II." Journal of American Folklore 90-357 (July-Sept. 1977): 316-30.

Freedom is the overarching theme in post-WW II blues lyrics. The singer of a blues song conventionally casts himself in the role of mistreated victim. As he draws up a bill of indictment against the mistreating lover, the drama turns on what he will do about it. Resignation resolves a small minority of blues lyrics, usually the singer acts to free himself from the mistreater. (author)

1735. TOWNLEY, Eric. Tell Your Story: a Dictionary of Jazz and Blues Recordings, 1917-1950. Chigwell, England: Storyville Publications, 1976. 416 pp.

1736. WOLFE, Charles K. "'Where the Blues is At': a Survey of Recent Research." Popular Music and Society 1-3 (Spring, 1972): 152-66.

A review-essay covering recent books by Paul Oliver, John Godrich, Harry Oster, and others.

IX. MUSICS OF VARIOUS ETHNIC TRADITIONS

In a sense, all people are "ethnic" in some way. In practical
American usage, however, the term ethnic normally denotes people
descended from non-English-speaking cultures. True, this
definition is not perfect, since Afro-Americans are usually not
thought of immediately as "ethnic." Obviously, there are people of
the so-called and alleged "melting pot" who have lost feelings of
ethnicity and might better be termed "generic Americans." But a
significant percentage of our population, for one reason or
another, retains feelings of ethnic identity, still reflecting a
non-American culture from which they or their parents or even more
remote generations came. They are the people who join the various
ethnic organizations which are represented at ethnic festivals or
who might describe themselves as hyphenated-Americans. Heretofore,
these have mostly been of European origin. For purposes of this
section, we have included Asians and Latin Americans as well.

Less research has been done on ethnic traditions in America
than one might have expected, and a good part of it has been
concerned more with the texts of songs than with musical aspects.
Certain nationalities have been studied by only one or a few
individuals, e.g., Hungarian (Stephen Erdely) and Irish (Lawrence
McCullough).

The least studied are the musics of Asian-Americans, partly
because many are recent arrivals, partly because some have come
from nations whose music is itself little known (e.g., the Lao).
Music in Hawaii was fairly thoroughly studied by earlier scholars,
which is fortunate because so little of it survives intact now.

A fair proportion of the material included here raises
questions about its "folkness." It was decided to err on the side
of generosity by including as many ethnic items as possible without
wringing hands too much over whether they were genuinely folk.
Similarly, it might be noted that much of this material would have
to be described as "music in America" rather than "American music,"
since to be ethnic it would not reflect a great deal of
acculturation. In some cases the United States provides a haven
for survivals from distant cultures where music has changed, but in

356

other cases the phenomena found here still exist and have been more thoroughly studied in their original contexts. This would seem to be so in the cases of, e.g., Jewish and Slavic musics.

General and Miscellaneous

1737. BLEGEN, Theodore C. "Singing Immigrants and Pioneers." In Studies in American Culture: Dominant Ideas and Images, pp. 171-88. Edited by Joseph J. Kwiat and Mary C. Turpie. Minneapolis: University of Minnesota Press, 1960.

This is a collection of song texts, but for no particular group, meant to illustrate how singers from various traditions felt about their New World experience, their hopes, and their homesickness.

1738. BORCHERDT, Donn. "Armenian Folk Songs and Dances in the Fresno and Los Angeles Areas." Western Folklore 18-1 (Jan. 1959): 1-12.

A description of the community, churches, the history of the Armenian immigrants and presents a collection of 50 songs and variants and 50 dances, some with tune transcriptions.

1739. COON, Leland. Traditional American Folklore and Folksongs of Minority Groups in Wisconsin. Washington, D.C.: Library of Congress, Archive of Folk Song, n.d.

1740. D'ARIANO, Regina and Roy. Italo-American Ballads, Poems, Lyrics, and Melodies. Parsons, W. Va.: McClain Printing Co., 1976. 265 pp.

Songs collected from immigrants with texts in Italian and English.

1741. ERDELY, Stephen. "Ethnic Music in the United States: an Overview." Yearbook of the International Folk Music Council 11 (1979): 114-37.

Introductory article to the subject, with discussions of the musical activities (e.g., singing societies, church music, etc.) of ethnic groups which arrived in the late nineteenth century. Other matters discussed include the mixing of ethnic and

art traditions, transmission, performance practices, and the
context of ethnic music in America.

1742. ERDELY, Stephen. "Research on Traditional Music of
      Nationality Groups in Cleveland and Vicinity."
      Ethnomusicology 12-2 (1968): 245-50.

Brief introduction to the kinds of musics found in
collecting c. 2,700 songs and instrumental pieces from Hungarian,
Slovak, Irish, Rumanian, Croatian, Greek, Scottish, and Afro-
American communities.

1743. HENRY, Mellinger Edward. A Bibliography for the Study of
      American Folk Songs with Many Titles of Folk Songs (and
      Titles that have to do with Folk Songs) from Other Lands.
      New York: New York Public Library, 1937. 142 pp.

A limited edition of 750 copies (consequently, rare),
this bibliography of song collections covers Scottish, English,
Irish, Puerto Rican, Jamaican, and Mexican songs among others.

1744. HOPKINS, Pandora. "Individual Choice and the Control of
      Musical Change." Journal of American Folklore 89-354
      (Oct.-Dec. 1976): 449-62.

A study which asserts that intentionality is the
determining factor in the occurrence (or non-occurrence) of change
in the United States. The author cites examples from Greek,
Norwegian, Finnish, Irish, and other traditions.

1745. KALOYANIDES, Michael G. "New York and bouzoukia: the Rise
      of Greek-American Music." Essays in Arts and Sciences 6-1
      (Mar. 1977): 95-103.

The author traces a progression in the development of
Greek-American music from the early 1900s to the present, seeing
the process changing from one of regional identity to first a
national one, then a Greek-American one.

1746. MARSHALL, Howard W., ed. Ethnic Recordings in America: a
      Neglected Heritage. Washington, D.C.: American Folklife
      Center, Library of Congress, 1982. 269 pp.

Collection of nine chapters, each by a different author, on different aspects of ethnic recordings: commercial, early field recordings, Irish, Mexican-American, Polish. There is also a general article, "Recorded Ethnic Music: a Guide to Resources" by Norm Cohen and Paul Wells which includes a discussion of the subject and classified lists by nationality of materials.

1747. The New Grove Dictionary of Music in the United States. S.v. "European-American Music" by Philip V. Bohlman. In press.

Both an introductory overview of European ethnic groups in North America and a discussion of the role of their organizations within ethnic communities. He concludes that these organizations both allow musical traditions to change but also protect them against disappearance. There is also a series of articles on the traditional musics of various ethnic communities, with some focus on historical background, important genres, and a description of contemporary musical life.

1748. PORTER, James. "Introduction: the Traditional Music of Europeans in America." In Selected Reports in Ethnomusicology, Vol. III, No. 1, pp. 1-24. Edited by J. Porter. Los Angeles: Department of Music, University of California at Los Angeles, 1978.

Because this introduction to a collection of articles is especially valuable for the non-specialist, it is cited separately from the following entry. In it the author discusses problems of terminology, the meaning of tradition, and explores the conceptual question of acculturation. He concludes with a six-page bibliography which includes valuable material on the subject generally.

1749. PORTER, James, ed. Selected Reports in Ethnomusicology, Vol. III, No. 1. Los Angeles: Department of Music, University of California at Los Angeles, 1978. 259 pp.

A collection of seven articles, including the previous entry, by specialists in various European-American traditions. These are: Claudie Marcel-Dubois, "Réflexions sur l'heritage musical Français en Louisiane"; Linda C. Burman-Hall, "Tune Identity and Performance Style: the Case of 'Bonaparte's Retreat'"; Stephen Erdely, "Traditional and Individual Traits in the Songs of Three Hungarian-Americans"; Ellen Koskoff, "Contemporary Nigun Composition in an American Hasidic Community"; Mark Forry, "Becar

Music in the Serbian Community of Los Angeles: Evolution and Transformation"; Christina Niles, "The Revival of the Latvian Kokle in America." The collection is concluded with a valuable un-annotated bibliography, pp. 241-58, which includes a number of master's theses not included in the present collection.

1750. ROCCO, Emma Scogna. "Italian Bands: a Surviving Tradition in Western Pennsylvania Milltowns." Ph.D. dissertation, University of Pittsburgh, in progress.

1751. TAWA, Nicholas. A Sound of Strangers: Musical Culture, Acculturation, and the post-Civil War Ethnic American. Metuchen, N.J.: Scarecrow Press, 1982. 304 pp.

Not especially about folk music but a major contribution on the subject of European and Jewish musics as they changed or were neglected in the context of America. Additionally mentions traditions brought from the Middle East, China, and Japan.

1752. WRIGHT, Robert L. "Scandinavian, German, Irish, English, and Scottish Emigration Songs: some Comparisons." In Ballads and Ballad Research: Selected Papers of the International Conference on Nordic and Anglo-American Ballad Research, University of Washington, Seattle, May 2-6, 1977, pp. 259-68. Edited by Patricia Conroy. Seattle: University of Washington, 1978.

Asian-American Musics

1753. HOFMANN, C. "Japanese Folksongs in New York City." Journal of American Folklore 59 (1946): 324-5.

Brief account of Japanese songs in Western style collected in New York in 1945.

1754. HOM, Marlon Kau. "Some Cantonese Folksongs on the American Experience." Western Folklore 42-2 (April 1983): 126-39.

This article has three stated purposes: 1) an introduction to Cantonese Chinese folksongs in America, 2) insight into the feelings of the singers, 3) the American experience of those who came around 1900 as seen in the songs.

1755. JAIRAZBHOY, Nazir, and DE VALE, Sue Carole, eds. Selected Reports in Ethnomusicology, Vol. VI: Asian Music in North America. Los Angeles: Department of Music, University of California, Los Angeles, 1985. 199 pp.

A collection of 12 papers read at the Symposium on Asian Music in the United States held at UCLA on October 17-18, 1984. After an introduction by Dr. Jairazbhoy, the following topics are covered: Karl Signell, "Music in a New World: Asian Musicians Speak"; Alison Arnold, Indian music in Chicago; Joan L. Erdman, Indian music and dance in Chicago; Gordon Thompson and Medha Yodh, "Garba and the Gujaratis of Southern California"; Amy Catlin, Hmong music; Terry Miller, Lao traditional music; Lou Harrison, "Thoughts on 'Slippery Slendro'"; Jo Anne Combs, "Japanese-American music and dance in Los Angeles, 1930-1942"; Christine R. Yano, Japanese bon dance in Hawaii; Susan Asai, Horaku Buddhist taiko drumming; Isabel K. F. Wong, Peking opera in San Francisco; Ronald Riddle, Korean music in Los Angeles.

1756. RIDDLE, Ronald. Flying Dragons, Flowing Streams; Music in the Life of San Francisco's Chinese. Contributions in Intercultural and Comparative Studies #7. Westport, Conn.: Greenwood, 1983. 249 pp.

A description of the history and activities of theatrical groups, clubs, and ensembles of the nineteenth and twentieth centuries.

1757. RIDDLE, Ronald. "Music Clubs and Ensembles in San Francisco's Chinese Community." In Eight Urban Musical Cultures: Tradition and Change, pp. 223-59. Edited by Bruno Nettl. Urbana: University of Illinois Press, 1978.

Describes the community, the Cantonese and Peking Opera clubs, instrumental music clubs, and how they function.

1758. SMITH, Barbara. "The Bon-Odori in Hawaii and in Japan." Journal of the International Folk Music Council 14 (Jan. 1962): 36-9.

Briefly describes and gives origin of the O-bon festival and how it is done in Hawaii in comparison to Japan.

Cajun or Acadian Music

1759. ANCELET, Barry Jean, and MORGAN, Elemore, Jr. The Makers of Cajun Music/Musiciens cadiens et creoles. Austin: University of Texas Press, 1984. 160 pp.

Lavishly illustrated with many color photos (by E. Morgan) and texts in French and English, side by side, this study consists of an introduction and sections on 18 individuals and groups, with many quotations from the musicians. Also includes discography, bibliography, filmography, and maps.

1760. BLANCHET, Catherine. "Acadian Instrumental Music." Louisiana Folklore Miscellany 3-1 (April 1970): 70-5.

1761. BRANDON, Elizabeth. "The Socio-Cultural Traits of the French Folksong in Louisiana." Revue de Louisiana/Louisiana Review 1-2 (1972): 19-32.

1762. BROVEN, John. South to Louisiana: the Music of the Cajun Bayous. Gretna, La.: Pelican Publishing Co., 1983. 368 pp.

Written by an English professor and scholar, this book is a history of artists and recordings of cajun, cajun-country, zydeco, blues, swamp-pop, and cajun revival musics.

1763. CLAUDEL, Calvin. "Mr. Doering's 'Songs the Cajuns Sing'." Southern Folklore Quarterly 8-2 (June 1944): 123-31.

Extensive critique of Doering's article (#1765) in which the author presents what he feels is better information and examples.

1764. DAIGLE, Pierre V. Tears, Love and Laughter: the Story of the Acadians. Church Point, La.: Acadian Publishing Enterprise, 1972. 140 pp.

The history of the Acadians, of musicians dead or retired, of musicians playing today, and an appendix of pictures, biographies, and a few tunes. Writes the author: "This book is for everybody, but only Cajuns will understand it."

1765. DOERING, J. Frederick. "Songs the Cajuns Sing." Southern Folklore Quarterly 7-4 (1943): 193-201.

After a brief introduction, a collection of French texts collected in Louisiana.

1766. LAGARDE, Marie-Louise, CHUTE, William, and REINECKE, George Fl. "Six Avoyelles Songs from the Saucier Collection." Louisiana Folklore Miscellany 2-2 (April 1965):1-26.

1767. LEADBITTER, Mike. From the Bayou: the Story of Goldband Records. Bexhill-on-Sea, Sussex, England: Blues Unlimited, 1969. 62 pp.

1768. MARCEL-DUBOIS, Claudie. "Réflexions sur l'heritage musical Français en Louisiane." In Selected Reports in Ethnomusicology, Vol. III, No. 1, pp. 25-76. Edited by James Porter. Los Angeles: Music Department, University of California, Los Angeles, 1978.

An extended study of a long example of text and music, providing background, comparison of the example in France and America, and a discussion of song types, scales, melodic structure, ornamentation, and use of the violin. 14 photos.

1769. POST, Lauren C. "Joseph Falcon, Accordion Player and Singer: a Biographical Sketch." Louisiana History 11-1 (Winter, 1970): 63-79.

The playing of Falcon (1900-65), from Acadia Parish, is examined in the context of a recording session, with excellent photos and discography.

1770. RODENBECK, Arlene, and FARRER, Suzanne. "A Brief Bibliography on Cajun Music." Washington, D.C.: Library of Congress, Archive of Folk Song, n.d. 26 entries.

1771. RUSHTON, William Faulkner. The Cajuns: from Acadia to Louisiana. New York: Farrar, Straus Giroux, 1979. 342 pp.

This general study of Acadian culture by a journalist includes on pp. 221-40 a description of French accordion music.

1772. WHITFIELD, Irène Therèse. Louisiana French Folk Songs.
Romance Language Series #1. University, La.: Louisiana
State University Press, 1939; reprint ed., New York:
Dover, 1969. 159 pp.

The writer provides first a 23-page introduction and
recital of the collecting process, then divides her material into
three groups according to linguistic distinctions: 1) Louisiana-
French, 2) Acadian or Cajun-French, 3) Negro-French or Creole.
The texts, in French and phonetics, and tunes with commentary are
given for each song.

1773. WILSON, Mary Louise Lewis. "Traditional Louisiana-French
Folk Music: an Argument for its Preservation and
Utilization as a State Cultural Heritage." Ph.D.
dissertation, University of Pittsburgh, 1977. 245 pp.

Partly a comprehensive survey of the Cajuns and Afro-
American Creoles, of the historical layers from 1699 and 1756
(when Acadians came from Canada), and partly an advocacy piece for
preservation. Discusses Cajun as related to the French language
vis-a-vis its preservation.

Musics of Germanic Peoples

1774. ALBRECHT, Theodore. "The Music Libraries of the German
Singing Societies in Texas, 1850-1855." Music Library
Association Notes 31-3 (Mar. 1975): 517-29.

A history of the singing societies of immigrants from
Germany in the 1840s and 1850s and their musical activities and
repertory, with a short list of works. Not folk per se.

1775. BOHLMAN, Philip V. "Deutsch-amerikanische Musik in
Wisconsin: Ueberleben im Melting Pot." Jahrbuch fuer
Volksliedforschung 30 (1985): in press.

Using both historical and ethnographic approaches, the
author examines persistence and change in German folk music in a
heavily German region of northern Wisconsin. Especially important
as agents for both persistence and change have been the
institutions of German Lutheranism, which have fostered the German
language and undergirded practices of traditional music. (author)

1776. BOHLMAN, Philip V. "Hymnody in the Rural German-American
       Community of the Upper Midwest." The Hymn 35-3 (July
       1984): 158-64.

       This article examines briefly the transformation of
religious German musical traditions to different types of
traditional and folk music. The interdependence of written and
oral musical traditions has effected this transformation,
especially in the heavily German areas of the Upper Midwest and in
communities where German Protestantism predominates. (author)

1777. BOHLMAN, Philip V. "Prolegomena to the Classification of
       German-American Music." Yearbook of German-American
       Studies 20 (1985): in press.

       This article proposes an approach to the examination of
German-American music as a reflection of diverse acculturative
responses. Based primarily on fieldwork in rural Wisconsin,
Chicago, and Pittsburgh, the study attempts to embrace a wide
range of repertories of German-American music and to stress the
need for understanding the interrelations among them. (author)

1778. BOYER, Walter E., BUFFINGTON, Albert F., and YODER, Don,
       eds. Songs Along the Mahantongo; Pennsylvania Dutch
       Folksongs. Lancaster: Pennsylvania Dutch Center, 1951.
       231 pp.

       A collection of song from central Pennsylvania with
headnotes, tunes, and words in German and English, preceded by a
14-page introduction.

1779. BUFFINGTON, Albert F. Dutchified German Spirituals.
       Pennsylvania German Society Publications, vol. 62.
       Lancaster: Fackenthal Library, Franklin and Marshall
       College, 1965. 239 pp.

1780. BUFFINGTON, Albert F. Pennsylvania German Secular
       Folksongs. Pennsylvania German Society Publications,
       vol. 8. Breinigsville: Pennsylvania German Society,
       1974. 182 pp.

       Field collected 1946-64 containing 97 songs and variants
with tunes and texts in German and English preceded by a preface
explaining background and methodology.

1781. BURKHART, Charles. "The Church Music of the Old Order
      Amish and Old Colony Mennonites." Mennonite Quarterly
      Review 27 (1953): 34-54.

      Description of the church, its origin and history,
contemporary usage, its services and types, performance practices,
and books. Concentrates on the musical practices of the Old
Colony (Dutch Mennonite) Church. Regarding its music there are
several transcriptions and analyses of hymns, with special
attention to ornamentation.

1782. BURKHART, Charles. "Music of the Old Colony Mennonites."
      Mennonite Life 7 (1952).

1783. DOLL, Eugene. The Ephrata Cloister: an Introduction.
      Ephrata, Pa.: Ephrata Cloister Associates, 1958. 32 pp.

      General introduction to the Cloister and its founder,
Conrad Beissel, with information on the musical practices and some
facsimile illustrations.

1784. ETTER, Russell C. "Extemporaneous Hymn-Making among the
      Pennsylvania Dutch." Journal of American Folklore 44-173
      (1931): 302-5.

      Description of the hymns, especially texts, of the United
Christian Church of the Lebanon County, Pennsylvania, area.

1785. FARLEE, Lloyd Winfield. "A History of the Church Music of
      the Amana Society, the Community of True Inspiration."
      Ph.D. dissertation, The University of Iowa, 1966. 929 pp.

      The Amana Community originated in Germany in the eight-
teenth century and came to southeastern Iowa in 1859. Their hymn
singing is traced to 1718 and the Protestant mainstream. This
work studies the performance practices, books, tunes, and use of
the Vorsanger, including in modern times.

1786. FARLEE, Lloyd. "Hymn-Singing in Amana." The Hymn 21-2
      (April 1970): 46-50.

      This article is a brief form of the above dissertation.

1787. FREY, J. William. "Amish Hymns as Folk Music." In
Pennsylvania Songs and Legends, pp. 129-62. Edited by
George Korson. Philadelphia: University of Pennsylvania
Press, 1949; reprint ed., Baltimore: Johns Hopkins
University Press, 1960.

The history, practices, and examples of Amish hymns,
including on p. 143 a transcription of "'S Lobg'sang" from a
Library of Congress recording.

1788. HOHMANN, Rupert K. "The Church Music of the Old Order
Amish of the United States." Ph.D. dissertation,
Northwestern University, 1959. 262 pp.

Based on literary sources and phonograph recordings, this
study emphasizes the history of Amish hymn singing while providing
a description and analysis of the texts and tunes.

1789. JACKSON, George Pullen. "The American Amish Sing Medieval
Songs Today." Southern Folklore Quarterly 10 (1946):
151-7.

Preliminary report asserting that the tunes are more than
two hundred years old. Also describes Der Ausbund, the hymnal of
the Amish and its relationship to the tunes.

1790. JACKSON, George Pullen. "Pennsylvania Dutch Spirituals."
Musical Quarterly 38 (1952): 80-4.

In this article the author demonstrates how the revivals
which swept English-speaking America also infiltrated into
Pennsylvania-German communities and their songs.

1791. JACKSON, George Pullen. "The Strange Music of the Old
Order Amish." Musical Quarterly 31 (1945): 275-88.

After briefly reviewing the origin and history of the
Amish, the author describes the sixteenth century hymnal, Der
Ausbund. Much of the remainder accomplishes two tasks, first to
review Yoder's collection of Amish hymns (see below) and second to
provide two tables listing Amish hymn tunes and their nearest
equivalents, to European folk tunes and American folk tunes
respectively. A few examples are given, some from Yoder.

1792. JOST, Walter James. "The Hymn Tune Tradition of the General Conference Mennonite Church." D.M.A. dissertation, University of Southern California, 1966. 318 pp.

The General Conference Mennonite Church, though having roots in the sixteenth century, was created in 1860 in North America combining Swiss and Dutch peoples. This a study of their hymnbooks and tunes, largely based on presentday life.

1793. KENNEY, Alice P. "Hudson Valley Dutch Psalmody." The Hymn 25-1 (Jan. 1974): 15-26.

A brief history and description of psalmody practices, the books used, and the controversies that resulted.

1794. MARTENS, Helen. "Hutterite Songs: the Origins and Aural Transmission of their Melodies from the Sixteenth Century." Ph.D. dissertation, Columbia University, 1969. 306 pp.

While the locale of this study is uncertain, it pertains to the American Amish, who sing some of the Hutterite songs from the sixteenth century.

1795. NETTL, Bruno. "The Hymns of the Amish: an Example of Marginal Survival." Journal of American Folklore 70-278 (Oct.-Dec. 1957): 323-8.

Introductory article and overview of the tradition, with one transcription of a hymn.

1796. SACHSE, Julius Friedrich. The Music of the Ephrata Cloister. Lancaster, Pa.: for the author, 1903 [copyright, 1902]; reprint ed., New York: AMS Press, 1971. 108 pp.

Although the music of the Ephrata Cloister was a complex, homophonic idiom entirely written out, the founder and main composer, Conrad Beissel, lacked training in standard harmony and consequently created a unique "primitive" (as in "primitive" American painting--unschooled) style. This work is a comprehensive study of that tradition with many examples and facsimiles, and also includes Beissel's "Treatise on Music" from the Preface of the 1747 manuscript "Turtel Taube."

1797. UMBLE, John. "The Old Order Amish, Their Hymns and Hymn
       Tunes." Journal of American Folklore 52-203 (Jan.-Mar.
       1939): 82-95.

       Excellent introduction to the Amish and their hymn
singing, giving the cultural and historical contexts of Der
Ausbund, and a description of the tunes with three transcriptions.

1798. WETZEL, Richard D. Frontier Musicians on the
       Connoquenessing, Wabash, and Ohio: a History of the Music
       and Musicians of George Rapp's Harmony Society (1805-
       1906). Athens: Ohio University Press, 1976. 293 pp.

       The Harmony Society, one of several German-origin
communal groups, included music as an important part of their
life. Led by millenial preacher, George Rapp, they came first to
Butler County, Pennsylvania in 1805 and dissolved in 1906. Not
folk music per se, for their style was closer to classic
traditions of Europe at the time.

1799. WETZEL, Richard D. "The Hymnody of George Rapp's Harmony
       Society." The Hymn 23-1 (Jan. 1972): 19-29.

       A distillation of the above book, with emphasis on the
hymn singing, hymnals, and poetry.

1800. WOLF, Edward C. "Two Divergent Traditions of German-
       American Hymnody in Maryland circa 1800." American Music
       3-3 (Fall, 1985): 299-312.

       Contrasts the music activities, particularly in hymnody,
of two churches, one in Baltimore representing the urban
tradition, and another representing the rural tradition still tied
up with singing schools and tunebooks.

1801. WRIGHT, Rochelle, and WRIGHT, Robert L. Danish Emigrant
       Ballads and Songs. Carbondale: Southern Illinois
       University Press, 1983. 302 pp.

       A 40-page introduction to dances in the New World is
followed by 116-song texts in Danish and English (pp. 47-242),
this being followed by 116 wordless melodies (music transcribed
and arranged by Richard P. Smiraglia) without analysis.

1802. YODER, Don. Pennsylvania Spirituals. Lancaster:
       Pennsylvania Folklife Society, 1961. 528 pp.

       A study of the Pennsylvania Dutch revivalist folk hymn,
with a collection of 150 songs with tunes. Yoder examines first
the origins of the American spiritual, summarizing also the
question of the provenance of the Negro spiritual and its relation
to the broader topic. He then describes and analyzes sociologi-
cally the Methodist camp meeting revivalism out of which the
Pennsylvania spiritual was born, tracing the spiritual tradition
in the state up to the 1960s. Specifically deals with Lutherans,
Reformed, Amish, Mennonite, Dunkards, and Bush-Meeting Dutch.

1803. YODER, Joseph W. Amische Lieder. Huntingdon, Pa.: Yoder
       Publishing Co., 1942. 114 pp.

       The author, a resident of Mifflin County, Pennsylvania,
collected these conservative hymns in the Kishacoquillas Valley.
He asserts that they derive from Gregorian chant. Finally, he
presents a number of hymns in Aikin's seven-shape notation with
texts in German (old typeface), hoping that this will encourage
the younger generation to retain the tradition.

Hawaiian Traditional Music

1804. EMERSON, Nathaniel B. Unwritten Literature of Hawaii: the
       Sacred Songs of the Hula. Washington, D.C.: Government
       Printing Office, 1909; reprint ed., Rutland, Vt.: Tuttle,
       1965; St. Clair Shores, Mich.: Scholarly Press, 1977.
       288 pp.

       A scholarly study of the ritual of the hula, the songs,
and the instruments, with several transcriptions and illustrations
of instruments.

1805. FELIX, John Henry, NUNES, Leslie, and SENECAL, Peter F.
       The 'Ukulele': a Portuguese Gift to Hawaii. Honolulu: by
       the author, 1980. 63 pp.

       Mostly photos and beginning instructions on how to play.

1806. FREEMAN, Linton C. "The Changing Functions of a Folksong."
       Journal of American Folklore 70-277 (July-Sept. 1957):
       215-20.

A case study of one Hawaiian song, its context, as social expression, and a comparison of it before, during, and after World War II.

1807. JOHNSON, Orme. "Musical Instruments of Ancient Hawaii." *Musical Quarterly* 25 (1939): 498-506.

A survey of Hawaiian music and its instruments as they are known today, the origin of the Hawaiian guitar, and descriptions of original instruments: ukeke, nose flute, etc. as well as the hula and drums. Three transcriptions are included.

1808. KAHANANUI, Dorothy M. "Music of Ancient Hawaii: a Brief Survey." Honolulu: by the author, 1960. 28 pp.

Introductory survey for non-specialists.

1809. KANAHELE, George S., ed. *Hawaiian Music and Musicians: an Illustrated History.* Honolulu: University Press of Hawaii, 1979. 543 pp.

This is the first comprehensive study since Helen Robert's 1926 book appeared (see below). But organization is somewhat like a dictionary, based around terms, places, and names. Also treats the development of popular styles and influences from the mainland.

1810. NOBLE, Gurre Ploner. *Hula Blues: the Story of Johnny Noble, Hawaii, its Music and Musicians.* Honolulu: E. D. Noble, 1984. 128 pp.

This work concentrates on present-day Hawaiian music and in particular the story of one man, Johnny Noble (1892-1944), who had great influence on it in recent times, as well as other leading musicians.

1811. OKIMOTO, Ray Ichiro. "Folk Music of the Dominant Immigrant Cultures of Hawaii as Resource for Junior High School General Music." Ed.D. dissertation, George Peabody College for Teachers, 1974. 171 pp.

Though not based on field work, the author advocates the use of Chinese, Japanese, and Filipino musics in the classroom in

the teaching of basic musical concepts, and provides examples of
how it could be done.

1812. PUKUI, Mary Kawena. "Songs (Meles) of Old Ka'u, Hawaii."
      Journal of American Folklore 62-245 (July-Sèpt. 1949):
      247-58.

      A study of poetry and its meanings.

1813. ROBERTS, Helen H. Ancient Hawaiian Music. Honolulu:
      Bernice P. Bishop Museum, 1926; reprint ed., New York:
      Dover, 1967. 401 pp.

      Still the best scholarly study of traditional Hawaiian
music, surveying both vocal and instrumental music, but stronger on
the latter. Includes maps, transcriptions, and illustrations.

1814. SMITH, Barbara B. "Folk Music in Hawaii." Journal of the
      International Folk Music Council. 11 (1959): 50-5.

      Introductory survey of the many types of music in Hawaii,
including Asian, native Hawaiian, and musical instruments.
Originally this was a paper read at an I.F.M.C. conference.

1815. SMITH, Emerson C. On Hawaiian Folk Music. Honolulu:
      Island Heritage, 1971. 68 pp.

      For the non-specialist, this item surveys song types and
texts and instruments, with drawings of the latter.

1816. TATAR, Elizabeth. "Hawaiian Chant: Mode and Music." Ph.D.
      dissertation, University of California, Los Angeles,
      1978. 354 pp.

      Based on recordings of pre-European chant made in 1923-4
and 1933 at the Bishop Museum in Honolulu, this work analyzes the
material in terms of its musical characteristics, voice quality,
and modality and as a reflection of social structure.

1817. TATAR, Elizabeth. Nineteenth Century Hawaiian Chant.
      Honolulu: Department of Anthropology, Bishop Museum,
      Hawai'i, 1982. 176 pp. and sound sheet.

This work is based on the author's dissertation (previous item), and is both detailed and scholarly. It discusses the sources, their context, types of songs, style, and then presents an extensive analysis and systematic theory, including the use of spectograms. A comparison with chant surviving today is made as well. There is also a disc recording illustrating this material, Pacific Anthropological Records #33 entitled "Nineteenth Century Hawaiian Chant."

1818. TATAR, Elizabeth. "Toward a Description of Precontact Music in Hawai'i." Ethnomusicology 25-3 (Sept. 1981): 481-92.

This is an attempt to reconstruct the style traits of precontact music, meaning before 1820. Based partly on melographs and therefore technical.

Hispanic Folk Music

1819. ALEXANDER, William Peddie. "Hispanic Folk Music in Intercultural Education in New Mexico." Ed.D. dissertation, 1961. 214 pp.

Towards the goal of using Hispanic folk music in intercultural education, the author provides background data, a description of style, and selected songs and dances for use by teachers in the classroom.

1820. ARMISTEAD, Samuel G., and SILVERMAN, Joseph H. "Hispanic Balladry among the Sephardic Jews of the West Coast." Western Folklore 19-4 (1960): 229-44.

Researched in 1957 among a population of 4,000 Sephardic Jews in Los Angeles, this article describes these people expelled from Spain and then focuses on their song texts. Thoroughly documented.

1821. BARKER, George C. "Some Aspects of Penitential Processions in Spain and the American Southwest." Journal of American Folklore 70-276 (April-June 1957): 137-42.

Interesting comparison of a penitential procession native to Spain and a survival of it among the Yaqui Indians of Arizona.

1822. BLOCH, Peter. _La-Le-Lo-Lai; Puerto Rican Music and its_
       Performers. New York: Plus Ultra Educational Publishers,
       1973. 197 pp.

       Lightweight but useful survey of the roots, of mountain
music, African influenced music, the danza, popular songs,
individual artists, and concert music.

1823. BLUM, Joseph. "Problems of _Salsa_ Research."
       Ethnomusicology 22-1 (Jan. 1978): 137-49.

       Partially a prologue to the study of popular music and
the problems involved, partly an initial study of salsa with an
attempt to define its origins.

1824. CAMPA, Arthur L. "Spanish Folksongs in Metropolitan Den-
       ver." _Southern Folklore Quarterly_ 24-3 (1960): 179-92.

       Describes the origins of the Spanish-speaking population
of Denver and its organizations, including those of the Sephardic
Jews. Surveys the types of songs encountered and gives examples.

1825. CAPPON, Clyde S. "Selected Spanish-American Folksongs of
       the Southwest and their Implication for Music Education."
       Ph.D. dissertation, Boston University, 1968. 201 pp.

       No abstract available.

1826. DICKEY, Dan William. _The Kennedy corridos: a Study of the_
       Ballads of a Mexican American Hero. Monograph #4.
       Austin: Center for Mexican American Studies, University
       of Texas, 1978. 127 pp.

       A discussion of the _corridos_ (dramatic narrative ballads)
written concerning President John F. Kennedy.

1827. DOWER, Catherine. _Puerto Rican Music Following the_
       Spanish-American War. Lanham, Md.: University Press of
       America, 1983. 203 pp.

       Not on folk music per se, but a source on a little
researched area. Concentrates on music since 1898, the political
context, festivals, religious feasts, and composers.

1828. ESPINEL, Luisa. Canciones de mi Padre: Spanish Folksongs
      from Southern Arizona. Tucson: University of Arizona
      Press, 1946. 56 pp.

   After a brief introduction the author presents 16 songs
arranged with piano accompaniment and words in English and
Spanish. The melodies were collected from her father, Don
Federico Ronstadt y Redondo.

1829. GRIFFIN, Robert J. "Teaching Hispanic Folk Music as a
      Means to Cross-Cultural Understanding." Ph.D.
      dissertation, The Ohio State University, 1973. 196 pp.

   With the goal of providing "matter" and "means" for
giving music teaching an Hispanic dimension, the author proposes
his plan in chapter 1, gives a panoramic view of Hispanic music in
chapter 2, examines in some detail the copla in chapter 3, African
influence in chapter 4, and finally describes how this music might
be taught to students in pursuit of cross-cultural understanding.

1830. HAGUE, Eleanor. "Early Spanish-Californian Folk-Songs."
      New York: Fischer, 1922. 23 pp.

   A set of songs harmonized for piano and voice by Gertrude
Ross.

1831. HAGUE, Eleanor. Spanish-American Folk-Songs. Memoirs of
      the American Folk-Lore Society #10. Lancaster, Pa. and
      New York: American Folk-Lore Society, 1917. 115 pp.

   A collection of 95 songs (tunes and words in Spanish and
English) from the New World (including California and Puerto Rico)
and a 15-page introduction.

1832. HAGUE, Eleanor. "Spanish-American Folk-Songs." Journal of
      American Folklore 24-94 (Oct.-Dec. 1911): 323-31.

   A set of 15 songs (melodies and texts) in Spanish
collected in Los Angeles and San Francisco.

1833. HANSEN, Terrence L. "Corridos in Southern California."
      Western Folklore 18-3 (July 1959): 203-32; 18-4 (Oct.
      1959): 295-315.

A study of narrative folk ballads collected in the late 1950s, the background of the genre, and 33 examples with tunes, texts, and translations.

1834. HEISLEY, Michael. "An Annotated Bibliography of Chicano Folklore from the Southwestern United States." Ph.D. dissertation, University of California, Los Angeles, 1977. 188 pp.

Section III, "Singing, Dancing and Music-making Traditions," covers materials, including unpublished theses and dissertations (without annotations) for five states.

1835. Una historia de la musica de la frontera (A History of Border Music). Arhoolie Records LP #9003-7, 9011-3, 9016-24. 16 33 1/3 rpm recordings, most with booklets.

Although recordings alone are not normally listed here, this set deserves mention because of its value. Genres covered include corridos, norteno acordeon, string bands, cancioneros de ayer, and various artists recorded in the 1920s to 1940s.

1836. KEIM, Betty. "Comparative Study of the Music of the Indians and the Spanish in Arizona and New Mexico: a Selective Bibliography." Current Musicology 18 (1975): 117-21.

An un-annotated list of materials, both published and unpublished, from several fields (e.g., folklore, anthropology, history) covering such topics as musical style, linguistic influences, musical influences, and historical and cultural data.

1837. LOPEZ CRUZ, Francisco. El aguinaldo en Puerto Rico: su evolucion [The aguinaldo in Puerto Rico: its evolution]. San Juan: Institute de Cultura Puertorriquena, 1972. 46 pp.

A study of the aguinaldo which includes analysis of various aspects (e.g., text, rhythm, melody, harmony) and a consideration of it as national Christmas carol and as folk song.

1838. LOZA, Steven. "The Musical Life of the Mexican-Chicano People of Los Angeles, 1945-85." Ph.D. dissertation, University of California, Los Angeles, 1985.

1839. LUMMIS, Charles F. "Spanish Songs of Old California." Los
       Angeles: C. F. Lummis, 1923. 35 pp.

       Fourteen songs with English and Spanish texts collected
starting in 1884, with piano accompaniments by Arthur Farwell.
Intended for the community song movement.

1840. MacCURDY, Raymond R., and STANLEY, Daniel D. "Judeo-Spanish
       Ballads from Atlanta, Georgia." Southern Folklore
       Quarterly 15 (Dec. 1951): 221-38. Reprinted in Music in
       Georgia, pp. 171-88. Edited by Frank Hoogerwerf. New
       York: Da Capo, 1984.

       The texts and translations of seven ballads recorded by
Mrs. Catina Cohen, a native of the Island of Rhodes who had been
living in Atlanta since World War I.

1841. McGILL, Anna Blanche. "Old Mission Music." Musical
       Quarterly 24 (1938): 186-93.

       This study was based on research among the Tigua Indians
from Ysleta who, together with many others, attended the Texas
Centennial Exposition in Dallas in 1936 and recorded a variant of
old mission music still carried by the tribe. The author presents
six songs in notation with comments on the performance.

1842. McNEIL, Brownie. "Corridos of the Mexican Border." In
       Mexican Border Ballads and Other Lore, pp. 1-34. Edited
       by Mody C. Boatright. Texas Folklore Society Publica-
       tions #21. Austin: Texas Folklore Society, 1946; reprint
       ed., Dallas: Southern Methodist University Press, 1967.

       A collection of tunes, texts, translations and discussion
preceded by a description of the field research and its
difficulties.

1843. MADRID, Miguel A. "The Attitudes of the Spanish-American
       People as Expressed in their Coplas or Folk Songs."
       Ph.D. dissertation, Columbia University, 1953. 139 pp.

       This work is based on the study of some 3,000 coplas found
in various printed editions representing speakers of Spanish from
various American countries, including the United States.

1844. PAREDES, Americo. "The Decima on the Texas-Mexican Border: Folksong as an Adjunct to Legend." Journal of the Folklore Institute 3-2 (1966): 154-67.

A study of the decima, its definition and relationship to stories, with some textual examples in Spanish.

1845. PAREDES, Americo. A Texas-Mexican Cancionero: Folksongs of the Lower Border. Urbana: University of Illinois Press, 1981. 218 pp.

A collection of songs (words and melodies) around which is given the history and customs of the people who made the songs.

1846. PAREDES, Americo. "With His Pistol in His Hand":a Border Ballad and its Hero. Austin: University of Texas Press, 1958, 1971. 262 pp.

A study of one particular corrido, that of Gregorio Cortez (1875-1916), and its hero.

1847. PAREDES, Americo, and GOSS, George. "The Decima Cantada on the Texas-Mexican Border: Four Examples." Journal of the Folklore Institute 3-2 (1966): 91-115.

In this article the authors define the decima, describe its collection, performance practices, and instruments. Included are the Spanish texts for four of them, with tunes separate.

1848. PENA, Manuel. The Texas-Mexican Conjunto: History of a Working-Class Music. Mexican American Monograph #9. Austin: University of Texas Press, 1985. 218 pp.

Comprehensive history of the conjunto, a kind of Mexican-American popular music played on accordion that began around 1930 and was recorded widely after 1935. Part I deals with the history of the genre up to modern times and Part II deals with the social dimensions.

1849. RAEL, Juan Bautista. The New Mexican Alabado. Stanford University Publications, University Series, Language and Literature, Vol. 9, No. 3. Stanford: Stanford University Press, 1951. 154 pp.

With a brief introduction, the compiler offers photos and 89 texts of religious songs from New Mexico in Spanish. The tunes for 88 are given separately, having been transcribed by Eleanor Hague.

1850. ROBB, John Donald. Hispanic Folk Music of New Mexico and the Southwest: a Self-Portrait of a People. Norman: University of Oklahoma Press, 1980. 891 pp.

Mostly a collection of nearly 700 songs, most with tunes and translations organized into Secular (with subtypes), Sacred (with subtypes), and instrumental melodies (with subtypes by function). There is brief commentary.

1851. ROBB, John Donald. Hispanic Folk Songs of New Mexico. Albuquerque: University of New Mexico Press, 1954. 83 pp.

Although there is a substantial 21-page introduction, the bulk is a collection of 23 songs in Spanish and English with piano accompaniments.

1852. ROBB, John Donald. "The Music of Los Pastores." Western Folklore 16-4 (Oct. 1957): 263-80.

Although the manuscripts of the plays have been previously studied, no one had before studied the melodies. The author describes the manuscripts as well as live performances in New Mexico, including the types of songs. Musical examples occupy pp. 275-80.

1853. ROBERTS, John Storm. The Latin Tinge: the Impact of Latin American Music on the United States. New York: Oxford University Press, 1979. 246 pp.

Although more concerned with jazz and popular styles than folk music, this book nonetheless traces the roots of Spanish influence in American music, especially from the 1930s to the 1970s, from jazz to the tango craze.

1854. RYBACK, Shulamith. "Puerto Rican Children's Songs in New York." Midwest Folklore 8-1 (1958): 5-20.

A study of 17 songs (tunes and words) in which the author compares versions from the upper West Side of New York's Manhattan with the original forms in Puerto Rico in order to determine what changes took place.

1855. SHOTWELL, Clayton Moore, Jr. "The Chicano Popular Corrido in Texas (1955-1982): a Musical Study of Commercially Produced Corrido Tunes." Ph.D. dissertation, University of Minnesota, in progress.

1856. STARK, Richard B., ed. Music of the Bailes in New Mexico. Santa Fe: International Folk-Art Foundation, 1978. 118 pp.

This is a collection of three lengthy essays: 1) COOPER, Reed. "Transcriptions of the Violin Tunes," pp. 1-71, biographies of three violinists (Meliton Roybal, Navor Lopez, and Gregorio Ruiz) and 58 transcriptions of tunes used in social dancing; 2) LUCERO-WHITE, Aurora. "Folk Dances of the Spanish-Colonials of New Mexico," pp. 73-107, a detailed description of colonial folk dances with tunes and diagrams, originally published in Santa Fe in the 1930s; 3) THOMAS, Anita Gonzales, "Traditional Folk Dances of New Mexico," pp. 109-18, a discussion of various dances of the Spanish people of New Mexico and the social function of dance.

1857. STARK, Richard B, PEARCE, T. M., and COBOS, Ruben. Music of the Spanish Folk Plays in New Mexico. Santa Fe: Museum of New Mexico Press, 1969. 359 pp.

Along with an edition of an old play (Los pastores) from the New Mexico-southern Colorado area from a manuscript in the Zimmerman Library of the University of New Mexico, transcriptions of several songs central to the play's repertory.

1858. VAN STONE, Mary R. Spanish Folk Songs of New Mexico, Collected and Transcribed by Mary R. Van Stone. Chicago: R. F. Seymour, 1928. 40 pp.

These songs, with texts in English and Spanish, have been arranged with piano accompaniment.

1859. VAN STONE, Mary R. Spanish Folk Songs of the Southwest. Fresno: Academy Guild Press, 1963; new ed., 1964. 45 pp.

Songs in Spanish and English with piano accompaniment.

Hungarian Music

1860. ERDELY, Stephen. "Folksinging of the American Hungarians in Cleveland." Ethnomusicology 8-1 (1964): 14-27.

A rather technical study of tune types collected at the Hungarian-American Singing Society in Cleveland, Ohio.

1861. ERDELY, Stephen. "Traditional and Individual Traits in the Songs of Three Hungarian-Americans." In Selected Reports in Ethnomusicology, Vol. III, No. 1, pp. 99-151. Edited by James Porter. Los Angeles: Department of Music, University of California, Los Angeles, 1978.

Cultural backgrounds and biographies of three Cleveland, Ohio, singers--Steve Martin, Mariska Szabo, and Janos Vasarhelyi-- who recorded nearly 100 folk songs of three types (old, new, and nineteenth-century popular). Analysis of style and many examples.

1862. WARE, Helen. "The American-Hungarian Folksong." Musical Quarterly 2 (1916): 434-41.

An essay-like introduction to the "birth" of Hungarian folksong in America followed by examples of both tunes and texts.

Irish Music

1863. BOHLMAN, Philip V. "The Folk Songs of Charles Bannen: the Interaction of Music and History in Southwestern Wisconsin." Transactions of the Wisconsin Academy of Sciences, Arts and Letters 68 (1980): 167-87.

This article examines the musical repertory of one of the most active Irish-American folksingers in an area characterized by pluralism. This repertory has been able to respond to diverse audiences and performance venues because of Bannen's understanding of his region and its complex culture. Also examined is the relation of the singer's melodic choices to his penchant for accompanying himself on a reed organ.

1864. CAZDEN, Norman. "Songs: 'The Foggy Dew' (Irish)." New York Folklore Quarterly 10-3 (Autumn, 1954): 213-7.

Songs collected in 1948 from George Edwards at Camp Woodland in the Catskills, their meanings, subjects, history, tunes, and texts.

1865. HEALY, William M. "Instrumentation and Repertoire in Commercially Recorded Irish Instrumental Music in the United States." In Folklore and Mythology Studies, Vol. 2. Edited by Jane E. Hartigan and Patricia Atkinson Wells. Los Angeles: Folklore and Mythology Program, Folklore Graduate Students' Association, University of California, Los Angeles, 1978.

1866. LAWS, G. Malcolm, Jr. "Anglo-Irish Balladry in North America." In Folklore in Action: Essays for Discussion in Honor of MacEdward Leach, pp. 172-83. Edited by Horace P. Beck. Publications of the American Folklore Society. Bibliography and Special Series, vol. 14. Philadelphia: American Folklore Society, 1962; reprint ed., Millwood, N.Y.: Kraus Reprint Co., 1972.

In this study of Irish ballads in the English language, the author stresses the importance of the Irish in the Anglo tradition. Also discusses the topics, themes, and texts of Irish ballads.

1867. McCULLOUGH, Lawrence E. "An American Maker of Uillean Pipes: Patrick Hennelly." Eire-Ireland 10-4 (July 1975): 109-15.

The background and biography of Hennelly of Chicago, the only maker of the uillean pipes in the United States.

1868. McCULLOUGH, Lawrence E. The Complete Irish Tinwhistle Tutor. Pittsburgh: Silver Spear Publications, 1976; rev. ed., 1980. 80 pp.

Self-instruction method, with introduction and historical notes. Uses staff notation for 68 pages.

1869. McCULLOUGH, Lawrence E. "An Historical Sketch of Traditional Irish Music in the United States." Folklore Forum 7-3 (July 1974): 177-91.

Introductory history, review of resources, discussion of context and acculturation, with a bibliography.

1870. McCULLOUGH, Lawrence E. "Irish Music in Chicago: an Ethnomusicological Study." Ph.D. dissertation, University of Pittsburgh, 1978. 449 pp.

Comprehensive study of Irish music in Chicago from the 1870s to 1978, the instruments, styles, repertory, and performance practices of both instrumental and vocal genres explored through social, psychological, political, economic, demographic, and musical factors.

1871. McCULLOUGH, Lawrence E. "Michael Coleman, Traditional Fiddler." Eire-Ireland 10-1 (1975): 90-4.

Coleman (1891-1945), from County Sligo and who recorded 80 record sides, was active in New York City. This article gives both his biography and musical career.

1872. MAGUIRE, Marsha, and SUTRO, Suzanne. "Irish Music in America: a Selected Bibliography." Washington, D.C.: Library of Congress, Archive of Folk Song, 1981. 10 pp.

A list of 115 items, including many master's theses.

1873. MALONEY, Michael. "Medicine for Life: a Study of a Folk Composer and his Music." Keystone Folklore 20-1/2 (Winter-Spring, 1975): 4-37.

A study of the folk process of composition in Irish music through an individual, Ed Reavy born in County Cavan in 1897. Mr. Reavy came to Philadelphia in 1912 and was a fiddler as well as composer.

1874. O'NEILL, Francis. The Dance Music of Ireland: 1001 Gems. Arranged by James O'Neill. Chicago: Lyon & Healy, 1907; reprint ed., Dublin: Waltons' Musical Instrument Galleries, 1965. 172 pp.

Both O'Neills were on the Chicago police force, but the elder, Francis, who had come from County Cork at age 16, was the instigator of the collections. An amateur traditional flutist,

383

Francis remembered many tunes from his native Ireland and sought out the many skilled fiddlers living in Chicago at the time. However, Francis asked the more musically skilled Sgt. James O'Neill to transcribe the music, but he, not being a traditional fiddler, tended to simplify the tunes and leave out the stylistic nuances that define the tradition. Nonetheless, these collections remain valuable resources.

1875. O'NEILL, Francis. Irish Folk Music: a Fascinating Hobby. Chicago: Regan Printing House, 1910; reprint ed., Darby, Pa.: Norwood Editions, 1973. 359 pp.

The reprint edition includes an introduction by Barry O'Neill.

1876. O'NEILL, Francis. Irish Minstrels and Musicians. Chicago: Regan Printing House, 1913; reprint ed., Darby, Pa.: Norwood Editions, 1973. 497 pp.

The reprint edition includes an introduction by Barry O'Neill.

1877. O'NEILL, Francis. O'Neill's Irish Music; 250 Choice Selections. First Series. Arranged by James O'Neill. Chicago: Lyon & Healy, 1908. 126 pp.

1878. [O'NEILL, Francis]. O'Neill's Music of Ireland: Over 1000 Fiddle Tunes. Edited by Miles Krassen. New York: Oak, 1976. 254 pp.

Excellent seven-page introduction to the O'Neills by the editor and notes on the authentic performance style.

1879. O'NEILL, Francis. Waifs and Strays of Gaelic Melody. Arranged by Selena O'Neill. Chicago: Lyon & Healy, 1922. 169 pp.

1880. One Thousand Fiddle Tunes. Chicago: M. M. Cole Publishing Co., 1940; reprint ed., 1967.

Evidently a reprint of one of O'Neill's collections, but no information given.

1881. STONER, Michael. "Narratives Associated with Irish Fiddle
       Tunes: Some Contextual Considerations." New York
       Folklore 2-3/4 (Summer, 1977): 17-28.

       This study is concerned with the relationships between
tunes and titles, based on work with Irish fiddlers in the
Rochester, New York, area. Author concludes there are three types
of relationships: 1) how the tune got its name, 2) how a tune was
created, and 3) how the tune was learned.

1882. TEAHAN, Terence "Cuz," with DUNSON, John. The Road to
       Glountane. Chicago: Real People's Music, 1980. 91 pp.

       A non-scholarly description of Irish musicians in
Chicago.

1883. WILGUS, D. K. "'Rose Connoley': an Irish Ballad." Journal
       of American Folklore 92-364 (Oct.-Dec. 1979): 172-95.

       The ballad "Rose Connoley," which has been widely
recorded in southern Appalachia, evidently had an Irish origin.
This study focuses on the text and lists 71 American performances.

1884. WILLIAMS, W. H. A. "Irish Traditional Music in the United
       States." In America and Ireland, 1776-1976: the American
       Identity and the Irish Connection: the Proceedings of the
       United States Bicentennial Conference of Cumann Merriman,
       Ennis, Aug. 1976, pp. 279-93. Edited by David Noel Doyle
       and Owen Dudley Edwards. Westport, Conn.: Greenwood, 1980.

       While the larger topic of the article is the contribu-
tions of Irish music to American folk music in general, it also
considers the survival of that music in America, dealing with
instrumental and vocal genres separately.

1885. WRIGHT, Robert L. Irish Emigrant Ballads and Songs.
       Bowling Green, Oh.: Bowling Green University Press, 1975.
       712 pp.

       A well-documented history of the Irish migration to the
United States and a vast collection of songs collected among
living musicians and from printed broadsides, many with tunes. In
the latter case, the original notation is reproduced. The

bibliography is especially extensive and a supplementary
collection is mentioned as being in progress.

Jewish Music

1886. ARMISTEAD, Samuel, and SILVERMAN, Joseph H., eds. Judeo-
        Spanish Ballads from New York: Collected by Mair Jose
        Benardete. Berkeley: University of California Press,
        1981. 149 pp.

        This collection of 39 ballads collected in the United
States is restricted to the Spanish texts, abstracts and notes for
each, and a 14-page introduction on the collecting of them.

1887. KOSKOFF, Ellen. "Contemporary Nigun Composition in an
        American Hasidic Community." In Selected Reports in
        Ethnomusicology, Vol, III, No. 1, pp. 153-74. Edited by
        James Porter. Los Angeles: Department of Music,
        University of California, Los Angeles, 1978.

        This article traces the history and philosophy of musical
composition in the Lubavitcher Hasidic community from its
beginnings in Eastern Europe in the eighteenth century to present
compositional practices in the United States. Traditional
practices of original composition and musical borrowing have been
continued here so that some contemporary nigunim have been
appropriated from the American folk and commercial traditions.

1888. KOSKOFF, Ellen. "The Effect of Mysticism on the Nigunim of
        the Lubavitcher Hasidim." Ph.D. dissertation, University
        of Pittsburgh, 1976. 232 pp.

        Nigun singing, a complex of music and meaning, is traced
historically and seen in relation to Habad philosophy. This study
concentrates on the Lubavitcher community, a branch of the Hasidic
family.

1889. KOSKOFF, Ellen. "Lubavitcher Women: Musical Behavior and
        Social Change." In Denes Bartha Festschrift. Edited by
        Norris Stephens and Irving Godt. Pittsburgh, American
        Musicological Society, in press.

        This study examines the role and status of women in
Hasidic and Lubavitcher society and their relationship to litur-

gical and para-liturgical practices. The research shows that women participate in music events previously thought to be solely male and that women from mainstream U.S. society who enter Lubavitcher society as adults (Ba'alei Teshuvah) have changed to some extent the traditional forms of music.

1890. MacCURDY, Raymond R., and STANLEY, Daniel D. "Judaeo-Spanish Ballads from Atlanta, Georgia." Southern Folklore Quarterly 15-4 (1951): 221-38.

This article studies Judaeo-Spanish ballads brought to Atlanta by Jews from the Island of Rhodes. Following the introduction is a set of seven untranslated ballad texts and tunes.

1891. RUBIN, Ruth. Voices of a People: the Story of Yiddish Folksong. New York: A. S. Barnes, 1963; 2nd ed., New York: McGraw-Hill, 1973. 558 pp.

A vast collection of Eastern European Yiddish folksongs also translated into English, but without tunes, and extensive commentary on them. Arranged by topic, such as children's world, marriage, and dancing songs. While these are not American Jewish songs, many have been retained in Jewish communities here.

1892. RUBIN, Ruth. "Yiddish Folksongs in New York City." New York Folklore Quarterly 2 (1946): 15-23.

This collection of texts provides a narrative about the Jewish experience in New York City.

1893. RUBIN, Ruth. "Yiddish Folksongs of Immigration and the Melting Pot." New York Folklore Quarterly 17-3 (1961): 173-82.

Essentially the same as the previous article, but focusing on songs of immigration and blending into American society.

1894. SLOBIN, Mark. "Klezmer Music: an American Ethnic Genre." Yearbook for Traditional Music 16 (1984): 34-41.

Klezmer is described as a secular, instrumental music of Jewish-American origin played by professional folk musicians.

Although it arose in the New World about 1910, it has Old World connections. Also discusses the infusion of the _doina_ and the revival of klezmer.

1895. SLOBIN, Mark. _Tenement Songs: the Popular Music of the Jewish Immigrants._ Urbana: University of Illinois Press, 1982. 213 pp. with cassette tape.

More properly a study of popular music than folk music, this well-documented work focuses on the musical life of Jewish immigrants on New York's lower east side during the period 1880–1920. Three sections cover "Before Ellis Island," "Entertainment in the Ghetto," and "The Sheet Music Microcosm."

Portuguese Music

1896. CUNEY-HARE, Maud. "Portuguese Folk-Songs from Provincetown, Cape Cod, Massachusetts." _Musical Quarterly_ 14 (1928): 35–53.

Massachusetts was home at that time to some 28,000 people of Portuguese descent, many of whom were fishermen. This article traces their coming and presents a series of songs (tunes and texts in Portuguese and English), discussion of their musical life, customs, and instruments.

1897. DaCOSTA FONTES, Manuel. "A New Portuguese Ballad Collection from California." _Western Folklore_ 34-4 (1975): 299–310.

Broad discussion of the ballad tradition among Portuguese in California, how they are transmitted, and an attempt to explain why only those born in Portugal seemed to retain the tradition. Discussion of 197 variants of 124 narrative ballads carried by 53 first-generation informants.

1898. PURCELL, Joanne B. "Traditional Ballads Among the Portuguese in California." _Western Folklore_ 28-1 (Jan. 1969): 1–20; 28-2 (Apr. 1969): 77–90.

Description of the Portuguese community, which began arriving in California in 1780, a report on field research and its problems conducted among them, and examples of seven song texts (English and Portuguese), variants, and tunes.

Scandinavian Music

1899. BLEGEN, Theodore C., and RUUD, Martin B., eds. Norwegian
Emigrant Songs and Ballads. London: Oxford University
Press and Minneapolis: University of Minnesota Press,
1936; reprint ed., New York: Arno Press, 1979. 350 pp.

The texts of classified songs and ballads collected both
in Norway and the United States, given in both Norwegian and
English with commentary. Eleven songs are presented in harmonized
arrangements.

1900. EDGAR, Marjorie. "Ballads of the Knife-Men." Western
Folklore 8-1 (Jan. 1949): 53-7.

Text-oriented study of the ballads of woodsmen and
hunters of Finnish descent living in northern Minnesota. Known as
hunters with the big knife (puukko), they were active in the
1890s. The article includes examples but no tunes.

1901. EDGAR, Marjorie. "Finnish Charms and Folk Songs in
Minnesota." Minnesota History 17-4 (1936): 406-10.

Briefly, on collecting the material with text examples.

1902. EDGAR, Marjorie. "Finnish Folk Songs in America."
Minnesota History 16-3 (1935): 319-21.

A brief and general introduction to the subject.

1903. EIDBO, Olav H. "Songs of the Norwegian Folk in Culture and
Education in the United States." Ph.D. dissertation,
University of North Dakota, 1956. 354 pp.

The author provides both history of the Norwegians in the
United States and, based on a questionnaire and interviews, data
concerning individuals, publications, and ethnic organizations.
An appendix includes 100 texts and tunes, some with English
translations, illustrating various types of songs and ballads.

1904. GRONOW, Pekka. Studies in Scandinavian-American
Discography (1-2). Helsinki: Finnish Institute of
Recorded Sound, 1977.

1905. HAUGEN, Einar. "Norwegian Emigrant Songs and Ballads."
Journal of American Folklore 51-199 (Jan.-Mar. 1938):
69-75.

An extensive review of Blegen and Ruud, Norwegian
Emigrant Songs and Ballads (#1899) with a number of text examples.

1906. JOHNSON, Aili Kolehmainen. "Finnish Labor Songs from
Northern Michigan." Michigan History 31-3 (1947): 331-43.

This article is a survey of labor songs from Ridge,
Michigan, giving background for them and their translated texts.

1907. LARSON, Leroy Wilbur. "Scandinavian-American Folk Dance
Music of the Norwegians in Minnesota." Ph.D.
dissertation, University of Minnesota, 1975. 507 pp.

This study of Norwegian music in Minnesota is based on a
corpus of 166 instrumental folk dance melodies collected from 48
informants in 14 counties. Some informants were also Swedish.
The author found that only 13 per cent of the melodies were of
Scandinavian origin, and many came from more recent phonograph
recordings and from the radio. They include the waltz,
schottische, polka, mazurka, two-step, square dance, and three
versions of "Nikolina." Instruments include accordion, violin,
harmonica, mandolin, banjo, piano, and guitar.

1908. NELSON, Carl L. "The Sacred and Secular Music of the
Swedish Settlers of the Midwest, 1841-1917." Ph.D.
dissertation, New York University, 1950. 167 pp.

A study of music composed and performed for a variety of
occasions, including church, home, school, and for the community.

1909. WRIGHT, Robert L. Swedish Emigrant Ballads. Lincoln:
University of Nebraska Press, 1965. 209 pp.

This body of classified song texts, with some of the
melodies in an appendix, includes examples in both Swedish and
English, the former not translated. A 29-page introduction
provides contextual and historical information.

Slavic Music

1910. BABCOCK, C. Merton. "Czech Songs in Nebraska." Western
       Folklore 8-4 (Oct. 1949): 320-7.

       The Czechs in Nebraska came starting in 1865 from Bohemia
to homestead. This article provides a number of texts with
minimal notes and no tunes.

1911. BALYS, Jonas. Lithuanian Folksongs in America: Narrative
       Songs and Ballads. A Treasury of Lithuanian Folklore,
       No. 5. Boston: Lithuanian Encyclopedia Publishers, 1958.
       326 pp.

       This extensive corpus of 472 untranslated song texts were
collected among first generation Lithuanians in the United States.
English summaries of the songs are provided.

1912. BALYS, Jonas. Lithuanian Folksongs in America: Second
       Collection. A Treasury of Lithuanian Folklore, No. 6.
       Silver Spring, Md.: Lithuanian Folklore Publishers, 1978.
       342 pp.

       The introduction is in Lithuanian, but there is a brief
English summary followed by 702 song texts in Lithuanian. There
are also photos of the singers who contributed songs.

1913. DAVIS, Susan G. "Utica's Polka Music Tradition." New York
       Folklore 4-1/4 (1978): 103-24.

       The musical life of Polish-Americans during the previous
100 years is viewed through a case study involving Utica, New
York, and the use of the polka in a variety of situations.

1914. ELZIARIA, M. "Notes on Polish American Music." Polish-
       American Studies 11-1/2 (Jan.-June 1954): 9-15.

1915. FICCA, Robert Joseph. "A Study of Slavic-American
       Instrumental Music in Lyndora, Pennsylvania." Ph.D.
       dissertation, University of Pittsburgh, 1980. 235 pp.

       Lyndora is a small milltown of about 2,400 residents 40
miles north of Pittsburgh with a population of Polish, Slovak,

Russian, and Ukrainian descent. This study is concerned with the impact of internal and external influences on the community in general and attitude changes towards instrumental music in particular during the period 1902-1980. It treats music in the contexts of dance, festivals, parades, and folk dances.

1916. FORRY, Mark. "Becar Music in the Serbian Community of Los Angeles: Evolution and Transformation." In Selected Reports in Ethnomusicology, Vol. III, No. 1, pp. 175-210. Edited by James Porter. Los Angeles: Department of Music, University of California, Los Angeles, 1978.

This article examines the genre called becar in Los Angeles, a type of music associated with predominantly male gatherings at both nightclubs and Orthodox Church Halls.

1917. HOFFMAN, D. "The Meaning and Functions of the Kolo Club 'Marian' in Steelton, Pennsylvania, Croatian Community." Keystone Folklore Quarterly 16-3 (1971): 115-31.

This study focuses on the development of an ethnic dance ensemble starting in 1954 led by Theresa Plasic of Steelton, a Croatian community just south of Harrisburg.

1918. KEIL, Charles. "The Dyna-Tones: A Buffalo Polka Band in Performance, in Rehearsal, and on Record." New York Folklore 10-3/4 (Summer-Fall, 1984): 117-34.

Part of a forthcoming book by the author and others (In Pursuit of Polka Happiness), this case study of a single group in three "takes" or "stop actions" is written in journalistic, descriptive style. It includes many quotations and photos as well.

1919. KLEEMAN, Janice Ellen. "The Origins and Stylistic Development of Polish-American Polka Music." Ph.D. dissertation, University of California, Berkeley, 1982. 370 pp.

Traces the development of the polka, both rural and urban, from Poland to the United States through recordings and living informants. The author documents a loss of rural style and changes in the urban style up to the present.

1920. KLYMASZ, Robert B., and PORTER, James. "Traditional
        Ukrainian Balladry in Canada." Western Folklore 33-2
        (April 1974): 89-132.

        Pp. 89-102 provide a review of literature, the function,
content, poetics, structure and style of traditional Ukrainian
balladry, and pp. 102-29 present 11 ballads with tunes, texts (in
both languages), and headnotes. Although this concerns Canada, it
was included because it is a substantial study of a little known
area which is not likely to be different in the United States.

1921. KOENIG, Martin, and RAIM, Ethel. "Tamburashi Tradition in
        America." In Balkan-Arts Traditions. Edited by Martin
        Koenig. New York: Balkan Arts Center, 1974.

1922. KOLAR, Walter W. A History of the Tambura. 2 vols.
        Pittsburgh: Duquesne University Tamburitzans. Vol. 1:
        The Tambura in Europe--its early Development, 1973. 28
        pp.; Vol. 2: The Tambura in America, 1975. 98 pp.

        This work traces the history of the tamburitza ensembles
both in Europe and in the United States, focusing on the Duquesne
Tamburitzans, through recordings and other documents. It also
treats outside influences and pedagogy.

1923. MARCH, Richard. "The Tamburitza Tradition in the Calumet
        Region." Indiana Folklore 10-2 (1977): 127-38.

        This informal overview of groups in the region was
written by a Croatian-American.

1924. NETTL, Bruno, and MORAVCIK, Ivo. "Czech and Slovak Songs
        Collected in Detroit." Midwest Folklore 5-1 (1955): 37-
        49.

        During the fall of 1954 the authors collected 13 Czech and
five Slovak songs from a single informant, aged 28, who was Czech.
These songs are given in English and Czech with tunes and some
analysis of style characteristics.

1925. NILES, Christina. "The Revival of the Latvian Kokle in
        America." In Selected Reports in Ethnomusicology, Vol.
        III, No. 1, pp. 211-39. Edited by James Porter. Los

Angeles: Department of Music, University of California, Los Angeles, 1978.

By the mid 1960s there were only about a dozen players of the kokle, a small wing-shaped zither, in the United States. This article studies the process of restoration of this nearly extinct tradition, now common in the United States and Canada, and changes that occurred.

1926. PAWLOWSKA, Harriet M. Merrily We Sing: 105 Polish Folk-songs. Detroit: Wayne State University Press, 1961. 263 pp.

This collection includes tunes and words in both English and Polish. There is some musical analysis by Grace L. Engel (pp. 219-23) and notes on the songs in an appendix.

1927. WASCHEK, Brownlee. "Czech and Slovak Folk Music in Masaryktown and Slovenska-Zahrada, Florida." 2 vols. Ph.D. dissertation, The Florida State University, 1969. 370 pp.

Although the ultimate goal was to collect music that could be used in public education, the author did extensive field collecting in two Florida towns. Besides providing background on the people and their music, he transcribed the songs into conventional notation and translated the texts. Vol. 2 is entitled "Arrangements of Representative Examples of Folk Songs Illustrating Their Adaptability to School Use."

403